SOUL MAGIC

© Konrad Gös

STEVE AYAN is a German psychologist, scientific journalist, and author. He studied psychology, literary translation, and science journalism in Berlin, Dusseldorf, Reading, and Naples. As a long-standing editor at the magazine *Gehirn&Geist / Scientific American*, Ayan's work specialises in consciousness research, moral psychology, and psychotherapy. He lives in Heidelberg.

MARSHALL YARBROUGH has translated books by Michael Kempe, Ulla Lenze, and Wolf Wondratschek, among other authors. He lives in New York City.

SOUL MAGIC

A Century of Psychotherapy

STEVE AYAN

Translated from the German
by Marshall Yarbrough

PUSHKIN PRESS

The people, places, and events described in this book are real and the accounts herein are based on a wide range of sources. Where gaps emerged, occasional fictional elements were added. These are grounded in the historical record and plausible, but speculative.

Pushkin Press
Somerset House, Strand
London WC2R 1LA

Soul Magic: A Century of Psychotherapy was first published as *Seelenzauber: Aus Wien in die Welt – Das Jahrhundert der Psychologie* by dtv Verlagsgesellschaft in Munich, 2024

First published by Pushkin Press in 2026

ISBN 13: 978-1-80533-237-4

A CIP catalogue record for this title is available from the British Library

The authorised representative in the EEA is eucomply OÜ, Pärnu mnt. 139b-14, 11317, Tallinn, Estonia, hello@eucompliancepartner.com, +33757690241

Designed and typeset by Tetragon, London
Printed and bound in the United Kingdom by Clays Ltd, Elcograf S.p.A.

Pushkin Press is committed to a sustainable future for our business, our readers and our planet. This book is made from paper from forests that support responsible forestry.

FSC www.fsc.org MIX Paper | Supporting responsible forestry FSC® C018072

www.pushkinpress.com

9 8 7 6 5 4 3 2 1

CONTENTS

For Erika,

the good soul

"I have the most peaceful disposition [. . .] —yes, one must forgive one's enemies, but not until they've been hanged."

SIGMUND FREUD
(QUOTING HEINRICH HEINE)

"Every founder of a branch of psychotherapy has attempted in his books to solve only those problems that he himself has suffered through."

VIKTOR E. FRANKL

1

THE UNCONSCIOUS

A LATE-ARRIVING GUEST

A man of short stature hurries down the street. Stepping briskly, he rounds the corner of a building, his hat pulled low over his face, his glasses speckled with rain. It's drizzling, and he's running late. The meeting begins at half-past eight, as it does every Wednesday evening, and the host doesn't like it when one of his guests arrives late. A glance at his pocket watch—the big hand is already scraping the six! Thankfully he's almost there.

In view of the weather and the rush he was in he had allowed himself a ride on the electric tram, leaving from Leopoldstadt, crossing over the Danube Canal and getting off at Schottentor. From there he had to continue on foot, past the Votive Church and down Währingerstraße for two blocks. Now he's on Berggasse. He can see the bright gateway arch at the entrance to number 19 shining at the far end of the street.

For a short stretch the street turns steeply downhill—careful not to slip on the slick pavement! A faded notice in a doorway catches his eye: *Tempters' meeting* . . . ?! Oh, wait—*tenants'!* He shakes his head. How quickly one's mind goes to the sexual. Is it really true that the libido lies hidden behind even the most trivial of thoughts? The colleague he's on his way to meet regards it as the driving force of the psyche, and maybe he's right, as outlandish as it may sound. Maybe its very outlandishness is proof that we repress what, deep down, makes us tick?

An icy evening wind heralds the arrival of winter. Only a handful of other people hurry past on the sidewalk, hidden under umbrellas. The man who is now ringing the bell at the entrance to number 19 is a physician—an ophthalmologist—and at just over thirty the youngest of those gathered here for this week's discussion. Dr. Freud, their host, will soon be fifty. Custom would dictate that the younger man keep his views to himself—especially since there's a lot he's not sure about, or at least not as sure as this Freud seems to be. He, the late-arriving guest, can sense that the differences between his and his host's ways of thinking will be considerable. There's something brewing inside him, something unique, something big—he just doesn't know what it is yet.

Flushed from the walk, our man takes a few deep breaths. The large wooden door opens with a creak. As he enters, it seems to him as though he were stepping through this door into an exciting new era.

. . .

The year 1902 is drawing to a close, and Vienna, the proud capital of the Austro-Hungarian Empire, is bursting at the seams. For years there has been incessant construction. The streets, especially east of the canal, in Leopoldstadt, are crowded with new arrivals from every corner of the Habsburg empire. They come from Bohemia, Moravia, Bukovina, Transylvania. Week after week, hundreds of people, many of them Jews, come streaming into the city on the Danube, fleeing poverty and persecution and in search of a better life. In the census of 1869, a year before our guest is born, Vienna's population is recorded at roughly 600,000 residents, including about 40,000 Jews, most of them from the eastern reaches of the empire.[1] In the thirty-odd years since then, the population has tripled. Soon the city will reach the two million mark.[2]

Industrialization is late to take hold in Austria, but when it does it arrives in force. Vienna is booming. Laborers are in demand everywhere, in the factories, in commerce, in government, in the press, in the courts and at the university. The face of the city is also quickly changing: ever since the medieval city wall was carted off and replaced with a wide, opulent boulevard, the Ringstrasse, the city center has been almost unrecognizable. Opera house and parliament building, city hall and

Burgtheater, university and Secession—everywhere one looks, testaments to Austria's importance soar into the sky. And that's leaving aside earlier monuments like the Hofburg, Heroes' Square, and Schönbrunn.

Elsewhere in the city, such as around the Prater in Leopoldstadt, tenement buildings are shooting up out of the ground, offering cheap living space for the masses: workers, day laborers, unskilled wage earners and their families. Here people live packed together in close quarters. Many can't afford their own apartment and leave their bed to someone else during the day while they're out toiling on fourteen- or sixteen-hour shifts, trying to make ends meet for themselves and their children. The hygiene conditions are miserable, sickness and contagious disease are ever-present.

Meanwhile, Franz Joseph's reign is entering its fifty-fifth year. As life in the shadows of the city's splendid façades grows ever more fast-paced, the Habsburg monarchy, with its dusty pomp and ceremony, seems a creature of another time. Since the World's Fair of 1873, all sorts of new innovations have arrived in Vienna: street lighting, the telegraph, the electric tram. Racing through the streets of late are vehicles that seem to move by themselves. Progress and the spirit of invention seem limitless, and the expectations for the future are commensurately great.

Alongside the hope that society is moving towards a golden age, however, all this newness brings with it a certain amount of agitation. Many feel overwhelmed by the rapid pace of change and are suffering from overstimulation and nervous anxiety. More and more people are coming down with fashionable illnesses like neurasthenia, a mix of restlessness and despondency, and hysteria, a complex condition prevalent among women. They are the maladies of what will come to be known as Viennese modernism.

Vienna is a melting pot and a laboratory for experimentation. Avant-garde movements in art, philosophy, and science are trying out new forms of thought and expression that break with a tradition seen as rotten and hollow. For all their differences, the innovators are united by a single vision: self-determination. Freedom from constraint and persecution, yes, but also the freedom to invent a new self in accordance with one's own unique capabilities. A person's fate should be determined not by fortune or birth, but by their own will and drive; their own talent and ambition should secure them a fitting outcome. While the nobility carries on with its opera balls and the proletariat struggles for survival, the ascendant bourgeoisie is developing its own system of values. Survival of the fittest, the law that, according to Charles Darwin, prevails in nature, should finally apply to society as well. Every individual is the author of their own happiness—a new age is dawning that turns on this central idea.

As the old order starts to falter, some cling to it all the more tightly. The guardians of the old ways and the skeptics of the new, overwhelmed by the changes brought on by modern life, go looking for a scapegoat, something they can fight to ensure that everything stays the way it is. This scapegoat is easy to find; it's been the same for centuries: the Jew. Even in liberal Vienna, antisemitism always rears its head whenever the economy takes a downturn. As it does, for example, in the summer of 1873, when the young Sigmund Freud is just about to begin his studies at the university. A speculation bubble driven primarily by German investors leads to the sudden crash of the Viennese stock market. Countless investors lose their money; companies go bankrupt. People say the Jews are to blame for the crash. The fact that it is for the most part Jewish investors who lose the largest sums in the panic does nothing to change this perception.

Up to this point, Jews have been able to climb the social ladder much more easily in Vienna than elsewhere. Here they can acquire property and pursue careers in government administration. By around 1890, roughly half of all doctors, lawyers, teachers, and civil servants in the city are Jewish, despite the percentage of Jews in the overall population being well under ten percent. Many assimilated Jews and Jews who have converted to Christianity even share in the antisemitic resentment; to them their origins are a blemish, the Jewish nature false and crooked. Our late guest is himself toying with the thought of becoming a Protestant, though in his case it's chiefly with practical considerations in mind: non-Jews have better chances of getting a well-paid position at the university or the polyclinic.[3]

In this time of upheaval shortly following the turn of the century, Vienna is awash in a "fertile torrent of ideas."[4] An active creative elite calls the city home, including the painters Egon Schiele and Gustav

Klimt, the writers Hugo von Hofmannsthal, Arthur Schnitzler, and Hermann Bahr, the composers Arnold Schönberg and Gustav Mahler, and the architects Otto Wagner and Adolf Loos, plus the essayist Karl Kraus and the critic and novelist Lou Andreas-Salomé. They loathe narrowmindedness and empty pomp, rebel against the widespread fulsome embrace of reason and progress. Death and eros are their subjects.

"That behind the façade of rationality something wholly other loomed [. . .] was for the artistic and intellectual avant-garde of the late 19th century a settled fact."[5] In order for the individual to come into their own, they must first conquer the dark terra incognita of the psyche, a realm ruled by lust and violence. They must subdue their inner demons, their unconscious, in order to become masters of their own self. Young Alfred Adler, handing his damp coat to the housemaid in the hallway, has no doubt that this is true.

In Vienna at the start of the 20th century, a truly epochal intellectual shift is in the making. And the members of the society that gathers every Wednesday at Berggasse 19 in the city's ninth district regard themselves as the vanguard of this movement.

. . .

It's just a few steps up to the upper ground floor. Quickly wiping his rain-spotted glasses and dabbing the sweat from his forehead, the new arrival steps into the waiting room, where the others are already seated. And smoking. Wilhelm Stekel is there, immaculately dressed as usual and in a chatty mood. Also present are the easygoing Max Kahane and the reserved Rudolf Reitler. And sitting, or rather enthroned, at the opposite end of the room, with his back to the veranda, is the host. He gives Adler a benevolent nod.

During the day Freud's patients sit here and look out through the large windows upon the chestnut trees in the courtyard. The practice is doing well, the host explains, even if the book on dreams has yet to meet with the success he had hoped for. A scant two or three hundred copies have sold, and you could count the number of reviews on one hand.[6] But it's no surprise that he would be dismissed and ignored, he says. The power of the unconscious and its driving force, the libido—above all however the pathological effect of repressed sexual desires—make people uncomfortable. They're uncanny; no one wants to hear about such things. But though the uncomprehending might shake their heads, Freud's conviction that he has uncovered a profound truth only grows.

Alfred Adler has more than one reason to feel at home at this address. His namesake, Victor Adler—no relation—lived with his wife in a modest, one-story building that once stood on this spot. Victor Adler was also a doctor and ran a practice that served the poor. In 1889 he and a few like-minded comrades founded the Social Democratic Workers' Party of Austria, of which Adler the ophthalmologist is himself an active member. The liberation of the proletariat is just a matter of time; the future belongs to socialism—this much is certain. Whether the same is true for psychoanalysis remains to be seen.

In the late 1880s Victor Adler's home is torn down and an imposing five-story bourgeois palace is erected in its place. In September 1891 the neurologist Sigmund Freud and his wife Martha move in with their young daughter Mathilde and two sons Jean-Martin and Oliver. Three more children follow over the next four years: Ernst, Sophie, and Anna.

Anna, the baby of the family, will soon be celebrating her seventh birthday. The family's apartment is located on the mezzanine level, one floor up from Freud's practice. Every day—in the morning, at midday, and late in the evening, when the last patient has left and the last of the correspondence has been taken care of—Freud goes up and down the two half-flights of stairs in the stairwell. Work and private life are kept separate, and yet they exist closely side by side.

Adler has known Dr. Freud for three years, but is still not really sure what to make of him. A chain-smoking doctor—he likes Cuban cigars best, but for the most part contents himself with the reasonably priced *trabucco* variety—he is also a knowledgeable collector of ancient artworks that he often brings back from trips to the south. The room where he sees his patients looks more like a museum than a doctor's office.

Freud's voice is warm, his judgment firm, but in person he often seems distant, almost unapproachable. He likes to speak with a sardonic undertone in his voice, but he doesn't handle criticism or disagreement well himself. And then his methods! Freud literally does nothing but listen to his patients talk—for several hours a week—and interpret what they say. The patients, predominantly upper-class women, are supposed to say everything that pops into their heads, unfiltered, no matter how unimportant or embarrassing it might seem. Freud calls it "unconstrained associating." He has the ladies lie on a chaise longue draped in cushions and blankets that was given to him by one of his patients. From where he's sitting, Adler can see a corner of the chaise in the next room, in front of the dark wall hanging.

And what is the purpose of this candid speech? From beneath the thoughts and associations brought to light in this way, Freud claims to uncover buried memories. The mind's repression of these memories is the cause of his patients' fears, compulsions, and hysteria. By unearthing these unacknowledged wishes and affects and making his patients conscious of them, he shows his patients a way to a cure. Freud is less a doctor than an archaeologist, descending into the burial chambers of the psyche.

But the success of his methods proves him right. The hectic nature of life in the city and contacts in well-heeled circles bring enough patients Freud's way to provide a comfortable living for himself and his family.

The most famous piece of furniture in the history of psychology: Freud's couch in Vienna

Mainly it is hysterics who seek him out, women who complain of pains with no discernible cause, lapses of memory and impaired speech, spasms or bouts of paralysis. Hysteria, along with neurasthenia, is *the* malady of the age. It afflicts almost exclusively women, hence the word's root, *hystéra* (Greek for uterus). But what exactly causes the mysterious disorder is to this point a mystery.

Adler can recall how fascinating he found the *Studies on Hysteria* that Freud published together with his colleague Josef Breuer in 1895. In the book the two doctors describe several cases from their respective practices in which they applied the new method of treatment. Based on its resounding success, Freud and Breuer conclude that "Hysterics suffer mainly from reminiscences."[7] That is to say: memories that are so upsetting or unpleasant that they must not be allowed to become conscious float around in the inaccessible part of the psyche until finally they come out as symptoms. In order to treat these symptoms, the therapist must bring the fragments of memory to light and know how to correctly interpret them. If the patients are then able to "act out" the inhibited emotion, the complaints disappear. Freud and Breuer call the effect cathartic.

In late 1899, a good four years after the *Studies*, Freud fires his next salvo, having benefited from more experience treating patients in the interim. On November 8, the Deuticke publishing house in Leipzig brings out *The Interpretation of Dreams*—with the forward-looking date of 1900 printed on the title page. For some the book is a revelation, for others an affront. But as yet no one suspects what explosive force is contained within.

A JOB, NOT A CALLING

On this rainy evening in late 1902, none of the five gentlemen in Freud's waiting room are expecting a revolution. But psychoanalysis, as Freud calls his treatment method,[8] will deliver a jolt to human self-conception and fundamentally change the individual's relationship to themselves and others. Its core idea is that all conscious experience has a deeper, hidden meaning. Every stirring of the psyche—feelings, thoughts, memories, desires, but also misconceptions, fears, or injuries—points to something else, has *something to say*. The notion that behind the masquerade of repression a truth lies waiting to be deciphered will become the dominant narrative of the new psychology of the unconscious.

The epicenter of this earthquake is Dr. Freud's waiting room at Berggasse 19, filled with conversation and smoke. And the topic for the first meeting of the Wednesday Society is aptly chosen: smoking. The air in the room is thick. Martin, as Freud's eldest son is called, will remember years later how as a boy he once entered the room after one of these gatherings and asked himself how people could even breathe in such an atmosphere, much less think.

Cigars are set out for the guests; the host himself is only smoking a pipe at the moment, on account of his heart. All the same, he refills it often. "Rarely have I seen a man smoke so much," Stekel notes. The neurologist got in touch with Freud in early 1900 after reading a review of *The Interpretation of Dreams* in the newspaper. It was he who suggested to Freud that he start a discussion group as a way of communicating his ideas. Stekel, who has a sideline as a journalist, soon becomes the unofficial PR agent for the budding psychoanalytic movement. The morning after this first meeting he pens an account of the evening at Freud's. Under the title "Conversations on Smoking," it appears in the *Prager Tagblatt* on January 28, 1903.

In Stekel's gossipy retelling, each participant receives a pseudonym. He himself is "the restless one," Adler "the socialist." Kahane, an ex-colleague of Freud's from his time at the Vienna General Hospital, gets the nickname "the comfortable one," and Reitler is "the silent one." Last but not least, there's "the master." The group quickly comes to speak about the stimulating effect of tobacco, which boosts one's mental and creative energies. Stekel claims to remember that his first fledgling efforts as a writer came precisely at the time that he first began to smoke. "This merely confirms my hypothesis that smoking counteracts self-criticism," Kahane teases. Freud responds: "Clever, but malicious."—"And wrong!" Stekel retorts.

Freud admits that for him cigars induce a kind of mild narcosis, a "sense of well-being of the nerves." He goes through up to twenty a day; he always needs "something warm between the lips." The phallic shape, the association with the child's suckling at the mother's breast—if they did come up in the discussion, Stekel kept it to himself. And anyway, how could he have written openly about such things in the newspaper? There is only one comment, attributed to "the socialist": "Smoking in many cases has intimate sexual connections." The remark is left unanswered, however; none of those present wants to turn the group into a confessional club on the very first night.

To give structure to subsequent meetings, Freud determines an order for the proceedings: each Wednesday gathering begins with a lecture, after which pastries and coffee are served and those present settle down to smoking and responding, each in turn, to what was said. It's left to Freud to deliver the last word before the meeting breaks up. Depending on how much there is to discuss, this can sometimes be past midnight.

It soon becomes clear, though, that Stekel takes certain liberties with the truth. His colleagues begin to suspect that when presenting cases of patients he is treating to the group, he adjusts the details in whatever way he deems fit. It's possible he just makes them up; no sooner has someone mentioned an interesting constellation of symptoms than the neurologist will exclaim: "Just this morning I encountered exactly such a patient . . ." Stekel's "Wednesday patients" become legendary.

All the while Freud acts the part of the benevolent patriarch whose authority goes unquestioned. As such he's unlikely to have admitted to his guests that his choice to practice medicine was a begrudging one. "Neither at that time, nor indeed in my later life, did I feel any particular predilection for the career of a doctor," he writes some twenty years later in a self-portrait.[9] His actual intention was to find success at the university and pursue a career in research. Neuropathology, the study of pathological changes in the tissue of the brain—this was his area of expertise. But every attempt at a major discovery failed; his big break never came. Meanwhile the competition wasn't idle.

The University of Vienna in the late 19th century is a gathering place for any number of distinguished figures. The psychophysicist and philosopher Ernst Mach teaches here, as do the zoologist Carl Claus (for whom Freud, after taking his exams, dissects hundreds of river eels in search of their testicles), the anatomist Hermann Nothnagel, and the brain researcher Theodor Meynert. After earning his M.D.

in March 1881, Freud works as a lab assistant, first for Meynert, then for the physiologist Ernst Wilhelm von Brücke, a stern Prussian and a charismatic teacher. One of the young doctor's projects is to work on a dyeing technique that is meant to make brain cells more visible under the microscope. But others beat him to it.

In 1884, Freud experiments with the euphoria-inducing effects of the alkaloid of the coca plant. He orders the substance from the Merck company in Darmstadt, samples it himself—and is thrilled! He sends a few grams in the mail to his fiancée Martha Bernays in Hamburg with a note saying that she simply has to try it. Just like that, Freud's melancholy is gone. And he's had plenty of reason to be melancholy, ever since Martha's mother took her daughter off to distant Hamburg. The older woman was probably trying to put an end to her daughter's attachment to this penniless doctor, son of a poor wool merchant from Moravia. What does Martha want with a man like that? This isn't the match Frau Bernays hoped to find for her eldest daughter.

Freud hastily pens a treatise on the miracle drug cocaine and travels to Wandsbek to see his fiancée again. As he learns upon his return a few weeks later, he's missed yet another opportunity. Instead of writing academic papers, his colleague Carl Koller went looking for a practical application for cocaine—and found it to be suitable as a local anesthetic for use during eye surgery. Due to the involuntary twitching that occurs during general anesthesia, patients previously had to endure the operations while fully awake. Their screams were unbearable to Koller. So he had an idea: he put a few drops of cocaine solution in his eye, and voilà, it immediately became numb to pain. The new approach made it possible to eliminate the worst of the patients' suffering.

Brücke has a heart-to-heart with his student. So does Freud's friend Josef Breuer, who is fourteen years older and helping him out financially. Breuer tells him that an academic career, while not out of the question, is still a less than likely proposition. Only by going into private practice and working as a doctor could he hope to earn enough to support a household of his own in the near future. And the thirty-year-old Freud wants this more than anything—for he is head over heels in love.

• • •

So what kind of person is Freud? Certainly not a simple one. There was no shortage of contradictory characters among the first cohort of psychoanalysts, but he may be the most contradictory figure of all. Freud is jovial and at the same time quick to anger. He insists on the scientific nature of his theories on the psyche, but makes for them a claim to truth that verges on religious certainty. Freud experiences bitter antisemitism and yet presents himself as more isolated than he is. He writes about addiction and ways to cure it and is himself severely addicted to nicotine—and arguably to gambling as well (he hardly lets a day go by without a game of his beloved tarot). He does away with the division between normal and pathological mental life, but castigates renegade pupils by labeling them "neurotic" or "anally fixated." He regards psychological suffering as the result of hidden trauma, but shows no interest in social reform; to the contrary, according to him, the pleasure principle which governs the mechanisms of the psyche inevitably collides with the demands of civilized life, the reality principle. His treatment method has a cathartic effect, and yet, according to Freud, it merely turns "hysterical suffering into common unhappiness."[10] The fact that he characterizes it as "whitewashing"[11] shows his limited optimism regarding his own therapy.

From childhood on, Sigmund has a contentious relationship with his father, the hapless wool merchant Jacob Freud from Freiberg in Moravia (present-day Příbor, Czech Republic). He vacillates between respect and loathing for the older man, who when his son is twelve years old tells him the following anecdote: once he was walking down the street in Freiberg when, without warning, an antisemite knocked his hat off his head. "Jew, get off the pavement!" shouted the man. But rather than fight back, Freud's father quietly picked up his hat and continued on his way. The young Freud is appalled by his father's cowardice.[12]

When Jacob Freud dies, in 1896, Sigmund skips the funeral. He then shows up late to the gathering afterwards, to the consternation of his sisters, who had cared for their sick father while Sigmund pursued his studies. It is in part for biographical reasons that the Ancient Greek myth of Oedipus, who (unwittingly) kills his father and marries his mother, resonates in Freud's thinking. Over time he will establish an entire school of psychology based on the classical myth.

Sigismund Schlomo Freud, born May 6, 1856 in Freiberg, is set apart even as a child. He reads excessively and is first in his class at the *gymnasium* year after year. His eagerness to learn is matched by his uncompromising nature. As an adolescent he shortens his name to Sigmund and decides that religion doesn't interest him, even though his family are observant Jews. In one of hundreds of letters to his fiancée Martha he later admits that "I do have a tendency toward tyranny."[13]

When Sigmund is four years old, Jacob and Sigmund's mother Amalia, who is Jacob's second wife and twenty years his junior (according to some sources she's his third), move the family to Leipzig. Jacob is hoping to enter the textile trade in the city, but he is denied right of residence. The family finally ends up in Vienna and, specifically, like many Jews, in Leopoldstadt. Sigmund is the oldest of seven children—he has five sisters and a little brother, Alexander, who is born in 1866, the baby of the family. Another brother, Julius, born a year and a half after Sigmund, dies in infancy. The eldest son quickly comes to occupy a special position in the family. His parents recognize his talent and hope he will bring the family prosperity. In the apartment where the Freuds live, Sigmund is the only child to have his own room, so that he can study without being disturbed. When the piano playing of one of his sisters interrupts his reading, the instrument is summarily carted out of the house. On a family outing to the Prater in 1867 a fortune teller prophesies that the boy will have a career at court—a prediction his parents are pleased to hear. A career in the civil service, maybe even a ministerial post, would suit them just fine.

After earning his *matura*, however, the seventeen-year-old chooses to study medicine. A lecture on the essay "Nature," commonly misattributed to Goethe, convinces him to give up his initial plan to become a jurist. Freud joins a reading group whose members hold intense discussions on Arthur Schopenhauer and Friedrich Nietzsche. Most of those involved in the club are alienated from the Jewish faith and are conscious of their position as outsiders. Freud, too, will write, looking back at this time: "When, in 1873, I first joined the University, I experienced some appreciable disappointments. Above all, I found that I was expected to feel myself inferior and an alien because I was a Jew."[14]

As is clearly evident from his correspondence with friends from his youth, Freud in his student days is proud, ambitious, scornful, and harsh in his judgments. His vindictive nature is also on display: he's not one to forget an injury, and cuts ties with people who disappoint him, usually for good. Freud's ambition is fueled by his and his family's experience of intermittent poverty following his father's failures in business.

In addition to his six siblings, Sigmund also has two half-brothers from Jacob's first marriage. One of them, Emanuel, is older than Freud's own mother Amalia, while the other, Philipp, is deemed by the young Freud to be a far better match for his mother than his own father is. In the mid-1860s both half-brothers move to Manchester, where Sigmund visits them in 1875.

He meets Martha Bernays for the first time in the spring of 1882. She is twenty, he is five years older. By June the couple are engaged. Now he needs a steady income, and quick. Faced with the choice between his dream of a career in research and the desire to stand on his own two feet, Freud chooses the latter and sets up as a neurologist. On April 25, 1886 he opens a practice at Rathausstraße 7, near the Ring. In the early days of the practice he has his sisters sit in the waiting room to make it look like his services are in high demand. Finally the way is clear: on September 13, Sigmund and Martha marry at the town hall in Wandsbek, near Hamburg, where Martha is still living at the time. Returning to Vienna after a honeymoon on the Baltic, Freud finds better premises on the northern Ring.

Here, in a building known as the Sühnhaus, built on the site of a burned-down theater, the couple's first child, Mathilde, is born in 1887. Next comes Jean-Martin in 1889. Martha is pregnant for the third time when, in September 1891, the family moves to Berggasse. For the next forty-seven years, until his flight from the Nazis in the summer of 1938, Freud will live, work, and write at this address. Outwardly his life follows a uniform course. September he usually spends traveling; the rest of the year is marked by the steady rhythms of his work life, seeing patients, attending to his correspondence, and writing, interrupted only by set times for meals and rest. All the adventures and affairs in Freud's life play out in the study and in the consultation room, in his conversations with his patients.

above: Freud in his early twenties stands behind his mother Amalia, surrounded by his siblings and other relatives.

right: Jacob Freud with ten-year-old Sigmund.

Freud is a dedicated worker—for one thing, he writes long letters almost daily, totaling around twenty thousand over the course of his lifetime—and committed to his role as patriarch. He insists on picking out his children's names himself. In the end Martha will give him three boys and three girls. The first-born, Mathilde, is named after Mathilde Breuer, the wife of his esteemed friend; Jean-Martin, Martin for short, after Freud's Parisian mentor Jean-Martin Charcot, with whom Freud studied for five months in the winter of 1885/86. Oliver is named after the English revolutionary Oliver Cromwell, who granted religious freedom to the Jews, and Ernst after Freud's teacher Ernst von Brücke. Daughters Sophie and Anna, born in 1893 and 1895, respectively, receive the names of his patron Josef Paneth's wife and of Freud's favorite sister.

. . .

In 1902, his "cause," as Freud calls psychoanalysis, is still in its nascent stages. Everything seems possible, from a hasty demise to a rapid ascent. On March 3, some eight months before the first Wednesday gathering, he is greeted with a modest success: sixteen years after giving up his academic career to go into private practice, Freud is appointed Professor Extraordinarius at the University of Vienna. To his friend Wilhelm Fließ in Berlin he writes impishly: "'The public enthusiasm is immense.' Congratulations and bouquets are already pouring in as though the role of sexuality had suddenly been realized by His Majesty, the importance of dreams confirmed by the Council of Ministers, and the necessity of treating hysteria by psychoanalytic therapy accepted in Parliament by a two-thirds majority!"[15]

From this point forward his circle of followers grows steadily. Another account of Stekel's survives chronicling the fourth or fifth meeting of the Wednesday Society. In addition to the four founding disciples—Adler, Kahane, Reitler, and Stekel himself—the account notes the presence of two more guests: the "moderate one," probably the music critic David Bach, as well as "the writer." This latter was probably Max Graf, whom we will meet again as the father of little Hans in Freud's first case study of a child suffering from phobia. In the years to come many other doctors will attend the meetings, but also non-physicians as well, like the trained machinist Otto Rank, the lawyer Hanns Sachs, and the publisher Hugo Heller. The core group of "Freudians" is starting to form.

Finally, in March 1907, there is a new guest at the weekly gathering, a young psychiatrist from Switzerland with whom Freud has corresponded for some years: Carl Gustav Jung. As a non-Jew and a renowned researcher at the Burghölzli, a psychiatric clinic in Zurich with an international reputation, Jung seems ideally suited to serve as the face of the movement. Freud thinks very highly of him and makes no attempt to hide the fact that he sees Jung as his heir apparent—to the chagrin of those who had hoped to receive this honor themselves.

In 1908 Freud moves his practice one story up, across the hall from the family's apartment. On April 8 of that year the Wednesday Society starts calling itself the Vienna Psychoanalytic Society and moves its meetings to Café Korb in the city center. Unlike Adler or Stekel, Freud isn't a big frequenter of coffeehouses, but at this point there simply isn't enough room for the group at his practice.

In 1910, Freud at last wants to found an international society. At the second-ever Psychoanalytic Congress in Nuremburg, Jung is to be selected as his lieutenant and elected president for life of the new International Psychoanalytical Association. Freud also wants to place the editorship of the *Zentralblatt*, the house organ of his movement, in Jung's hands. But Adler and Stekel rebel against this plan; they fear a veiled censorship if Jung, as Freud's right-hand man, has the power to determine what gets published. In the end a compromise is reached: Jung becomes president with a limited term in office, and Adler in return is named head of the Vienna chapter, with Stekel as his deputy.

But if there's anything Freud can't forgive, it's a challenge to his authority. His resentment toward Adler and Stekel festers for two years, then he summarily removes both from their posts. In 1913, Jung, the "crown prince," will also be cast aside, a falling out that echoes the ending of Freud's earlier friendships with Wilhelm Fließ and Josef Breuer. Jung, like the others, had gone his own way and strayed too far from psychoanalytic dogma. Freud nevertheless feels that it is the others who are at fault. He cannot suffer any divergent opinions; only faithful followers will he tolerate in his orbit. Freud's irreconcilable nature, and the impact it has on his relationships, form a common thread running throughout his life.

When a former patient of Jung's decides to become a psychoanalyst herself and travels to Vienna to meet Freud in 1911, Jung advises her: "Approach him as a great master and rabbi, and all will be well."[16] After the young Sabina Spielrein has attended several meetings of the Vienna Psychoanalytic Society, she tells the patriarch that he "didn't look malicious, as she had imagined [he] would."[17] Freud laughs it off; after all, the jibe comes from a woman.

The decade following the publication of *The Interpretation of Dreams* in 1899 witnesses the formation of an international organization and a truly unprecedented science of the soul—and more than that, it also sees the emergence of a new cultural movement that Freud directs with a firm hand. He propagates a heretofore non-existent view of what drives the human individual deep within, and of the relationship between body and psyche, brain and mind. To understand how this works and where it comes from, let us look briefly at the first stage of Freud's medical career, when the young doctor was still earning his wages at the Vienna General Hospital. It was here where his ideas first took shape.

THE SOURCE OF SUFFERING

It is late one evening in the early 1880s, and a light is still burning in the physiological department. A research assistant is fumbling with his specimen. Carefully he dissects a human brain, cutting it into paper-thin slices. The microtome, a precision instrument specially designed for this purpose, works its way through the tissue, slice by slice, as if it were a wheel of cheese. The assistant has quickly grown accustomed to working with the tool, even developing a certain dexterity. But his attempt to dye the delicate samples in order to make the basic elements of the cerebral cortex, the neurons, visible under the microscope, just isn't working out. Sometimes the dye is too strong, sometimes too faint; sometimes the procedure damages the tissue, sometimes the specimen bursts apart as it dries. It's maddening!

Freud has been working at the General Hospital for several years now. With over two thousand beds, it is one of the largest hospitals in Europe. He cycles through all the major departments, from anatomy and surgery through internal medicine and pediatrics and on to neurology. After conducting studies in comparative anatomy under the zoologist Carl Claus, at one point spending several weeks studying in Trieste, in October 1876 he begins a position as an assistant in Ernst von Brücke's laboratory. Freud is twenty and has a head full of plans.

At this time the brain, from a scientific standpoint, is still unconquered territory. It's the place where body and mind meet, that much is clear. But how this transpires, what exactly this three-pound lump of furrowed nerve tissue has to do with thinking, feeling, wanting, and memory, is still a mystery. And no wonder, since researchers can only look at the dead organ. Observing a living brain at work and studying its functions is impossible. Thus even the experts disagree as to whether the brain is made up of several distinct units or constitutes one cohesive mass. Its basic elements, the brain cells or neurons, may be easily recognizable under the microscope if dyed in the correct fashion; but whether they are connected, and how they function, no one knows.

Freud is depressed. He can't get a toehold; every attempt he makes, hoping for a breakthrough, only ends in failure. In 1873—when Freud was just beginning his studies—the Italian Camillo Golgi discovered the *reazione nera*, or black reaction, an initial method for dyeing brain tissue, and in doing so opened up a new universe to research. Will he too be able to find a way to penetrate deeper into the human interior? Freud has his doubts. He is even more skeptical, however, of one of the foundational principles of medicine at this time, which holds that all psychological suffering, whether it be madness, hysteria, melancholy, anxiety, or compulsive behavior, is rooted in physical defect. Old medical dogma has it that when the psyche falls ill, what is in fact sick is the brain. Couldn't mental illness simply be "psychogenic" in origin, without there being an underlying defect in the nervous system? This is the question the young Freud is asking himself.

As stubborn as his colleagues are in their attempts to trace everything related to the psyche back to a physical substrate, they are just as incapable of pinning this substrate down. Staring down at the gray mass of brain tissue on his dissecting table, Freud wonders: where does the human will reside? Where do fears and memories dwell amidst all the grooves and convolutions? Will it ever be possible to peer within these layers, to push ahead to the very nature of consciousness?

The biological dogma of his time rests in part on a groundbreaking scientific achievement whose influence has extended to many areas of natural science. The talk these days is centered on the successful study of infectious diseases. After doctors like Louis Pasteur and Robert Koch discovered pathogenic microorganisms, it seemed to be just a matter of time until similar explanations could be found for other ailments: if gangrene and tuberculosis are caused by tiny bacteria invisible to the naked eye, this could also be the case for disorders of the psyche. Do toxins produced by such pathogens throw the cognitive organ out of whack? For a time Freud plays with the thought that hysterical over-excitation might be traced back to the effects of a "sexual toxin." He soon abandons the hypothesis, however.

For him the question of the somatic roots of the psyche is of pivotal importance. For if the hypothesis that all psychological suffering has a physiological cause is true, then physically healthy people who present with symptoms of anxiety, paralysis, or other impairments can really only be either hypochondriacs or malingerers. If emotional strain or the circumstances of one's life do not qualify as potential triggers, then that leaves only a lack of will or a desire to escape into illness. That is to say: these sufferers *want* to be sick; they choose to be sick as a way of seeking shelter from the demands of everyday life. Freud doesn't rule this idea out—after all, illness certainly has its advantages. But surely only a very small number of patients could *consciously* decide to be sick. If they are putting on an act, the act is also for themselves—lacking insight, as they do, into their actual motives.

For the most part, people suffering from mental illness find neither understanding nor any real help from doctors of this era. The psychiatry of the time institutionalizes patients, observes them, and refines its diagnoses. There are no real therapeutic methods; hydrotherapy and electrotherapy, though often used, are quite evidently useless. The ice-cold affusions and electric "current cures" have the sole purpose of driving away mental suffering and replacing it with suffering of a different, physical kind. The use of suggestion under hypnosis does work sometimes, but often it doesn't. The method, which Freud becomes familiar with during his time studying at the Salpêtrière in Paris, is not very reliable.

When Freud opens his practice in 1886, he too has a device for transmitting electric stimuli. But he hardly ever uses it. He prefers the power of talking, a treatment "by measures which operate in the first instance and immediately upon the human mind. Foremost among such measures is the use of words; and words are the essential tool of mental treatment."[18] As yet there is no mention of psychoanalysis; this term first appears in May 1896, in Freud's essay "Further Remarks on the Neuro-psychoses of Defense."

Imagine the relief that people must have felt at not having to fear mistreatment or criticism from the person from whom they sought treatment in their time of need. Allowing a patient to express themselves, to say what is worrying them and how they feel while trusting the expertise of the doctor—this is the great advantage of Freud's method of psychological treatment.

But we're not quite there yet. For now Freud is a frustrated young doctor in a giant hospital who is still in search of his calling. It's late, his eyes are aching, he can wait until morning to look at the newly sliced specimens. Plus he has an uncontrollable urge to smoke. He places the brain back in its jar and carries it back to the anatomical collection. Then he turns out the light, leaves the hospital through the imposing main gate and lights himself a cigar as he steps out into the street. Exhaling smoke with pleasure, he turns up his collar and heads off toward home.

PSYCHOLOGY WITHOUT THE PSYCHE

What a sad hick town Batesburg is. The days crawl past, each one the same as the one before, their monotony exceeded only by the endless rows of cotton in the fields. His job at the school is a torment to him. Here he's expected to instill the bare minimum of knowledge into the dunces that the local farmers call their children. And it hasn't even been a year since he first started working here. This job was the only suitable position he could find after five years at Furman University in Greenville, a Baptist college, like so many in the South. He received his master's there. Now, at twenty-one, he's principal of the "Batesburg Institute," as the school pretentiously calls itself. If there's one thing John Broadus Watson knows, it's that he has to get out of here. The sooner the better.

Around the time that Freud is eagerly awaiting the response to his dream book in Vienna, Watson the college graduate, six thousand kilometers away in South Carolina, is cursing his fate. He's poor, a country boy with a master of arts degree whose deeply pious mother had scrimped and saved to pay for his studies. Watson has neither top grades (he graduated fourteenth out of a class of twenty-two) nor friends in positions of influence. But he attempts the impossible: on July 20, 1900, he writes a letter to William Rainey Harper, the president of the University of Chicago, founded just a few years earlier. He begs Harper for a scholarship or a break on tuition and promises his complete dedication. Watson is inspired to make something of his life, and his only chance is a degree from "a real university."[19] He gets some help from the president of his alma mater, who provides a flattering letter of recommendation to include with his application. He calls Watson "one of our strongest men [. . .] a gentleman of marked ability, very studious, a successful teacher, and a man of high character."[20] This is, to put it mildly, a shameless exaggeration.

. . .

Born on January 9, 1878, John B. Watson grows up in a small town surrounded by cotton fields. He is the fourth of six children. When John is thirteen, his father, a drinker and a braggart, walks out on the family. His wife Emma is left with just one option: she sells the farm and moves the children to nearby Greenville. There the children go to school, and John attends college. His mother wants him to become a preacher.

He is named after John Albert Broadus, a renowned theologian admired by his mother. Twenty years later Watson will give the pseudonym "Albert B." to an infant whom, in a famous experiment, he teaches to experience awful fright at the sight of anything fluffy—a late act of revenge against his namesake, perhaps? Despite her good connections to the Baptist church, Emma doesn't earn enough money to support her family.

John is a loner—taciturn and quick-tempered, with an arrogant streak. In the judgement of one professor, he is "more interested in ideas and theories than . . . people" and "[thinks] too highly of himself."[21] But Watson has ambition and big plans. His boldest idea will be to found his own, strictly scientific research discipline: a psychology without consciousness. As a young man, however, he often finds himself in trouble with the law. He is not ill-disposed towards alcohol and is often picking fights; on one occasion the police arrest him for firing a gun in the middle of town.

Whatever it was that inspired him to write his entreaty to Harper, Watson is rewarded: in the fall of 1900, at the dawn of the new century, he enrolls at the University of Chicago as a student in experimental psychology. The city on the shores of Lake Michigan is exhilarating; he throws himself into the bustle of big city life. While the Viennese celebrate splendor and glory, here architects like Louis Sullivan and Frank Lloyd Wright build functional skyscrapers, the cathedrals of the future. And like these colossi of steel and concrete, the dreams of the city's inhabitants soar high into the sky.

The philosopher John Dewey, founder of pragmatism, has taught in Chicago since 1894. Watson takes a seminar on Immanuel Kant, but can't make much of his speculations on the "conditions of the possibility of knowledge." He's looking for something tangible, something that will change people's lives. And so he finds his way to psychology.

But his preferred object of study isn't, say, the thorny human psyche. Rather it's . . . the lab rat. Under the guidance of the biologist Jacques Loeb, Watson investigates how rodents navigate their way through mazes, make note of places to find food and react to sensory stimuli. Loeb is from Germany and advances a strictly mechanistic view of living things. Man is nothing but a biochemical machine that obeys objectively describable natural laws. "Our instincts are the root of our ethics," says Loeb, and these instincts "are just as hereditary as is the form of our body."[22] Thought, consciousness, will—for the scientist these are causally irrelevant side effects of neural activity. This reductionist worldview impresses Watson.

In 1903, as the university's youngest doctoral candidate to date, he hands in his PhD thesis. The focus of the dissertation is the connection between the brain development of rats of various ages and their behavior in the maze. A substance called myelin, as we now know, speeds up the transmission of stimuli along the neural pathways, which is a precondition for associative learning. In the years to come, Watson will stick with his animal studies. In sometimes grisly experiments, he will gradually rob animals of their sensory organs and investigate how they orient themselves without sensory stimuli.

Watson doesn't resist the temptations of the big city. He frequents bars, theaters—and brothels, too. Until he establishes himself as a behavioral researcher, he steadily takes on debt in order to stave off bankruptcy. His straitened circumstances fuel his desire to make it big someday.

Women are drawn to the dapper Watson. He courts several of his fellow students, chief among them a young woman named Vida Sutton. Sutton gives him the brush-off, however; it seems not everyone cares for his brash manner. Then, in a seminar, Watson meets nineteen-year-old Mary Ickes. The two of them grow close, keep their relationship a secret and finally marry on December 26, 1903. They will go on to have two children, whom they'll name after themselves, Mary and John.

What Watson fails to reckon with, however, is the insistent distrust of his brother-in-law, Harold Ickes. Ickes can't stand Watson and accuses him of cheating on Mary with Vida Sutton. Ickes even hires a private detective to tail his brother-in-law, but the detective can't find anything conclusive. True, Watson does meet with Sutton occasionally, but there's no indication that their relationship is intimate. This doesn't stop Ickes from taking his accusation to the university administration and demanding Watson's firing. The case is investigated and dismissed for lack of evidence.

After making a name for himself with his meticulous studies in the laboratory, in the fall of 1908—the Psychoanalytic Society has just been founded in Vienna—Watson moves to Johns Hopkins University in Baltimore. He makes shrewd use of offers from other universities—some real, some invented—to drive up his own price. When, soon after his arrival in Baltimore, a sex scandal forces the head of the Department of Philosophy and Psychology, James Mark Baldwin, to resign, Watson senses his chance. The gifted lab researcher and resolute empiricist takes over the top post at the age of thirty.

Watson works incessantly, often to the point of exhaustion. Alongside his work in Baltimore he conducts field studies in a breeding colony of migratory birds on a group of islands off the coast of Florida, gives guest lectures at various universities, edits scientific journals, and writes articles for popular magazines. Watson recognizes that bringing his bold theories to the public will benefit his career.

In 1910 he pens his first manifesto, which appears in *Harper's* magazine under the title "The New Science of Animal Behavior."[23] In it, he counters the speculative metaphysics of the psyche by putting forward a progressive psychology of behavior. No different from physics or biology, this new discipline describes universal laws, like those that the Russian scientist Ivan Pavlov had discovered with his conditioning of dogs. An initially neutral ("unconditioned") stimulus, like the ringing of a bell, if combined with a biologically relevant stimulus, like food, can soon trigger on its own the reactions typical to the biological stimulus. Pavlov's dogs began to slobber as soon as the bell rang.

In the spring of 1913, at Columbia University in New York, Watson proclaims the beginning of a new science. Shortly thereafter, one of his lectures appears in print under the title "Psychology as the Behaviorist Views It."[24] The term "behaviorist" is an invention of Watson's, meant to convey what he considers the only sound basis for psychology: measurable data, taken from observable behavior. The behavior could be that of humans or of animals; it doesn't matter, since there's no fundamental difference between the two. Language and abstract thinking expand the behavioral repertoire considerably, true, but, according to Watson, the similarities outweigh the differences.

A scientist on the make: the psychologist John B. Watson as a young man

His psychology is "a purely objective experimental branch of natural science. Its theoretical goal is the prediction and control of behavior."[25] Not only does Watson reject all speculation about the unconscious, he also breaks with the (to that point dominant) branch of psychology that conducted empirical consciousness research. The pioneers of the discipline, like

Wilhelm Wundt of Leipzig and his students, hope to identify the elements of thought and perception through systematic self-observation. They turn their gaze inwards, describe feelings and associations, draw parallels between objective sensory stimuli and their subjective perception. Watson rejects such methods, deeming them unreliable. "The time seems to have come," he writes, "when psychology must discard all reference to consciousness; when it need no longer delude itself into thinking that it is making mental states the object of observation."[26]

This claim justifies the program of a science of behavior. It differs radically from the approach prescribed by psychoanalysis, which calls for interpreting mental conflicts and making the patient conscious of them. Behaviorism places the focus on behavior, or, to be more precise, on patterns of stimulus and response and the laws about learning that can be inferred from them. From this point of view, psychotherapy is nothing other than a targeted learning process.

Though Watson has no interest in developing a therapeutic method, he founds a branch of research out of which behavioral therapy ultimately emerges. There is a certain irony in the fact that a man for whom "the psyche" was nothing but a pretty fiction would become a founding figure of modern psychotherapy. In 1890 the philosopher William James wrote: "[Psychology] is no science, it is only the hope of a science."[27] The ambitious Dr. Watson wants to turn this hope into reality.

THE MIRACULOUS HEALING OF ANNA O.

The first psychoanalytic treatment worthy of the name is conducted a good decade and a half before the term "psychoanalysis" is born—between the final months of 1880 and the summer of 1882. And it's conducted not by Freud, who at this time is still dissecting brains, but rather by a Viennese internist named Josef Breuer, whom Freud gets to know through his boss, Ernst von Brücke. As for the patient, whom we might call "patient zero" in the history of modern psychotherapy, she quite literally has a lot to say on the matter.

Bertha Pappenheim, who will become famous as "Anna O.," more or less prescribes herself the "talking cure," as she calls it. The smart and sensitive future women's rights campaigner sometimes refers to the treatment in jest (and with a frank sexual allusion) as "chimney sweeping." She uses those exact words, since one aspect of her condition is that she goes through periods of speaking only English. Her doctor's role in the procedure is little more than to serve as prompter and notetaker. It is mid-November 1882 when Breuer tells his colleague Freud of the curious case, which will lead the younger man to draw far-reaching conclusions about the origins of hysteria. How did it all come about?

Bertha Pappenheim comes from a prosperous merchant family and is friends with Martha Bernays, the woman to whom Freud becomes engaged in the summer of 1882. When Bertha is eleven years old, the Pappenheims—father Siegmund, mother Recha, Bertha, and her little brother Wilhelm—move to Liechtensteinstraße in Vienna's ninth district, just a few steps away from Freud's future practice. The family likes to spend the summer months in the mountains, at the spa town of Bad Ischl. There Bertha's father, whom she loves deeply, falls gravely ill. Deeply worried, the twenty-one-year-old keeps watch at his bedside. And here her unusual ailment begins.

First Bertha is plagued by fears and hallucinations. She sees snakes and evil, hideous faces. Next she loses her capacity for speech: for days at a time she can't speak or can only say things in English, French, or Italian (as a daughter of a well-heeled family, she enjoyed a multilingual education). Added to these difficulties are acute pains in her face, deafness, and paralysis of the limbs on one half of her body; she starts to squint, her vision is blurred; at times she can barely eat, and her memory fails her. In short: she displays almost every known symptom of hysteria.

In the late 19th century, so many women are afflicted with these distinctive pains, spasms, speech impairments, and lapses of memory that it comes to seem like an epidemic. As with a contagious infection, the cases spread, but it is almost exclusively the daughters of upper-class families who are stricken. Women from the working classes are as good as immune. What's more, it is mainly young women who get sick. Clearly the ailment must have something to do with the living circumstances of those who suffer from it.

On the one hand, women from bourgeois families are privileged in many respects: they are better nourished, better educated, face fewer physical demands, and suffer through fewer traumatic experiences. On the other hand, in one key respect, they are under almost round-the-clock pressure: they must always maintain decorum and self-control. In fin-de-siècle society, there is an obligation to suppress all physicality.

The women's girdles are as constricting as the rules for class-appropriate behavior. To have a sense of self-regard means to observe the proprieties. One must never permit oneself to sweat, nor give off any odors, nor make any uncouth sounds—and above all else, one must not think of sex, much less talk about it! Ladies regularly have fainting spells; in many homes, tins of smelling salts are kept at the ready in case of such an event. Sex education is not provided, or at least not officially. Is it possible that the cause of hysteria lies in this denial of physical needs? This at least would explain why working-class women aren't susceptible to the condition: though their lives are marked by many hardships, they at least get to stink and have sex. But to point this out in the pleasure-phobic society of the time is completely unthinkable.

With a scholarship in hand, Freud travels to Paris in October 1885 to study under Jean-Martin Charcot, the famous professor at the Salpêtrière. The guest from Vienna attends Charcot's hysteria demonstrations in the medical department's auditorium. He looks on as the professor uses hypnotic suggestion to free patients from paralysis and put an end to their fainting spells. The hypnoses, conducted with great flair, captivate an audience that extends far beyond the circle of young doctors. Charcot's cures are nothing short of miraculous. His method is to induce a shock by touching the hypnotized patients on their stomach or shoulders, after which the women seem to have been rid of their symptoms, often instantly. It will later come to light that Charcot would give some of his patients instructions on how they should respond to his laying on of hands, while others would dutifully act out the role of convalescent, eager to fulfill the expectations of the professor and his audience. Where exactly the border between magic and medicine lies, no one at these demonstrations can really say. What counts is having faith in the therapeutic effect.

Nevertheless, the patients' suffering isn't merely simulated. Freud suspects that the hysterics are pretending, but that they themselves don't know it. Which is to say: the symptoms function as a release valve for conflicting forces within the psyche, but the mechanism that makes this possible remains hidden to those afflicted. They aren't faking their hysteria; ascribing it to pure imagination or a weak constitution doesn't explain things either. Freud believes there's more to it than that.

Together with Breuer he pens a "Preliminary Communication" covering a few cases of hysteria that appears in 1893 in the *Neurologisches Zentralblatt*. Two years later they include this paper as the first chapter in their book *Studies on Hysteria*. In it they write: "Hysterics suffer mainly from reminiscences."[28] In other words: the symptoms result from the repression of unconscious, because sexual, wishes, and from experiences that are inaccessible to memory.

But how did Freud come up with this idea? At first, Breuer scarcely knew how to treat Anna O. and her rapidly mutating complaints. He limited himself to observing her behavior and letting her talk. To encourage her to talk freely, without restraint, he did his best to put her in a trance-like state of deep relaxation. In this state, she was supposed to attempt to remember the origin, the first appearance of each symptom. This method turns out to be a winner. "When this happened for the first time—when, as a result of an accidental and spontaneous utterance of this kind, during the evening hypnosis, a disturbance which had persisted for a considerable time vanished—I was greatly surprised,"[29] notes Breuer. The procedure was now clear: Bertha was to deliberately seek out the moment that each of her symptoms made its first appearance.

One indicative session focuses on Bertha's inability to drink—at this point in her illness she relies solely on melons and other fruits to quench her thirst because she finds water and other drinks revolting. Under hypnosis she connects this to a long-forgotten event: in the room of her English lady's companion, she had observed a small dog, a "horrid creature!", drinking out of a glass. The memory makes her very agitated; full of rage, she inveighs against the little mongrel. "After giving further energetic expression to the anger she had held back, she asked for something to drink, drank a large quantity of water without any difficulty and woke from her hypnosis with the glass at her lips; and thereupon the disturbance vanished, never to return."[30]

This was the cathartic method, taken from the Greek word *kátharsis*, or purging. "Abreacting" an emotion makes the patient aware of the hidden source of the malady and eliminates it at the same time. Freud will further refine this principle in his 1914 essay "Remembering, Repeating, and Working-through," but the idea remains essentially the same: let it out! Give repressed feelings and thoughts space, then the demons of the unconscious will flee of their own accord!

The whip and hat suit her: A buttoned-up Bertha Pappenheim

It probably wasn't quite so easy, however. Breuer's account does end with the triumphant announcement: "Since then she [Anna O.] has enjoyed complete health."[31] But the fact that after concluding his treatment he sent Bertha to the Sanatorium Bellevue outside of Vienna suggests that her recovery wasn't so complete after all. Moreover, Bertha will continue to be visited by recurrent hysterical attacks afterwards. "[I]t is ironic that Anna O.'s unsuccessful treatment should have become, for posterity, the prototype of a cathartic cure," writes medical historian Henri Ellenberger.[32]

Freud doesn't get bogged down in such details. Decades after the fact, in a letter to the writer Stefan Zweig, he describes what led to his brilliant inspiration: "On the evening of the day when all her symptoms had been disposed of, [Breuer] was summoned to the patient again, found her confused and writhing in abdominal cramps. Asked what was wrong with her, she replied: 'Now Dr. B.'s child is coming!' At this moment he held in his hand the key that would have opened the 'doors to the Mothers,'[33] but he let it drop. With all his great intellectual gifts there was nothing Faustian in his nature. Seized by conventional horror he took flight and abandoned the patient to a colleague."[34] According to

Freud, the key to the mystery lies in Bertha's having imagined a romantic relationship with her doctor; her repressed libido is the actual source of her suffering.

"I admit," writes Breuer to the psychiatrist Auguste Forel twelve years after publication of the *Studies*, "that immersing myself in the theory and practice of sexuality is not to my taste."[35] Disagreement over the question of whether hysteria is exclusively sexual in origin, as Freud believes, puts a strain on the two doctors' friendship. Initially Freud holds the view that the symptoms must stem from a real trauma that the patient has experienced. According to this hypothesis, which he calls the "seduction theory," every hysterical woman was abused in her childhood or adolescence, usually by her father or another relative.

Freud presents his idea on April 21, 1896 at a meeting of the Verein für Psychiatrie und Neurologie (Organization for Psychiatry and Neurology) and is met with general bafflement and even, from some members, enraged protest. Richard von Kraft-Ebbing, the famous professor of psychiatry at the University of Vienna, calls Freud's theory a "scientific fairy tale." After all, hysteria in its various guises is so widespread that, if Freud were right, it would mean that tens of thousands, if not millions, of girls had been sexually abused and raped by their fathers, uncles, brothers, or employers, or by strangers (even if terms like "sexual abuse" and "rape" wouldn't have been used at the time).

It can certainly be assumed that, given the patriarchal conditions of the time, abusive sexual behavior is not at all rare, or in any case is more widespread than Freud's contemporaries are prepared to accept. The male head of household's rule over his wife, children, and domestic staff is absolute. Neither his offspring nor the maids are safe from him, especially since corporal punishment and other forms of violence are considered normal methods of child-rearing. However, given the wealth of symptoms, there surely cannot be a *single* type of hysteria; rather it seems more likely that there are various forms of distress that all get lumped in together. Sartorial fashion alone is responsible for fainting spells, breathing difficulties, and feelings of constriction. On top of that comes a daily routine which is permeated with prohibitions and violence. For young ladies especially, remaining in sound mental health amidst the social constraints of the late 19th century is a challenge.

The fact that the phenomenon of hysteria is unknown to present-day medicine has a lot to do with the greater degree of freedom and self-determination in our lives today, as well as to the strides towards women's equality. Psychological syndromes are always, at least in part, a product of particular living conditions. Freud's choice to raise the suppressed libido to the status of anthropological constant, rather than understand it as a phenomenon linked to a particular age, was a consequential error.

The case of Anna O. marks the debut of an idea that lives on today: there is healing power in awareness! Facing the hidden sources of one's suffering, gaining an understanding of one's injuries and desires and acting out the emotions associated with them leads to the disappearance of one's illness. This claim appears again and again, in many different forms, throughout the history of psychology. But as old as this credo is, it has always been accompanied by the suspicion that it is a myth.

THE TANGLED WEB OF THOUGHTS

"Hot."
"*Cold.*"
"Woman."
"*Man.*"
"Love."
—"*Marriage.*"
"Children."
. . . "*Have.*"
"Mother."
. . . —"*Death.*"

The test goes on forever. Word by word, the man leading the experiment goes down his list, his face expressionless. In a monotone voice he reads one prompt after the next, and in response the test subject is supposed to say the first word that pops into her head. All the while she grips two small metal knobs, one in each hand, that are hooked up to the galvanometer. A weak continuous current runs through this device, allowing it to register the slightest changes in the level of skin conductance. The polygraph that comes into use years later will function according to the same principle.

The association experiment is supposed to bring to light unconscious psychical reactions that are triggered by the prompts. The list contains hundreds of words; the test takes a while. After going through the list once, the leader and patient go through it again a second and often even a third time, since divergences from the first round's responses are an opportunity to glean more information. The analysis looks at the literal sense and character of the responses given, as well as tempo, intonation, and any potential stuttering or mixing up of words—plus of course the electrodermal response. Which stimulus words get the subject worked up? Which cause her to hesitate or produce odd, uncommon associations? Adding up all these factors, a gaggle of young psychiatrists at the Burghölzli in Zurich then draw conclusions about what they call "emotionally accentuated complexes"—a person's emotionally charged, hidden desires and thoughts.

The conscientious Dr. Franz Riklin encounters the method shortly after the turn of the century during a guest stint at Emil Kraepelin's clinic in Munich and brings it back with him to the Burghölzli—a one-of-a-kind institution for treating the mentally ill that has stood on a hilltop amidst the vineyards outside of Zurich since 1870. The goal here is not merely to put patients away, but to cure them. The head of the fortress-like institution, which is surrounded by a three-meter-high wall, is the psychiatrist Eugen Bleuler, who took over in 1898. He and his junior colleague Carl Gustav Jung recognize the potential of the association method when Riklin explains it to them. Right away they decide to try the method out on a few patients—hysterics, lunatics, patients with dementia, alcoholics—and, for purposes of comparison, healthy people as well. In 1904 the first studies on the association experiment appear, authored by Jung and Riklin.

Wilhelm Wundt, the founding father of experimental psychology, had long employed the method at his world-famous Leipziger Institut. But the attempt to draw conclusions about a person's psychological state from spontaneous answers to stimulus words can originally be traced back to an eccentric English gentleman: Sir Francis Galton.

In 1883 Galton had published a book with the title *Inquiries into Human Faculty and Its Development*, a collection of musings on various topics related to biology. Among other things the book discussed the peculiar characteristics of self-observation. While strolling down London's Pall Mall, Galton had noticed that many people, buildings, shops, and other objects awakened memories and images from his youth and triggered various thoughts. Meticulous chronicler that he was, Galton recalled "about 300" objects to which he had one or several associations. Many of the associations repeated. His thoughts, he mused, were "like the actors in theatres where large processions are represented, who march off one side of the stage, and, going round by the back, come on again at the other."[36] There must be, Galton conjectured, "deeper strata of mental operations"[37] where experiences that had left an impression were conserved. This was the starting point for studying complexes of ideas, an approach that placed the Zurich psychiatrists at the forefront of neuropsychiatry at the beginning of the 20th century.

Jung and his colleagues suspect that even the seemingly confused fantasies of psychotics have an internal coherence and are more meaningful than they would appear to be at first glance. According to this

A therapeutic institution, not a detention center: the Burghölzli psychiatric clinic in Zurich, circa 1900

hypothesis, these patients' hallucinations, and the often disturbing images and thoughts that accompany them, follow patterns. There is a method to the madness, and psychiatric research can decipher it with the help of the association method—of this Jung is convinced. Nowhere is this technique applied more creatively and systematically than at the Burghölzli. In hundreds of test series, Jung, Riklin, and their colleagues go hunting for clues to the unconscious.

Their findings seem perfectly aligned with Freud's theory of repression: if test subjects hesitate for a particularly long time in giving an answer, or respond using very emotionally charged words, this points to a trauma, a buried memory, or a wishful fantasy. Jung explains: "In earlier writings I have already pointed out that the association experiment devised by me gives the same results in principle, and that psychoanalysis is really no different from an association experiment."[38] Jung's approach to exposing the nodes of the unconscious provides psychoanalysis with the scientific affirmation that Freud has longed for. Up to this point it has been little more than the hobby horse of an unknown Viennese neurologist. With the Swiss psychiatrist's help, Freud hopes to finally receive the recognition he deserves from the medical community.

But not all of those working in this field are dedicated followers of Freud like Jung. In May 1906 the psychiatrist Gustav Aschaffenburg delivers a fierce attack against psychoanalytic interpretations of the association experiment.[39] He argues that the reactions recorded in the test by no means reveal unconscious sexual desires and conflicts—these are drawn from wide-ranging assumptions that are anything but convincing. According to Aschaffenburg, the psychiatrists in Zurich are coming to unreliable conclusions based on the content and latent meanings of words that have myriad sources. They are assigning more significance to the whole procedure than is really there.

Aschaffenburg cites a case from Jung's post-doctoral thesis *Studies in Word Association*.[40] An obsessional neurotic patient whom Jung introduces in the last chapter of his thesis, hearing the stimulus word "tree" (*Baum*), responds without hesitation with the word "plum" (*Pflaume*). Jung then explains: "The German *Pflaume* (plum) is, like Swiss *Zwetschge* (plum), a popular sex symbol in our colloquial language." In another round of associations the patient hesitates when prompted with the words "yellow," "custom," "hated," "dear," "part," and "old" and responds several times with the word "child." Jung's conclusion: "The patient feels herself to be old and ugly, is very sensitive about her sallow complexion, above all pays anxious attention to her body; in particular she does not like being so small. Presumably she has a great desire to get married; she would certainly be a loving wife to her husband and she would like to have children. Behind these not very suspicious erotic symptoms, however, there seems to lie a sexual complex that the patient has every reason to repress. There are signs that allow the conclusion that she pays more than usual attention to her genitals. In a well brought-up and educated woman this can only refer to masturbation."[41]

Aschaffenburg's bafflement is evident in his response. "I am completely incapable of following this reasoning. I cannot concede that this interpretation can make any claim whatsoever to probability."[42] One reason for his skepticism is that many associations simply follow ordinary habits: spontaneous thoughts aren't necessarily expressions of one's innermost mental life; rather it's possible they simply relate to the prompt itself, or sound similar. Thus "small" comes after "big," "chair" comes after "table," and "house" comes after "mouse." And since the examiner is never fully acquainted with a test subject's habits or the circumstances of their life, they cannot know whether banal everyday experiences have found their way into the answers. In short, says Aschaffenburg, his colleagues in Zurich saw in the responses what they wanted to see, and then tried to talk their patients into believing their conclusions. This, like psychoanalysis as a whole, is a novel form of suggestion: "Freud's manner of proceeding is an association method. The patient indiscriminately relates whatever occurs to him. Then, however, the investigator, by means of questions and occasional interpretations, steers things in a certain direction, and indeed a direction that leads to sexual interpretations."[43]

Jung sees things quite differently. According to him, he revealed numerous sexual fantasies held by his obsessive patient, who fears she could be responsible for the death of other people. These fantasies trigger a sense of unease; in response, her conscious mind goes looking for a "screen cause" (*Deckursache*), a seemingly plausible reason, and comes up with the fear of killing others. It turns out that as a child the woman once eavesdropped on her parents having sex. According to Jung, the repressed memory of this event triggers an obsessive preoccupation with the sex act. The idea that a young woman might have sexual fantasies even without the trauma of overhearing her parents mid-coitus doesn't concern Jung. For him, the pressure that the secret exerts on the patient's psyche explains her obsessions and anxiety. "Pathological ideas can be definitely submerged only by a strong effort. People with obsessions and compulsions are weak; they are unable to keep their ideas in check."[44]

In his autobiography, *Memories, Dreams, Reflections*, Jung also describes his treatment of a depressive woman at the Burghölzli. In anguish over a man she had loved in her youth, the woman had given her children unclean river water to drink. Her four-year-old daughter contracted typhoid fever and died; shortly thereafter the mother came to the clinic for treatment. Jung writes: "From the association test I had seen that she was a murderess, and I had learned many of the details of her secret. It was at once apparent that this was a sufficient reason for her depression."[45] How the details of such a grave secret could be ascertained from responses to stimulus words, Jung doesn't say—the reader must be content with his "it was at once apparent."

Despite its imponderability, the association experiment at the turn of the early 20th century is one of the keenest tools in the rather meager toolbox of psychiatric diagnosis. While there is a range of typical symptoms and behaviors known to practitioners, including cognitive, perceptual, and emotional impairment, these don't add up to a coherent set of distinct syndromes. As a result, most patients get lumped into one of two broad categories that go back to Emil Kraepelin: manic-depressive psychosis or dementia praecox (in layman's terms: premature dementia). In addition, patients are coming down with fashionable syndromes like somnambulism (disorientation with trance-like moments of inspiration), neurasthenia (nervous restlessness and anxiety), and, of course, hysteria.

In part on the basis of association studies, the head of the Burghölzli, Eugen Bleuler, proposes at a scientific congress in late 1908 that "premature cerebral softening," as dementia praecox is also known, be renamed "schizophrenia." The new term is meant to express the understanding that the heart of the illness is not the failure of the patient's mental faculties, but rather a detachment of thinking and feeling from reality. This psychotic disorder, which afflicts most of the patients at the Burghölzli, fascinates Jung. Because he doesn't believe in random coincidences, he suspects that an underlying structure lies concealed within the patients' fantasies. But how to cast light on this web of connections? To him the best means seems to be a precise measuring of the patients' associations, with no outside influence steering them one way or another. The question is: does the person leading the experiment not (unconsciously) steer them more than he suspects?

. . .

The association test is an early entry in the genre of psychological procedures that turn statistical probabilities into unambiguous conclusions about individual cases. Another is the inkblot test developed by a later Burghölzli psychiatrist, Hermann Rorschach, which posits that the stories that test subjects invent about symmetrical patterns supposedly reveal something about their mental state. And there's also a method that will come into fashion half a century later in US courts of law: the polygraph or lie detector. This test purports to detect the presence of hidden knowledge—about, say, a crime—based on the degree of emotional agitation or nervousness an examinee displays when answering related questions. The method certainly isn't airtight: some people could just be nervous, even if they had nothing to do with the crime under investigation, while a coldblooded psychopath might not bat an eyelid. Nevertheless, polygraph test results are frequently admitted as evidence in court.

Jung himself writes a paper on the question of whether his association test is suitable for forensic investigation. The paper appears under the title "On the Psychological Diagnosis of Facts" in 1905, at almost the same time as Freud's classic *Three Essays on the Theory of Sexuality*. By this point Zurich has established itself alongside Vienna as a second center of psychoanalysis. The Burghölzli's renown increases the Swiss doctors' chances of gaining international recognition. A motley crew of independent physicians who meet to discuss their cases can hardly compete with institutional Swiss expertise. Freud recognizes that Jung will secure more recognition for his movement than he himself ever could. And so he does everything he can to win the Swiss psychiatrist's commitment to his cause.

Meanwhile Jung's pride and his big ideas are already causing headaches for his boss Bleuler. The director has trouble convincing his young colleague to take on onerous assignments. Bleuler is well within his rights—but Jung doesn't like taking orders. When Auguste Forel, Bleuler's predecessor as director of the Burghölzli, visits Zurich to inquire about the state of research at the institution, he asks in amazement: "Who is the boss in this hospital, Dr. Bleuler or Herr Jung?"[46] The latter is so full of self-confidence that he seems to feel his boss is actually his subordinate.

Jung's ego stems in part from his background. Born in 1875 to an ecclesiastical family, he grows up in Kleinhüningen, near Basel. His father, Johann Paul Achilles Jung, is the village pastor; his mother Emilie is the daughter of Samuel Preiswerk, another well-known clergyman. His paternal grandfather and namesake Carl Gustav Jung believes himself to be an illegitimate son of Goethe—a legend that his grandson proudly repeats. Jung will also feel a lifelong connection to the august poet. Another quirk that runs in the family is a penchant for the supernatural: Jung's cousin Helene Preiswerk is a successful medium who delivers messages from the beyond at hundreds of séances and occult meetings—until one day she is found guilty of fraud.

Jung's own imaginative gifts reveal themselves early. From childhood on he has vivid dreams. In one, the ten-year-old dreams that a colossal dung heap falls from the sky and buries the venerable old Basel minster. Jung takes this as a sign not to follow in his father's footsteps. Nevertheless, he will have an affinity for the spiritual throughout his life.

In 1895 Jung begins to study medicine in Zurich. He specializes in psychiatry and starts working at the Burghölzli in 1900. Jung concludes his studies in 1902 with a dissertation, "On the Psychology and Pathology of So-called Occult Phenomena," in which he reckons with his cousin's spiritualism—though with an eye as well to his scientifically minded professors. "In the dissertation," writes Jung biographer Deirdre Bair, "his intention was to make the point that psychic powers emerge from psychological states of mind and have nothing to do with the so-called supernatural."[47] Jung's decision to talk openly about his own experiences with Preiswerk's séances casts a pall over his relationship with his mother's side of the family.

Despite his strict scientific education, telepathy and precognition remain incontestable reality for Jung. This is evident from an episode that takes place during his first visit to Vienna in the spring of 1907. On March 3, he and his wife, along with his colleague from the Burghölzli Ludwig Binswanger, pay a visit to Berggasse. At this first meeting Freud and Jung talk for almost thirteen hours, from midday to deep into the night. Late in the evening, when they're still up conversing in Freud's study, a sudden loud creak comes from the bookshelves that extend along almost the full length of the back wall. "Now this is a so-called catalytic exteriorization phenomenon," Jung declares. It's a marvel that, after talking with Freud all day, he still manages to say such a thing without tripping over his tongue. "Exteriorization" is the term used to characterize the mind's purported ability to act upon the physical world. Jung believes the sound to be the result of the surplus energy emitted by their exchange. Freud dryly responds: "Oh, no, that is complete nonsense." This prompts Jung to predict a recurrence of the sound. And voilà, a few seconds later there is "an indescribably terrible noise in the cabinet!"[48] Freud remains unimpressed. His rationalistic way of thinking leaves no room for the occult.

Years later Jung will give an account of another meeting with the Viennese doctor: "I can still recall vividly how Freud said to me, 'My dear Jung, promise me never to abandon the sexual theory. That is the most essential thing of all. You see, we must make a dogma of it, an unshakeable bulwark.'" To Jung's question, "A bulwark?—Against what?" Freud answers: "Against the black tide of mud," and after hesitating adds, "of occultism."[49]

Jung is aware that "a dogma, that is to say, an indisputable confession of faith, is set up only when the aim is to suppress doubts once and for all. But that no longer has anything to do with scientific judgment; only with a personal power drive."[50] Scarcely two years later, this power drive bears fruit: Freud and Jung are both invited to the United States to give lectures at an elite East Coast university.

"It was these association studies which [. . .] procured me my invitation to Clark University," Jung writes in his autobiography. "The association experiment and the psychogalvanic experiment were chiefly responsible for my reputation in America."[51] Unlike Freud, who maintains a skeptical attitude towards the American "dollar uncles," Jung quickly establishes contacts with businessmen and influential figures who are interested in his psychology of the unconscious. The philosopher James Putnam, a noteworthy supporter of psychoanalysis, helps make introductions; after the festivities in Worcester, Putnam, Jung, and Freud all spend time together at a lodge in the mountains.

In June 1909, a few months before his trip to the New World, Jung resigned from his post at the Burghölzli. His relationship with Bleuler had long been strained. Later that same year, shortly after his return from the US, Jung, his wife Emma, and their children move into a

A happy couple: Carl Gustav and Emma Jung, née Rauschenbach, were married on February 14, 1903.

large house in Küsnacht on Lake Zurich. Jung himself has a hand in the house's design. In it he opens up his own practice. Emma Jung, née Rauschenbach, is one of the richest heiresses in Switzerland and will later become an analyst herself. Her father made a fortune running the IWC watch company, which after his death in 1905 passed to his widow and daughters. By that point Carl Gustav and Emma had already been married for two years. Thanks to this marriage, Jung, the psychiatrist drawn to higher things, was now free from all material worries.

WHAT DORA DOESN'T KNOW

In January 1907, two months before Jung's first audience with the master, a different young doctor from the Burghölzli pays a visit to Berggasse. His name: Max Eitingon. He travels to Vienna for the express purpose of finding out more about the Freudian school; while the doctors at the Zurich clinic are receptive to psychoanalysis, information on its methods is scarce. Eitingon wants to get a sense of it first-hand. But the impression his Viennese peers make on him is vexing to the young psychiatrist. They spend their time attacking one another; each seems to feel nothing but scorn and gall towards his colleagues. Even over fundamental matters there is disagreement: where do neuroses come from? What effect does analysis have? What role does sexuality play? There seem to be more opinions on these subjects than the group has members.

Eitingon wasn't expecting so much discord. He feels what is needed is a set of clear rules to contain the dissent. A few years from now Eitingon will become an important figure on the "secret committee," the circle of Freud's close confidants who, beginning in 1912, will keep watch to ensure adherence to the true doctrine. The psychoanalytic movement will owe Eitingon a lot, including in a material respect. With the fortune amassed by his father, the fur dealer Chaim Eitingon, he finances, among other things, the Berlin Psychoanalytic Institute founded in 1920. Soon enough a bon mot starts making the rounds among analysts, punning on the words for cases ("Fälle") and furs ("Felle"): "The finest cases in psychoanalysis are old man Eitingon's furs."[52]

And speaking of cases: Freud's clinical studies, which are all published in the first decade of the 1900s, make for fine literature. The fates of the hysterical Dora, the five-year-old phobia-plagued Hans, the "Rat Man" Ernst Lanzer, or the "Wolf Man" Sergei Pankejeff all appear at first glance to be authentic case histories. But they are meticulously composed works, both at the level of language and thought, and are unmistakably meant to serve a purpose: to help validate Freud's approach.

To be sure, he does refer in these texts to his own lack of knowledge, to mistakes and false leads; but ultimately his doing so only demonstrates how rocky the road to knowledge and healing is, while imbuing the reading experience with a special frisson of suspense and persuasive power. The fact is, his "clinical material" is gap-ridden, his need to interpret overweening, and his willful stylizing plainly evident. It is this unlikely combination of contradictory elements that makes these stories as worth reading as they are dubious.

Physicians have always used anecdotal case studies as fig leaves. In the absence of generalizable patient data, selectively chosen observations are meant to serve as evidence for the utility of an applied method. True, for a long time psychiatrists hadn't even felt it necessary to look at facts or outcomes; in light of what came before, the rise of case studies in the late 19th century was progress. But the practice of describing individual outcomes, especially when the doctor who administered treatment is the one doing the describing, was at best only a tentative first step toward evidence-based medicine.

To present treatments in a comprehensible manner is better than merely claiming to have healed a patient. But even if the author is at pains to remain objective, individual cases reveal little about the virtues of a method, since success can also be due to chance, spontaneous recovery, or the placebo effect. Only by looking at many treatments together can one draw reliable conclusions. Thus above all else, Freud's psychoanalytic case histories satisfy one thing: the desire for a good story.

. . .

One such good story is Freud's famous case history of a girl whom he calls "Dora." He publishes the study in 1905, after long hesitation, under the title "Fragment of an Analysis of a Case of Hysteria."[53] It is a fragment because the patient, whose name was Ida Bauer, broke off treatment after just eleven weeks. This was on December 31, 1900, well before Freud publishes his account. Freud finishes the manuscript by late January 1901, but he has reservations about going public with it. Firstly because the therapy had of course failed, and secondly because the treatment involved Freud speaking frankly about sexual practices and desires with a young woman who was just eighteen years old—something which at that time was utterly scandalous. The way that Freud presses the young woman to reveal her intimate secrets (or what he assumes her secrets to be) draws outrage from medical circles. However well-disposed toward the libido theory they might be, for many this type of inquisition goes too far.

By Freud's standards as well, Dora is a young patient. She seems to have suffered for several years from periodically recurring facial pains, coughing fits that lead to her losing her voice, fainting spells, and cramps. Dora is brought to Freud's practice by her father after she has expressed a desire to commit suicide. Thus Freud finds himself face to face with a young woman who is more or less compelled to submit to the talking cure, rather than beginning it of her own accord and hoping it will lead to recovery.

Freud begins his account by describing Dora's family life. The whole description recalls an Arthur Schnitzler-style chamber play centered around hidden eroticism, power, and decadence. Dora's father, a businessman, has long been bored with his wife, the mother of Dora and her older brother. On top of that, he has health problems. He had undergone treatment with Freud before, for symptoms caused by syphilis, so the two of them know each other well. Now enter the married couple K., close friends of Dora's family. Frau K. shows a touching concern for both Dora's sick father and Dora herself. So it happens that an affair likely begins between Dora's father and the attractive Frau K.

Then, soon after the onset of the affair, Herr K. makes advances on Dora during a walk. She is horrified and confides in her parents. But her father is more worried about his own relationship potentially coming to light, and makes Dora out to be a liar. She must have imagined the attempted come-on because she reads "books of that sort" (meaning erotic novels). Freud believes that Dora feels more for Herr K. than she is willing to admit. But her affection for Herr K. is in turn only a way of concealing the true object of her love: her father.

Over the course of the treatment Dora relates a dream that Freud interprets in a way that lines up fully with his hypothesis. While Dora's family is fleeing from a burning house, her mother wants "to stop and save her jewel-case." Her father reacts furiously—there's no time for that now! No sooner does everyone make it out safely than the dream ends and Dora wakes up. Freud explains to the young woman that "jewel-case [*Schmuckkästchen*]" is a frequently used metaphor for the female genitals. Dora's mother doesn't want to surrender hers to Dora's father; Dora meanwhile would very much like to surrender her own.

As he does in this instance, Freud will repeatedly confront Dora with references to sex. She is in love with Herr K., he says, even if it's only to conceal her sexual attraction to her father. On top of that, Freud sees a homoerotic component to Dora's relationship with Frau K., whose "adorable white body" she admires. Freud overlooks his own role in the drama, which he later describes using the terms "transference" and "countertransference." Dora unconsciously "transfers" her affection for her father onto the therapist, and thus displays a similarly overt dislike for him—this way her love won't come to light. Freud's experiences with Dora lead him to think deeply about the doctor-patient relationship. Regardless of whether the transference is expressed as enamored adoration or as its opposite, as dislike, it makes it more difficult, indeed it thwarts on several levels the therapeutic goal of making repressed thoughts conscious. Per Freud, this phenomenon is ultimately to blame for the failure of Dora's therapy. In order to avoid the problem in the future, he recommends a radical measure: strict neutrality and distance on the part of the analyst, aimed at preventing the formation of any kind of emotional connection. The therapist should function exclusively as a mirror in which the patient can recognize themselves.

Dora rejects Freud's explanations, but he views her rejection as being itself confirmation of the repression he suspects. Before he is able to work through the conflict that has been revealed, however, Dora breaks off the treatment.

Freud's description is suffused with a self-certain importunity that was shocking even to many of his contemporaries. Let us look, for instance, at the passage where Freud interprets Dora's mysterious coughing fits, which have no discernible physical cause. The doctor connects them to Dora's unconsciously imagined ideas about the precise nature of the affair that her father is having with Frau K. Freud writes:

"She [Dora] had once again been insisting that Frau K. only loved her father because he was '*ein vermögender Mann*' ['a man of means']. Certain details of the way in which she expressed herself [. . .] led me to see that behind this phrase its opposite lay concealed, namely, that her father was '*ein unvermögender Mann*' ['a man without means']. This could only be meant in a sexual sense—that her father, as a man, was without means, was impotent. Dora confirmed this interpretation from her conscious knowledge; whereupon I pointed out the contradiction she was involved in if on the one hand she continued to insist that her father's relationship with Frau K. was a common love-affair, and on the other hand maintained that her father was impotent, or in other words incapable of carrying on an affair of such a kind. Her answer showed that she had no need to admit the contradiction. She knew very well, she said, that there was more than one way of obtaining sexual gratification. (The source of this piece of knowledge, however, was once more untraceable.) I questioned her further, whether she referred to the use of organs other than the genitals for the purpose of sexual intercourse, and she replied in the affirmative. I could then go on to say that in that case she must be thinking of precisely those parts of the body which in her case were in a state of irritation,—the throat and the oral cavity. To be sure, she would not hear of going so far as this in recognizing her own thoughts; and indeed, if the occurrence of the symptom was to be made possible at all, it was essential that she should not be completely clear on the subject. But the conclusion was inevitable that with her spasmodic cough, which, as is usual, was referred for its exciting stimulus to a tickling in her throat, she pictured to herself a scene of sexual gratification *per os* between the two people whose love-affair occupied her mind so incessantly."[54]

To put it bluntly: according to Freud, Dora's coughing stems from her repressed fantasy of her father having Frau K. perform oral sex on him. (At the time, men were considered "impotent" if they were incapable of having conventional intercourse or producing offspring; this incapacity could include the inability to get an erection, but did not necessarily have to.) The journalist Dieter E. Zimmer, in his critical commentary on this scene, points out that the crux of Freud's diagnosis hinges on evidence that is extremely thin: based solely on "certain details of the way in which she expressed herself," Freud concludes that the word used by Dora, "*vermögend*," in truth means "*unvermögend*," i.e., "impotent."

What is one supposed to imagine he means by "certain details of the way in which she expressed herself"? A moment of hesitation, a clearing of the throat, a note of uncertainty in Dora's voice, a tormented facial expression? Whatever it might have been, surely it wasn't anything that could have justified such a bold theory: the young woman's refusal to admit to "her thoughts"—which in fact come from Freud—results in the manifestation of symptoms. The young woman's coughing proves that unconscious fantasies are at play. And because at the moment of realization the symptoms promptly disappear, the explanation is clearly correct. Published as a "study," the example is taken thenceforward as incontestable confirmation of the origin of nervous coughing.[55]

This episode is enough to illustrate why psychoanalytic logic calls to mind an old joke: if there were a cat sitting on the chair, you would see it. On the chair, however, no cat can be seen—so it must be invisible! Looking at other passages as well, Freud's interpretation of Dora's case, for all its claims to logical consistency, proves to be tenuous. In one instance, Freud explains the young woman's shortness of breath and elevated pulse by saying that these are "detached fragments of the act of copulation." Thus nervous asthma can be "traced back to the same exciting cause—to the patient's having overheard sexual intercourse taking place between adults."[56] Zimmer summarizes this conclusion as follows: "Dad breathes hard while having sex, so his little girl gets asthma and wheezes."[57]

According to Zimmer, Freud left behind priceless moments of unintentional comedy in his case histories, in which he "makes grotesque leaps, so that in the end he can declare this or that hypothesis to have been proven beyond all doubt."[58] For the literary historian Frederick Crews, Freud's case studies consist "in large part of self-serving anecdotes, disarming literary parallels, artful fendings-off of objections, promises that the evidence will come later or false assurances that it was given earlier." His summing up: "Freud, while continuing to profess that psychoanalysis was a rigorous natural science, had simply resigned from the wider scientific community and founded a cult of his personal authority."[59] Nevertheless, his theory will become a major force in modern thought. The mix of penetrating insight and nearly unassailable certainty would appear to be too seductive.

. . .

The year 1905 marks a turning point in psychoanalysis's journey from method of treatment to broadly recognized science of the soul. In just a short period of time, Freud publishes several books that seek to explain not only the origin of neuroses, but also the psychological activity of healthy individuals. Along with the "Fragment," these writings include *Jokes and Their Relation to the Unconscious* as well as the *Three Essays on Sexuality*. From this point forward, the suppression of the libido becomes a universal explanatory model. The inventory of unconscious defense mechanisms, such as repression (failing to remember an experience), rationalization (using flimsy reasoning to justify an action), projection (ascribing one's own motives to others), displacement (redirecting the libido toward fetish objects or the ego), and sublimation (satisfying sexual desire by means of other activities, for example artistic endeavor), contains more than just the components of a theory of illness; it comes to describe everything that goes on in the psyche.

The fundamental principle remains the same: resistance to psychoanalytical interpretation confirms its accuracy. Moreover, Freud's theory and praxis back each other up: what works in treatment must surely have scientific validity; and by the same token an explanation elaborated in psychoanalytic terms can hardly go wrong in practice. In the afterword to *The Question of Lay Analysis*, published in 1927, Freud speaks of the "inseparable bond between cure and research" that has accompanied his teachings from the start.[60] The rapid ascent of psychoanalysis is an impressive example of how greatly our own wishful thinking shapes our image of what we take to be true.

Dora, though, has had enough, at least for the time being. After she breaks off her three-month course of treatment with Freud, silence ensues. Not until a year and a half later, in early April 1902, does she come back seeking help for a painful case of facial neuralgia. Dora reports that she confronted Herr and Frau K. The wife admitted to her affair with Dora's father, and Herr K. likewise admitted to having sexually harassed Dora. After that she had been symptom-free for a time.

Ever the egomaniac, Freud attributes Dora's return to her having read in the newspaper about his recent appointment as professor extraordinarius. He generously sets aside the sense of grievance that Dora's abrupt departure had left him with: "I promised to forgive her for having deprived me of the satisfaction of affording her a far more radical cure for her troubles."[61] Whether he was able to cure the neuralgia, Freud doesn't say.

Finally, in 1904, Dora marries, moves away from Vienna and takes on the name Adler, which makes it possible for Freud to publish her case history. Ida Adler, née Bauer, flees to the United States to escape the Nazis and dies shortly before Christmas 1945 in New York.

DREAMY PROSPECTS

Today the name Alphonse Maeder is familiar only to diehard students of psychoanalytic history. Maeder, though, deserves praise for an achievement that was far ahead of its time. Before the First World War, Maeder develops a functional theory of dreaming. He considers the imaginative journeys people go on at night to be, in simplified terms, dry runs of the mind. They serve a similar function as play does for children: they are rehearsals, necessary for practicing actions, thoughts, and emotions, for reinforcing what we've learned and steeling ourselves against future challenges.

At the time, hardly anyone takes this idea seriously. Even Freud, the inventor of modern dream interpretation, is skeptical. He dismisses Maeder's approach, calling it "mystical" and "dangerous"; it goes too far against his own notion of the dream as the guardian of sleep. According to Freud, dreams are psychological release valves that allow the energy from the drives that we have worked so hard to suppress to escape without causing harm. The reason the imaginative images they sometimes present are so far from reality is that this avoids the risk of them disturbing our sleep through their unsettling character. This leads Freud to the theory that wishes always appear in dreams in disguised form.

But Maeder won't relent and finds himself caught between the front lines of the conflict then raging between Jung and Freud over their different views of the libido. While Freud disparages Maeder by calling him an antisemite, the other party to the conflict, Maeder's ex-colleague from the Burghölzli, simply ignores him: Jung keeps delaying publication of Maeder's paper stating his theory in the *Blättern für Psychopathologische Forschung und Psychoanalyse*—the difference of opinion with Freud has him emotionally on edge and he doesn't want to pour more oil on the fire. Thus a promising approach sinks into oblivion. Maeder will continue to practice psychiatry in Zurich for years to come, but won't play any major role in the history of psychoanalysis from that point forward.

Behind his hunch is an idea that scientists who study dreams will take up many years later. In order for the scenarios playing out at night to have surplus value that carries over into waking life, they *must* go beyond the limits of the real. If everything in dreams were normal, within the bounds of our usual perceptions, there would be little to gain from them. Today's artificial intelligence experts are familiar with the phenomenon of "overfitting": if you feed machine learning systems on limited, self-similar input, it's harder for them to form and predict patterns. In this process, outliers and extremes are clearly necessary; the fantastic functions as a corrective. It is presumably for similar reasons that our mind, when dreaming, so often leaves the terra firma of the plausible—doing so makes it better able to find its bearings. Put another way: we dream of flying because it helps us keep our balance when we walk.

The often irrational character of dream activity doesn't escape Freud either. In "A Note on the Unconscious in Psycho-Analysis" he writes: "There is one psychical product to be met with in the most normal persons, which yet presents a very striking analogy to the wildest productions of insanity, and was no more intelligible to philosophers than insanity itself. I refer to dreams."[62] It is to dreams that he devotes what is by far his most famous work. Published on November 8, 1899, it begins with the words:

"In the following pages I shall provide proof that there is a psychological technique which allows us to interpret dreams, and that when this procedure is applied, every dream turns out to be a meaningful psychical formation which can be given an identifiable place in what goes on within us in our waking life. I shall further try to explain the processes that make the dream so strange and incomprehensible, and infer from them the nature of the psychical forces in their combinations and conflicts, out of which the dream emerges."[63]

A sensational opening. Preceding it is an epigraph in Latin: *Flectere si nequeo speros, Acheronta movebo* ("If Heaven I cannot bend, then Hell I will arouse.") The quote comes from the *Aeneid* by the Roman poet Virgil and had been used before by the labor leader Ferdinand Lasalle—though, as Freud notes, Lasalle was referring "to social—not psychological—classifications."[64] He himself chooses to understand the epigraph as follows: "The wish rejected by the higher mental agencies (the repressed dream wish) stirs up the mental underworld (the unconscious) in order to get a hearing."[65] There is also a personal dimension to his choice of quote: in Virgil's epic, Aeneas travels to the underworld to ask his father Anchises's advice. Freud's book is also the result of an intense bout of introspection that followed the death of Jacob Freud in 1896. Freud's biographer Ernest Jones explains: "His father's death was the stimulus for [self-analysis] as much as for composing the book."[66]

In *The Interpretation of Dreams*, Freud elaborates for the first time a detailed mechanism of psychological processes and ascribes to them a function: to conceal what motivates us and preoccupies us deep down. Some of the terms he uses, like "repression," "transference," or "projection," will enter the lexicon of everyday speech. Psychoanalytic nomenclature will have a lasting impact on how people think and talk about themselves, even today. Naturally this transformation doesn't happen overnight, but rather occurs over an extended period of time.

For Freud, the interpretation of dreams is the *via regia* to the unconscious. Anything that appears in a dream is significant. Every image, every action, every emotion, as confused as they might seem, contains a message. "[I]f we follow the method of dream-interpretation indicated

DIE

TRAUMDEUTUNG

VON

DR. SIGM. FREUD.

»*FLECTERE SI NEQUEO SUPEROS, ACHERONTA MOVEBO.*«

LEIPZIG UND WIEN.

FRANZ DEUTICKE.

1900.

A book that makes history: Freud's *The Interpretation of Dreams* is published in November 1899, but bears the date 1900 on its title page.

here, we discover that dreams really do have a meaning [. . .]. *After the work of interpretation has been completed the dream reveals itself as a wish-fulfilment.*"[67]

Regarded thus, the psyche comes to resemble a sophisticated wish machine. Impulses and ideas that are fed by the instinctual wellsprings of the unconscious must be actively hidden from the conscious mind because they are incompatible with the demands of life in society. The result is an ongoing process of self-deception, as seen for instance in the "distortion" of dream activity. This results from what Freud calls the compromise between moral demands and the dynamic of our inner drives. His explanation of exactly how this mechanism works extends over several hundred pages.

Freud highlights two processes in particular in *The Interpretation of Dreams*: displacement and condensation. These are "the two foremen in charge of the dream-work, and we may put the shaping of our dreams down mainly to their activity."[68] The "latent" content is displaced by a censor that recognizes material which, because it is potentially disturbing, is inadmissible, and defuses it by disguising it with the "manifest" (evident) dream content. Instead of a penis, what appears in the dream is, say, a snake or a cigar, instead of the vagina a box or a dark shaft. Condensation in turn means that in the dream various layers of the remnants of the day, that is, experiences that have occupied our minds in the waking hours, are stacked one on top of the other. Thus we find for example that a dream figure appears to be put together from elements of several real people—a so-called collective or composite figure.

One arrives at the latent content of dreams through the work of interpretation. Freud demonstrates this procedure by means of numerous examples, including a dream that came to him one summer night in 1895. It becomes famous as the "dream of Irma's injection."

"Irma" is a real patient of Freud's who suffers from inexplicable pains, dizzy spells, and (presumably pre-menstrual) bouts of depression. It is highly probable that Irma is in fact the future women's rights activist Emma Eckstein. She has been socially acquainted with the Freuds for some time; it's possible that Freud treats her as a personal favor. Freud can't really seem to do much for his patient's multiple complaints, however, and refers her to his friend Wilhelm Fließ, an ear, nose, and throat specialist in Berlin. Fließ has for some time subscribed to a "nose reflex theory," which holds that nosebleeds in men are the equivalent to the female cycle. It sounds rather abstruse—and even at the time is fairly out there—but Freud thinks highly of Fließ's "discovery." In any case the Berlin ENT specialist is firmly convinced that in men and women there is a psychophysiological connection between the olfactory organ and the genitals. This theory forms the backdrop for the drama that subsequently unfolds.

Fließ operates on Emma's nose, suspecting that the cause of her ailment is to be found there. The patient's condition doesn't improve, however. To the contrary: soon she develops an infection of the mucus membrane, accompanied by frequent nosebleeds. Back in Vienna, the young woman undergoes further treatment from Freud, who for his part believes he is dealing with a case of psychogenic hysteria. He is unsure of himself, however, and calls in a surgeon friend of his on March 8, 1895. While Freud looks on in horror, this surgeon removes "at least half a meter of gauze" from the patient's nasal cavity! Fließ must have left it in during his operation, a grievous blunder. "The next moment," Freud writes in a letter to Fließ, "came a flood of blood. The patient turned white [. . .] So we had done her an injustice; she was not at all abnormal."[69]

This, then, is what actually happened. Only recently did it become possible to reconstruct these events, based on the surviving correspondence between Fließ and Freud. In *The Interpretation of Dreams*, however, we don't hear a word about any of this. In the book we are told only that Irma has not accepted Freud's "solution" to her ailment. At this point the doctor is struck with the fear that he could have overlooked a physical cause for the pains she is experiencing.

In his dream, Freud thoroughly examines the patient's throat and nose. In the throat he discovers yellow spots, in the nostrils "greyish-white scabs." Other doctors appear and one of them declares: "No doubt about it, it is an infection." Then it suddenly occurs to the dreamer that a colleague had recently given her an injection. The account ends with the words: "Probably the syringe was not clean, either."

If one knows the real backstory, the meaning of the dream seems obvious: Freud is tormented by the thought that, as a result of his own failure, he may have increased his patient's suffering, rather than eased it. An anxiety dream, in other words. The fear of malpractice has dogged Freud at least since the time when an unsuccessful cocaine therapy that he recommended led to the ruin of his friend Ernst Fleischl von Marxow. Fleischl was a talented colleague of Freud's, a physiologist in Brücke's laboratory who, suffering from severe, chronic pain, had started to inject himself with morphine. The cause of the pain was an infection that he had contracted from a cadaver during his dissection work. One of his thumbs was amputated, but Fleischl continued to suffer from severe pain at the site of the amputation, as well as in other parts of his body. It wasn't long before he was severely addicted to morphine. Freud hoped to rid Fleischl of his morphine addiction through the administration of what he believed to be a non-addictive drug, cocaine. In the end however the unfortunate Fleischl suffered from a double addiction, which quickly took its toll on his health. Fleischl died in October 1891, shortly after Freud had moved his practice to Berggasse. In his study he kept a portrait of his late colleague as a constant admonition.

Freud's explanation of "Irma's injection" in *The Interpretation of Dreams* is a mysterious hunt for clues that plays out over more than a dozen pages. After taking his dream apart line by line, image by image, he concludes that in his nocturnal fantasy he was trying to absolve himself of guilt: if there was a physical basis for Irma's suffering, like an infection, then Freud's hysteria treatment naturally couldn't have succeeded. In the dream he assuages his conscience, while the sexual allusion present in the reference to the injection makes the colleague who is responsible for it seem especially villainous. "*After the work of interpretation has been completed the dream reveals itself as a wish-fulfillment*"—thus Freud's much-cited conclusion.

He has the dream while staying at the Villa Bellevue on Himmelstraße, a few kilometers north of Vienna. Freud regularly travels there in the summertime to escape the city. To Fließ he writes: "Do you suppose that someday one will read on a marble tablet on this house:

Here, on July 24, 1895,
the secret of the dream
revealed itself to Dr. Sigm. Freud."[70]

Where the building once stood (it was torn down in the 1950s), this quote from Freud's letter now adorns a memorial plaque. What a remarkable form of self-fulfilling prophecy.

"Irma's injection" is only one of a good two hundred dreams recounted in Freud's book, forty-three of them his own nocturnal adventures. The author, to be sure, does discuss certain problems with his approach. Fairly early on he writes: "For after all we know only of its [the dream's] existence from our recollection of it after waking."[71] But Freud resolutely ignores the very crux of the matter. For what he actually analyzes are not dreams, but rather *accounts* of dreams, reconstructions which, through the process of remembering and verbalizing them, have been reshaped many times over. Everyone knows from their own experience how fragmentary dreams often appear, how difficult it is to separate what one has dreamed of from what is added after the fact, to discern between sleeping and waking consciousness. In a certain sense all memories are fictions; depending on mood and situation, we take what we have experienced and fashion it into stories that appear meaningful, piecing things together, embellishing, changing things as we go. To remember is to reinvent, adding and filling in elements to round out the picture. What one has *really* dreamed is a mystery, and will remain a mystery.

This imponderability doesn't bother Freud in the least. He relates the events of a dream with the skill of a dramatist—and ignores the fact that the account of the dream and the dream itself are not the same thing. Often his analysis relies on a formulation that he himself has chosen. If for example he recounts that at the sight of a sinking ship he "was greatly alarmed," the interpretation that follows is built upon this "strong affect." But his account of the dream isn't an objective fact; rather it is a product of his own imagination, mediated through language, which is intent on coherence and intelligibility. Freud describes what he dreamed, then declares the description to be "the dream"—an equivalence that, on closer inspection, seems invalid.

People have ascribed prophetic power to their dreams from time immemorial. Joseph in the book of Genesis interprets a dream for the Egyptian pharaoh: seven fat cows appear, followed by seven thin cows who eat the fat ones. Joseph takes this to mean that Egypt would face seven years of famine. In the second century AD the physician

Artemidoros of Daldis, who lived on the coast of Asia Minor, offered readers of his *Oneirocritica* a diverse set of interpretative markers: quails appearing in a dream are harbingers of misfortune, winged ants represent a dangerous journey, and frying pans mean fines. As strange as it sounds, Artemidoros also offers individually tailored predictions. Thus sex with one's own mother (in a dream) can point to the imminent death of one's father and might promise bountiful income or power. It depends entirely on the circumstances.

Artemidoros doesn't provide evidence for this schema, unlike Freud, who, consistent with his claim to scientific authority, presents his findings as the result of impressive deliberations. Nevertheless, as the journalist Stefan Klein notes, Freud's approach is not dissimilar to that of his ancient predecessor, since both writers' interpretations are essentially impossible to disprove. The Viennese writer runs into the same difficulty that Artemidoros faced, namely that every interpretation is necessarily undertaken by the waking mind. "From the superior vantage point of reason one looks down at the images of the night and searches for their meaning using the logic of language," Klein writes. "But what if daytime logic is incapable of fully comprehending the experience of another state of consciousness?"[72] As it happens, dreams for Freud always seem to follow a plan. Wishes arising from the unconscious are checked by the censor for delicate content and if necessary manipulated, disguised, or displaced and sent elsewhere. Only in this way can the energy stemming from our urges be channeled into tolerable pathways.

Freud is not the first to hit upon the idea that dreams are wish-fulfillments in disguise. He cites for example Wilhelm Griesinger, an early pioneer of psychiatry, who formulated this notion in 1845. Freud had his predecessors, then. But whereas someone like Artemidoros searched for prophetic meaning in dream symbols, Freud's approach is more subtle. According to his theory, unconscious thoughts are disguised as harmless notions so that they don't produce any turmoil. In order to see through this, one has only to "make the symbols speak." And how does one do this? Through free association. This method allows previously forgotten or overlooked aspects to come to the surface. These could also just be creative elaborations on what the dreamer "remembers"—but this he ignores.

What is new in Freud's approach is that he seamlessly incorporates dream interpretation into the complicated machinery of the psychical apparatus that he mapped out in his paper "Project for a Scientific Psychology" from 1895.[73] According to this system, everything in the dream points to something else—and first and foremost to sexual desires. Thus long and narrow objects like canes, umbrellas, zeppelins, or ties are guises of the phallus, while hollow objects like wardrobes, boxes, cans, cartons, or rooms represent the vagina. Symbols for castration, the primal male fear, are also present in abundance, and include above all activities that have to do with trimming or cutting (cutting hair, mowing grass, hemming a garment).

Freud's dream interpretation is less formulaic than Artemidoros's, but it is burdened with similar difficulties. The philosopher Philipp Hübl points to one of them: a wish that appears in another form becomes at that point a *different* wish. Wishes are defined by their relation to an object; a wish cannot be relabeled by transferring its object from a "latent" to a "manifest" one. Or at least not without creating a new wish. Hübl gives the following example: in the psychoanalytic interpretation, fetishism arises from a boy's shocked discovery that girls don't have penises. This provokes fear in the boy, who is now afraid of being castrated himself. As a result he goes looking for a substitute, something that he can touch and possess; this act of touching and possessing takes away his fear of losing his member. The *actual* wish (not to be castrated) appears in the guise of a lustful fixation on, say, lacquer or boots.

The problem with this wishful arithmetic: wanting to lick a boot is something fundamentally different from the endeavor to keep one's penis. The connection is fabricated. "Freud imagines wishes to be like bronze statues that one can melt down and shape into new figures," Hübl writes. "But when dealing with wishes and other mental states, material and form are identical; there is no raw wish material that can be reshaped again and again."[74]

Drawing analogies, making interpretations, connecting the unconnected—these are the domains of art and literature. It's no surprise that in the beginning Freud's ideas found far more supporters among writers and artists than among physicians. "It still strikes me myself as strange that the case histories I write should read like short stories and that, as one might say, they lack the serious stamp of science," Freud writes.[75] His analytical oeuvre, beginning with the *Studies on Hysteria* from 1895 and extending all the way to the unfinished *An Outline of Psychoanalysis* published posthumously in 1940, is a testament to how easy it is for us to allow elegant language and observational skill to distract us from certain weaknesses in a writer's argument. If it's beautifully written and well thought out, then surely it's got to be true! Without the refined style and rhetorical finesse that Freud brings, his work would hardly be so influential—or fascinating, as it still is today. At the same time it serves as a warning to us that intellectuality is no protection from error; sometimes it only prevents us from taking our own fallacies seriously. It did not hamper the success of Freudian psychodynamism.

THE LAST SHALL BE FIRST

What Max Eitingon encounters during his visit to Vienna in early 1907 threatens to become an obstacle to the spread of psychoanalysis. Discord and animosity among the members of Freud's circle cloud the image of a theory and therapeutic method that is meant to be clear and easily disseminated. Freud knows that he must close the ranks of his followers and take action against dissidents, and he isn't shy about severing ties, even those formed over many years. He has already dropped his old friend Wilhelm Fließ and his mentor Josef Breuer without a trace of remorse. It's only a matter of time before the next falling out.

One pillar of Freud's theory in particular meets with skepticism even among his close allies, though most only voice this skepticism behind his back: it is the assertion that all neurotic symptoms are sexual in origin. At first Freud even believes that hysteria is always the result of repressed sexual trauma. From this "seduction theory" he soon pivots to a new idea known as "psychogenic etiology": even imagined events and desires can cause psychological stress that manifests in neurotic symptoms.

Reading the minutes of the Wednesday Society—which since 1906 have been taken by Otto Rank—one can see that there are reservations toward the libido theory.[76] Among the critics is Alfred Adler, who treats an array of nervous disorders himself at his practice on Czerningasse near the Prater. Only a few of his patients come from the well-to-do circles to which the majority of Freud's clients belong. Adler sees white-collar and blue-collar workers and even artists involved in the nightlife scene. The denial of sexual desire is less prevalent in these milieux. For proletarians and the petite bourgeoisie, sex isn't that big of a problem; Freud's theory seems mainly to apply to those who, even if they do have sexual intercourse, are never permitted to think or talk about it.

Bit by bit, Adler develops a different idea of what drives the psyche, whether healthy or sick: according to him, a child's first experience is the experience of their own incapacity. The child's feeling that they are small and weak and dependent on care from others, their observation that everyone else has mastered things that are unattainable for them—starting with the ability to hold their head up, pick things up, or walk—this, per Adler, produces insecurity, unease, and anxiety. In adolescence and adulthood as well, every individual necessarily runs up against limits, experiences frustration and defeats. "To be human means to feel inferior," Adler declares.[77] For him, everything else follows from this feeling. The fact that he bases his entire approach on the feeling of inferiority has a lot to do with his own difficult childhood.

. . .

Adler is born on February 7, 1870. He is the second child of a wheat merchant from the Burgenland and his wife. The family lives in Rudolfsheim, just outside of Vienna, not far from Schloss Schönbrunn; as a boy, Alfred often wanders through the palace gardens. Shortly before Alfred's fourth birthday, in January 1874, his younger brother Rudolf dies of diphtheria. During the night the eight-month-old suffocates in his bed, which is next to Alfred's own. Alfred himself develops a severe case of rickets and suffers from periodic spasms of the larynx that are accompanied by shortness of breath and a terrible fear of suffocating. By the time he starts school, Alfred feels neglected by his mother, who doesn't think her sickly son capable of much, unlike his older brother, a year-and-a-half his senior, who—as fate would have it—shares a name with Alfred's later father figure: Sigmund.

While his relationship with his mother is fraught, Alfred gets along famously with his father—another reason he can't really get behind the Oedipus complex posited by Freud the "mama's boy." Adler gets his medical degree in 1895, and shortly thereafter goes into private practice, working as a general practitioner with a specialty in ophthalmology. In late 1902 he joins Freud's circle.[78]

By all accounts the young Alfred has several reasons to feel inferior. Because everyone experiences this condition—so he believes—the desire to overcome it and compensate through achievement and renown must also be universal. Adler's idea of the individual compensating for real, or even just perceived, insufficiencies ties into a notion that is widespread in this era: physicians often explain physical illness as the result of a weakened organ triggering compensatory activity in other parts of the body. Adler, seeking a plausible explanation for why, as he suggests, hearing problems often occur in musical families or impaired vision among painters, applies this pattern to the psyche. He even cites the Greek politician Demosthenes as evidence: in the 4th century BC, the stutterer was considered the greatest rhetorician in the ancient world.

But these compensatory efforts are not always successful. Far from it: they can also overshoot the mark or miss it entirely. The resultant neurotic fixation usually begins in childhood and has a lasting impact on the personality. Children who receive too little praise from their parents develop a narcissistic craving for recognition; others who are subject to constant prohibitions reject rules. Adler extends his explanatory approach as far as birth order: the baby of the family has to prove his independence, the eldest tries to escape responsibility, and the only child is always waiting for someone to help her. According to Adler, both emotional frigidity and coddling will damage a child's psychological development.

Already it is clear how deeply Adler is drawing from the wellspring of popular views and prejudices. More than any other psychologist, he will put popular assumptions about the psyche on a scientific footing. His approach makes no sharp distinction between the normal and the pathological; after all, every individual is confronted with their own inferiority. Everyone feels compelled to overcome and compensate for their shortcomings; only when this leads to the denigration of or even aggression towards others, to envy, tension, or megalomania, does it become problematic. Once tendencies of this sort come to dominate a person's "life plan," they become very difficult to cast aside. For that reason, Adler places great emphasis on the early phases of a child's development and upbringing: here it is still possible to affect fundamental attitudes—and avoid more severe outcomes.

In his 1904 treatise "The Doctor as Educator" Adler discusses his pedagogical idea for the first time at length. Confidence in one's own abilities, courage, and self-reliance are for him the central goals of child-rearing. "Courageous children," he writes, "both in childhood and later in life as well, will not look for their fate to come from outside of themselves; rather they will expect it to arise from their own strength."[79] His appeal for a nourishing, affectionate form of child-rearing breaks with the then-dominant ideal of toughening children up through privation and punishment. Children at this time are subject to regular violence or left to fend for themselves. In this Adler sees a primary cause of mental suffering. But he also opposes lavishing *too much* love and indulgence on one's offspring.

Like Freud, Adler mainly presents anecdotal reports to provide evidence for his concept of inferiority and compensation. His writings include numerous examples and situations that he analyzes from the standpoint of his own theory. Adler possesses keen powers of observation and strong psychological intuition. Nevertheless, in the absence of facts, some of his generalizations seem questionable. We know now, for example, that the claim that birth order among siblings has any discernible effect on the personality doesn't hold up. In spite of this, clichés like that of the "difficult" first-born or the lazy only child continue to live on.

Adler's essays and books are full of myths that contribute to the popularity of his theories but often border on the trivial. The notion that heroes only become strong by overcoming their weaknesses is one of them. Such a figure appears in countless fairy tales and legends, and in our daily lives we often explain certain distinctive traits in others by saying that they are overcompensating for something: someone who puffs himself up and acts important actually feels "two feet tall," the class clown is concealing her melancholy, and a disobedient child is in reality afraid of losing his parents' love.

But there's one thing that doesn't represent a primary motive in human inner life: the sex drive. At the meetings of the Psychoanalytic Society Adler initially sweeps his lack of interest in this point discreetly under the rug. Instead of infantile sexuality and the Oedipus complex he posits the existence of an innate "need for affection" which prompts the infant to seek devotion and protection. Adler also considers the aggression drive significant, since this is the means through which the neurotic goes on offense and confronts his feeling of inferiority. It is this point that triggers the first conflict with Freud, who makes his stance clear: "I cannot bring myself to assume the existence of a special aggressive instinct alongside of the familiar instincts of self-preservation and of sex, and on an equal footing with them."[80]

In many respects Adler is Freud's opposite. While the latter remains stuck in the mold of the nineteenth-century scholar, Adler is a man of the modern age. Freud communicates through untold numbers of lengthy letters; Adler usually sends telegrams. Freud regards women as inferior; Adler advocates for equal rights and considers the notion of the "weaker sex" an invention of the patriarchy. Freud, though not religious, wears his Jewishness with confidence; Adler converts to Protestantism. Freud has his patients lie down on a couch and sits in an armchair behind them; in Adler's sessions, doctor and client sit in chairs facing each other.[81] Freud directs his psychoanalytic movement from the comfort of his practice and study; Adler spends his time in public and loves coffeehouses and the theater. Freud is an intellectual overachiever; Adler's grades in school were mediocre, and a more prestigious career at the university is closed to him. Freud is fastidious about his appearance, Adler dresses carelessly. Freud is authoritarian, Adler jovial, Freud a pessimist, Adler an optimist.

More than anything, however, Adler is a socialist. As a boy he runs around with street urchins, playing in empty lots on the outskirts of Vienna. Throughout his life he will be proud of his humble origins and his Viennese accent. In 1897, in a Marxist student group, he meets Raissa Timofejewna Epstein. The young Russian comes from a wealthy Moscow family and is a dedicated communist. The two marry on Christmas Eve of that same year.

Once, at a meeting of the Wednesday Society, Adler gives a lecture on "Psychology and Marxism." In the lecture he explains, in line with his compensation theory, that the class struggle of the working classes arises out of a feeling of humiliation that must be overcome. But, as Adler presciently notes, rather than a government of the people, the revolutionaries are interested only in obtaining unlimited power for themselves. The Adler home is occasionally the site of intense disagreements between the staunch communist Raissa and her more moderate Alfred.

Adler has prepared another lecture for November 7, 1906.[82] He has been attending the meetings of the Freud group for a good four years now, and as yet has never clearly laid out his own position. On this day, however, in a lecture with the title "On the Organic Foundations of Neuroses," he finally devotes himself to the subject that has occupied his mind for some time now. In his minutes for the meeting, Rank notes his decision not to include a lengthy transcript of the talk, "in light of Adler's mention of the prospect of his work being published soon."[83] This work is the *Study of Organ Inferiority and Its Psychical Compensation*, published in 1907, in which Adler offers a comprehensive presentation of his view. On the November evening in question he may have spared his listeners, among them Freud and Stekel, especially since the time allotted him to speak was limited to half an hour. The reactions to his lecture are mixed, but on the whole favorable. Freud even offers praise: through Adler, the "knowledge of the organic bases of neuroses has certainly been expanded."[84]

For a subsequent lecture of Adler's in March 1907, the group plays host to their colleagues from Zurich, Jung and Binswanger. Adler discusses his treatment of an obsessional neurotic patient who, among other symptoms, has the compulsion to dunk his face in a full water basin and count to three, seven, or forty-nine—in the last case, often to the point of near-suffocation. Adler's theory: the young man, after comparing himself to his brother, discovered that the brother was superior to him with respect to both penis size and amount of pubic hair. In conducting his strange dunking ritual he is trying to prove what he is capable of, despite his physical inferiority.

The discussion of the case quickly veers away from the drive to compensate for perceived deficiencies and instead gets hung up on the relative size of Jewish and Christian penises. Rank declares that the seven represents the small penis, forty-nine on the other hand the large penis.

Freud posits that the three was probably to be regarded as the equivalent of the Christian genitals, while the seven and the forty-nine stood for the small and large Jewish penis, respectively. The guests from Zurich are more than a little taken aback by all this phallic numerology. As Binswanger remembers, looking back years later, Freud took him aside after the meeting and asked him, with a glance at the others: "So now you've had a good look at this bunch, huh?" Clearly he didn't think too highly of his retinue.

Adler is conspicuously absent from the discussion that he himself launched. Does he feel that he's not being taken seriously? Is he afraid of conflict? Or does he simply feel it's unnecessary to sew discord? The minutes give no indication. Nevertheless, around this time Adler begins to separate himself more and more from Freud's dogmas. Similar to Jung, the sexual theory will be the point of contention. Adler sees the source of unconscious psychological conflicts not in the libido, but in the experience of deficiency and helplessness.

. . .

In his 1907 book *Study of Organ Inferiority and Its Psychical Compensation*, Adler outlines a theory of neuroses in which the unconscious and sex play mere secondary roles. For him they are important aspects of one's overall psychological well-being, but they are not etiological. The sexual realm is simply the easiest place (for the man) to exert power, for which reason it is here in particular that neurotics often strive to compensate and exhibit their virility. At heart their intent is to demonstrate their strength: the neurotic associates his inferiority with the feminine, against which he raises his "masculine protest." In Adler's nomenclature this expression is by no means limited to men, however; the "masculine" part of the psyche that is directed toward power and greatness can seek to assert itself in a woman as well.

Adler's writings are nowhere near as polished as Freud's. There is much that he merely touches on; at other times he repeats himself. Much remains unclear. Later on, instead of the "masculine protest," he will come to speak, with a nod to Friedrich Nietzsche, of the "will to power"—this even though protest, which is directed *against* something, is very different from mere will. And then there is the portentous sense of community that Adler contrasts with the typical egocentric quality of the neurotic—but what exactly this sense of community is remains an open question.

Adler's stroke of brilliance is to take the thinking of his era, shaped, as it is, by Charles Darwin's theory of evolution, and place it on its head. By recasting weakness as something beneficial—only by compensating for their weakness do individuals acquire strength—he breaks with the notion that those who are *naturally* stronger are the ones who prevail. It is not the fittest per se who have a leg up, but those who are most adept at making up for their deficiencies. Anyone can overcome their shortcomings and make something of themselves—this is Adler's hopeful message. The philosopher Ernst Bloch will at one point refer to this dismissively as a "pure psychology of competition."[85] And it's true that without the individualistic, capitalistic way of thinking, geared toward self-improvement, that arises in the years between the two world wars, Adler's theory would hardly have met with such success. He has his finger on the pulse of his time.

If one takes Adler's premises to their logical extreme, then any achievement or character trait can be explained by its ostensible opposite. Wherever someone displays an extraordinary talent, one can suspect a hidden fault. This inspires a mocking comment from Robert Musil in his novel *The Man without Qualities*: "Our nature always digs a ditch first when it wants us to build a mountain over it."[86] What's more: Adler looks with suspicion on anything maladjusted or out of the ordinary. If someone is very ambitious, this indicates a secret fear of failure; if they act obsequiously, then in reality they have a problem with authority. Nor is Adler shy about making moral judgements: dominant behavior is just as wrong as passive retreat; the healthy individual is both strong-willed and at the same time oriented toward the common welfare. Adler embodies a type that many later therapists will rush to emulate: instead of merely easing suffering, they want to instruct people on how to lead a better life, how to live the right kind of life.

Over the years the conflict between Adler and Freud continues to escalate. But before their final falling out, something astounding happens: quite unexpectedly, psychoanalysis gets a major showcase on an international stage—thanks to a friendly invitation from across the Atlantic.

ANCHORS AWAY

In early September 1909, three men arrive in the city of Worcester, Massachusetts, some two hundred miles northeast of New York, hoping to conquer the New World with an idea. The controversial Dr. Freud from Vienna is accompanied by the Hungarian Sándor Ferenczi and Carl Gustav Jung from Switzerland. With them are Ernest Jones, an Englishman, and Abraham Brill, an Austrian by birth who now lives in New York, both of them enthusiastic proponents of Freud's theory. All have accepted an invitation from psychology professor Granville Stanley Hall to celebrate the twentieth anniversary of the founding of the prestigious Clark University.

Hall pulls out all the stops in his determination to land the Viennese neurologist and his entourage as guests of honor for the celebration. An initial attempt in the spring foundered when Freud feared too much lost income from missed appointments. After Hall raises the honorarium again and suggests a time in September, the month when Freud usually goes on vacation, the master accepts his offer. On August 20 the delegation of psychologists sets sail from Bremen.

Before they board the *George Washington*, one of the largest luxury liners of its time, and cross the Atlantic, they meet for a noteworthy dinner. Freud, Ferenczi, and Jung dine at the Essighaus in Bremen. To celebrate their trip together, Jung, normally a strict teetotaler, has a glass of wine or two. Alcohol is prohibited at the Burghölzli, where Jung has worked since 1901; patients, nurses, and doctors (most of whom live at the clinic) can't touch a drop, officially at least. And so, as might be expected, the alcohol quickly goes to Jung's head. During the meal he talks nonstop, going on and on about a subject that fascinates him: in certain peatlands in North Germany, mummified bog bodies had been discovered, their age and origin unknown. Jung can't get enough of these horror stories, and neither Freud nor Ferenczi can get him off the topic. Finally Freud, already feeling ill—the smoked salmon served at dinner doesn't agree with him—has had enough: "What is it with you and these corpses? Wouldn't it be better if you admitted that you wish I would drop dead?"[87] Jung is taken aback. Evidently Freud interprets his dwelling on the subject of death as an instance of unconscious rebellion against the "master," as though Jung wished him, his psychoanalytic foster father, in the grave.

It's all too much for Freud, weakened by the long journey and his protesting stomach: he faints. Together Jung and Ferenczi carry him into another room, where he quickly regains consciousness. And so concludes this boozy evening before the big journey to America.

On the ship Jung stays in a first-class cabin, as befits the husband of an heiress to a Swiss watch empire; Freud and Ferenczi make do with second class. The group meets on deck and discusses the previous night's dreams, as well as their expectations for the journey. Freud is amused to discover that one of the ship's officers is reading his *Psychopathology of Everyday Life*. When the ship lands at Hoboken, New Jersey, Freud supposedly quips: "Do they have any inkling that we're bringing them the plague?" This would be in keeping with Freud's dark sense of humor, but on the other hand his critics often ascribe such sinister motives to him. At this point in time he could hardly have expected the triumph that psychoanalysis would soon meet with in the US, too great seem the prudery and superficiality of the Americans. In fact, however, within a few decades the study of the unconscious will become a key pillar of American self-improvement and therapy culture.

It's true that a good two dozen other guests of honor are present at Clark University to mark its twentieth-anniversary celebration, among them the famous physicist Ernest Rutherford and the psychologist William Stern from Hamburg. But while the others are put up at hotels, the esteemed analysts stay at Hall's private home and are waited on by Hall's wife and servants. Their host is hoping that Freud's visit will generate a ton of publicity. And indeed, the gambit pays off. The visit from the scandalous "Dr. Sex" causes a stir in the East Coast papers. Ten years have passed since the publication of *The Interpretation of Dreams*, four since Freud described the infantile libido and the Oedipus complex in his *Three Essays on the Theory of Sexuality*.

An illustrious group: In 1909, G. Stanley Hall (seated center) invited a delegation of psychoanalysts, including Jung (seated right) and Freud (seated left) to Worcester for Clark University's twentieth-anniversary celebration.

During his stay in the US, Freud does far more than present a method for treating cases of hysteria and other neurotic ailments. He stirs controversy with his theory that everyone, including people who are physically and mentally healthy, is ruled by sexual drives. Fantasies of lust and violence must constantly be kept out of the conscious mind; they must be repressed, disguised, and sublimated, lest they disrupt social coexistence. Because the censorship never functions perfectly, however, some of these impulses break through and manifest as slips of the tongue, lapses of memory, or dreams—or they impel people to achieve great feats of culture. In order to uncover the true motivating forces behind these actions, Freud says, one has only to interpret the signs correctly.

After many years of concerning himself with hysteria and cases of obsessional and anxiety neurosis in his practice in Vienna, starting in 1905 Freud takes a decisive step from pathology to the psychology of the "normal" individual. He claims that even the most banal quotidian events—whether it be slips of the tongue, a baby's suckling at the mother's breast, or dreams of long trains and dark tunnels—draw from a hidden source: the libido. In order to expose the pleasure-seeking motivation that has been so painstakingly disguised, one must drill down to the "latent" contents on the other side of the psyche's resistance.

This is a conception of enormous import. It says nothing less than this: we humans, despite all notions to the contrary, are not the master of our own selves; we're merely following orders. In the lower depths of the psyche, amoral forces are at work that have only one goal: instinctual gratification. In order for life in common to be possible, the reality principle must prevail over the pleasure principle, and the drive or instinct must continually be suppressed or channeled; individuals must mask their desires, renounce pleasures, and find substitute forms of satisfaction. If no other means of release is possible, the libido finds a safety valve in the form of phobias, compulsions, or other symptoms.

On his first and only visit to America in this late summer of 1909, Freud presents his view to a thoroughly receptive audience. He gives five lectures on campus over five consecutive days. Jung also speaks in Worcester about his association experiment and its connection to the unconscious. It's a once-in-a-lifetime chance to finally gain recognition. Psychoanalysis to this point has only reached small circles in Berlin, Vienna, Budapest, and Paris. This limited reach is due above all to resistance on the part of the scientific establishment. Its representatives reject Freud's speculations about the hidden life of the psyche. His ideas might speak to an artistic elite fascinated by notions of eros and inner demons—but they have nothing to do with serious research. The trip to America, Freud and Jung hope, might help to revise this image.

One of those who attend Freud's Worcester lectures is the philosopher William James. Sixty-seven years old and suffering from cancer, he travels from Cambridge, Massachusetts specifically for the purpose. After a walk around campus, James predicts big things for the Viennese analyst: "The future of psychology belongs to your work."[88] So reports Freud's biographer Ernest Jones, at least. In private letters, however, James calls the symbolism of psychoanalysis "dangerous" and says it verges on charlatanism. James recognizes the problem posed by the absence of any means of verifying the analysts' claims. As Freud argues in his lectures, not only dreams, but also lapses of memory, slips of the tongue, mistakes, and sudden flashes of inspiration are full of significance. Nothing happens by chance; every utterance, every action reveals some truth once it is interpreted in the light of psychoanalytic theory. And if anyone disputes the psychoanalytic interpretation, that merely increases the likelihood that it is accurate, since the critic clearly doesn't want to admit the truth. It's hardly possible to refute such tricky logic, James observes.

The immunity to criticism that characterizes Freudian thought proves to be both a drawback and a recipe for success. While many experts like James shake their heads, among the wider public Freud enjoys a reputation as the man with the penetrating gaze who knows the depths of his clients' psyches better than they do themselves. What for empirically-minded scientists is a congenital defect of psychoanalysis turns out to be an advantage in the budding market for psychological help. Freud is the author of a narrative that remains persuasive today: you are not what you think you are. You have no awareness of the motives that guide you, and overlook the influences and conflicts that fuel your mental life. Thus all of a sudden psychotherapy becomes a kind of expository act that resolves blockages and makes self-knowledge possible.

With this shift, the therapist slips into a flattering new role, revealing things of which the client had no prior inkling. What's more: ever since the failure of his treatment of Dora, Freud has come to consider the mechanism of transference to be a key feature of the therapeutic process. Patients project onto the therapist libidinous affects originally directed toward a parent. That is to say: they fall in love with him and, for that very reason, unconsciously reject him. This dynamic burdens the analyst with enormous responsibility, for he must overcome his patients' resistance and at the same time resist their concealed sexual advances; he must lay bare what patients don't want to accept while he himself becomes an object of their love. Inherent in this process is the risk of transgression—a problem that will preoccupy many analysts to come.

According to Freud, the pleasure principle is *the* motor of the psyche. No member of his society is permitted to dispute this premise. But the split with Adler and Jung occurs over this very point, not long after the trip to America. The first fissures in Freud's relationship with the Swiss psychiatrist are already starting to show on the trip back from their weeks-long sojourn in the US. As the hours crawl by on board the *Kaiser Wilhelm*, making its eight-day journey from New York back to Bremen, the men pass the time by analyzing one another's dreams. When Jung has trouble with a dream of Freud's, he asks for more details from the older man's personal life. "Freud's response to these words was a curious look—a look of the utmost suspicion. Then he said, 'But I cannot risk my authority!' At that moment he lost it altogether. [. . .] Freud was placing personal authority above truth."[89] It will take another five years, however, for the two of them to part ways for good.

. . .

Meanwhile, back in Vienna, Adler is growing more self-confident in advocating for his own position, distinct from Freud's. Some in the Psychoanalytic Society respect him for it, but often he encounters only whispers or embarrassed silence. Now Adler finally wants to land a major blow. He is working on a book that is meant to provide the necessary foundation for his approach. The basic idea is easily stated: out of a feeling of incapacity, the natural deficiency of the infant, arises the entire inner dynamic and personality of the human individual. The infant is dependent on others; they can do basically nothing for themselves: they can't grab hold of things, can't walk, can't soothe themselves, can't obtain food. The infant is a helpless bundle that is in constant need of care.

In the first part of his book, Adler draws many parallels to organ inferiority. The body, Adler argues, often compensates for physiological dysfunctions by stimulating other organs or faculties to develop in response, sometimes to a greater extent than necessary. Adler sees the same principle at work in the formation of character as it aims to overcome its own inferiority.

It is here that Adler breaks decisively with Freud. "The neurotic does not suffer from reminiscences; he makes them," he writes.[90] Where for Freud neurotic impulses are rooted in repressed infantile sexuality and traumatic experiences, for Adler everything starts with the wish to escape from one's own deficiency.

Since the second Psychoanalytic Congress in Nuremberg in 1910, at which the International Psychoanalytical Association was founded and Jung was elected president, Adler has led the Vienna chapter. He and Stekel also edit the *Zentralblatt für Psychoanalyse*, one of the two main journals of the movement. But in February and March 1911, the conflict with Freud comes out into the open. At several meetings of the Society there are tense debates over Adler's positions. The dissident seeks to shift the focus from the unique past of the neurotic individual toward a fundamental constant of human experience. Literally everyone starts off feeling small and weak and must learn to deal with this indignity. Adler's approach widens the field of those who are in need of therapeutic guidance: everyone strives for security, greatness, power; the neurotic simply does so in an extreme, uncontrollable fashion.

Freud criticizes Adler on two fronts: first, he "eliminates the sexual" and disputes the etiological role of the repressed libido. And second, he advances an ego psychology that fails to peer into the depths of unconscious motives. There is some truth to both criticisms: for Adler the sexual is a symptom. The individual can demonstrate his power by showcasing his virility or asserting dominance over a woman, but nevertheless, sexual lust is not the cause of neurosis. Adler actually adopts a teleological position that asks what a psychical process is for, what purpose it serves. For him, every person develops their own life plan, which they apply to every new situation. The neurotic is "nailed to the cross of his fiction," as Adler puts it.[91]

On May 24, 1911, almost nine years after his first invitation to Freud's Wednesday gathering, he takes part in a meeting of the Vienna Psychoanalytic Society for the last time. Over the ensuing summer break he starts his own Society for Free Psychoanalytic Research. The name says it all. At the first meeting of the Psychoanalytic Society after the summer recess, on October 11, Freud tells his followers that no one can belong to his society and also belong to the society led by Adler. The differences, he says, are too great. In response, seven members announce their resignation. A period of mutual invective and animosity ensues.

Finally, in 1912, Adler publishes his magnum opus, *Über den nervösen Charakter* ("On the Nervous Character"; the book will be published in English as *The Neurotic Constitution*). "Nervous" here means essentially neurotic, over-anxious, ruled by complexes. The book offers a recap of the fundamental concepts of inferiority, compensation, and of neurosis as an exaggerated, sclerotic striving for power. The next year Adler renames his group the Society for Individual Psychology, which, in contrast to the dissecting approach of analysis, is meant to emphasize the totality of the individual. The term "individual psychology" makes it sound as though the primary focus here were the individual and their needs. But ironically, the social feeling, the orientation toward the collective, plays a central role in individual psychology.

The vagueness of many of Adler's terms makes his theory accessible to various movements—including those that he himself denounces. He is read not only in Marxist circles, but in nationalist-conservative circles as well, where the "will to power" and the notion of severity towards one's self find a receptive audience. Whether consciously or not, Adler fails to specify what kind of community he has in mind. Could he mean the community of the Aryan *Volk*? And doesn't *too strong* a communal sense lead to self-sacrifice and ideological blindness? Adler stresses that solidarity is at the forefront of a healthy orientation toward the collective, but solidarity as a rule is limited to a clearly defined group—family, like-minded individuals, the nation—and excludes others. Right-wing ideologues will understand how to exploit this open flank in Adler's approach for their own ends.

The fundamentally optimistic nature of Adler's thinking contributes to its attractiveness. "The views of our individual psychology require the unconditional dismantling of the striving for power and the development of the social feeling," he writes in 1922 in the foreword to the third edition of *Über den nervösen Charakter*.[92] Ten years prior he put it somewhat differently: at that time, before the horrors of the world war, Adler called his universal mechanism for the enhancement of the ego the "will to power." To be sure, even at the time he condemned the tendency towards self-aggrandization and warned of its destructive power. But because Adler sets weakness and passivity against the heroic conquest of self, he provides psychological fodder to a wealth of different worldviews.[93]

On a personal level, Adler, unlike Freud, is very much inclined toward conciliation. In *Der Sinn des Lebens* ("The Meaning of Life";

published in English as *Social Interest*), from 1933, looking back at the early years of the movement in Vienna, he writes that Freud was "the first to attempt to form a scientific theory of dreams. This is a lasting merit that no one can lessen." He continues: "He seems to have known much more than he understood. It was inevitable, however, that he should go wrong when he forced himself to group all psychical phenomena round the single ruling principle that he recognizes—the sexual libido."[94]

. . .

Late one night on the return trip from the US in September 1909, Jung is lying in his cabin. The seas are calm, but the bed is too short for the nearly six foot two Jung. He feels hemmed in, restless. Suddenly he gets up and finds himself standing, as if liberated, in a roomy house. This is *my* house, thinks Jung. Not bad! He looks around, curious. He is standing in a kind of living room on the upper level, furnished in the finest rococo style, with velvet-upholstered armchairs, a stately writing desk, and expensive paintings on the walls. He decides to check out the rest of the house, and takes the stairs down to the ground floor. Here the atmosphere is suddenly gloomy; the low ceiling and narrow windows give the room a medieval feel. The simple, crudely-fashioned furniture and antiquated tools hanging on the walls suggest that this part of the building dates back to the 15th or 16th century.

Under a hatch Jung discovers a stone staircase leading down to the basement; he descends. The clay brick walls remind him of Roman buildings; it smells musty; stone slabs are visible beneath a layer of dust on the floor. On one of them he discovers an iron ring. He pulls on it and the slab lifts up with astounding ease. It reveals a cave; Jung, not sure what's going on, descends even further.

It is pitch black; his feet sink into the sandy ground beneath him; suddenly he steps on something hard. Jung bends over. He can see gleaming white bones, and there, right at his feet, two half-decayed skulls. At this moment he awakes.

. . .

After his return from the US Freud is more certain of his cause than ever before. His topography of the psyche, divided into three systems—conscious, unconscious, and preconscious—is now firmly established. "Thus an unconscious conception is one of which we are not aware, but the existence of which we are nevertheless ready to admit on account of other proofs or signs," he writes in 1912.[95] What kind of proofs and signs could these be? Freud offers post-hypnotic suggestion as one example. People under hypnosis are prompted to perform certain actions, with the hypnotist whispering to them that when they awaken from their trance they should do this or that. The hypnotized individuals, after emerging from the trance, do in fact sometimes (though certainly not all the time) detect such an impulse, without suspecting where it comes from.

"The mind of the hysterical patient is full of active yet unconscious ideas; all her symptoms proceed from such ideas," Freud explains.[96] "If the hysterical woman vomits, she may do so from the idea of being pregnant. She has, however, no knowledge of this idea. [. . .] If she is executing the jerks and movements constituting her 'fit,' she does not even consciously represent to herself the intended actions. [. . .] Nevertheless analysis will show that she was acting her part in the dramatic reproduction of some incident in her life, the memory of which was unconsciously active during the attack. The same preponderance of active unconscious ideas is revealed by analysis as the essential fact in the psychology of all other forms of neurosis."[97]

Freud also distinguishes between the preconscious and the unconscious. The latter term is understood to comprise all elements that are cut off from conscious perception, memory, and reflection. Preconscious, on the other hand, refers to what can *potentially* become conscious. Though it is the case that "every psychical act begins as an unconscious one,"[98] how and why something is shifted from the realm of the unconscious to that of the preconscious is unclear—such a transition must take place, however, because otherwise everything that is unconscious would stay unconscious. "The distinction between foreconscious[99] and unconscious activity is not a primary one, but comes to be established after repulsion has sprung up."[100] Meaning, in other words: a thought or desire is preconscious if it can pass into conscious awareness without being repressed or defamiliarized; if not, it remains unconscious.

This point of view contains a subtle flaw: thoughts, intentions, memories, perceptions, decisions—these things aren't sitting in some corner of the brain's attic, waiting either to step out into the bright light of consciousness or to have their way barred by certain defense mechanisms. We don't carry around an archive of finished thoughts in our heads. If I remember the previous evening, for example, I'm not accessing fully-formed thoughts and notions; rather I'm creating the reminiscences anew in the very moment of remembering. The brain actively reconstructs what we have experienced or intended from lots of different fragments. In Freud's unconscious, however, all the "material" is lying there ready to be shipped here or there or disguised by the censor. The substance is the same; all that changes is where it's located and the form in which it appears.

This system corresponds to a static, mechanistic notion of the mind as a filing system that keeps compromising documents under seal or disguises them through encryption. The idea that there might not be pre-formed mental states, that instead we are constantly, creatively generating thoughts, feelings, and conceptions, might have been conceivable in Freud's time, but was not yet established knowledge. Thus many contemporaries, above all people outside of the medical field, accepted his concrete division of the realms of the mind without hesitation.

Another drawback to Freud's model is the waste of resources it entails: the unconscious as the stronghold of amoral desires serving the goal of gratification would require an arsenal of defense mechanisms to keep watch over it around the clock and ensure that its true activity remained hidden. But why all the effort? Is it all just to keep the individual from becoming aware of their animalistic roots? Without the late 19th century's hostility toward sex and the body, this whole construct collapses like a house of cards.

If all the mind's activity really were directed toward lending a touch of civilization to our libidinous urges, if our psyche really were involved in such a complex system of double-entry bookkeeping, the required energy consumption would be tremendous. The opposite is likely the case: it is not the unconscious that is pressing to become conscious; rather everything that does not require our conscious attention proceeds to carry on automatically. The brain is a high-efficiency machine—a discovery that will first be made possible by modern imaging neuroscience; for Freud, the Victorian, this knowledge is still a long way off. In the age of the steam engine, energy wasn't something one had to budget. From today's perspective, however, the constant denial, repression, and sublimation of libidinous energies hardly seems compatible with the idea that the machinery of the psyche works as economically as possible.

In one respect, however, Freud's approach represents major progress. He breaks with the attitude of "therapeutic nihilism" held by many physicians at the time, which called for merely observing sick individuals without listening to them, and of diagnosing them with no intention of healing them.[101] Freud, on the other hand, puts the promise of recovery at the center of his psychological treatment method.

Uncovering and "working through" neurotic complexes is the purpose and aim of psychoanalysis. At one point, later in life, Freud declares with demonstrative modesty that he had had the good fortune to discover the unconscious. This is stretching the truth, to say the least. The awareness that we aren't master of our own house dates back well before Freud. The difference is that others, like the Romantic poets or the physician and natural philosopher Carl Gustav Carus, regarded unconscious notions as a positive force that brought about inspiration and loftier insights. The proponents of the 18th- and early 19th-century Enlightenment fought heated battles with the spiritualists over this question.

Freud filled the blank space that the unconscious has always been with assumptions that reflected the realities of his own life. He then coupled these assumptions with the task of investigating the stirrings of the psyche as a way of deciphering their true significance. Nothing is as it seems; everything points to something else, be it a traumatic experience, an early impression, or repressed immorality. Freud's achievement is therefore not to have discovered the unconscious, but rather to have been the first to regard thoughts, feelings, fantasies, and desires as purely psychological phenomena, and to deal with them accordingly. Ever since he gave up his original goal of a career as a researcher,[102] his interests were directed toward one subject and one subject alone: the hidden depths of the soul.

A GIRL NAMED FRANK

The First World War has not yet broken out when Freud parts ways with another apostate, the man on whom he had once pinned his hopes: Carl Gustav Jung. Once again the split is preceded by an act of blasphemy. The year 1912 sees the publication not only of Adler's *Über den nervösen Charakter*, but also of Jung's *Wandlungen und Symbole der Libido* ("Transformations and Symbols of the Libido," published in English first as *Psychology of the Unconscious* and later, in revised form, as *Symbols of Transformation*). In the book, the thirty-six-year-old rejects Freudian sexual theory in no uncertain terms and develops a theory of the unconscious that goes beyond mere individual experience.

In the years since the publication of *The Interpretation of Dreams*, Freud has come up with a complex nomenclature to label all the mental processes that regulate the border traffic between consciousness and the unconscious. Of particular importance to this system is infantile sexuality. The idea that even infants feel sexual pleasure, the notion that children harbor Oedipal death wishes towards their fathers or fantasies of becoming one with their mothers, that boys feel an unconscious fear of castration and girls penis envy—all these Freud regards as constants of psychological development. Jung isn't convinced. He develops his own approach which transcends the individual. According to Jung, suppressed libidinal energy doesn't create neuroses; rather these are the product of ancient conflicts rooted deeply in all people that reveal themselves in myths and symbols. Whether they are inherited or culturally disseminated, Jung can't say (at this time people know neither what genes are nor how memory works). The key point, as he sees it, is that one doesn't need to catch mom and dad having sex or wish for either of their deaths to become neurotic.

In their correspondence, Jung and Freud debate questions of this sort quite openly at first. It doesn't make sense to Freud why Jung insists on seeing traditional patterns at work in causing neurosis when a far more plausible explanation seems to be that real-life experiences are the culprit. Jung for his part is convinced that individual impressions alone do not account for the character of the unconscious. Based on his dream of the house with the skulls inside, which greatly preoccupies him, he concludes that there are also layers of consciousness that are as old as human history. This is how Jung interprets the medieval-style ground floor, the Roman cellar, and the prehistoric cave: the historical eras represent various levels of consciousness, as if in a "structural diagram of the human soul."

A further source of inspiration for Jung is the case of Emil Schwyzer, son of a Zurich coppersmith, who lived at the Burghölzli for many years and was treated there by Jung and his colleague Johann Honegger. Schwyzer fell ill around the age of twenty with schizophrenia, as "precocious madness" (*dementia praecox*) has been known since 1908 at the suggestion of Eugen Bleuler.[103] After an odyssey that takes him through various clinics, Schwyzer is finally brought by relatives to the institute in Zurich. His psychotic episodes are so severe as to make it impossible to have anything close to a normal conversation with him. Nor can he follow the prompts of the association experiment. Schwyzer's thinking and speech seem fully steeped in delusion. Jung and Honegger notice that he sometimes tosses his head energetically from side to side. As they discover through intensive probing, Schwyzer believes that by moving his head in this way he can influence the weather. There is, he explains, a large, phallus-like appendage that hangs down from the sun; by setting the appendage in motion through his own actions, he regulates the sun's radiance.

Around the same time, Jung is studying mythology and stumbles on a staggering coincidence: this same kind of "solar phallus" existed in Mithraism! The adherents of this mystery cult, which was prevalent in Asia Minor, North Africa, and Greece in the first centuries after the birth of Christ, believed that a lengthy appendage on the lower edge of the sun conveyed its warmth down to the earth.[104] Given Schwyzer's lack of education, he can hardly have gleaned this knowledge from books. According to Jung, this can only mean one thing: within the unconscious there are images that have been inscribed there over generations. These images get passed down in a social or ethnic community and influence the particular manifestations of each individual's psyche. In some people they come to light in the condition of madness or through some other mental disturbance; these individuals have access to the profound layers of the unconscious. Thus the idea of the archetype is born.

In March 1911, without warning, Jung's assistant Honegger commits suicide with an overdose of morphine. As he experienced the early stages of a mental illness that had afflicted his father before him, it had become increasingly impossible for him to work.[105] In Honegger's writings, Schwyzer's perspective often blurs with Honegger's own. After his assistant's death, Jung takes possession of his manuscripts and expands on the ideas contained within them. Some of his colleagues suspect that in doing so Jung also took the notion of the collective unconscious from Honegger. Even if that is the case, however, Jung himself significantly elaborated on the concept and breathed life into it.

The first part of *Wandlungen und Symbole der Libido* appears in 1911 in the *Jahrbuch für psychoanalytische und psychopathologische Forschung*, the second part in early 1912.[106] This book marks Jung's departure from the "constricting atmosphere of Freudian psychology and its narrow outlook," as he writes in a foreword.[107] It is a highly complex, meandering stream of thought in which dreams, poems, and literary allusions mix with historical episodes, fragments of myth, and psychological interpretations—a wild ride through Jung's intellectual universe.

Featured prominently in the book is a case of exuberant youthful imagination that Jung takes from a professional journal. The personal

Pioneer with principles: Eugen Bleuler led the Burghölzli in Zurich from 1898 to 1927 and coined the term "schizophrenia." He left the Psychoanalytic Society after less than a year, accusing it of sectarianism.

testimonial of a young American woman named Frank Miller was first published in French by the Genevan psychologist Théodore Flournoy.[108] Jung has never met the young woman himself and repeatedly veers off track in his discussion of the case. Not only does he assume her name is a pseudonym (she was in fact named Frank, after her father); he also goes so far as to pronounce via remote diagnosis that she is in the "prodromal state" of psychosis—i.e., the early stages of schizophrenia. But Miller, who studied with Flournoy, was a poet and stage performer who impersonated historical figures as part of her act; by all accounts she wasn't sick in the psychiatric sense.

Whatever the case may be, from the account of the unconventional young woman, Jung draws wide-reaching conclusions about humanity's unconscious inheritance. One of Miller's astounding capabilities is to identify with figures unknown to her, often from the distant past, and to speak as if she were they. On reading *Cyrano de Bergerac*, for example, she feels the same intense burning sensation in her chest that the hero feels when he is stabbed during a duel. When she steps out of the bath with a towel wrapped around her head like a turban, she suddenly feels like an Egyptian from the time of the pharaohs and starts to move exactly like the figures represented in the hieroglyphs found in ancient tombs. Along with these episodes, Jung interprets in all earnestness three of Miller's imaginative works, the poems "Glory to God" and "The Moth and the Sun" as well as the Aztec drama "Chiwantopel." Miller claims to have conceived these texts on her travels while half-asleep.

Before Jung gets down to the work of exegesis, he distinguishes in a central chapter of his book between two fundamentally different types of thinking: the logical type, which is tied to concepts, and the analogical type, which is "emotionally toned, pictorial, and wordless," an "inner-directed rumination on materials belonging to the past."[109] The latter is the form of thought that draws from the unconscious. His name for this descent into hard to articulate archaic patterns is "introversion." If this process gets out of control, the personality risks being overtaken by analogical thinking. The result: a psychosis.

The conclusion he draws from the mythological spectacle inspired by Miss Miller follows this same logic: "The psyche is not of today; its ancestry goes back many millions of years. Individual consciousness is only the flower and the fruit of a season, sprung from the perennial rhizome beneath the earth."[110]

Freud isn't having any of it. True, he too has a weakness for mythological subjects, as shown by the 1910 essay "Leonardo da Vinci and a Memory of His Childhood," in which, drawing on Egyptian mythology, he explains that da Vinci's homosexuality and creative energy were a product of his excessive love for his mother. But for Freud, the myths only serve as a historical backdrop against which the individual biography comes into sharper relief. Jung, on the other hand, regards the individual himself as a manifestation of the "mythos."[111] For Freud, the ancient myth of Oedipus is the prototype of an ancient father complex; according to Jung, however, the myth is part of the collective unconscious.

The conflict between the two points of view comes out at first in subtle digs and hints, but their work together on the shared project of advancing psychoanalysis keeps it from spilling out into the open. Over time the differences grow more acute, and the tone of the discourse between the two men becomes more abrasive, with each insinuating that the other is neurotic. After a period of intensive mythological study, Jung writes to Freud in May 1911, almost apologetically: "Please don't worry about my wanderings in these infinitudes I shall return laden with rich booty for our knowledge of the human psyche. For a while longer I must intoxicate myself on magic perfumes in order to fathom the secrets that lie hidden in the abysses of the unconscious."[112] But a year later, after the publication of *Wandlungen und Symbole*, a deep rift opens up in their relationship, and the professional disagreement takes a sharp turn into personal antipathy.

At first the conflict revolves around Jung's turning away from the libido theory. For Jung the libido is not the source of the psyche's conflicts, but rather the place where they play out: "The sexuality of the unconscious is not that which it appears to be, it is merely a symbol."[113] At a meeting between the two men in Munich in November 1912, Freud again has a fainting spell, for the second time since the memorable evening that preceded their departure for the US. Again the incident involves the question, so disturbing for Freud, of "patricide." The two men are arguing over whether the Egyptian pharaoh

Amenhotep, believed to be the founder of monotheism, was right to have his father's name expunged from all public buildings. Before introducing the new religion, says Jung, he first had to remove all traces of the old divine ruler. Freud sees this claim as yet another veiled attack against his authority.

It's true that Jung has continued to build his group of contacts since their trip together to the US, where he had given well-regarded lectures and gained influential supporters. In letters he accuses Freud of pathologizing his followers as soon as they depart from orthodox doctrine. Freud angrily denies this and withdraws into himself. In January 1913 he writes to Jung: "Accordingly, I propose that we abandon our personal relations entirely."[114] The Swiss psychiatrist replies dryly: "I accede to your wish that we abandon our personal relations, for I never thrust my friendship on anyone. You yourself are the best judge of what this moment means to you. 'The rest is silence.'"[115]

In October Jung officially resigns his post as president of the International Psychoanalytical Association. What began six years earlier with a marathon thirteen-hour discussion meets an abrupt end. The two men, who in their letters would occasionally address one another as "dear friend," now become rivals and adversaries.

Shortly before the conclusive break with Jung, Freud clearly suspects that something bad is in the works. One can "expect wicked things" from him, he writes to Ferenczi in May 1913. Naturally "everything that strays from our truths has official applause on its side. It is quite possible that this time they will really bury us after they have so often sung us the dirge in vain."[116]

The pattern resembles that of Freud's previous ruptures. Initial effusiveness is followed by estrangement, then discord, and finally a breaking off of contact. In the end what remain are grievance, silence—and a dogged insistence on one's own point of view. Jung isn't the last pupil with whom Freud grows close and then cuts ties; a long trail of such disputes runs alongside the history of psychoanalysis. Even devoted followers who remain loyal for years, like Sándor Ferenczi and Otto Rank, will go their own way in the 1920s. Ferenczi calls for the therapist to show empathy and engage with patients, which goes against Freud's law of abstinence; Rank, meanwhile, favors a psychoanalysis that doesn't merely root around in the past but changes thought patterns in the here and now. Both of them, as we shall see, will become important and influential figures for a new generation of psychotherapists.

The schism between Freud and Jung is rooted in their different ideas of what the unconscious should be. The historian and psychologist John Kerr explains it as follows: "Jung seems always to have wanted an 'unconscious' that he could talk to, one that might counsel and guide him, even help him heal the divisions in his personality. Freud, on the other hand, sought no such personal relation with the inner world. Fundamentally, he appears always to have wanted an 'unconscious' that he could examine like an arcane text, one that required deciphering and exegesis."[117]

For all his disappointment at the loss of his "crown prince," Freud claims to be undaunted: "[This] will change much in our fate, but nothing in that of science," he writes to Ferenczi. "We are in possession of the truth; I am as certain as I was fifteen years ago."[118]

SWORN BROTHERHOOD

What sort of science do these words call to mind? In a word, a dogmatic one. Early evidence of this can be found in an episode from the fall of 1906. The medical student Fritz Wittels is attending a lecture given by Freud at the University of Vienna. The professor is pontificating about the weaknesses of experimental psychology. Its leading exponent, Wilhelm Wundt, founded the world's first psychological institute in Leipzig in 1875 and trained almost the entire cohort of early psychologists. Freud compares him to Orlando from Ariosto's epic and muses sarcastically: "We cannot help thinking that the old psychology has been killed by my dream doctrine; but the old psychology is quite unaware of the fact, and goes on teaching as usual."[119]

This is typical Freud. He lends himself an avant-garde aura by criticizing the establishment and at the same time limiting entry to his own circle. Freud doesn't let non-medical students sit in on his lectures except with special permission. And to be admitted into the Psychoanalytic Society is a difficult undertaking.

For the prestige of the movement, the fact that the Zurich crowd centered around Bleuler, Jung, and Binswanger support psychoanalysis is of immense value. Some of Freud's disciples, like Max Eitingon and Karl Abraham, who will later belong to the "secret committee," began their careers as junior physicians at the Burghölzli. But at least one person at the institute—its director, Eugen Bleuler—has concerns about the sectarian tendencies of his Viennese colleagues.

Freud convinced Bleuler to join the Psychoanalytical Association at a meeting in Munich around Christmas 1910, but Bleuler resigns the following November. His reason: "This 'whoever isn't for us is against us,' this 'all or nothing,' is in my opinion necessary for religious communities and useful for political parties. I can therefore understand the principle as such. For science, however, I consider it harmful. [...] It isn't a *Weltanschauung*, after all."[120] Meanwhile the Viennese are greatly reliant on their predominately non-Jewish colleagues in Zurich. "We need our Aryan friends," Freud tells Ferenczi. This is one reason why he had chosen Jung—"Siegfried," as he's known in Vienna—as his heir apparent.

More than once, in the early years of psychoanalysis, Freud mentions the prospect of writing a guide, a handbook with rules for interpretation. But aside from a few essays here and there on the practice of analysis, he fails to produce this long-awaited manual. Instead he publishes novella-like case studies and a bevy of theoretical texts. What is missing is a readily understandable technique, a scaffolding for aspiring analysts to build on.

Freud is in a bind. On the one hand, every form of medicine rests on the principles of transparency and conveyability. Not just the odd talented pupil but every sufficiently trained professional should be capable of applying the method. Only then can a given therapy establish itself on a widespread scale. It's certainly true that some physicians have more talent than others, and that each has individual predilections, strengths, and weaknesses. But what good is an approach if only its inventor and a few adepts could ever master it? To fail to provide a schema laying out which methods are to be used to treat which types of condition is to practice not medicine, but art.

Nevertheless Freud is brilliant at boosting the attractiveness of his own system of meaning by contrasting it with the old ways. Even as he is splitting with Jung he is putting together the aforementioned "secret committee," made up of several faithful followers. Rank, Abraham, Jones, Ferenczi, and Sachs are charged with policing adherence to the true doctrine. (Max Eitingon joins a few years later.) As a sign of their conspiratorial bond, each receives a ring from Freud's hand. Transparency and skepticism, which for true science are indispensable, are made subordinate to loyalty. What's right is what the "master" says is right, not what stands up to fact-based scrutiny. Freud must have the last word, just as he did at the first meetings of his Wednesday Society.

Imagine if the most eminent physicist of that era, Albert Einstein, had started a club to disseminate his views about the universe, and made his colleagues—Niels Bohr, Max Planck, Werner Heisenberg—sworn members. Thanks to the power of his intuition, he has come up with subtle explanations for the functioning of gravity, the movements of particles, and time and space. To support these ideas he has offered

The Secret Committee: in 1912 Freud assembles his innermost circle, tasked with protecting his theory from attacks and dissenters. From left: Otto Rank, Sigmund Freud, Karl Abraham, Max Eitingon, Sándor Ferenczi, Ernest Jones, Hanns Sachs.

anecdotal evidence. What's more, his discoveries can only be deduced indirectly, they can never be measured or verified; indeed he would have categorically rejected the validity of such a review. Now let's imagine further that "Master" Einstein had demanded unconditional loyalty from his followers and dismissed dissenting views as illegitimate or pathological. Would this Einstein fellow have made it as a scientist? Probably not. Why, then, did other standards seem to apply for psychology?

What makes physics different from the psychology of this era is the touchstone of empiricism: universally comprehensible data. Predictions based on this data must provide the best-possible explanation of observed reality and, what's more, must remain valid in the light of new findings. No authority or theory, not even a plausible one, gets to decide what is true or false. One can come up with a lot of ideas, but one must also present facts that no one can dispute.

In his paper "The Foundation of the General Theory of Relativity," published in May 1916, Albert Einstein claims that the sun's gravity slightly deflects the light that passes through the center of the solar system. As a result, the position of many stars appears to shift when viewed in proximity to the sun. By Einstein's calculation, the extent of that shift was 1.75 arcseconds (this is about the width of a quarter seen at a distance of several kilometers). Is this true? On May 29, 1919, the occurrence of a total solar eclipse presents an opportunity to test Einstein's prediction. Sir Arthur Eddington of Great Britain dispatches two expeditions equipped with telescopes and photographic gear, one to the island of Príncipe off the coast of Spanish Guinea, the other to Sobral in northern Brazil. Both locations, for reasons of climate and geography, offer the best guarantee of making a successful measurement. Conditions are difficult; in the end, only a few of the photo plates taken during the solar eclipse are usable. But a comparison of the evidence yields a conclusion: the apparent position of the stars as measured in the vicinity of the solar disc does in fact differ slightly from their previously observed position. According to a follow-up experiment conducted with modern instruments in 1978, the difference is around 1.90 arcseconds.

Because Einstein's predictions line up with the data thus obtained, there's no contesting the truth of his theory—at least until a new theory comes along that offers a more elegant explanation of the facts, or new facts emerge that call the model into question. Why was something similar not conceivable with regard to the psyche? Why can't psychologists give to their discipline a degree of clarity similar to that which exists in physics, chemistry, or biology? Unlike the unconscious, which everyone fills with their own fantasies, the universe can be observed and measured. The psyche, on the other hand, the "clinical material" of psychology, is unintelligible without subjective interpretations and premises. Freud's case histories are literary gems, but scientifically they are of little value.

And there's another part of the equation as well: from the beginning, psychoanalysis is accompanied by distortion and acrimony. One analyst portrays his patient's suffering as more severe that it actually is; another claims to have cured a patient, when in fact the treatment yielded only modest success; and a third insinuates that his critics have "defects" as a way of undermining their authority. Disagreement sometimes even serves as proof that the person voicing it is wrong—for clearly the critic hasn't overcome his resistance yet. Karl Kraus coins a witticism for this phenomenon: "Psychoanalysis is the disease for which it considers itself the therapy."

All that notwithstanding, many of Freud's contemporaries eagerly swallow his theories. After all, there's no better remedy on offer. Freud created a myth that satisfied a universal need: to see more profoundly than everyone else. And so it came to pass that, as John Kerr writes, "psychoanalysis early ceased to be merely a clinical method—it was never a science—and became instead both a movement and a *Weltanschauung*."[121]

2

SEX

THE FIND

The Palais Wilson perches majestically on the western shore of Lake Geneva. Built in the 1870s as a grand hotel in classical style with more than two hundred rooms, in 1920 the building was made the headquarters of the newly-founded League of Nations. Four years later the palais was renamed in honor of US President Woodrow Wilson, one of the League's architects. It bears that name still, and today houses the Office of the United Nations High Commissioner for Human Rights (UNHCR).

By the mid-1970s the building is in dire need of renovations. When, in 1977, workers enter one of the rooms in the catacomb-like basement, they find a stained old suitcase in a corner, covered in spider webs. The suitcase is opened, and there beneath a blanket of dust are dozens of handwritten notes, letters, and postcards, plus a moldering stack of diaries.

A good half a century earlier, the University of Geneva's Jean-Jacques Rousseau Institute was located in this part of the building. It was here that Jean Piaget, the famous pioneer in the field of cognitive development in children, conducted his research. Did the documents date back to that time? An expert in the history of the Geneva institute is summoned. He lives far away, in Rome, and so asks a friend of his, the analyst Aldo Carotenuto, to inspect the find on Lake Geneva.

Carotenuto can't believe his eyes. He immediately recognizes Freud's looping script and Jung's economical Swiss hand. As he leafs through the nearly seventy-year-old papers, Carotenuto suspects what sort of treasure it is that he holds in his hands: eighty-one letters—originals, copies, drafts, and fragments—from and to Sabina Spielrein, who carried on a lively correspondence with Jung and Freud that began in 1908. He also discovers diaries kept by the Russian woman from 1909 to 1912. During that time she was undergoing training to become an analyst with Jung—who was first the doctor in charge of her treatment, then her boss, and finally her lover—while at the same time corresponding with the patriarch of the movement in Vienna.

The suitcase left behind in Geneva proves to be an explosive discovery for the history of psychoanalysis, filling in several puzzle pieces and helping to complete the picture we have of its protagonists.

. . .

In the spring of 1923 Sabina Spielrein is packing up the last of her things. She is about to leave for Moscow, where she will be reunited with her husband Pawel Scheftel. After living apart for years, the couple plans to start a new life together. He had gotten homesick and returned to Russia from Switzerland, where the two of them had sought refuge at the start of the First World War. Swept up in the fervor of the revolution, he wanted to help build a new society, a collective of free people. She however was committed to her work at the University of Geneva, where she was making important contributions to the field of child psychoanalysis. She couldn't just give up her research and trade it in for an uncertain future in the land of Bolshevism.

But Pawel, who like her is also a physician, gushes to her in his letters about the forward thinking and spirit of awakening in the young Soviet Union. All over the country progress was being made, and not just economic progress; there were also advances in cultural life and in science. Under the guiding hand of People's Commissioner Leon Trotsky, psychoanalytic institutes and clinics were popping up all over the place, and Moscow even had the world's first state-run training institute for psychoanalysis. Spielrein is optimistic that, in her home town of Rostov, she'll be able to continue her work in the field of child psychology, finding her own way to help people liberated from czarism. In the last twenty years she has witnessed—and personally experienced—enough Western decadence and double standards.

When Sabina Spielrein was nineteen years old, her mother checked her into the Burghölzli psychiatric institute in Zurich. Eva Lyublinskaya Spielrein didn't know what else to do. At the elegant Hotel Baur on Paradeplatz, where the family often stayed in the summer, her daughter had started lashing out with her fists, screaming, and generally going berserk. The fits of anger were only the tip of the iceberg, the most acute symptom in a hysterical condition that had grown ever worse over the years.

Tall and proud: the young assistant physician Carl Gustav Jung outside the Burghölzli.

During the night of August 18, 1904, Eva Lyublinskaya, her raving daughter, and a servant drive up to the main gate of the insane asylum, as the Burghölzli is officially known. Shortly after being admitted the patient calms down, and the next morning she is asked to recount her medical history. The young woman is placed in the care of junior physician Carl Gustav Jung. He is twenty-nine years old and has been married to his wife Emma, daughter of a wealthy watch manufacturer, for a little over a year. In a photo taken around this time, Jung poses self-confidently in front of the same gate that Sabina Spielrein passes through when she is brought to the institute.

Her family, from the southern Russian city of Rostov on Don, is also wealthy. Her father Nikolai, a fertilizer and animal feed manufacturer from Warsaw, is a clever businessman. As the head of the family he runs a strict household and regularly punishes the children, three boys and two girls, by spanking them on their bare bottoms. He also decrees that the family will speak a different language on each day of the week: Mondays German, Tuesdays French, Wednesdays English, Thursdays Russian. Little Sabina soon becomes fluent in all of these languages. When and where her putative hysteria began is a mystery. Jung hopes to suss out her repressed complexes with the help of his trusty association method.

As he soon realizes, the patient has suffered through several traumatic experiences. When she was sixteen, her beloved six-year-old sister Emilia died. The unbending severity of her father's regime is a heavy burden on Sabina. She hates her father's tyranny and at the same time idolizes him. Since finishing school, Sabina has been adrift, living aimlessly from day to day. At this time the indignities of life in imperial Russia are becoming ever more substantial. Women in Russia aren't permitted to go to university; all a woman of her class can hope for is to marry well, have children, and while her boredom away in cultivated salons. That's not the life she wants!

Nevertheless, what exactly Sabina Spielrein is suffering from remains unclear. Decades later, based on Jung's presumably exaggerated description, some psychiatrists will suspect paranoid-schizophrenia, others a borderline personality disorder. It's possible however that Spielrein is just going through an acute adolescent crisis. Her remarkably quick recovery at least suggests the latter.

It doesn't take long after her arrival at the Burghölzli for Spielrein to begin feeling better. In October 1904, barely two months after her admission, Bleuler writes to inform her father in Rostov of the "cheering fact that Fräulein Spielrein has now decided to begin studying medicine here in Zurich next spring." Thus the highly intelligent young woman quickly finds herself on the other side of the patient-doctor divide: where before she was Jung's patient, now she becomes his assistant, accompanying him on visits with patients and relieving him of bothersome paperwork. She takes part in medical consultations and in the daily discussions at the doctors' table about diagnoses and how patients' conditions are progressing—all without any academic training.

When Spielrein enrolls at the university, she takes a small apartment in the city and continues to consult Jung on an irregular basis. The meetings sometimes take place at the Burghölzli, where Jung lives, and sometimes at her apartment. At some point the relationship between patient and doctor—or has he ceased to be her doctor by then?—grows more intimate. In her diary, Spielrein starts writing effusively about the "poetry" that connects her with Jung, her "poet"—language which at that time is a not uncommon euphemism for sex. In light of her childhood experiences and the pleasurable role occupied by pain and beatings, one can assume that Spielrein has pronounced masochistic tendencies. Even as a small child, for example, she derives great pleasure from holding back her feces, pressing her buttocks together until it's close to bursting out. It's fair to assume that the tall Jung, who not for nothing has been nicknamed "Siegfried" by the members of the Vienna Psychoanalytic Society, explores a type of erotic play with Spielrein that is unknown to his wife Emma.[1]

The sources don't reveal when exactly the affair begins. Certain passages in the letters suggest that both at first fought back the transference and countertransference, the erotic attraction between doctor and patient. It's likely in the summer of 1908 that Jung chooses to ignore his scruples. It's no coincidence that shortly before then he spends several weeks treating a colleague with an addiction to cocaine and morphine. This charismatic oddball by the name of Otto Gross preaches the casting off of sexual inhibitions. He sees the path to healing, for the individual and society alike, in unattached love, in freely pursuing one's desires outside of bourgeois convention. It's very much possible that he inspires Jung to view sex with a patient not as a problem, but as part of the solution.

. . .

The two psychiatrists first meet at a congress in 1907. After the encounter Jung writes to Freud: "Dr. Gross tells me that he puts a quick stop to the transference by turning people into sexual immoralists." According to Gross, "the truly healthy state for the neurotic is sexual immorality."[2] Behind these words is a vision that many apostles of liberation will subscribe to: the individual must cast off the fetters of an uptight society and overcome pathological conventions in order to live in harmony with themselves.

The charismatic Gross is not the only one preaching disinhibition at the time. A group of free thinkers and artists who call themselves "the moderns" is trying out alternative forms of living, shuttling back and forth between the bohemian Munich neighborhood of Schwabing and a commune called Monte Verità near the Swiss town of Ascona on Lago Maggiore. There, under the southern Ticino sun, they combine vegetarianism and nudism with anarchist thinking. And while the communards don't subscribe to any single comprehensive worldview or vision, nevertheless most of them view monogamy with suspicion.

Chastity and nuptial vows are considered means of female oppression, the denial of desire a direct path to neurosis. Perverse behavior (which at the time includes not only sodomy and sadomasochism but also homosexuality and cross-dressing) is a natural part of the personality; the patriarchy only seeks to suppress them because inculcating a hostility towards pleasure is a way of exerting power over the people. The fundamental nature of the human individual is bisexual and polyamorous, and only the most broad limits, if any, should be placed on the varieties of the libido's expression.

The fact that Gross is not the type to impose limits is evident not only from his semi-regular intake of several grams of cocaine and morphine per day, but also his sexual escapades. He sleeps with his female patients, conceives children out of wedlock with two of them, and moves restlessly back and forth between Schwabing and Monte Verità. Gross's tragic fate, which we will soon turn our attention to, gives an early taste of how easily the liberation from all constraints can lead to the psychological abyss. But let us first follow the patient-turned-psychoanalyst Sabina Spielrein as she attempts to untangle the different strands of pleasure, love, and aggression.

LABORATORY EXPLOSIONS

In the draft of a letter that Spielrein will send to Freud in summer 1909, she reports: "He [Jung] no longer wishes to suppress his feelings for me."[3] Clearly Jung, inspired by his colleague Otto Gross, has arrived at a different view of polyamory. How long Jung's affair with Spielrein lasted, we don't know. As Spielrein's diary reveals, however, she suffers from all the secretiveness involved. Because she also fears that she's not the only "poetic" friend of Jung's, she briefly thinks of suicide. But instead of harming herself, she throws herself into her work.

In early 1911 Spielrein concludes her studies with a dissertation, "On the Psychological Content of a Case of Schizophrenia (Dementia Praecox)." It is the first PhD thesis in psychoanalysis by a woman, and with Freud and Jung's support it is published that same year in the *Jahrbuch für psychoanalytische und psychopathologische Forschung*. The young analyst spends the following summer in Munich. Here she develops nothing less than a new theory of the sex drive. She sees a profound antagonism at work, which Freud won't seek to excavate until years later when, influenced by the slaughter of the First World War, he writes his book *Beyond the Pleasure Principle*.

The questions that Spielrein asks herself are: how are pleasure and love related to aggression and hate? Can there be a life-negating tendency in the human individual, or even a death drive, even though all existence is ultimately directed toward survival and growth? Others wrestled with this problem before Spielrein, including Alfred Adler and Theodor Reik. But it's one thing to posit the existence of several contradictory principles in the human psyche, another to find a meaningful basis for the claim. Spielrein hits upon a more elegant solution: the tendencies of love and hate that appear so contradictory are in fact mutually dependent; they are two sides of the same coin. Thus there is only *one* driving force within the psyche, comprised of two elements that are inextricably bound.

The title of Spielrein's 1912 study reveals her approach: "Destruction as the Cause of Coming into Being." In order for the new to emerge, the old must pass away; indeed, the living being, *in the very act of* striving to reproduce, ultimately works toward its own downfall, the dissolution of its self. From the beginning, destruction is inevitably inscribed in pleasure.

In the fall of 1911 Spielrein travels to Vienna and applies, with Freud's approval, for membership in the Vienna Psychoanalytic Society. After

Patient, lover, pioneer: Sabina Spielrein's theory of the two sides of pleasure bore a close relation to her own life.

a heated debate, her application is accepted over the objection of a few members.[4] One can only imagine: a polyglot, attractive woman of twenty-five in a club of older gentlemen who like to talk shop about infantile lust and female hysteria, masturbation and perversion! After a few meetings on Berggasse she notes: "Freud's students are like his children, he shapes them according to his will."[5] Freud is taken with Spielrein's verve. She thinks independently, exercises her own judgement, and eyes with contempt the craving for recognition she sees in the men. Clear-eyed, she notes that "In science, the true thirst for knowledge is replaced by the thirst for admiration, the thirst for power."[6]

Ernest Jones, Freud's right-hand man and later biographer, can't stand the Russian and doesn't mention her once in his account of Freud's life. Nor does the master himself, well-disposed toward her though he may be, go to much trouble to acknowledge Spielrein's contributions. In the end she is mentioned in his work only in a single footnote, in a book in which he contrasts the life-affirming power of the libido with that of a death drive. In *Beyond the Pleasure Principle*, published in 1920, Freud appends the following note to a passage which examines masochism as an instance of the individual's death drive turning inward, toward their own ego: "A considerable portion of these speculations has been anticipated by Sabina Spielrein (1912) in an instructive and interesting paper which, however, is unfortunately not entirely clear to me. She there describes the sadistic components of the sexual instinct as 'destructive.'"[7]

And yet here Freud fundamentally misunderstands Spielrein's intention. She by no means believes that the individual has an independent death drive; she considers such a construct far-fetched even by Freud's standards. Rather what she is getting at is that "psychologically speaking, the reproductive drive is made up of two antagonistic components and therefore is as much a becoming as a destructive drive."[8] Or in simpler terms: loving means wanting to die. Freud thus co-opts Spielrein for a position that she doesn't actually share.[9]

. . .

Carl Gustav Jung first presents the "Spielrein case" at the International Congress for Psychiatry and Neurology in Amsterdam in 1907. He probably portrays her symptoms as being somewhat worse than they actually were, thus making the success of the treatment appear all the greater. There is (naturally) no mention of the attraction between the two. It's possible too that the affair doesn't begin until late May 1908, because shortly beforehand Spielrein complains about Jung acting so aloof towards her: "It is humiliating if I now go to see him."[10] On the other hand, this very aloofness could have stoked her desire.

Jung's wife Emma soon grows suspicious and writes an anonymous letter to Sabina's mother in Rostov in which she criticizes her daughter's loose lifestyle. On receiving the letter, Eva Lyublinskaya plans to inform Jung's boss Bleuler. Even by the standards of the time, for a doctor to begin an intimate relationship with a patient entrusted to his care counts as a severe instance of professional misconduct. In order to limit the damage to his career and his marriage, Jung ends his relationship with Spielrein—and writes her mother in a distant tone to inform her that further treatment of her daughter would cost a fee of ten francs per session. Sabina Spielrein finds out about this and lets Jung have it. Afterwards their relationship cools.

In a letter to Freud dated July 10, 1909, Jung expresses his gratitude for the older man's support in what he calls the "Spielrein matter, which has now settled itself so satisfactorily."[11] Earlier, in a sympathetic, between-us-men tone, Freud had sought to boost his spirits, saying in essence that this kind of thing could happen to anyone: "Remember Lasalle's fine sentence about the chemist whose test tube had cracked: 'With a slight frown over the resistance of matter, he gets on with his work.' In view of the kind of matter we work with, it will never be possible to avoid little laboratory explosions. Maybe we didn't slant the test tube enough, or we heated it too quickly. In this way we learn what part of the danger lies in the matter and what part in our way of handling it."[12]

Freud himself adheres rigidly to his self-imposed abstinence rule, which he also tries to drum into his students: "Analytic treatment should be carried through, as far as possible, under privation—in a state of abstinence."[13] Or in other words: The (male) therapist keeps a low profile, doesn't comment, speaks no more than absolutely necessary, doesn't reveal his own feelings and desires, and rebuffs all signs of affection and loving entreaties from the (female) patient. Some of Freud's followers, like Otto Rank and Sándor Ferenczi, will one day deviate from this doctrine and develop an "active technique" that includes even physical contact. But Freud sticks with abstinence throughout his life; this, he believes, is the only way to prevent an ersatz gratification from arising out of the affection given by the analyst that fixes the symptoms in place rather than alleviating them. In psychoanalytic jargon this is called "secondary gain."

There are good reasons for maintaining distance, because the interplay of repression and transference all but invites transgression. On the one hand the analyst must overcome the patient's resistance in order to bring her latent desires to the surface; on the other hand he quickly becomes an object of desire himself. For those of less steady character than Freud, this is a challenge. But as Freud's talk of "laboratory explosions" shows, it is easy for an analyst to blame his own weaknesses on the fickle nature of the object of study. A few years after the "Spielrein matter," Jung has another brief affair with a patient who, like Spielrein, becomes a colleague: Toni Wolff. Emma has to swallow her disappointment at her husband's infidelity while the pretty Fräulein Wolff often dines with the family at lunch. Emma is a resolute woman and hardly of a mind to share her husband with another woman. On the other hand, for the sake of her four children, she doesn't want to put the family's harmony in jeopardy—and so she grudgingly submits to the all-powerful libido.

ONAN THE BARBARIAN

The fact that the new psychology of the unconscious devotes so much energy to sexual concerns is due in no small part to the obsessions of its chief exponents. As soon as the Freud circle forms, shortly after the turn of the century, the intimate details discussed by the group engender a distinct conspiratorial mindset among its members. This attitude also shapes Freud's relationship with Wilhelm Stekel, the first mouthpiece of the movement.

On May 21, 1904, an article appears in the Viennese newspaper *Die Wage* under the title "Autoerotismus und Gesundheit"—"Autoeroticism and Health." The article reports: "In a small company of physicians there unfolded not long ago a lengthy debate about the harms of masturbation. Is onanism harmful? And if yes, how much so?" This small "company" is Freud's Wednesday group—the author of the article no other than Stekel. What the paper's readers don't know: Stekel has suffered for some time from impotence. What's more, it would appear, based on certain indications in the correspondence between Freud, Stekel, and others, that he masturbates excessively.[14] While on his own, trembling beneath the touch of his own hand, he is capable of getting an erection and having an orgasm, but when performing his "marital duty," Stekel's member falls down on the job. How frequently he pleasures himself and what effect this has on his personal life, no source reveals.

Stekel is eloquent and extroverted, a prolific writer who isn't exactly a stickler for the truth. His contribution to psychoanalysis comes more from his writing for the feuilleton than from his work as a scientist and physician. In fact, the internist Stekel is Freud's first and most assiduous PR agent. "His panegyrics were continually appearing in the daily press," Fritz Wittels writes of his colleague in 1924.[15] It was an effusive review of *The Interpretation of Dreams* that paved the way for Stekel's first encounter with Freud. Stekel is one of a select few who address the master not as "Herr Professor" but simply as "Freud." His copy of the book, given to him by Freud, includes a dedication: "To Herr Dr. W. Stekel. With heartfelt thanks for his great service in garnering recognition for my book."

In the years to come Stekel will praise the head of the movement and his achievements in more than three hundred essays, most of them for a popular readership. In them, Freud features as the "famous authority on the sick psyche," the "first-rate psychologist" and "most significant dream researcher now living," whose "brilliant work" and "excellent researches" represent the "greatest advance in the field of psychology."

Shortly after they first came to know one another, likely in 1901, Stekel undergoes an analysis with Freud. In Stekel's telling, the treatment only lasts for eight sessions, because he displays "no repression." At this point in time, Freud still considers it conceivable that practices like coitus interruptus and masturbation trigger the release of a sexual toxin that causes neurasthenia, a common form of nervous exhaustion. In Freud's view, some symptoms are not necessarily rooted in unconscious conflicts, but are caused instead by the patient's current behavior, for which reason he calls such disorders "actual neuroses."[16] In concrete terms, what this means is that if, instead of having sex, one resorts to ersatz actions like masturbation, the stored-up libidinous energy is insufficiently discharged. This makes you sick, because in terms of instinctual gratification, pleasuring yourself is only a pale imitation of the true experience of making love.

Freud differentiates between anxieties of this sort, which result from a backup or "retention" of the libido, and other neuroses for which modern life is to blame, chief among them neurasthenia or "nervous debility." The latter was first described by the American neurologist George Beard in 1870. Because its symptoms, like fatigue, headache, restlessness, and impotence, are largely rooted in the hectic daily life of the city-dweller, the only sensible cure consists of an ample amount of rest and relaxation—at a sanatorium, for instance, with lots of fresh air, quiet, and good food.

Stekel summarily rejects Freud's diagnosis of his complaint. The way he sees it, masturbation is not at all harmful to the organism; on the contrary, it fosters relaxation and an even temper. Why he ever sought treatment from Freud in the first place is unclear. It's possible he simply wanted to get close to the man he admired and submitted to an analysis that he soon came to regret.

At the start of the 20th century, physicians, educators, and clergymen are quick to condemn any sexual practice that isn't marital sex for the purpose of conception. "Squandered" amorous energy is declared the source of a whole range of afflictions—which ties into the notion, prevalent since the 18th century, that onanism makes you sick. Spilling one's seed is not merely a sign of weakness of will and immorality, it's also bad for one's health. According to this view, self-pleasuring is right up there with sodomy, which category includes not just sex with animals but also intercourse between partners of the same sex.

Unsatisfied with his interpretations, Stekel breaks off his analysis with the master. Naturally he must have revealed a fair amount of intimate details about himself. Since Freud now knows what fantasies occupy Stekel's mind, Stekel would do well not to get on his bad side.

Stekel's treatment shortly after the turn of the century doubles as the first psychoanalytic "apprenticeship" and creates a pattern that will be imitated many times over. The principle of the training analysis ties the teaching of the analytic method to the close one-on-one relationship between analyst and student. It bears emphasizing that this practice demands a degree of self-exposure that far exceeds the disclosing of personal secrets that might occur in ordinary interpersonal situations. This is the foundation for a dependent relationship: the teacher finds out far more about the student than the student might like—while the amount of communication coming from the other direction tends to be near zero.

The delicate knowledge Freud is in possession of might explain why Stekel remains loyal for so long, even though his opinion differs from Freud's on many points. He even puts up with Freud claiming credit for the discovery of infantile sexuality after sketching it out in his 1905 book *Three Essays on the Theory of Sexuality*. In fact, Stekel had written about it long before then. In *The Interpretation of Dreams*, published just six years prior to the *Three Essays*, Freud stated that infants had no noteworthy sexual feelings, and certainly no spontaneous ones. In Stekel's 1895 essay "Über Coitus im Kindesalter"—"On Coitus in Childhood"—on the other hand, he writes at length about the intimate desire of the infant.[17] Freud at first regards sexual feelings in children as the byproduct of traumatic experiences, like watching adults have sex or receiving excessive stimulation from the mother. Not so with Stekel: according to him, small children feel spontaneous pleasure when playing with their genitals and simulating the sex act. Parents who suppress this behavior by means of scolding and punishment produce anxieties and neuroses.

The tensions between Freud and Stekel grow worse over the years, especially after the rebellion against Jung's appointment as president for life of the Psychoanalytical Association. Freud never forgives Stekel for his revolt and in 1911 expels him for good. Stekel promptly founds his own school and starts up a society for "active psychoanalytic therapy." In choosing this name, he means to distinguish his approach from Freud's passive therapeutic stance. Stekel also argues for a shorter timeframe for treatment, an approach that the less well-off can also afford. Rather than having to commit to several sessions of therapy a week for months or years, success, according to Stekel, is often possible within a few weeks. It's simply a matter of exposing the patient's conflicts and speaking about them openly, thus "planting" them in the patient's conscious mind. There's only one downside to this approach: a doctor who treats patients for less time is more often in need of new clients. It's more practical to bind a small number of loyal patients to yourself for a long time, as Freud does.

TOWARD PLEASURE, TOWARD FREEDOM

The ladder, nearly three meters tall, leans against the ivy-covered wall, a silent witness to the drama that has just unfolded. A patient climbed the wall in broad daylight and leapt down to reach the other side. There lay the freedom that means everything to him.

"Patient escaped! Patient escaped!" a nurse cries. While making her rounds she noticed the man was missing. She runs through the halls and reaches the consultation room, where Dr. Jung is already expecting her. He stands there, calm and composed, as if he's long known about the escape. He must at least have suspected that the patient, *his* patient, wouldn't submit to being cooped up at the Burghölzli for long.

It is June 17, 1908. Five weeks earlier, on May 11, Otto Gross and his wife Frieda had turned up at the clinic outside of Zurich—on the same day, as chance would have it, that Sabina Spielrein took her preliminary exam at the medical faculty. Gross's treatment seemed to be going well at first—though at times Jung did ask himself who was actually analyzing whom.

That's because Dr. Gross is a physician himself, and a brilliant one at that. The outside lecturer in neuropathology at the university in Graz is just as well versed in the subtle psychoanalytic technique of deciphering complexes as Jung is. Gross's obsessive relationship with his own father can hardly be characterized as a *repressed* complex; the two are bound by a profound mix of love and hate. Otto is an only child, intensely adored, and has suffered under his father's dominance ever since he was a child. Hans Gross is considered one of the most influential sociologists and criminologists in Austria, maybe even in all of Europe. He does everything for his son, but he also intends to mold him in strict accordance with his own ideals, while Otto's mother Adele submits to the patriarch's will without resistance. Economically dependent on his all-powerful father, Otto nevertheless finds his own way to rebel. In that sense the ladder is a fitting symbol for the eternally restless son, who runs away and ascends on the strength of his own visions—to a place where there is nothing to hold him back.

During the weeks that Otto Gross spends at the Burghölzli, he and Jung talk a great deal, once for almost twelve hours nonstop, until their heads "drooped down like ripe oranges," Jung reports to Freud. Gross seems to Jung like a twin brother, the talented scion of a respectable household, born only two years after Jung, on March 17, 1877. His parents coddle him so much that he never has to make his own decisions, even though he's highly intelligent. His father Hans trains his son to be nothing less than an academic wunderkind. Otto however reveals his tempestuous temperament early on. An early childhood memory of Otto's captures the moment when his father warns a guest about his then five-year-old son: "Watch out, he bites!" Otto will keep that irascible spirit throughout his short life.

He wants for nothing; money is no object, and his parents are loathe to refuse any of their son's requests. In the absence of any practical experience in life, Gross lapses into "continual theorizing," as Jung puts it in his medical report. After receiving his doctorate Gross signs on as a ship's doctor and travels to South America, where he is introduced to cocaine. The depressive young physician is delighted by the drug's euphoria-inducing effect—the same effect that Freud had enjoyed before him. After his return he serves stints as an assistant physician, first under the Graz psychiatry professor Gabriel Anton, then under the famous Emil Kraepelin in Munich, whom Freud derisively dubs the "Oberpapst"—the supreme pope.

Captivated by psychoanalysis, Gross doesn't just want to devote himself to ridding individual patients of their neuroses. What he has in mind is nothing less than healing all of humanity. "The psychology of the unconscious is the philosophy of the revolution," he writes in a 1913 essay for the expressionist magazine *Die Aktion*. Psychoanalysis is "liberation of the individuality constrained by one's own unconscious. It is called to make people inwardly capable of freedom, called to serve as the *preliminary work* of the revolution."[18]

Gross takes part in the first congress of the Psychoanalytical Association in Salzburg in April 1908. His paper on "The Societal Role of Psychoanalysis" is swatted aside by Freud with the words "We're doctors, and doctors we'd like to remain."[19] The master has no sympathy for free love or any other appeals for liberal sexual mores. On the contrary, he fears that anarchistic free spirits like Gross could harm the reputation

Sex, drugs, and visions: Dr. Otto Gross from Graz was the *enfant terrible* of the psychoanalytic movement.

of his movement. In his *Introductory Lectures on Psychoanalysis* from 1916, Freud declares categorically: "A recommendation to the patient to 'live a full life' sexually could not possibly play a part in analytic therapy."[20]

More than a few of Freud's contemporaries—and those who come after him as well—see things differently. They want to help their patients overcome their false shame and the impulse to deny their desires. The dream of an unrestrained, self-determined sexuality heralds the arrival of a better society, an innocent paradise in which everyone pursues their own form of pleasure and finds happiness. Freud calls for self-control, for the subordination of baser drives to the reality principle. It is this notion of restraint that young wildmen like Gross and, later, Wilhelm Reich will radically call into question.

. . .

One place where this paradise is meant to become reality, at least on a small scale, is the aforementioned Monte Verità overlooking the town of Ascona on Lago Maggiore. The name itself is an exaggeration—to call the scraggly hilltop rising just three hundred meters above sea level a "mountain" requires a fair amount of imagination. Gathered here are vegan ascetics, anarchists, artists, spiritualists, and other seekers. The commune was founded by a group of six led by the music teacher and protofeminist Ida Hofmann and Henri Oedenkoven, son of an industrialist.

In the fall of 1900, using Oedenkoven's money, they buy the hilltop from the Swiss politician Alfredo Pioda, who had wanted to build a theosophic monastery there. Instead the young communards, hungry for sun and fresh air, build a kind of sanatorium that offers fasting cures, nudism, and expressionist dance, as well as a strict vegetarian diet. The name "Monte Verità" first appears in a promotional brochure from 1902. Writers like Erich Mühsam and Hermann Hesse come here to take the cure with like-minded bohemians (and occasionally sneak down to the village for a roast). And they're not the only ones. Otto Gross likely pays his first visit in 1905. In the years to come he shuttles back and forth between Schwabing, the heart of Munich bohemia, and "Mount Truth." He dreams of starting an anarchist school in Ascona.

At home in Graz, Otto's father Hans is horrified. He appeals to Freud to take his son on as a patient, hoping that he can treat the young man's drug addiction and paranoid personality. Freud himself had experimented with the invigorating effects of cocaine until the death of his friend from his student days, Ernst Fleischl von Marxow. In weak, occasional doses it brightens the mood and reduces inhibitions—but in the quantities that Gross consumes it's undoubtedly harmful, especially since the intoxicating effect diminishes over time, requiring ever greater doses to produce the same result.

Freud suspects that a temperament like that of the young Gross would only bring him trouble. He refers him to the Burghölzli; to start with, Jung could at least get him off the drugs. Freud generously offers to take the difficult patient on himself starting in October. Until then, his colleague in Zurich could deal with the eccentric young man.

Jung and Gross, two kindred spirits, get to work exploring Gross's psyche. They get off to a euphoric start, as Jung reports to Freud: doctor and patient have achieved "all manner of scientifically wonderful results" and worked through "infantile complexes." Gross even limits his drug

Monte Verità: In 1900, a hill overlooking the town of Ascona on Lago Maggiore becomes home to an experiment in new ways of living.

intake, though he suffers from withdrawal symptoms that ultimately make his flight inevitable. Jung's patient proves intractable in another respect as well: Gross hates monogamy. He enters into love affairs with the sisters Else and Frieda von Richthofen, whom he "psychoanalyzes" on debauched nights out at Café Stefanie in Schwabing. Else, technically married to the economist Edgar Jaffé, gives birth to Gross's son Peter in 1907 (a few months earlier, Frieda Schloffer, whom he met in Graz and married, had herself given birth to a son named Peter). The depressive poet Regina Ullmann also becomes pregnant and in 1908 gives birth to their daughter Camilla. Hans Gross's refusal to pay for the children's upbringing meets with a shrug from Otto. He leaves Regina with a large quantity of drugs, probably hoping that she will use them to commit suicide. Instead she writes poems and plays that garner praise from the likes of Rainer Maria Rilke.

For others, Gross's moral indifference bears more fruit, albeit of the poison variety. On April 1906 the mentally unstable Charlotte Hattemer, one of the founders of the community on Monte Verità, commits suicide with a drug cocktail mixed by Gross. Five years later, in March 1911, a long-time patient and lover of the analyst meets a similar fate in the same spot. The painter Sofie Benz also met Gross in Schwabing. She suffered from anxiety and heard voices; he immediately began to analyze her. No sooner has he slept with her than, like a man obsessed, he starts manipulating her in other ways to free her from her demons. Sofie takes up cocaine herself and starts sleeping with other men who Otto picks out for her. As time goes on the relationship spirals ever more out of control under the strain of constant drug use and ongoing psychological crises.

In early 1911 Otto and Sofie travel to Monte Verità for a "cure." After threatening several times to leave him for good, on March 3 Sofie takes an overdose of cocaine and opium, both of which Gross always has with him in ample supply. The drama, in Gross's telling, unfolded "three steps behind me, as I was sitting at the hearth and staring into the fire"—i.e., without his involvement. It's impossible to judge how much of this account is an attempt to absolve himself of blame. After his involvement in the suicide of Sofie Benz, however, Gross is a wanted man. In early 1914, police officers, acting on orders from Gross's father—who, being a criminologist, is eminently well-connected—raid Gross's hideout in Berlin and bundle the "deranged anarchist" onto a train bound for Austria. There he is detained at the Tulln sanatorium outside of Vienna.

All the while Hans Gross is working to have his son declared legally incapacitated—and ultimately succeeds: for a few months Hans becomes his son's guardian, until a court grants Otto's objection. On top of that Hans Gross is also pursuing a lawsuit against his daughter-in-law Frieda for custody of his young grandson. The effort fails. The sociologist Max Weber, who advises Frieda Gross in the legal battle, is certainly not wrong in saying that the young people are "caught up" in "a powerful web of gross self-deceptions." Nevertheless, Gross seems to be of sound mind, and his support among intellectuals is considerable.

Aside from his reputation as a desperado, what is it that makes Gross's thinking attractive to so many of his contemporaries, men and women? In his roman à clef *Heart on the Left* the writer Leonhard Frank describes a Dr. Kreuz, who is meant to stand in for Gross: "Dr. Kreuz, thirty and married, had studied psychiatry at the University of Graz. [He had] blue, childish, innocent eyes, a hooked nose and full lips that were always a little apart, as though, noiselessly panting for breath, he carried all the woes of the world on his shoulders. [. . .] No one could easily forget that fanatical, birdlike face, which seemed to consist of faintly tinted china. [. . .] Dr. Kreuz was a theoretician with a bold and original mind, but in daily life he was the worst possible judge of character, childishly and blindly credulous."[21]

Jung's conversations with Gross, who teetered between naïveté and megalomania, contribute greatly to his change of heart toward his relationship with Sabina Spielrein. The timing is striking: no sooner has Gross expounded on his vision of overcoming bourgeois sexual morality than Jung begins an affair with his Russian patient. In order to minimize his failure in Gross's case, Jung will later reach for the same excuse that Gross uses to explain many of his own failed analyses: the patient's resistance was insurmountable. Though shortly before Gross's escape he had regarded him as being on the road to recovery, no sooner has the patient fled than Jung diagnoses him with the most severe of conditions: dementia praecox.[22] In other words: the man was beyond help anyway.

But while Gross may be a lot of things—an addict, paranoid, lacking in self-control, reckless—he isn't schizophrenic.

He wants to reform people by employing the knowledge and methods of his utopia of pleasure. In order for this to happen, it is necessary to overthrow those power structures that are based on the suppression of "matriarchy," of the woman's freedom to choose her sexual partner. Gross develops a psychologically grounded theory of liberation that will travel by way of Wilhelm Reich and Herbert Marcuse to the neo-Freudian Erich Fromm and ultimately finds many adherents in the student movement of 1968.

The idea that the way to salvation lies through free expression of the sex drive resonates with the Wandervogel and German Youth Movement in the lead-up to the First World War: for these young people Gross becomes a cult figure, a symbol of the rebellion against their fathers' generation. The goal is a self-determined, more authentic life. "Among young people," writes the sociologist and historian Michael Schröter, "the mix of introspection, social critique, grandiose theories about humanity and culture, sexual liberation, and a promise of personal healing that psychoanalysis offered landed on particularly fertile soil."[23] This seems all the more stunning when one considers that for years Gross devoted himself to an intoxicating drug habit that ruined his health.

Finally, in the fall of 1919, the impoverished, mentally wrecked visionary is taken in by a friend from his Munich days, the writer Franz Jung, then living in the Berlin neighborhood of Friedenau. Gross's wife and other former comrades have long since turned away from him. The second winter after the war is hard, food and coal are scarce, the Great Influenza epidemic claims hundreds daily. Gross is at the end of his rope. He wanders aimlessly through the city, sits in cafés warming up over a bowl of broth that he pays for with an impromptu monologue, like in the good old days in Schwabing. In February 1920 he gets in an argument with Franz Jung, who refuses to lend him money for drugs. Gross storms off in a rage. He doesn't come back.

Jung and others comb the city streets. They finally find Gross on the night of February 11, lying half-frozen in the entrance to a courtyard. He dies two days later, in a hospital in Pankow, a month shy of his forty-third birthday.

A SCHOOL FOR ANALYSTS

The day after Gross's death, the Berlin Psychoanalytic Polyclinic opens its doors, just a few hundred meters away from Potsdamer Platz, the vibrant center of the city. On the fifth floor of the building at Potsdamer Straße 29 (today 74), Max Eitingon rents a spacious apartment with room enough for seeing patients and training aspiring analysts. There are five consulting rooms, a reception area, a seminar room, and an adjoining apartment for the resident doctor, Anna Smeliansky, a nearly blind former girlfriend of Eitingon's from their student days. The rent isn't exactly cheap, but neither is it beyond the means of the son of the Leipzig fur dealer Chaim Eitingon.

The polyclinic's services are explicitly geared toward the lower rungs on the social ladder; its stated goal is that members of the petite bourgeoisie and the proletariat should also be able to enjoy the benefits of psychoanalysis. What's more, the rising generation of therapists needs hands-on study material. The patients pay a reduced hourly fee, or in individual cases no fee at all, and the gap in revenue is filled by membership fees, the tuition paid by candidates, donations, and—Eitingon. Keeping the polyclinic going costs him a good 10,000 Reichsmarks per month (the equivalent today, in Euros, of a high four-figure sum). He acts as director of the institution, alongside Karl Abraham. Eitingon selects both the cases to be treated and the candidates to undergo training.

Without such a patron, psychoanalysis would never have been able to establish itself in the heart of the German capital so soon after the end of the war. Eitingon doesn't advertise his financial involvement, and deliberately so. In fact, the original inspiration for founding a psychoanalytic "poor clinic" came from the Hungarian philanthropist and brewery heir Anton von Freund, who wanted to bankroll a similar institution in Budapest. In September 1918 Freud presented a lecture on "Lines of Advance in Psycho-Analytic Therapy" at the Psychoanalytic Congress in the Hungarian capital, and praised von Freund's plans in the highest terms. It was necessary, said Freud, to appeal to the conscience of society for the means to provide psychological support to the less well-off, even if it meant alloying "the pure gold of psychoanalysis"[24] with the less valuable methods of suggestion or hypnosis. One could hardly ask the uneducated to grasp the art of analytic interpretation; they had to be treated with disciplinary authority and demands that would be inappropriate in "better circles."

But von Freund, plagued by ill-health, dies before he can realize his plans for the clinic. To make matters worse, a large portion of his fortune is lost to the psychoanalytic movement when in November 1919 a rightist regime under Admiral Miklós Horthy takes power and starts hunting down Jews and people on the left. Several Budapest analysts flee to Berlin, where, thanks to Eitingon, they find a new place to practice their craft.

Boomtown Berlin: The Psychoanalytic Polyclinic opens in early 1920 on the bustling Potsdamer Straße.

From the start, philanthropy isn't the only motivation for the founding of the polyclinic. By this point, so many candidates are pouring into Vienna and Berlin—not only from Austria and Germany but also from abroad—that training analyses are in high demand. By the same token, the new generation of therapists, who are paying for their training, need patients on which to try out their know-how. Some days, the offices of the Berlin institute host sessions from morning to night; at any given time there may be more than a hundred analyses in progress, so that over the course of the Weimar years roughly eight hundred people receive the benefit of psychoanalytic treatment. Here it's worth noting as well that such treatment involves several sessions a week—even daily sessions are not uncommon—over many months.

More and more medical students and fully-fledged physicians from the US, Great Britain, and other European countries are digging deep into their pockets to undergo a training analysis with a noteworthy analyst. Because Freud asks for at least forty Kronen per session (about 250 Euros today), the master remains out of reach for many. This means all the more applicants are lining up to undergo training with Freud's entourage in Vienna, or with Karl Abraham, Hanns Sachs, Sándor Radó, or Karen Horney in Berlin. On the Spree there's also a whole curriculum of theory courses available to them, and they can immediately apply their knowledge and skills in actual therapy sessions.

Thus the crucial question soon presents itself: who should be admitted for training, and who shouldn't? How to assess whether a candidate is suitable to become an analyst? Should candidates be required, at a minimum, to have completed medical school, or should the opportunity be open to anyone with enough talent, time, and money? Up to this point, someone who wanted to be a psychoanalyst had to convince one of the pioneers in Vienna, Budapest, or Berlin to take them on as a student. During their months-long training analysis, the candidate revealed a lot about themselves, which deepened their dependence on their teacher. A formal course of training, with a curriculum and a diploma, didn't exist. Starting in 1923, the institute in Berlin seeks to fill this gap by developing a multi-year course of study. The polyclinic opens up an affiliated educational institute and from now on calls itself the "Berlin Psychoanalytic Institute (Polyclinic and Academy)." It quickly becomes the premier destination for those who want to learn psychoanalysis from the ground up. Vienna can't compete with the scope and quality of the Berlin curriculum; not a few in Freud's orbit look with envy at the training ground on the Spree.

Three of Freud's close associates—Hanns Sachs, Theodor Reik, and Otto Rank—will also move to Berlin over the course of the 1920s. None of them has studied medicine. To such "laymen," as they are known, somewhat condescendingly, in medical circles, Prussia, unlike Austria, offers the freedom to offer therapeutic services even without medical training.

At this time, Karl Abraham of Bremen is acquiring a reputation as Freud's most gifted adept. Abraham, the son of a religion teacher, first studies medicine in Würzburg before going to Zurich in 1904, where he works under Bleuler and Jung as an assistant physician and is introduced to psychoanalysis. In 1907 he becomes part of the Freud circle in Vienna, staying there a few years until he moves to Berlin and opens up his own neurology practice in 1909. He can't complain of a lack of demand for his services; the ranks of neurotic city-dwellers are constantly expanding. In a letter to Freud from May 16, 1909, Abraham reports: "I am busy for the greater part of the day with long-term treatments. I have nine patients tomorrow, six of them psycho-analytic cases. A year and a half ago I would not have dreamt of this. [. . .] I now see that psychotherapy can be a very exhausting business."[25]

But how do you teach the tools of the psychoanalytic trade to others? Studying Freud's writings is all well and good, but it doesn't make you a skilled analyst. While the method of training analysis invented in Vienna, involving intensive self-examination led by an experienced colleague, has established itself as the norm, it remains up to the discretion of the usually older training analyst to decide whom they will take under their wing, and when. Besides that, the training analysts' didactic gifts often leave something to be desired, and ambition can be a factor as well. For that reason the Berlin curriculum, as a way of supporting its candidates, includes so-called control analyses. Candidates discuss their own cases, going over symptoms and therapy plans with a colleague, who assumes a critical stance. Today such "supervision" is a regular component of any course of psychotherapeutic training.

A long-simmering conflict revolves around the pros and cons of lay analysis: should non-physicians be permitted to practice psychoanalysis? Freud argues in his 1926 book *The Question of Lay Analysis* that a medical degree isn't necessary so long as the analyst acquires the necessary theoretical and practical foundation. On the one hand, this stance arises out of the desire not to limit too greatly the circle of those who can help spread the word. Even opponents of lay analysis, like Abraham, concede how important it is for the spread of the school that teachers, early childhood educators, lawyers, criminologists, and others also be introduced to analysis. On the other hand, the guild needs limits on admission if it is to prevent the career of psychoanalyst from losing its prestige.

In Berlin, only doctors are officially admitted to train at the Psychoanalytic Institute, but there are exceptions. Sachs and Rank are accorded the privilege of membership by dint of their personal connection to Freud. To be sure, not every psychiatrist makes a good analyst, while on the other hand people from different backgrounds can be sensitive therapists. Nevertheless, Abraham and Eitingon essentially keep the doctors-only restriction in place, for reasons that mainly have to do with internecine politics: this way they maintain control over the contents of the curriculum and the choice of candidates. Ironically, the lawyer Sachs of all people will become the most hard-working training analyst at the Berlin Institute.

Another fixture of the institute is a woman who confidently pushes back against Freud's phallocentrism. Karen Horney of Hamburg doesn't share the view that girls and women, owing to their lack of "real genitalia," suffer from penis envy and consider themselves deficient. Horney posits, to the contrary, that men are afraid of women's hidden genitals and feel inferior because they can't bear children. Despite her fundamental critique of the Freudian view of women, Horney is entrusted with many training analyses, including that of a certain Wilhelm Reich. Even the antipathy of the Viennese patriarch has no effect on her involvement with the Berlin Institute, which shows just how far the teaching there has distanced itself from Viennese orthodoxy.

. . .

Life in Berlin in the 1920s is marked by sharp contrasts and tensions. The city plays host to a wild profusion of political and ideological movements, all locked in a bitter struggle against one another. Among them are monarchists, revanchists, anarchists, Communists, socialists, German Nationalists, liberals, clericalists, and—as yet a peripheral phenomenon and source of derisive amusement—Nazi brownshirts. The misery of the tenements forms the backdrop for the drama of everyday life, with adventurers and upstarts peddling common wares on the black market, anything from potatoes and coal to alcohol and sex.

The notion that repressing the libido makes the psyche ill and that one must resolve inner conflicts by overcoming unconscious resistance becomes a broadly accepted narrative over the course of the 1920s. At its heart is the opposition between inner and outer, self and other, individual and society. This is fitting for a time of upheaval, in which the old, authoritarian order is overthrown, in which fealty to the emperor and unconditional love for the fatherland give way to the yearning for personal growth and happiness. Slumbering beneath the conventions the individual is raised to accept is something real, something authentic, which must be laid bare if self-knowledge is to be attained: "You're like that because . . . "; "You only do that because . . . " Every stirring of the psyche has a deeper meaning, and it takes patience and knowledge to discover what it is—knowledge that a new profession is ready to provide.

The euphoria of the early days of the Weimar Republic soon cools after the hyperinflation of 1923 ruins countless livelihoods. Added to the pressure of coping with daily life is an uncertainty that brings ideologues and prophets of all different stripes onto the scene. They offer up competing visions of salvation, be they Marxist, fascist, or esoteric in nature. In this environment, the image of the psyche as a force to be unleashed and perfected acquires an explicitly political dimension.

PHYSICAL THERAPY

When Wilhelm Reich steps off the train at Vienna's Central Station on a late summer evening in 1918, he doesn't have a penny to his name. The life of the twenty-one-year-old looks like one long series of catastrophes. His parents are dead; the estate he grew up on is lost, probably destroyed. The horrors of the war, which he experienced first-hand as a lieutenant in the Austrian army at Isonzo in Northern Italy, seem to him a bitter farce, collateral damage in a back-and-forth between great powers that has ground up an entire generation of young men for no purpose whatsoever.

For a long time Reich has been plagued by recurrent bouts of psoriasis, a terribly itchy rash that spreads over large parts of his skin. He can thank this condition for his early discharge from military service, which allows him to come join his brother Robert in the city on the Danube. Robert, who is three years younger than he, is all he has left.

The two brothers, born in 1897 and 1900, respectively, grow up in an assimilated Jewish family on the eastern periphery of the Habsburg empire. Their father, Leon Reich, owns an estate near the hamlet of Yuzhynets and raises cattle, whose meat he sells at great profit; the German army is his best customer. Wilhelm and Robert are taught by private tutors. They are not allowed to play with the Ukrainian children, nor are they allowed any contact with the Yiddish-speaking Jews in the nearby village. The two boys spend endless afternoons watching the cattle graze and mate.

Their father is violent, a tyrant. Reich's first published work, an autobiographically tinged "case study," reveals many details about his own childhood, despite being written in the third person. He writes that he was "raised very strictly, always had to achieve more than the others to satisfy his father's ambition." He "was attached from earliest childhood to his mother, for whom he felt intense tenderness, and who often protected him from his father's violent outbursts. His parents' marriage wasn't a happy one, in so far as his mother suffered terribly from his father's jealousy."

Even if the circumstances aren't the best, still Reich feels something inside himself, driving him on. "Quick to reach sexual maturity—even at five years old there were 'no secrets' for him—and physically strong as well, he had intercourse for the first time at age eleven and a half with the housemaid, albeit at her instigation."[26] As an adolescent he has sexual fantasies about his mother, well knowing that she will remain unattainable for him.

What follows is a tangled web of tragic events that ultimately leads to the death of both parents. One night when Reich is around twelve years old, he sees his mother sneaking into the room of the tutor, who lives with the family on the estate. Whatever it is that compels him to tell his father about the brief nocturnal escapade, whether he was acting on a rash whim or out of a desire for revenge,[27] the result is that the notoriously jealous Leon Reich flies into a rage. He humiliates and beats Reich's mother, and in the ensuing months he makes her life hell. Her situation seems inescapable to her and she tries to poison herself. In the fall of 1910 she finally succeeds: Cäcylia Reich dies at the age of thirty-five.

But the tragedy doesn't end there. Reich's father regrets his ruthlessness. He withdraws more and more into himself and becomes depressive. Finally he ups the amount of his life insurance policy and devises a plan to depart from this earth without drawing notice. Putting a bullet in his head or hanging himself is out of the question, since the insurance won't pay out in the case of suicide. Leon Reich decides to seek death in another fashion. In the winter he walks across the fields for hours, through ice and snow, clad only in scanty clothes. He doesn't have to wait long before he's contracted an infection. Pneumonia sets in, fever, delirium. Three and a half years after his mother's death, Reich's father follows her into the grave. It is May 1914. Leon Reich dies believing that he has done everything to ensure that his sons will be provided for. But the insurance company judges his death to be intentional—and refuses to pay.

Thus Wilhelm Reich, barely seventeen years old, is an orphan with a younger brother to take care of and a cattle ranch to run. Even if he could hardly have foreseen the consequences of his betrayal, it is he who brought about his family's ruin. One can imagine how heavily the boy's guilt weighed on him.

After receiving his *Abitur* in 1917 he volunteers for the army, abandons his parents' farm, and is soon promoted to lieutenant, while his brother Robert finds a job in Vienna. Wilhelm fights in bloody battles for patches of territory that are just as quickly given up again. What, he asks himself, does he have left to lose?

The only bright spot is an affair with an Italian farmgirl that he writes about in his diary. She instructs the young man in the ecstasy of orgasmic bliss; his uninhibited sex with her will help shape his notion of the all-controlling energy of the libido that strives for release.

Not long after he has put his time in the army behind him, Wilhelm makes a pact with his brother Robert in Vienna. Wilhelm, the older, more gifted of the two brothers, will go to university, while Robert supports him financially by working a job at a shipping company. Naturally this arrangement will only last until the older brother earns enough to pay back his debts. Wilhelm enrolls as a law student, but switches to medicine in the first semester.

It is an extremely difficult time to begin one's studies: many Viennese are starving and freezing. The university is unheated; in the lecture halls the students sit wrapped in threadbare military coats and blankets. Reich is soon earning his share of living expenses by giving private lessons.

One day, when he is in his third semester, Reich is attending a lecture and notices a slip of paper being passed around: fellow student Otto Fenichel is looking for like-minded peers for a "sexuological seminar," organized by the students themselves, that will deal with questions that don't appear in the official curriculum. The project, beginning in 1920, consists of a handful of medical students enlightening one another on sexual theory, which they view as neglected. Reich is tasked with obtaining the necessary reading materials. Shortly before then, in March 1919, he records in his diary: "[F]rom my own experience, and from observation of myself and others, I have become convinced that sexuality is the center around which revolves the whole of social life as well as the inner life of the individual."[28] For the student-led seminar Reich obtains case material from various analysts and finally makes contact with the circle orbiting the professor on Berggasse.

Freud's personality makes "the strongest and most lasting impression" on Reich. "Stekel tried to please. Adler was disappointing." Not Freud. "To begin with, he was simple and straightforward in his attitude. Each one of the others expressed in his attitude some role: that of the professor, of the great *Menschenkenner*, or the distinguished scientist. Freud spoke to me like an ordinary human being. He had piercingly intelligent eyes; they did not try to penetrate the listener's eyes in a visionary pose; they simply looked into the world, straight and honest."[29]

These few words alone reveal an important aspect of Reich's character: his enthusiasm. His life will come to revolve around his conviction that he has discovered the biological basis for Freud's libido theory in what he calls "orgastic potency." Reich turns Freud, who is forty years his elder, into the father he wishes he'd had; and Freud for his part takes a liking to the bright student who so admires him. Though only halfway through his medical training, Reich receives permission to practice as an analyst.

Reich's winning manner, along with his contacts to older colleagues, bring the first patients his way. Wasting no time, he begins a love affair with his second-ever patient, who is nineteen years old. A few months later the young woman is dead. Her parents want Reich held accountable, but their suspicion that their daughter died of complications from an illegal abortion can't be confirmed. Reich denies the accusations—and keeps working as an analyst. He takes on another patient, and then another: a friend of the deceased woman, the student Annie Pink. Once again the law of transference and countertransference comes into effect: Annie and Wilhelm fall in love. Reich is certainly aware of the Freudian imperative of abstinence, but this doesn't stop him from submitting to his sexual feelings for the attractive and intelligent Annie. He does at least suggest that she find another analyst, which she in fact does.

Reich studies at the Vienna Psychiatric Clinic under Julius Wagner-Jauregg, future winner of the Nobel Prize. When, in 1920, Reich delivers lectures there on psychoanalytic technique, he is drawing on his experience of treating a total of four patients, two of whom he started relationships with. Soon afterwards Annie's parents catch the two of them *in flagrante*. After much discussion they coerce the couple into marrying. Wilhelm and Annie Reich say their vows in Vienna on March 17, 1922. They may be bowing to convention, but the marriage itself is anything but conventional. Each partner maintains their own bank account, and Annie, after finishing medical school, also works as an analyst. Most notably, they grant each other the right to have sexual relationships outside of the marriage—a right that Wilhelm makes far more use of than Annie.

Because every aspiring analyst, Reich included, has to complete a training analysis with an experienced colleague, the quite conservative-minded Freudian clique is soon thoroughly well-apprised of the young man's sexual liberality. His reputation as a ladies' man and his obsession with the orgasm will have consequences.

. . .

A look back through history teaches us how closely our understanding of sickness and recovery is connected to the times in which we live. People in different historical eras, in seeking to describe and alleviate mental illness, have entertained various explanations which they consider plausible. Freud's assertion that repressed sexual thoughts were chiefly responsible for the formation of neuroses comes out of the highly rigid sexual mores of the late 19th century. Meanwhile the theories of the early psychoanalysts themselves often reflect an astounding level of inhibition. It seems antiquated today that any mention of sex, such as a patient's experience of overhearing their parents having intercourse, would lead to murmurs of excitement and the invocation of trauma.[30] Why should witnessing coitus, the "primal scene," be so shocking to a child? Why should seeing one's naked mother or an exposed member cause lifelong anxiety? According to Freud, boys who see a naked girl are beset with fear that someone will cut their penis off, too; and this castration phobia casts a pall over their lives. Girls, on the other hand, envy boys for their member, that visible symbol of power. How is it that such fantasies were raised to the status of scientific fact?

One reason is surely that the repression and stigmatization of sexual needs that was prevalent in the early 20th century drove many people to develop guilt complexes. But analysts, for the most part, are not free spirits; they don't plead for more flexible morals, much less live according to such an outlook. They are, like Freud, strict Victorians who consider it inevitable that the libido be channeled and sublimated. Characters like Otto Gross and Wilhelm Reich are exceptions to the rule. No sooner have the "young wildmen" called for tearing down sexual barriers as a way to heal the individual and society than they feel the icy breath of the establishment blowing in their face.

. . .

At just twenty-three years old, Wilhelm Reich is the shooting star among Viennese analysts. Freud thinks highly of the confident young whippersnapper. A lecture offering an interpretation of the fantasies of Peer Gynt, the title character of the play by Henrik Ibsen, paves the way for Reich to join Freud's Psychoanalytic Society. Just a few years after Gross's death, Reich resurrects his vision of a liberated sexuality. The suppression of the libido keeps the patriarchal order intact, at the cost of the individual's psychological well-being. Reich makes it his life's work to overthrow this pathological order. But he's not quite there yet; for the moment he is standing firmly on the ground of established psychoanalytic theory and practice.

Even before he concludes his studies and earns his MD in 1922, Reich is already giving lectures before the Psychoanalytic Society on libidinous energy and the theory of neurosis. Two years later he is director of Vienna's technical seminar in psychoanalysis, whose founding he himself helped bring about. As he himself found out while experiencing his own growing pains, there was up to that point no standardized course of training for analysts in Vienna. "There was neither a training institute nor an organized curriculum. The counsel to be had from older colleagues was meager. 'Just go on analyzing patiently,' they would say, 'it'll come.' What would come, and how, one did not quite know."[31]

Reich leads the technical seminar from 1924 until his move to Berlin in September 1930. His teaching is instructive because he mainly talks about therapeutic failures. Instead of giving success stories that gloss over details, he presents everything that went wrong during a course of treatment. There is an observation that Reich makes frequently during this time: merely informing the patient of the psychoanalytic interpretation of a symptom or dream has almost no impact. The patient's resistance must be overcome first before explaining unconscious mechanisms can have a healing effect.

"First the resistance, then the interpretation," as Reich's maxim has it. As such he places the attempt to dismantle the patient's barriers at the center of his approach. "The technique of analysis of resistances, although theoretically formulated, was not practiced . . . If one told the patient, 'You have a resistance,' he would look at one uncomprehendingly. If one told him that he 'defended himself against his unconscious,' one was no better off."[32] Talking alone doesn't seem to be helpful in all cases, but if talking doesn't work, what then?

Reich is creative and very taken with himself and his approach. Therapy with him is not a delicate procedure. Whenever he deems it appropriate, he gets clients to assume certain physical positions, repeat gestures, or let out their emotions. For Reich the libido is a real physical tension that has to be "discharged," while constant resistance leads to excess strain. In his eyes neuroses are a kind of sclerosis, a "character armor" that must be broken open, and not just verbally, but in a real, concrete sense. He massages his patients, stretches and loosens muscles and sinews to stimulate the free flow of vital energy. These are the beginnings of the physical therapy for which Reich in the mid-1930s coins the term "Vegetotherapy." Over the years it will inspire a wealth of therapeutic approaches, from bioenergetics to dance therapy.

But all this is yet to come. In his 1925 book *The Impulsive Character*, Reich shows himself to be an astute diagnostician. He broadens the spectrum of mental illnesses by speaking for the first time of character neurosis, which for him is a disorder in its own right between neurosis and psychosis. Where neurosis manifests in symptoms like compulsive actions, pains, or phobias, and psychosis is marked above all by hallucinations and delusion, character neurosis lies in between: it is expressed primarily in distorted sensory impressions, mood swings, and aggressive or self-destructive behavior. Because of its position on the border between the two conditions, it enters psychiatric manuals as "borderline personality disorder."

In addition to running his own practice, Reich helps out at an outpatient clinic for patients without means, where he mostly treats lower-class blue- and white-collar workers. He considers the meetings of the Freud circle "frightfully boring." A key experience for him will be his training analysis with an older colleague, the Hungarian Jenö Harnik, who barely says a word during their sessions; even when a session is over he only indicates this by scraping his foot. Reich has no use for this extreme abstinence. He even suspects some analysts of falling asleep while their patients pour their hearts out to them.

Reich is aware of his talent, and considers many of his colleagues mediocre blowhards. Of one gathering he reports: "About eight or ten people would sit around, and it was awfully dull [. . .] Everybody had an opinion about this or that. [. . .] I acted like a shark in a pond of carps. When I came in, everything somehow began to stir."[33]

. . .

It is now becoming ever more clear that the talented Dr. Reich will be going his own way someday. It's also clear what path he will take. Some apostates refuse to follow Freud because they don't want to join the dance around the golden calf of the libido. There are also those, however, who draw conclusions from the theory of sexuality that go even further than the master himself. Among this latter group, Reich turns out to be the most significant. Over the course of the next decade, he distances himself ever more from Freudian psychoanalysis and sketches an image of the psyche dominated by biophysical terms like "energy fields" and "energy currents." Reich considers the physical substrate of the libido to be the universal life energy, and one's ability to practice "ultimate vegetative involuntary submission" to be indispensable.[34] The key to curing neuroses lies not in interpreting the unconscious but in reducing the backup of the libido. Removing such "inhibitions to arousal" and allowing the energy to flow freely is the prerequisite for health.

Reich is at least as much of a physical therapist as he is a psychotherapist. Through physical intervention he hopes to rouse the emotions that bring his patients' buried memories to light. But unlike, for example, the autogenic training developed by Johannes Heinrich Schultz or Edmund Jacobson's progressive muscle relaxation technique, Reich's approach is aimed at cracking open the patient's "body armor"; he's interested not merely in promoting relaxation and well-being, but also in dismantling the psyche's defensive architecture.

Freud himself once laid the track for this approach. In his theory of actual neurosis he declared the "sexual build-up" to be the source of many symptoms. Moreover, in the 1908 article "'Civilized' Sexual Morality and Modern Nervous Illness," Freud suggested that rigid sexual mores cause psychological suffering. But he consciously avoided calling for the solutions his own diagnosis seemed to suggest, like social reforms or the founding of new, maybe even socialist communities. Now Freud can't rid himself of the spirits that he himself summoned; he fears the potential harm to his "cause" if psychoanalysis acquires the reputation of being an amoral club of revolutionaries.

Not only does Reich's biology-oriented thinking appear unorthodox, his method of treatment is new and different as well. For Reich, the sure path to individual liberation is to break open the hardened layers of the character armor. The key to healing is not the word, but the body, not understanding things intellectually, but acting them out emotionally. In order to head off rumors, Reich is careful to have his patients at least keep their underwear on during his physical exercises. By this time, Freud's psychoanalysis, which began with the famous Anna O. "acting out" her memories, has evolved more and more into an interpretive art that focuses on the reading of symbols and fantasies. In a sense, Reich is returning to the catharsis of the early days.

"On his hobby horse": Wilhelm Reich in his time as the most talented of Freud's students in Vienna.

ALL GENITAL?

According to Wilhelm Reich, all neurotics suffer from a genital disorder. Repression of their natural need for sexual satisfaction prevents the complete discharge of the libido, what Reich calls a "blockage neurosis." The sadism and megalomaniacal fantasies of many (usually male) patients are a potential consequence of this inhibition, but so are obsequiousness, excessive regard for others, or detachment.

Reich develops the concept of orgastic potency, by which he means the ability to achieve spontaneous physical surrender in the moment of ecstasy. He distinguishes between two phases of the sex act: first the moment of penetration and the ensuing build-up, with the pleasurable—for both partners—gradually accelerating rhythmic movement (friction) of the penis against the vaginal wall. And second, the actual climax, the moment of pure ecstasy, during which conscious awareness is reduced and sexual energy is "discharged" into the body through contractions of the pelvic muscles. This surge of pleasure is followed in turn by a phase of profound relaxation, gratitude, and closeness. That's the theory, anyway.

Reich constructs an ideal of fully developed "genitality," compared to which all other sexual practices, whether they be masturbation, coitus interruptus, oral sex, or petting, are inferior. Though these ersatz actions might seem liberating initially, the free flow of genital desire is the hallmark of the mature character. Thus Reich dismisses many erotic preferences as inferior, indeed pathological, a notion that lines up seamlessly with the idea that achieving climax through clitoral stimulation is less "valuable" than the ability to have vaginal orgasms. Mental health is a matter of having the right kind of sex.

Between Reich and many of his colleagues, including Freud, a conflict arises over the question of whether there can be neurotics with sound genital sexuality. For Reich this is a contradiction in terms. Freud on the other hand insists that there isn't only *one* cause of neurosis; he rejects the idea that genitality is a universal cure.

For Reich, there's nothing devilish about giving free rein to the libido; in fact, it's vitally necessary. Only where sexual energy flows without impediment are there no inhibited emotions. And because blockages, once they have formed, take great effort to clear, it's better to prevent them in the first place: which means teaching children about sex as early as possible, and in a comprehensive manner, promoting the pleasure of touching and being touched even in early childhood and giving adolescents access to contraceptives so that their love lives are free of constraint. The opposite approach, involving threats of punishment, embarrassment, and evasiveness, only creates an atmosphere of guilt that acts as a hotbed for neuroses. In his 1933 book *The Mass Psychology of Fascism*, Reich argues that the suppression of sexuality creates anxious and authoritarian-sadistic characters on a massive scale, who can then be manipulated by demagogues for their own ends.

Freud finds such theories horrifying, but for a time continues to tolerate Reich as the director of the technical seminar. He writes to Lou Andreas-Salomé in May 1928: "We have here a Dr. Reich, a worthy but impetuous young man, passionately devoted to his hobby-horse, who now salutes in the genital orgasm the antidote to every neurosis."[35] A year earlier, when Reich presents him with a signed copy of his book *The Function of the Orgasm* on the occasion of his seventieth birthday, Freud replies dryly: "That thick?"[36]

The leading role that Reich plays within the Viennese community of psychoanalysts stands in sharp contrast to the silence that surrounds him in print. His name barely appears in Freud's writings, while others ignore the notion of "orgastic potency" completely. Only the approaches Reich develops for character and resistance analysis are well-received. His major work on the function of the orgasm isn't reviewed in a psychoanalytic journal until a full three years after publication, albeit in a very favorable notice by Otto Fenichel, Reich's old friend from university.

In 1926 Freud denies Reich's request to complete a training analysis with him, saying that he didn't want to analyze any more colleagues who lived in Vienna (by that point many doctors from the US are lining up outside his door). This rejection, which Reich takes as a major slight, is the beginning of his rupture with Freud. A short while later the assiduous model student commits yet another act of defiance against the patriarch: Reich becomes a Communist.

. . .

We know the exact date when Reich's political consciousness is awakened: July 15, 1927. On this day the Vienna police brutally suppress a workers' uprising. Eighty-nine people die, more than a thousand are injured. The backstory is easily told: in January members of a right-wing paramilitary group kill two people, one of them a child, when they fire shots at a gathering of workers in the town of Schattdorf bei Wien. The court in Vienna, notorious for its leniency toward right-wing offenders, lets the shooters off. This brings hundreds of incensed workers out into the streets. Some force their way into the courthouse and set it alight. Police arriving on the scene suddenly open fire; Reich and his wife, who are in the crowd, find themselves in the line of attack. At the last possible moment they take cover behind a row of trees. This incident shocks the thirty-year-old Reich. From now on he calls for answering violence with violence, and becomes active both in the left wing of the Social Democratic Party and in the Communist Party, despite the fierce enmity that divides the two groups.

Frustrated by the fact that even the most polished rhetoric can't incite the masses to overthrow the prevailing order, Reich tries a new strategy: subversion has to start at the bottom, with the everyday needs of the lower classes. Together with a few like-minded doctors and educators he founds an organization for sexual-political enlightenment, the Sexpol movement. Using his own money, Reich prints handbills that he and his comrades post in doorways and public squares in workers' districts. The members of the movement hold outdoor counseling sessions, providing information about sex and abortion and handing out contraceptives. This is illegal; abortion is a punishable offense under Austrian law. Bolder still, Reich's campaign is aimed primarily at young people, to whom he recommends a free sex life as a "prophylactic against neuroses." The Sexpol teams regularly have to flee from police.

Reich's next big project is an attempt to combine Freud's psychology of the unconscious and the repressed libido with the social theory of Karl Marx. His theory of sexual economy is a forerunner of the Freudo-Marxism that will reach intellectual maturity in the Frankfurt School. Given the circles he moves in, however, Reich's project seems destined to land him in no man's land. On the one hand, most psychoanalysts harbor a deep skepticism toward revolutionary theories of liberation. On the other hand, the leaders of the Social Democrats and Communists regard psychoanalysis as a product of bourgeois decadence that is incompatible with the Marxist-materialist view of humanity. As soon as the proletariat takes power, unconscious conflicts and suppressed drives will vanish into thin air—this is their conviction. In the view of many comrades, the birth of a new Communist society is imminent, its emergence predicted by natural laws in accordance with historical and dialectical materialism. To Reich, the scientist, this view is still very much unproven. He decides to get his own idea of the political situation, and in September 1929 he and Annie set off to spend several months traveling through the Soviet Union. They leave their children, Eva and Lore, just five and one years old, in the care of their grandparents.

Less than a year after the Reichs return, they head to Berlin, the biggest Communist stronghold in the German-speaking world. They find an apartment near an artists' colony in southwest Berlin. During the day, Reich runs his practice out of the bedroom. Fees from patients and candidates make up the main source of the family's income, which Reich supplements by giving lectures and consulting on questions of sexuality and child-rearing.

Lore, the younger of the Reichs' two daughters, goes to a Communist daycare, where the little ones are supposed to grow up "without an Oedipus complex." But this apparently isn't enough for Reich. Sexual impulses and the pleasure to be derived from playing with one's own and others' genitals should be not suppressed, but promoted. Thus the girls are permitted to watch their parents have sex in the shower and marvel at the "very swollen" genitals.[37]

Early on, in *Three Essays* (1905), Freud distinguished between different phases of early-childhood sexuality. Oral satisfaction of desire, which dominates in the first year, is followed by an anal phase, in which defecating brings the greatest pleasure. These are followed by the phallic and finally the genital phase. If a person gets stuck, emotionally speaking, in any one of these stages, this regression is expressed in typical patterns of behavior: the orally-fixated character, for example, is susceptible to addiction; the anally-fixated individual tends to be greedy and excessively controlling; the phallic type displays "polymorphous perversity in object selection," which means, put simply, that the libido becomes attached to objects, imbuing them with a fetishistic character, but not allowing a true channeling of the libidinous impulse. This, as Freud himself saw it at the time, is only possible through fully-developed genital sexuality. Reich adheres to this view, but believes that the social environment has a greater influence: constant admonishment, punishment, or embarrassed silence leads children to grow up in an atmosphere of fear and guilt. This impedes the development of orgastic potency and ultimately produces neurotics.

Shortly before moving to Berlin in September 1930, Reich pays Freud a visit in his summer house on the Grundlsee. His former mentor appears saddened by Reich's having strayed from the "middle way" of psychoanalysis. There isn't only one single cause of neurosis, Freud says, and the complete orgasm isn't the means to alleviate it. Reich regrets the disagreement between them, but insists on his point of view. A few months prior, at a congress of the World League for Sexual Reform, he had called for a packet of measures whose implementation would likely have been possible only under socialist rule: provide taboo-free sex education, make abortion and contraception available at no cost, dissolve the traditional, monogamous family. In place of "lifelong compulsive marriage," communal child-rearing would give early childhood sexuality its due. For guardians of traditional morality, Reich's proposal is a cabinet of horrors.

Freud thinks a lot of Reich, the "best mind" among Vienna's analysts, but fears that such demands could damage the movement. "It is not the task of psychoanalysis to save the world," Freud says[38]—especially since a condition of happiness "is not included in the plan of 'Creation.'"[39] Thus things play out as they must: no sooner has Reich moved to Berlin than he is dismissed from his post as director of the technical seminar. He also loses his seat on the executive committee of the Vienna Psychoanalytic Society. Freud declares that, should he return to Austria, Reich could take up his positions again at any time—"if he has not become impossible."[40] By the following summer he will have sidelined Reich entirely.

"FREE ME FROM REICH!"

In August 1934, a married man and his mistress go on a camping trip. They travel from Denmark to Switzerland by car, covering the first leg of the journey by ferry from Copenhagen to Holland. Traveling through Nazi Germany would be too dangerous for the man, a Jew, Communist, and sexual reformer. The trip is tricky enough already, since Reich and his girlfriend Elsa Lindenberg have his two underage daughters with them, ten-year-old Eva and six-year-old Lore. Staying at any hotel could cause a stir—so the four of them camp out!

Reich's marriage is in ruins, but you wouldn't know it to look at him. He's in love with Elsa, a dancer for the Berlin Opera, and to the children their father seems transformed, his violent temper replaced by a cheerful, carefree air. This summer they stop wherever they feel like, go swimming, buy their food from farmers, dance in the moonlight and slink wearily back to their tent after long evenings by the campfire. Wilhelm and Elsa feel free again, unbound, filled with love.

The journey's destination is Lucerne. There, on the shores of the lake, the thirteenth Congress of the International Psychoanalytical Association (IPA) is being held from August 26 to August 31. IPA president Ernest Jones of Great Britain recently assured Reich that he would be able to plead his case for being allowed to remain in the association, despite his, well, unorthodox views. The same Jones had said to Anna Freud back in May 1933 that it would be best if "the madman" left of his own accord.

Shortly before setting out on his camping trip Reich receives a letter from the head of the Berlin chapter, Carl Müller-Braunschweig, informing him that he will not be appearing on the list of participants at the congress. He was still welcome to speak as a guest, of course; the fact that he would soon be joining the Norwegian chapter meant that his membership was assured (Reich has been living in Oslo since spring 1934). But at this same time high-ranking German analysts are issuing warnings to their colleagues in Norway—if they let Reich in, they'll risk being expelled themselves. Reich learns in passing that he has long since been taken off the membership roles of the Berlin Psychoanalytic Institute.

Reich, Lindenberg, and the girls don't stay at a hotel in Lucerne, either, but instead camp out in the sprawling park on the shore of the lake. Reich wears a dagger in his belt that Elsa gave him. This is pure fodder for his enemies in the Psychoanalytic Association, who are already calling him "crazy." Reich's estranged wife Annie is herself a psychoanalyst and is here in Lucerne, as is his friend from his student days, Otto Fenichel, and his former training analyst Sándor Radó. All three help spread the rumor that Reich suffers from a slowly progressing case of psychosis.

The sting of disappointment lingers on August 30, when Reich gives his lecture "Psychic Contact and Vegetative Current." He opens the lecture with these words: "After fourteen years as a member, I speak for the first time as a guest of the Congress."[41] Reich sticks to the matter at hand, even though inside he is seething. He explains that the patient's lack of contact to themselves, their "contactlessness," hinders the flow of "vegetative energy." The physical tension that builds up in the organism must be channeled somewhere, however, otherwise it leads to the formation of rigidities. This idea forms the basis for all of Reich's subsequent research. His colleagues clap politely—and silently move on to the next order of business.

After this noteworthy final appearance among psychoanalysts, henceforth Reich's work will only be published by his own Verlag für Sexualpolitik ("Sexual Politics Press"). In 1933 he'd been expelled by the Communist Party in response to his *Mass Psychology of Fascism*. Freed from all artificial constraints, Reich now follows his thirst for knowledge and adopts an ever more venturesome tone. The path he is on leads finally to his vegetotherapy, based on the dubious notion of vital energy that he terms the "orgone," and a self-built device, the Orgone Accumulator, which will be his ruin two decades later when he tries to sell it.[42]

For Freud, only one thing matters: he wants to protect his movement from views that will damage its reputation. To achieve that end, the seventy-eight-year-old, suffering intensely from oral cancer, is once more prepared to sacrifice a years-long friendship. He wishes to say nothing more about Reich publicly. The split culminates in an almost plaintive request to Felix Boehm, later chairman of the Berlin Pyschoanalytic

Society: "Free me from Reich!" Boehm, like Carl Müller-Braunschweig, is not Jewish. Under pressure from the Nazis—and with the consent of Freud and his innermost circle—both were quietly handed their positions. Instead of disbanding, the society complies with the demand for "Aryanization," probably in the hope that the storm will soon blow over. To ensure the survival of psychoanalysis, Freud's daughter Anna and IPA President Ernest Jones in London agree to a change in the society's bylaws: thenceforth, in Germany, only non-Jews will be admitted as members.

It thus comes to pass that Eitingon, who is himself Jewish, instructs the Jewish Wilhelm Reich not to set foot in the polyclinic's offices anymore, effective immediately. Many of those who hope that the political winds could still shift and the Nazis would be driven from power will pay for this mistake with their lives. To avoid arrest, the Reichs flee to Scandinavia just in time. Wilhelm the Freudo-Marxist can get no residency permit in Denmark and continues on to Oslo. Here he remains for six years, until he makes his next escape. In August 1939, on the eve of the start of the Second World War, Reich catches sight of the Statue of Liberty in New York Harbor.

3

FEAR

THE PROFESSOR AND GOD

Hans is afraid. So afraid! An uncanny terror takes hold of the boy every time he sees a horse anywhere near him—which in Vienna in 1908 is just about unavoidable. It's gotten to the point where the five-year-old would rather not leave the house at all. He's afraid that the big animals will bite him, or that one of them will fall and crush him. And what if a horse comes into his room and tries to hurt him?

Hans is particularly impressed by the animals' enormous "widdlers."[1] Believing that every person has genitals like this, he suspects that his mother has a "widdler like a horse" because she's so big. The boy found out long ago that the penis isn't just for urinating; it feels good to touch it, too. Every night when he goes to bed "he puts his hand there." His mother threatens him: if he doesn't stop it she'll cut his widdler off! Clearly she subscribes to the then-widespread notion that masturbation makes you sick.

Hans's affection for his mother manifests in his constant desire to be near her and to cuddle with her—and in his simultaneous fear of losing her, of his father taking her away. When the family is on vacation—and Hans's father, Max Graf, has to work and can only be with the family for part of the time—Hans enjoys the bliss of his mother's constant companionship. One day during the holiday the boy observes a scene that stays with him for a long time afterward. Another father warns his child not to pet a horse: "Don't put your hand there or it'll bite you!" The same expression, "put your hand there," describes both touching one's genitals and petting a horse. And clearly there is danger involved with both actions.

Freud's occasional mentions of the clever Hans and his fascination with widdlers date back to 1904, the year the music critic Max Graf first starts attending the Wednesday gatherings. It seems he amuses the master with stories of his little boy. The two men met when Hans's mother, Olga Graf-Hoenig, saw Freud for treatment. But it's not Freud who goes to work on Hans's phobia; rather it's his father, under Freud's expert guidance, beginning in the spring of 1908. In exchange for the quality "material," Freud tells Hans's father what steps to take in leading the boy's treatment.

So, what to do? The obvious, Freud says. Hans's father should explain to the boy that his idea about horses was "a bit of nonsense"; nobody was going to bite him. He also prescribes some sex ed: Hans should learn that men and woman, like stallions and mares, are biologically different, and that his mother doesn't have a penis at all. Hans's father follows the first instruction, but declines initially to explain sex to his son this early. When he finally does say something to that effect, however, Hans isn't buying it: he stubbornly insists that he has seen his mother's widdler.

Little by little, careful not to jump the gun, Freud puts the pieces together and finds a case of neurotic phobia triggered by repressed sexual desire. At the center is Hans's tender love for his mother and the fear of his father that is bound up with it, which is at the same time fear *for* his father. This is because, as much as Hans would like to have his mother all to himself, he also fears losing his father. This conflict causes the fear to attach itself to another object: horses.

Freud himself meets Hans, whose actual name is Herbert, for just one brief consultation at his practice. This takes place on March 30, 1908, in the presence of his father. When the two men touch on the boy's still pronounced fear, Hans reveals that "he was particularly bothered by what horses wear in front of their eyes and by the black round their mouths." The boy speaks in riddles! Then Freud has an epiphany: "But as I saw the two of them sitting in front of me and at the same time heard Hans's description of his anxiety-horses, a further piece of the solution shot through my mind [. . .]. I asked Hans jokingly whether his horses wore eyeglasses, to which he replied that they did not. I then asked him whether his father wore eyeglasses, to which, against all evidence, he once more said no. Finally I asked him whether by 'the black round the mouth' he meant a mustache; and I then disclosed to him that he was afraid of his father, precisely because he was so fond of his mother. It must be, I told him, that he thought his father was angry with him on that account; but this was not so, his father was fond of him in spite of it, and he might admit everything to him without any fear. Long before he was in the world, I went on, I had known that a little Hans would come who would be so fond of his mother that he would be bound to feel afraid of his father because of it."[2]

On the way home, Hans asks his father, awestruck: "Does the professor talk to God, as he can tell all that beforehand?" Freud couldn't have asked for a better compliment.

As Hans moves toward recovery, the meaning behind the occasional mysterious dream he has becomes clear. One night, for example, Hans dreams of two giraffes, one big and beautiful and the other "crumpled." The big one lets out a terrible scream because Hans tries to take the crumpled one away from it. As Freud explains, the big giraffe stands for Hans's father (the long, strong neck symbolizes his penis), while the small one represents his mother. Hans demonstratively sits down on top of the crumpled giraffe at the end of his dream, as if to say: scream as much as you want, Mama belongs to me! On another occasion Hans dreams of a plumber who "screws off" his bottom and penis and replaces them with larger ones. Shortly after that his horse phobia is gone.

Freud draws two important conclusions from this case: first, that children too are ruled by pleasure and unpleasure and have repressed wishes; they just tend to express them in more imaginative ways than adults. With this first assertion, Freud lays the groundwork for studying the psychological expressions of even the youngest of patients, in line with the motto: "The arbitrary has no existence in mental life."[3] The second lesson for Freud is to see in Hans the confirmation of his theory that repressed desire comes out as fear and, because it can't simply disappear, "affixes" itself to another object. Thus anything can potentially trigger the fear. Understanding what actually lies at the root of the phobia brings quick relief, even to a five-year-old.

The astounding thing about this is that the boy continues to have repressed desire; he still longs for a union with his beloved mother and isn't permitted to achieve it. The source of the fear doesn't dry up, then, it simply becomes manageable. Freud explains: "Analysis replaces the process of repression, which is an automatic and excessive one, by a temperate and purposeful control." Unlike those revolutionaries of Wilhelm Reich's ilk who preach the liberation of desire, Freud sees the internal conflicts brought about by the libido as inevitable; the goal is merely to ensure that they don't lead to neurotic symptoms, but rather are controlled in a healthier, accepted fashion. Or as Freud puts it in a later dictum, perhaps his most famous: "Where id was, there ego shall be."[4]

Whether it was the conversations with his father—with Freud offstage giving cues—that brought about Hans's recovery, and not simply habituation, maturity, or the passage of time, is a question that cannot be answered. Children grow and mature; feelings and thoughts, fears included, come and go. Only by comparing the cases of many children of the same age with similar issues, some of whom receive treatment, others of whom do not, could one draw conclusions as to what makes for an effective method of child analysis. As a doctor in private practice Freud can't afford to go to such efforts—nor does he want to. A good case history is proof enough for him.

The account of little Hans appears in 1909, in the same volume of the *Psychoanalytisches Jahrbuch* in which Jung, inspired by Otto Gross, publishes his essay on the role of the father. Freud's study is the first instance of remote diagnosis in psychoanalysis and the first analysis of a child. The practice of therapists receiving expert guidance or "supervision" from their colleagues will only become common in the 1920s at the training institute in Berlin. In these early years, when analysis is still in its infancy, the idea hasn't yet occurred to anyone. Each analyst heals—or fails to heal—in his own way.

In April 1922 the professor and Hans, aka Herbert, Graf meet for a second and final time. Herbert, now nineteen years old, perfectly healthy and mentally well-adjusted, doesn't remember his former fear of horses. He is only aware of the treatment led by Freud by way of his father from reading his own case study, which stoked his curiosity about the wise doctor of the soul. Herbert Graf studies music history like his father, and goes on to become a successful opera director.

FIGHTING FIRE WITH FIRE

Summer 1914. Suddenly the world is at war. Europe marches with eyes wide open into a catastrophe whose scope no one is yet capable of imagining. To the contrary, enthusiasm for the war is enormous, and both sides—the Central Powers, led by the Habsburgs and the Hohenzollers, and the Entente, consisting of France, England, and Russia—are convinced that triumph is just a matter of weeks. The most bitter realization to come from this First World War will be how little humanity knows itself; how greatly we underestimate our capacity for blind, all-consuming, destructive madness.

In April 1914, Carl Gustav Jung, having fallen out with Freud, resigns his post as president of the International Psychoanalytical Association. Two months later, on June 28, the Serbian nationalist Gavrilo Princip carries out one of the most consequential assassinations in history. He shoots and kills the heir to the Austrian throne, Archduke Franz Ferdinand, and his wife Sophie as they drive through Sarajevo in an open car. A month passes before Austria-Hungary declares war on Serbia on July 28. In a cascade of mobilizations and pledges of support, the major powers of Europe, and eventually even China, Japan, and finally the United States, initiate a ruthless bloodbath.

With the outbreak of war the first phase of the psychoanalytic movement's progress comes to an abrupt end. Most of the members are doctors, and as the fighting drags on they are called up to serve in the army or in field hospitals. Alfred Adler is at first exempted from military service, but then in 1916 he is drafted after all. He treats wounded soldiers in various locations—though not with psychoanalysis; rather his orders are to get the wounded men physically and mentally fit for combat again, or as close to fit as possible. Attrition warfare takes its toll; the number of "depleted" men soon climbs into the hundreds of thousands. With the army's reserves dwindling, the wounded men are to be sent back to the trenches as quickly as possible. The doctors' mission is not to alleviate suffering and cure illness, but rather to supply battle-ready cannon fodder.

Over time the demand within the military for psychological know-how starts to grow. Fallen soldiers and amputees are only part of the generals' woes; the country is also awash in soldiers suffering from so-called *shell shock*. There are thousands of men who can't sleep, lose control of their bladder, and tremble uncontrollably. To many patriots, the neurotics, or those anyway who have been spared lost limbs and shrapnel wounds, are nothing but shirkers and fakers. Meanwhile the criteria for draft-eligibility are being expanded. Asthma, poor eyesight, a weak constitution—conditions like these are no excuse for not serving the fatherland.

An old dogma persists in the minds of many doctors of this period: soldiers with psychological conditions must have hidden brain injuries, triggered perhaps by the concussion of exploding shells—either that, or they are weak-willed cowards. Freud breaks with this inhumane view by stressing the psychological nature of the symptoms.

At first no one can explain the large number of shell-shocked troops in the army. Only gradually does the idea start to take hold that psychological factors could contribute to the phenomenon. This view holds that the soldiers are torn between the desire to flee and a sense of duty, between the natural instinct to stay alive and their orders to fight and, if need be, die for the fatherland. Though the condition seems to have little to do with conflicts arising from the libido, the massive numbers of shell-shocked troops seem to confirm the hypothesis that psychogenic causes of illness do exist.

"Treatment" for those afflicted involves neither making inner conflicts conscious nor a display of compassion and understanding. Rather the goal is to make the price of illness as high as possible so that disability is no longer "worth it." Physicians resort to brutal methods to force war neurotics to rejoin the ranks. One favorite method: electroshocks that far surpass the pain threshold. War neurotics are literally supposed to lose their desire to be neurotic. The repertoire of "will power training" also includes ice-cold baths, forced exercise, and artificially-induced shortness of breath, brought about by inserting ball bearings into the larynx. None of this is of any use as therapy, of course; it's simply torture. As such it succeeds in getting some shell-shocked soldiers to return to battle rather than endure the hell of the field hospital any longer. But it doesn't yield soldiers who are fit for service, as the army leadership also comes to recognize.

A mixture of ignorance and wishful thinking leads some military leaders to put their hopes in a quick, long-lasting fix through psychoanalysis: in September 1918, at the fifth congress of the International Psychoanalytical Association in Budapest, representatives of the German, Austrian, and Hungarian military command float the prospect of lucrative contracts for the treatment of war neurotics. If psychoanalysis is so capable of healing the mind, can't it also provide soldiers with a fresh jolt of courage and dedication?

As far-fetched as the plan sounds, it is inspired by success stories like those reported by Ernst Simmel, a doctor at a field hospital in Posen, who in 1917 is the first to attempt psychoanalytic treatment of traumatized soldiers. At the congress in Budapest he explains: "A combination of analytic-cathartic hypnosis and waking analytic articulation and dream interpretation [. . .] enabled me to develop a method that results in relief from war-neurotic symptoms in two or three sessions on average."[5] Cured of shell shock by talking and having your dreams interpreted? And not, as in classic analysis, over the course of months and years, but within days? Simmel is promising the moon. Whether the ministry officials would have awarded the promised contracts is an open question—surrender renders the plans moot.

The debate over war neuroses has at least one positive side effect: a psychical genesis of even the most severe physical symptoms now seems plausible. Or are shell-shocked troops just shirkers after all? Freud himself has spoken of the benefit that war neurotics get out of escaping the meatgrinder of trench warfare. But this alone can hardly explain the thousands of cases.

While Jung in neutral Switzerland hears little of all this and devotes himself to the study of archetypes on his estate in Küsnacht on Lake Zurich, Freud, a good sixty years old by this point, is actively following the events of the day. Since patients are limited in the war years, he devotes all the more time to his writing. In 1916 he publishes a preliminary distillation of his writings, the *Introductory Lectures on Psycho-Analysis*. Toward the end of the war, influenced, among other things, by the millions of casualties, Freud begins to consider whether the cause of this aggression and destruction might be found in a possible death drive. For decades he has defended the libido as the sole source of instinctual activity; now, to the astonishment of many of his colleagues, Eros is joined by Thanatos, the Greek god of death.

Freud comes into occasional contact with wartime psychiatry in his capacity as a medical observer. Shortly after the war is over, a lieutenant colonel in the Austro-Hungarian army named Walter Kauder accuses the Viennese professor Julius Wagner-Jauregg of having tortured soldiers with electric shocks. A "Commission for Investigating Derelictions of Military Duty" calls on Freud to provide his professional opinion. In his assessment, Freud pronounces Wagner-Jauregg free of any personal guilt, but sharply criticizes the common use of electroshock therapy.[6] The intent of this treatment, Freud says, was to minimize the benefit that shell-shocked troops received from their exemption from war service by subjecting them to horrible torment. Because there is no proof of Wagner-Jauregg being directly involved, the court ultimately acquits him.

The strategy of using one ill to drive out another will serve Wagner-Jauregg well a few years later, when it provides him with the biggest success of his career. In 1927 he receives the Nobel Prize for Medicine or Physiology for using malaria inoculation to treat progressive paralysis. Neurosyphilis is a condition caused by the syphilis pathogen. It is characterized by the degeneration of certain parts of the brain, and with it the loss of mental capacity in those afflicted. Wagner-Jauregg noticed that those suffering from this form of paralysis often showed signs of improvement after a bout of fever. Could an artificially-induced fever possibly slow the course of the cerebral degeneration? Wagner-Jauregg managed to achieve that very result when he infected patients with malaria pathogens. Using one evil to drive out another remained the most important approach for treating the effects of late-stage syphilis until the discovery of antibiotic treatment.

On the other hand, Wagner-Jauregg's research gave new momentum to the notion that mental disorders stemmed from physical damage to the brain. Accordingly, many physicians considered disorders of the psyche to be the aftereffects of infections, hereditary defects, or the loss of tissue during war service. It took a scientific exotic like Freud to break with this dogma and push for the view that mental suffering is psychogenic.

. . .

The war leaves deep scars on the map of Europe. It lasts more than four years, till November 11, 1918, and takes the lives of seventeen million people. No sooner do the guns go silent than the Great Influenza epidemic sweeps across the globe and carries off millions more. In 1920 Freud's daughter Sophie dies of the virus. The displaced and wounded sleep on the streets of Vienna. The war had robbed many families of their livelihoods; food and fuel for heating are scarce. Little remains of the splendor of the Habsburgs. The multi-ethnic empire is reduced to a rump state, the new Republic of Austria. Where Austria-Hungary had nearly eighty million subjects, the new country counts only eight million citizens. The economy and infrastructure are in a woeful state.

Soon the social tensions find an outlet in violence. Brawls, shootouts, and outright battles in the streets are regular occurrences. Socialists and German Nationalists, Communists and anarchists, Marxists and Trotskyites, liberals and revanchists—the political landscape is chaotic. Many groups maintain armed paramilitary units to bolster their claim to power.

During this time, Alfred Adler's socialist convictions grow even stronger. In *Die andere Seite* ("The Other Side"), he attempts to explain in psychological terms how the powerful misled the people and drove them to blind enthusiasm for the war. Like many on the left, Adler is troubled by a seeming paradox: why do insecurity and hardship lead so many people to cast their lot with the right wing, whether it's national conservatives or fascist ideologues? Why can they not grasp that it is these very forces that exploit their hardship for their own ends and ultimately exacerbate it? What has to happen for them finally to support progressive forces?

Adler suspects that what lies behind this phenomenon is a sort of perverted thirst for power. The oppressed nation dreams of fame and greatness, ultimately as a way of salving its wounded ego. Ten years later, when the fragile era of peace ends with the National Socialists' seizure of power, another theorist will offer a mass psychological answer to the same questions: Wilhelm Reich sees in the suppression of sexuality the central mechanism in the production of subjects who are obedient to authority.

But for now there is still hope. Progress, peace, and a democratic future can still be saved. In the mid-1920s a period of upheaval begins. Despite crushing reparations, things start to look up for the economy, and not just in Weimar Germany. The golden age of the left-wing-dominated "Red Vienna" is beginning; Austria's capital becomes the first European city ever to get a Social Democratic mayor. Adler, with good connections among politicians and the administration, founds numerous child guidance centers, the grass roots of his individual-psychological movement.

LEARNING TO FEAR

Meanwhile, in Baltimore, John B. Watson is preparing to strike a blow against the psychoanalysis he so loathes. Over the winter of 1919/20, he and his assistant, Rosalie Rayner, plan an experiment that is meant to bring the curtain down on the newfangled method of probing into the unconscious. He wants to expose Freud's theory, which posits that fear stems from the repressed libido, for the fiction he believes it to be. To do so, all he must do is show that there are simpler, more obvious explanations for fear—and thus that there's no need to mess around with unconscious forces. All Watson is missing is a suitable guinea pig.

In 1908, at just thirty years old, he was named Professor of Psychology at the venerable Johns Hopkins University. He has been at the elite university for eleven years when he meets the talented student Rosalie Rayner. She moved to Baltimore in the summer of 1919 after getting her Bachelor's degree at Vassar College. The tall twenty-one-year-old catches Watson's eye and he offers her a job as an assistant in his lab. His attention is not limited to academic matters.

The two of them begin a love affair that Watson makes little effort to conceal. This is partly to do with his freewheeling disposition. What others feel or think about him is of little concern; he prefers to follow his instincts and his mood. Speaking to a friend, he describes what he and Rosalie have in common: "We both have the power of getting what we go for."[7]

In his classes he has nothing good to say about psychoanalysis. On a fundamental level, he argues, no one who undergoes such a "treatment" knows what is happening to them. Both the goal and the path taken to reach it remain opaque; after the patient offers up random thoughts and scraps of memory, the mostly silent analyst cobbles together a diagnosis based on the most outlandish of premises. If anything brought relief, then it was only the patient's unreserved and awestruck belief in the correctness of the insights brought about through psychoanalysis. The analysts themselves meanwhile aren't exactly overflowing with optimism; even Freud, at the end of his *Studies on Hysteria*, had admitted that therapy could only "turn hysterical suffering into common unhappiness."[8]

In his furious paper "Psychology as the Behaviorist Views It,"[9] published in 1913, Watson put forth a very different vision. "Psychology as the behaviorist views it is a purely objective experimental branch of natural science. Its theoretical goal is the prediction and control of behavior. Introspection forms no essential part of its methods, nor is the scientific value of its data dependent upon the readiness with which they lend themselves to interpretation in terms of consciousness."

In other words: what the individual thinks and believes she knows about herself is irrelevant. Her behavior is subject to natural laws that can be objectively measured and described. Watson's approach is based on the principle of conditioning developed by Ivan Pavlov. This principle states that the association of an initially neutral stimulus with other experiences, pleasant or unpleasant—reward or punishment, for instance—leads to a learned and thus "conditioned" response. Pavlov demonstrated this principle by way of the salivating reflex of dogs. Shortly before presenting each dog with a bowl of food, he rang a bell. After just a few repetitions, the ringing was enough to cause the dogs to salivate.

Because Watson sees no fundamental difference between human and animal, he concentrates his efforts on a species that no one suspects of conscious thought: rats. This earns him the mocking title of "rat scientist," given to him by others in the field. Though he considers the psychoanalytic idea of uncovering and working through hidden conflicts humbug, he basically follows a similar pattern. The premise is ultimately the same: The individual doesn't know why they do what they do. Like a puppet, they are controlled by invisible strings—the difference between Freud and Watson comes down to the type of strings: where the one posits dark libidinous energies at work, the other sees predictable learning schemata.

Watson wants to show that speculating about the unconscious is unnecessary for explaining and changing human behavior. To this end he designs a study that even for the time is remarkable for its disregard of ethical standards. He wants to prove that fright and phobias aren't based on sexual fantasies of the kind that Freud ascribed to small children, but rather are acquired, according to the simple laws of conditioning. Fear is learned. Which means, logically speaking, that it can also be *unlearned*.

Together with Raymond, Watson comes up with an audacious plan: he wants to teach an infant how to fear. The task falls on nine-month-old Albert B., who recently started going to the daycare run by the university. His single mother works long shifts as a nurse, which gives the scientists enough time to win the child's trust—while his mother likely has no inkling of the exact nature of the "pedagogical" experiment that the researcher couple are planning.

First Watson and Rayner present the cheery little boy with a rat from their laboratory. The boy approaches the animal without hesitation and allows it to be placed on his lap. After repeating the encounter a few times, Watson positions a steel bar right behind Albert's back and strikes it with a hammer as soon as the child sees the rodent. As one would expect, the earsplitting noise frightens the boy, and he starts to cry. After another few repetitions with the fear-triggering stimulus, the tool is put away and the boy is confronted with all manner of objects, like a stuffed animal, a fur coat, or a cotton ball. Voilà: Anything fluffy only arouses his aversion; the boy turns away in tears. His fear is "generalized." And if the experiment leaders try to show him the rat itself, he's so frightened he almost falls off the table on which the experiment is being conducted.

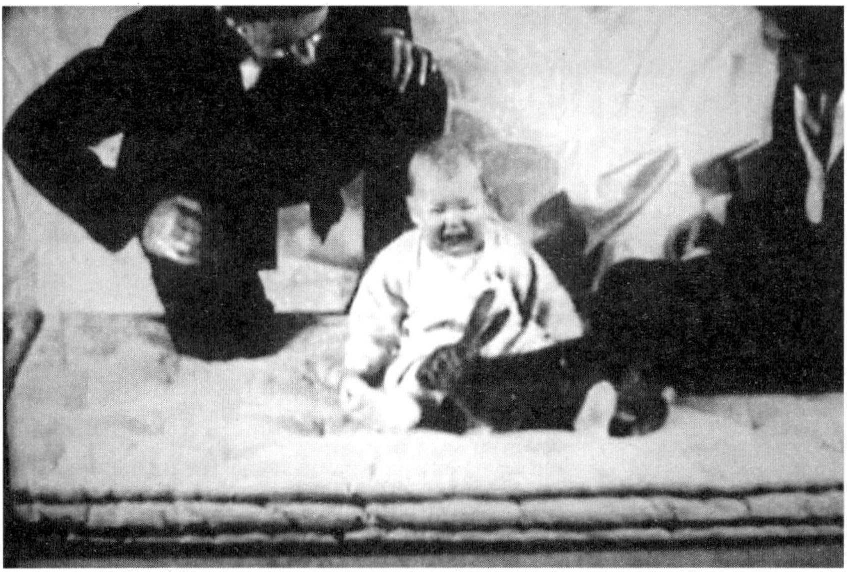

Who's afraid of the big bad bunny: Watson and Raynor in 1920 conducting their "experiment" with little Albert.

Not only is the experiment with little Albert highly dubious from an ethical standpoint; it's also methodologically weak. Watson does the very thing for which he criticizes the psychoanalysts: he bases his argument on a single case. What's more, the original account of the study published in 1920 gives only vague information about what exactly happened with Albert, how severe his fear was and to what extent he transferred it to other objects. Over two separate sessions with a few days in between, Watson seems to have struck a bar with a hammer a total of seven times while the boy saw the rat in front of him or had it on his lap. A month later, however, the child permitted physical contact with the animal without showing any great discomfort. Watson credits his experiment with proving that phobias are learned and by no means triggered by inner conflicts, as Freud believes. But Albert's spooked reaction demonstrates neither that *all* fears are acquired, nor that the boy's reaction will persist.

When delivering lectures, Watson frequently shows a film he made of the experiment, which contributes to its widespread renown. No other study since has been cited more in psychology textbooks.

Little Albert was probably William Barger, born in 1919, the illegitimate child of an employee at the university's hospital.[10] A few weeks after the experiment, before it occurred to Watson to reverse the negative conditioning he had imposed, both mother and son moved to another city. Barger died in 2007 at the age of eighty-seven. Whether he still felt a sense of unease around furry animals as an adult is unknown.

. . .

Meanwhile Watson is all too careless about how he carries out his liaison with his student and assistant. Just a few months earlier, the university's president, Frank Goodnow, had generously raised Watson's salary, hoping to make the celebrated researcher unreceptive to offers from the competition. Watson thinks he's untouchable and fawns over Rosalie on campus, writing her soulful love letters almost daily. "Every cell I have is yours, individually and collectively," he writes in one of them. "Could you kiss me for two hours right now without ever growing weary? I want you all 24 of the hours and then I'd quarrel with the universe because the days are not longer. Let's go to the North Pole where the days and nights are 6 mo. each."[11]

But Watson misjudges several factors. First and foremost, he fails to take into account his wronged wife's desire for revenge. After an earlier dalliance, Mary Watson has become deeply mistrustful of her husband and only keeps up a show of comity out of a sense of duty toward her children. In the summer of 1920 it's an open secret that Watson is having an affair—and what's more, that it's with a woman who works for him. At this time the Watsons are regular guests at the Rayner family home, which may reflect a somewhat naïve attempt on Watson's part to hide his love of Rosalie with a show of demonstrative nonchalance.

On one of these evenings at the Rayners', Mary sneaks into Rosalie's room on a pretense. In a desk drawer she finds a stack of her husband's love letters and takes them. In the large, very public divorce proceedings that Mary initiates the following November, these letters will be of great value to her. Mary's lawyer leaks them to the press, which makes hay out of the professor's scandalous relationship with a student half his age. In prudish East Coast society, sex outside of marriage is a severe breach of taboo, and the offense is twice as grave when it's a teacher getting involved with a student under his tutelage. Some newspapers print Watson's avowals of affection in full, like a serialized novel. The ensuing scandal feeds on a mix of vicarious embarrassment and voyeurism.

Watson's second mistake concerns Rosalie's family. The Rayners aren't just anybody; in fact, they're one of the wealthiest families in Maryland. Rosalie's grandfather, William Solomon Rayner, made a fortune in railroads, shipbuilding, and mining; her uncle Isidor even served as a Senator in Washington. This same Isidor Rayner had recently given a generous $10,000 donation to Johns Hopkins University. The university administration certainly doesn't want to spoil its relationship with such a munificent donor. As far as the family is concerned, the fact that Rosalie is ardently in love with Watson, and therefore hardly an innocent victim, mustn't come to light. There's only one solution: Watson must be punished for his actions, and the punishment must be so severe that not a trace of suspicion can fall on the daughter from the respectable home.

Finally, Watson overestimates the protection afforded to him by his venerable position. As it turns out, his scientific reputation doesn't keep the dean from making an example of him. To be sure, Goodnow and many of Watson's colleagues are very much upset about the star scholar's tragic fall. Adolf Meyer, for one, a Swiss-born psychiatrist, voices his dismay that Watson would "ruin his career for a girl." But faced with the choice between the potential loss of prestige and money on the one hand and breaking with one of its luminaries on the other, the university doesn't hesitate: Watson's got to go!

Goodnow, in a conversation in October 1920, warns Watson that he is facing termination. In a final act of defiance Watson scribbles a resignation letter on a sheet of paper in his boss's office and storms out. Just like that, his relationship with Rayner puts an end to a career more than twenty painstaking years in the making. Watson may at first have hoped that he could continue his research at another college, but after all the coverage in the press this is out of the question. No academic institution of any stature can afford to have such a skirt-chaser on its faculty. Thus the once-celebrated Watson has no choice but to go looking for a new job.

He soon finds work in an industry for which he has long had a special affinity: advertising. For $25,000 a year—more than four times his professor's salary—he takes a job at J. Walter Thompson Advertising Company, one of the biggest ad agencies in the US. The new position isn't just a step up financially, it's also an excellent platform for self-promotion. Ironically enough, it's only after his career change that Watson becomes a celebrated behavioral expert; his most successful books are all published after his departure from active research. In hundreds of articles, interviews, and lectures, Watson promotes his view of human nature.

In an age that is drunk on visions of progress, many believe it is the ultimate goal of science to exercise deliberate and fundamental control over human behavior. With great fervor Watson writes: "Give me a dozen healthy infants, well-formed, and my own specified world to bring them up in and I'll guarantee to take any one at random and train him to become any type of specialist I might select—doctor, lawyer, artist, merchant-chief and, yes, even beggar-man and thief, regardless of his talents, penchants, tendencies, abilities, vocations, and race of his ancestors."[12]

This passage is often cited as proof of Watson's fantasies of omnipotence. But more than anything his words give expression to an unbridled desire for freedom: according to Watson, the human individual is not bound by background or destiny; we can do anything and make anything of ourselves if the conditions are right.

In the midst of profound social unrest, Americans dream of making the ups and downs of the individual's life predictable and controllable. A sober assessment of the behaviorists' results shows that they fall far short of these high-flying hopes, but that doesn't bother Watson and his followers much. The mere expectation that behavioral science will revolutionize the world leads it to become the dominant trend in psychology over the course of the 1920s—with Watson its most prominent exponent.

SECRETS OF A SOUL

Martin Fellmann is no looker. Short and pudgy, with a weak chin and goggle-eyes, he and his conspicuously attractive young wife Martha live in an elegant townhouse on a no less elegant street. To cinemagoers it's immediately clear: if a guy's got money, he doesn't need to be Romeo. Fellmann has made it. His job as a chemist in a futuristic-looking laboratory clearly brings in enough dough. Seeing the man ambling cheerfully into the bathroom in the morning, you would scarcely believe that a dark secret slumbers within him. Not even he himself suspects it.

Fellmann is shaving when his wife, seated at the makeup table in the bedroom, calls over to him. Could he please come here and cut off the pesky curl that keeps tickling her? He ambles over, sets the blade against her immaculately white neck—and is suddenly interrupted by loud screams. Next door, the neighbors' maid is standing at the window, gesturing wildly: "Help, help!" Her mistress has been killed—murdered with a razor! Cut back to the bedroom, where wouldn't you know it, Fellmann's blade has left a bloody scrape on his wife's neck. The wound is dressed, and as the ambulance arrives next door, Fellmann heads off to work, brooding darkly.

A little while later, his wife calls to tell him that cousin Erich is coming to visit that evening. Erich, who lived for a long time in India, has sent gifts ahead of him: a statue of an Oriental fertility goddess and a beautifully ornate dagger. Again Fellmann feels uneasy. The mere thought of blades frightens him; he dreads even reaching for the butter knife. He can't touch it, he won't touch it; he has no idea what's the matter with him. What a nuisance this knife phobia is!

Fellmann's fear grows with each new day. At dinner with his wife and Erich he can't bring himself to touch the silverware. Filled with shame, he runs off and wanders the streets, finally stepping inside a café. A patron at another table notices him. When Fellmann leaves the café, he forgets his umbrella. The stranger follows him; they get to talking.

Cut to an expressionistic dream sequence. Fellmann steps out of his house and finds cousin Erich sitting in a tree and threatening him with a gun. Then Fellmann floats up into the air like a balloon; he sees locomotives speeding through tunnels and finds himself suddenly among houses and towers jutting high up into the sky. He hurries up one of them, in which his wife's head and the heads of other women are ringing like bells, swinging wildly to and fro. Then he spies his dear Martha with her cousin in a rowboat. She pulls a child out of the water and solemnly hands it to Erich.

What a stroke of luck that Dr. Orth, the stranger from the café, is a psychoanalyst! At his office, he has Fellmann free associate. Soon enough, the source of his fear is found: a memory from his childhood, when the three of them—Erich, Martha, and Martin—played together in harmony. Back then Fellmann looked on as Martha gave Erich a doll, just like the baby in his dream. At the time he was beside himself with jealousy, but after all these years he had forgotten it completely.

The parallel to the boat scene is obvious, as is the solution to the phobia: behind Fellmann's fear of knives is a childhood trauma of unrequited love and the unacknowledged desire to revenge himself on his beloved wife. As soon as he realizes this, he is cured. The movie ends with Fellmann fishing in an idyllic natural setting. He hurries home with a bounteous catch, and there Martha receives him with an infant in her arms. Filled with fatherly pride, Fellmann lifts the rosy-cheeked boy into the air—and all is well.

Geheimnisse einer Seele—Secrets of a Soul—premieres on March 26, 1926 at the Gloria Palast in Berlin. UFA gives the film the rating "*volksbildend*"—edifying. The first feature film about psychoanalysis lays out the premise of this therapeutic method and explains how it works. Talking frees you from childhood traumas, the repression of which causes fears and phobias.

A critic for the *Lichtbild-Bühne* praises the film for "painlessly instructing the viewer in the most necessary points in modern education." The review ends with the words: "This film touches on the great question of our time. The hearty applause proved it. It will likely find a global audience." The *Berliner Tageblatt*, on the other hand, opines "that the analysis might heal the patient, but doesn't convince the viewer." It does in fact seem contrived, the idea that a touch of childhood jealousy would decades later give rise to the wish to murder one's own wife—and consequently to a phobia of knives. But so it goes in the wonderful world of psychoanalysis: a trivial experience or a fleeting fantasy are enough to saddle the psyche with a heavy burden. Nothing is too incidental; anything can pave the way for suffering.

The combination of X-ray vision, drama, and the expectation of a cure make psychoanalysis a beloved subject for novels and films in these years. In a move that recalls the old device of the bump on the head that's enough to wipe out a person's entire memory, the analyst in the movie reveals the repressed childhood memory that casts a shadow over everything, only to render it harmless in the very next instant. This is one of the many unwittingly comical clichés to be found in this film. But many cinemagoers take it at face value, as a realistic portrayal of what analysts are capable of.

Freud himself thought little of the flick, and of cinema in general. He was skeptical of the "new medium." The makers of *Secrets of a Soul* received expert advice not from Freud, but from Karl Abraham and Hanns Sachs. Their participation renders a service to psychoanalysis as it moves toward public recognition. In those interwar years the divide between the academic science called psychology and this publicly-propagated cliché of mind doctoring grows ever greater. According to the latter, dark wishes and taboos are lurking everywhere, and with them revealing slips of the tongue and dreams that long for interpretation. The image of the individual as someone who doesn't know his own mind becomes commonplace. No wonder that ever more people in these years believe that they have to work through their true desires and memories before they can be happy.

EMOTIONAL CONJUNCTURE

In his autobiography, the writer Elias Canetti describes the atmosphere in Vienna in 1924: "There was hardly a conversation in which Freud's name did not pop up," Canetti recalls. "Freudian slips [. . .] had become a sort of party game. In order to use this buzz word frequently, slips were produced in spates. During any conversation, no matter how animated and spontaneous it may have sounded, there arrived a moment when you could read on your interlocutor's lips: here comes a Freudian slip. And it was already out; you could already start analyzing it, uncovering the processes that had led to it, and thereby you could talk about your private life in tireless detail, without seeming overbearingly intimate, for you were involved in shedding light on a process of universal, even scientific, interest."[13] And indeed, "talking about your private life" will become a favorite activity for enlightened city dwellers in Europe and the US during the "Roaring Twenties."

The pace of economic recovery accelerates around the middle of the decade, even in Germany, which is groaning under the burden of the reparations imposed by the Versailles treaty and still recovering from the hyperinflation of 1923. After the introduction of the Rentenmark, living conditions quickly improve. The availability of radios and the invention of the rotary press for newspaper printing lead to an unprecedented boom in the media and advertising industries. To be up to date, have your finger on the pulse, follow the latest fashion—for most residents of Berlin, Vienna, Paris, or New York, being *au courant* takes on special importance. This goes hand in hand with a rapid revaluation of the self: rather than subordinate one's self to others and quietly bear one's fate, now it becomes important to showcase one's personal talents and strengths; the ego reigns. Self-reflection is no longer the privilege of a wealthy elite. Now everyone wants to be somebody, and to show it, too. "Self-rationalization" is the word of the day; economic principles are applied to all aspects of life, the personal sphere included.

Americans in particular are obsessed with efficiency and self-improvement. If you want to make something of yourself, you have to be better than the rest—faster, stronger, more clever. You have to use your potential and never get discouraged. Concepts like cost and benefit, outlay and yield are applied to the framing of individual lives: what will help me get ahead? How much should I invest? Which of my potential strengths can I develop? Two decades earlier, hardly anyone would have asked themselves questions such as these.

The Australian psychologist and sociologist Elton Mayo, originally a follower of Jung's, turns to the field of industrial psychology after moving to the US. In 1927 the Western Electric Company in Chicago hires him to lend his scientific expertise to a study. The company, which produces parts for telephones, is known for paying above-average wages and for the good working conditions in its factories. At a factory complex in Cicero, Illinois known as the Hawthorne Works, Mayo's team is asked to look for other factors that might help boost productivity.

Is there too little daylight in the workshops? Do the workers need longer or more frequent breaks? Or shorter shifts? Does it help to divide people into teams? Over several months, the psychologists keep making one adjustment after another—and finally conclude that whenever they tweaked conditions slightly, like making a five-minute break a ten-minute break or serving the workers a sandwich for breakfast "on the house," output increased. If on the other hand a given measure was discontinued and the old order reintroduced, this too seemed to have a positive effect on productivity. The workers were grateful for just about every change, no matter what kind.

Next Mayo conducts interviews with managers and assembly-line workers. The explanation for the rise in productivity seems to lie in workers simply being given the opportunity to talk about their grievances and feeling that they are being taken seriously. From these data Mayo draws a striking conclusion: the most important factor isn't the objective working conditions, so long as these don't fall below a minimum standard. Far more significant is the attention that management pays to workers, its interest in and openness to their needs and concerns—and, by the same token, their subjective impression that they are valued. What counts, in other words, is the "human touch"![14]

Up to that point, feelings were psychology's blind spot, especially since it went against the behaviorist ideas then dominant in the US to attach great significance to subjective states. The best way to deal with feelings—so the thinking went—was to ignore them and replace them with rational arguments. Emotions should be banished to make room for reason, planning, and optimization. Mayo's discovery lights a fire: feelings, personal satisfaction, and subjective well-being increasingly become crucial markers of success in life. The goal is to feel needed; good social relationships, a sense of connection, and respect are of primary importance.

This view is shared by an early confidant of Freud's who threatens to split the psychoanalytic camp even further. In 1924, Otto Rank, who for years has taken the minutes for the Vienna Psychoanalytic Society, publishes a book that instantly draws the ire of the Freudians: *The Trauma of Birth*.[15] In the book he advances the theory that every person bears within them a trauma—the experience of being forced out from the warmth of the mother's body into the cold of existence. Freud receives it graciously at first, viewing it as a kind of biological foundation for the

Oedipus complex. What could be more present in the human psyche, as much for the existentially abandoned child as for the grown man, than the desire to return to the mother's womb, even if it's only symbolically, through the act of coitus? Seen in this light, the wishful fantasy of incest forbidden by the father and the moral conscience he represents loses its far-fetched character.

Rank draws important conclusions from his version of the psyche's fundamental conflict. In a book published shortly after the birth trauma book,[16] Rank and his co-author, Sándor Ferenczi, introduce the concept of an "active therapy." As we recall, Freud believed that the therapist must remain distant so that the process of transference and counter-transference doesn't get in the way of the patient's insight. Ferenczi and Rank, however, favor an engaged attitude, which is receptive to the patient's hurts, desires, and needs.

From this point forward the two psychoanalytic schools will stand opposed to one another, with "free-floating attention" as the guiding concept on the one side and "corrective emotional experience" on the other. The first characterizes Freud's ideal of the restrained observer, who lets the client do the talking and only offers occasional interpretations. The latter refers to the idea of the therapist as an empathetically receptive and reciprocating interlocutor. This is the seed of an imperative, still present today, for therapists to be engaged and encouraging. The distant stance of the analyst must be replaced with honesty and trust, say Rank and Ferenczi. It is a demand that not all therapists can or want to meet.

. . .

The early 1920s are a time that sees the first significant splitting of psychotherapy into various branches. Three days in Baden-Baden in the spring of 1926 offer a chance at rapprochement, a thaw between the enemy camps. It almost seems as though treating patients will take precedence over ideological arguments and disputes about the distribution of economic benefits. But the hope doesn't last for long.

In April 1926 the spa town on the northern edge of the Black Forest is host to the first congress of the General Medical Society for Psychotherapy. There psychoanalysts are just one faction among many. Eighteen participants from the ranks of the International Psychoanalytical Association, among them the director of the Berlin Institute, Ernst Simmel, as well as Karl Landauer, Karen Horney, and Felix Boehm, are met by an equally large contingent of Alfred Adler's individual psychologists. There are also practitioners of hypnotherapy, the method out of which psychoanalysis developed; pedagogical therapists and will therapists; so-called psychagogues; and representatives of the more biologically-oriented field of psychiatry. The gathering takes place on the initiative of the Munich doctor Wladimir Eliasberg. He wants to compare notes with representatives of all the major schools in order to search for possible common ground and together cultivate the growing field of psychotherapy.

But the three major luminaries of the discipline—Freud, Adler, and Jung—give the conference a pass. Simmel confidently asserts that "The fundamental form of training for any future psychotherapy is Freudian psychoanalysis." Whispers of disbelief fill the hall. Now Simmel doubles down: "Every doctor, no matter which specialty he devotes himself to, should undergo a thorough psychoanalytic training." Every doctor? Even, say, a surgeon or a hematologist? This year's congress and the ones that follow revolve primarily around internecine politics: participants discuss questions of training, quality control, and billing psychotherapy as an insurance benefit. Everyone is intent on securing as big a piece of the pie as possible for their own particular club.

One participant at the fifth psychotherapy congress in Dresden in 1930 notes the presence of a "growing feeling of shared belonging [. . .] we've become like one big family."[17] This assessment might however reflect naïve wishful thinking more than reality. Why are the representatives of the major schools unable to establish an overarching discipline of psychotherapy? Would it not be in everyone's best interest to bring together the most effective approaches? Two factors work against this. The first is the "fickle nature of the object": mental illnesses and their treatment are still too undefined, the knowledge about them still too rudimentary; to do without blanket claims and dogmatic theoretical assertions would mean giving up a baseline sense of order and control.

And secondly: who would benefit if everyone were tugging on the same thread? To establish one's own approach, one has to radiate competence—and this works particularly well if one casts doubt on the competence of others. One's own brand becomes all the more attractive the more ineffectual the others appear. The logic of supply and demand dictates that one should praise one's own mode of psychotherapy and cast aspersions on others'.

PETER AND THE HARE

The first behavioral therapy session in history takes place at Columbia University in late 1923. It is led by Mary Cover Jones, a college friend of Rosalie Rayner's, who is now Mrs. Watson. The two women met at Vassar College in Poughkeepsie, north of New York City. When Rosalie moves to Manhattan, Mary follows a short time later. She attends Watson's lectures at the New School for Social Research, where each week he presents his psychological theory to a wider public. Cover is among those fascinated by the science of behavioral control that Watson paints in the most dazzling tones.

In the classic experiment featuring little Albert, a boy was trained to fear a rodent and then transferred this fear to all manner of fluffy things. Such generalized emotional reactions could explain why in many cases the original trigger is not always apparent. But Cover asks herself a different question: what is the practical value of conditioning? Following the principle that links a given stimulus to a given reaction, can one also achieve the opposite effect and cure an existing phobia? If it were possible to associate the object of a phobia with a positive stimulus, would this succeed in dispelling the fear? Cover is the first to make the attempt at using conditioning for therapeutic ends.

A boy named Peter becomes something like the counterpart to little Albert. He is two years and ten months old when the experiment begins at Teachers College at Columbia University. How exactly Cover becomes acquainted with the boy is unclear. In any case the child seems suitable, since he displays a great aversion to furry animals. Maybe he once had an unpleasant encounter with a cat or a dog; maybe he's just generally very sensitive. As described in Cover's report, Peter's mother seems insecure and overwhelmed. She is plagued by various anxieties;

when her son is playing outside, she grows upset and calls him in with the words: "Come in Peter, some one wants to steal you."

At this time psychologists are still quite careless in the application of their methods. No one checks to make sure that Peter is healthy or to see if he suffers from any other disorders; no one inquires into his family history or tries to rule out other possible influences that might have led to the boy's fearfulness. All anyone knows for certain is that if someone puts a rabbit cage a few feet away from him, he gets upset and starts to cry.

The deconditioning begins on December 4, 1923 and ends in March of the following year, though during that time a bout of scarlet fever and subsequent quarantine keep Peter away for two months. Cover puts the child in a high chair and gives him what he likes most: candy. While Peter eagerly devours the sweets, he casts occasional glances at the rabbit, as if to say: stay away from me, you! Then, little by little, the experimenter slowly moves the animal closer to him. When it's barely three feet away from Peter, quietly nibbling and minding its own business, the boy breaks into tears.

Cover tries several desensitizing techniques at once, so it remains unclear which one in particular is responsible for the improvement. Could learning by example have helped? Peter is especially fond of "Dr. S.," a student assistant. Sometimes he even calls him "papa." Peter is also placed in the company of other children who display no shyness around rabbits. In her report, Cover writes: "Laurel, Mary, Arthur, Peter playing together in the laboratory. Experimenter put rabbit on floor. Arthur said: 'Peter doesn't cry when he sees the rabbit come out.' Peter, 'No.' He was a little concerned as to whether or not the rabbit would eat his kiddie car. Laurel and Mary stroked the rabbit and chattered away excitedly. Peter walked over, touched the rabbit on the back, exulting, 'I touched him on the end.'"

Peter's fear disappears. True, there are setbacks, for example when the boy and a nurse are jumped on by a dog on their way to Teachers College. Immediately after this incident Peter wants nothing to do with the rabbit and again reacts with discomfort at the sight of it. Meanwhile, another boy, Lawrence, likes rabbits and pets them without a second thought. Whether it's the sweets that ease Peter's anxiety or the example of others is hard to say. Maybe not having to sit in the high chair also helps, since he can move away whenever things get to be too much for him.

According to the behavioral theory of learning, once a fear has been acquired, there are only two ways in which a person can get rid of it. The first is to let it fade with time. This phenomenon, called "extinction," is akin to a gradual forgetting and primarily occurs when the fear remains without consequence. Without a persistent threat or painful consequences there is no negative reinforcement of the behavior. The second option is to link the fear-inducing stimulus to another stimulus or to a reward. Through this process of counterconditioning, the new association switches the fear off, as it were.

Serious phobias rarely fade on their own, however. They even have a peculiar way of taking on an independent life and growing more intense: soon the person with the phobia comes to fear not so much the object of their fear as their own reaction to it—they panic at the prospect of panicking.

The article about Peter that will earn Mary Cover Jones renown and turn her into the "mother of behavioral therapy" leaves many questions unanswered. Who was this Peter? How did Cover find him? What exactly brought about his fear of rabbits? Watson, who serves as Cover's thesis advisor, regards a single case study as insufficient. Thus before attempting individual therapy, Cover studied a group of seventy children in total and tested their reactions to various fear-inducing stimuli. What do the little ones between the ages of three months and seven years do when you step out of the room or leave them in the dark; when they hear a loud sound; or when you confront them with frogs, a snake, or a rabbit? For those who showed fear, Cover proceeded to a second step and tested various countermeasures like distraction, habituation, talking to the child, and even subjecting them to the teasing of their peers. All in vain. Only two things proved helpful: the example of other children who weren't afraid and counterconditioning through rewards.

The same Peter who appears in the individual study appears as case number 30 in Cover's group study, in which he responds well to the "treatment." Cover writes: "Peter. Age 2 years, 10 months. March 10, 10:15 A.M. Peter sitting in high chair, eating candy. Experimenter entered room with a rabbit in an open meshed wire cage. The rabbit was placed on the table 4 feet from Peter who immediately began to cry, insisting that the rabbit be taken away. Continued crying until the rabbit was put down 20 feet away. He then started again on the candy, but continued to fuss, 'I want you to put Bunny outside.' After three minutes he once more burst into tears; the rabbit was removed."[18]

A month and a half later the boy appears transformed: "Peter standing in high chair, looking out of the window. He inquired, 'Where is the rabbit?' The rabbit was put down on the chair at Peter's feet. Peter patted him, tried to pick him up, but finding the rabbit too heavy asked the experimenter to help in lifting him to the window sill, where he played with him for several minutes."

Cover's article appears in 1924 in the *Journal of Experimental Psychology*, which Watson edits.[19] That same year he publishes a book that some praise as a milestone of behavioral science, while others see it as a slipshod work full of prejudices and exaggerations. By the middle of the decade, *Behaviorism* has become a bestseller. Watson can thank the obsession with efficiency and control that characterizes his age.

If everything is learned, then it's all the more important to apply scientific methods even when dealing with the youngest of children. In 1928 Watson and his wife Rosalie publish a book of parenting advice, *Psychological Care of Infant and Child.* Parents and educators eat the book up, but many of the tips it contains are dubious. Watson singles out the practice of "coddling" children and giving them emotional support, regarding it as a form of poison with which mothers "destroy the child from the moment it is born."[20] Following his advice, even infants and toddlers should be treated like little adults.

Watson and his wife recommend: "Never hug and kiss [your children], never let them sit on your lap. If you must, kiss them once on the forehead when they say good night. Shake hands with them in the morning. Give them a pat on the head if they have made an extraordinarily good job of a difficult task. Try it out. In a week's time you will find how easy it is to be perfectly objective with your child and at the same time kindly."[21] Only in this way can one avoid all the "weaknesses, reserves, fears, cautions, and inferiorities," in short, the "destructive" and "devastating" effects of "mother love."[22]

Watson's eldest son William suffered all his life from his father's emotional frigidity. In an interview he reported that Watson hugged him and his brother James only once—when their mother died of pneumonia in 1935. Only then did he see his father cry. When John B. Watson is seventy-six, William commits suicide. In fact, three of Watson's four children will attempt suicide during their lives, though only William will die from the attempt. Callous old man that he now is, Watson doesn't speak of it. In an unpublished manuscript with the title "Why I Don't Commit Suicide," he explains: "The best, sanest and quickest acting thought I can give to one brooding over taking his own life is this: Run away for a week, a month or a year. There is no psychological medicine so potent in this wide world as a *new environment*."[23]

As he grows older Watson becomes increasingly isolated. He lives in the country home he built for himself in Connecticut, together with his beloved dogs and horses, and takes to drinking. Watson is nearing eighty when one evening his secretary finds him in front of the fireplace, consigning page after page of his correspondence and manuscripts to the flames. The secretary tries to convince him to leave the documents to posterity, but Watson dismisses the idea: "When you're dead, you're all dead."[24] He dies at his farm on September 25, 1958.

. . .

His student Mary Cover Jones will go on to contribute several important insights into the development of psychological resilience in children. First however she meets an elegant fellow student at Columbia University named Henry Jones and falls in love with him. When, in 1927, Jones receives an offer to establish an Institute for Child Welfare at the University of California, Berkeley, the two of them leap at the opportunity and move with their two young children to the West Coast, across the bay from San Francisco.

Mary Cover Jones continues her work in California, working above all with children from disadvantaged backgrounds. She contributes to three longitudinal studies, including the "Oakland Growth Study," which stretches over sixty years and provides valuable data for resiliency research. The study is the first to show that children's social skills—the ability to interact with others, ask for help, and build stable relationships—are often crucial to the development of mental and emotional resilience. Children who managed to cultivate a good relationship with a mentor or seek support from some other source were more rarely unsettled by violence and negative life experiences than others of their age cohort who tried to make do on their own. Watson's own children seemingly lacked such a positive role model in their lives.

Cover Jones dies in the summer of 1987 in Santa Barbara. Shortly before her death she says to her sister: "I am still learning about what is important in life."[25]

THE BEGINNING OF THE END

On Tuesday, October 29, 1929, sixteen million stocks change hands at the New York Stock Exchange on Wall Street. What sounds like brisk business is in reality a sell-off. The industrial firms that are listed on the Stock Exchange lose around $14 billion in value on this "Black Tuesday." This follows a twelve-percent drop in stock prices the day before, meaning that the total value of the most important stock exchange in the world has shrunk by almost a quarter within forty-eight hours. The result is panic.

Millions of Americans had invested in stock in the hopes of steadily-rising prices, many on credit. A mad rally had pushed the Dow Jones to a peak of almost four hundred points on September 3, 1929; now a dramatic drop in prices ensues. It would still have been possible to recover from the two jet-black October days if they hadn't completely ruined the confidence of many investors. Some firms can't find buyers for their shares, which drives prices down even lower. By the summer of 1932 the Dow has fallen below fifty points, an eighth of its value three years before. It will take a quarter century for stock prices to return to their pre-crash level.

Not only does the crash bankrupt thousands of publicly-shared companies, it also ruins many private individuals as well. Credit dries up, workers lose their jobs, families are made homeless because they can't pay the interest on their loans. The Wall Street crash is the beginning of an economic crisis, the "Great Depression," that lasts for years. When US banks ask for repayment of the billions they've lent to Europe, the continent's economies start to teeter, too, and global trade collapses. By mid-1932, almost every other German is out of work. Hunger, misery, and crime are rampant.

For those trapped in poverty, what matters is sheer survival. People are afraid of starving, getting caught stealing or trading on the black market, or becoming sick and losing their ability to work and, with it, their last glimmer of hope. The immiseration of large portions of the population leads to political radicalization. The moderates increasingly go quiet, propaganda and disinformation stoke tensions, the atmosphere is charged. Germany in the early 1930s is like a powder keg—only the fuse is a lot shorter that most people suspect.

In August 1930 Sigmund Freud is awarded the Goethe Prize by the city of Frankfurt. The award, which is endowed with a prize of 10,000 Reichsmarks, honors outstanding public figures. When the prize was first awarded in 1927, the choice fell on the poet Stefan George; the following year it went to physician and philosopher Albert Schweitzer. After being nominated in 1929 (and passed over in favor of the now-forgotten cultural philosopher Leopold Ziegler), the time seems ripe for Freud to receive the honor. The board of trustees chooses Freud in a vote of seven to five. Two members remain steadfastly opposed to the ennoblement of psychoanalysis and refuse to attend the award ceremony. In his laudatory speech, Frankfurt Mayor Ludwig Landmann praises Freud as the "master of demystification, who, as it were, divests the depths of the primordial world of the psyche of their magical allure."[26]

For health reasons, the guest of honor doesn't travel to Frankfurt. His daughter Anna reads his acceptance speech. The most important advocate for Freud was Alfred Döblin, himself a psychiatrist and a writer who works for a time at the Berlin Polyclinic and causes a furor with his 1929 novel *Berlin Alexanderplatz*. Once again it is not scientists who celebrate Freud, but writers and artists. Newly-minted Nobel laureate Thomas Mann declares that one is "lit up by Freud's ideas as if by a bundle of X-rays."[27] The myth of the analyst with the X-ray gaze lives on.

Even before the Nazis seize power in Germany, the first wave of psychoanalysts leaves the country: important figures like Franz Alexander,

Sándor Radó, Karen Horney, and Hanns Sachs leave Berlin to build a life on the other side of the Atlantic. That antisemitism and fascism are both gaining strength in Europe plays a role in their decisions, but many analysts simply see the New World as the new El Dorado for psychology. The quintessentially American quest for self-improvement provides the right environment, allowing the ideas of Freud, Jung, Adler, and others to spread like wildfire throughout the country; for many, depth psychology has by this point taken on a role as a kind of ersatz religion in scientific garb.

With Hitler's appointment as German chancellor on January 30, 1933, the situation comes to a head for those who have stayed home. Those who before now had barely taken the Nazis seriously suddenly find themselves in mortal danger. At first the SA goons set their sights on Communists and other opponents of the regime; the effort to hunt down Jews begins later. Wilhelm Reich flees to Scandinavia, Max Eitingon to Palestine; Adler has been a professor at Columbia University in New York since 1932. Franz Alexander and Karen Horney are starting their own institute in Chicago, where they profit from the large number of Americans who learned the analytic craft in Berlin or Vienna. Hanns Sachs and Otto Rank also move west. Theodor Reik is hired by a businessman to be his personal on-call therapist. Freudo-Marxists like Erich Fromm, meanwhile, find an intellectual home at the New School for Social Research. There is one man, however, who does not follow the exodus: Freud stays put in Vienna.[28] For now at least.

Meanwhile the center of psychoanalysis is shifting to the English-speaking world, with London as the seat of the International Psychoanalytical Association. Although the Nazis castigate Freud's theory as the product of "international Jewry" and burn his writings along with those of Adler, Reich, and others on May 10, 1933, the Psychoanalytical Association proves astonishingly quiescent in adapting to the new regime. Instead of dissolving the German chapter or moving it into exile, the choice is made to comply with the demand for "Aryanization." While almost all Jewish members emigrate from Germany, the non-Jews Felix Boehm and Carl Müller-Braunschweig take over the leadership. The survival of the movement would seem to have top priority, even in Nazi Germany. Meanwhile the head of the

International General Medical Society for Psychotherapy (IAÄGP), a certain Carl Gustav Jung, is holding forth about the difference between the Jewish and the Aryan unconscious. One is decadent, the other "youthful-barbaric." *How* barbaric would soon be evident.

By 1935, Carl Müller-Braunschweig is writing a memorandum to the Prussian Culture Ministry and sketching the prospect of a "psychoanalysis of German coinage," which would take "weaklings," "the instinctually inhibited," "out of touch fantasists," and those "at the mercy of their libidinous impulses," and "[re]integrate them within the newly emphasized bounds of a heroic, reality-minded, constructive conception of life."[29]

One mustn't underestimate the dilemma that the members of the Psychoanalytical Association who remain in Berlin and Vienna find themselves in: should they give up their livelihood or try to adapt? Without seeking to relativize the horrible crimes of the Nazis and their thugs, the record must show that Freud and his entourage make far-reaching concessions to ensure the continued existence of psychoanalysis in Germany and Austria. Do they believe the association will actually be able to continue its work under the Nazis? Or do they hope Hitler's government will soon be gone? Either way, the opposite happens. In 1936 the German Psychoanalytic Society is absorbed into the newly-created German Institute for Psychological Research and Psychotherapy. The institution is led by the physician Matthias Göring, a cousin of Hermann Göring. He dreams of a "German psychiatry."

. . .

The flowering of Soviet psychoanalysis is similarly brief. Soon after Stalin drives his rival Trotsky into exile in 1929, the political purges begin. That same year, psychoanalysis is outlawed in the Soviet Union; it is now considered bourgeois. The age of awakening and of experimentation is over. Little by little the pressure on doctors and intellectuals to swear off the psychology of the unconscious increases. Even worse: many of them simply vanish without a trace. They end up in labor camps, locked away on flimsy charges, tortured or left to die of starvation. Adler's eldest daughter Valentine, who had moved to Moscow full of enthusiasm, is one of them: just like that she is gone; it's as if the earth had swallowed her up. All attempts to locate her come to naught, and the uncertainty weighs on her parents and siblings.

In 1937 Sabina Spielrein's name appears for the last time on the Psychoanalytical Association's list of members. With the start of the Second World War and "Operation Barbarossa," the German invasion of the Soviet Union that begins in June 1941, the final chapter of her tragic life begins.

On November 20, the Wehrmacht takes control of Rostov on Don, but a week later the Red Army successfully drives the Germans back. From their bridgehead in Taganrog, eighty kilometers west of the city, the Germans launch a new offensive in the summer of the following year. In late July 1942, Rostov falls and is occupied by a mountain corps and the SS's Wiking tank division. No sooner is the position secured than the SS begins its "Entjudung." Soldiers scour apartments, basements, and barns, rounding up all the Jewish residents of the city. Neighbors look on helplessly as the fifty-six-year-old Spielrein and her daughters Renate and Eva are driven out of the city. They are among the approximately twenty-seven-thousand people whom the Germans take to a ravine a few kilometers outside the city in August 1942. In Rostov it's known as "the ravine of the snakes."

The sound of machine gun fire drowns out the sound of bodies falling into the ravine. No one hears them die.

4

THE EGO

WEAKNESS MAKES YOU STRONG

By the mid-1920s, a good two decades after his break with Freud, Adler is riding high. His renown exceeds even that of his one-time spiritus rector. And no wonder, since Adler is far more adept than Freud is at using the new channels of mass communication. He gives countless interviews in newspapers, magazines, and on the radio; writes articles, brochures, and books for a popular audience; gives lectures at home and abroad; and on top of that conducts seminars and consultations at universities, academies, and clinics. He is indefatigable, traveling constantly in service of his own mission. Outside of Austria and Germany, Adler's preferred destinations are the Benelux countries, France, and England. In 1926 he sets foot on US soil for the first time—and is spellbound.

The "American way of life," this very un-Austrian mix of optimism, the pursuit of happiness, and prudishness, fascinates him. Aren't the Americans collective proof of the idea that success comes from the protest against personal limits and the triumph over the self? That the fit individual will separate himself from the masses by working, with burning ambition, on his own transformation? The "from dishwasher to millionaire" mentality is nowhere so garishly celebrated as in New York, the city of skyscrapers and ostentatious luxury. Here, Alfred Adler, son of a modest grain dealer from the outer districts of Vienna, feels like he's in a dream.

At the same time he recognizes what an opportunity the New World holds for him. Millions of US citizens thirst for psychological know-how to help them master life's challenges. How do I develop my talents? How do I cultivate advantageous relationships without being exploited? What's the right way to raise my children? How do I find happiness and fulfillment in life? To all these questions and more, Adler provides answers. In his 1927 bestseller *Understanding Human Nature* he writes that "the communal life of mankind is accompanied by constant self-measurement which gives rise to the desire for superiority, and the hope of success in competition."[1] This speaks directly to the hearts of the advancement-obsessed Americans. "Adler's temperament, his vitality, and the direction of his thinking," writes his biographer Alexander Kluy, "reflect these years in the socio-cultural development of the United States."[2]

Adler is the master of multiuse. He often recycles portions of older texts; he takes notes and sketchy thoughts and pieces them together

The self-made psychologist: Alfred Adler at the zenith of his international renown.

into drafts that others revise or translate for him. In this way he quickly churns out enough child-rearing guides, self-help books, and reflections on the philosophy of life to fill an entire bookshelf. All the while, Adler quickly adapts his arguments to the spirit of the times. If at first the individual's orientation toward his fellow man played a subordinate role in the school of individual psychology, over the course of the 1920s Adler comes to imbue it with ever greater significance, finally declaring the "social feeling" (*Gemeinschaftsgefühl*) the highest principle guiding the healthy psyche. According to this view, the individual acquires his sense of self-worth not merely by striving for power and greatness, as Adler first asserts, but also by placing himself in the service of a common cause. The neurotic lacks the ability to commit himself to a collective idea that transcends himself; he must learn to think and feel within larger, communal bounds.

While in Europe the right and left are hopelessly at odds with one another, American society is shaped by an ideal that bridges many divides. Every dollar bill carries the motto "E pluribus unum," or, roughly translated, "united in diversity." True, the US has divides that are no less sharp—between rich and poor, puritans and free spirits, bigots and technocrats. "The pursuit of happiness" is a right enshrined in the country's founding document, the Declaration of Independence. As the old societies across the Atlantic fall apart, the universal promise of happiness brings Americans together.

In his books, Adler explains how to turn weaknesses into strengths and gives tips on how to deal with feelings, children, one's spouse, and psychological burdens of every variety. His ideal is encouragement. Overcoming weakness, compensating for shortcomings—these actions form the blueprint for the solution to any problem. Franklin D. Roosevelt offers up a living example: since contracting polio at age thirty-nine, the popular politician uses a wheelchair and can only walk on his own for short distances at a time. Despite this handicap Roosevelt first becomes the governor of New York and then, on November 8, 1932, wins the presidential election in a landslide. Roosevelt will become the only person in US history to win election to the country's highest office four times. If a man with such a handicap can make it so far, it seems clear: compensating for their deficiencies drives people to major achievements.

Unlike Adler, Freud remains wary of the US throughout his life, despite the recognition that his visit to Worcester in 1909 brought him. On Berggasse, to say something is *echt amerikanisch* is another way of saying it's superficial and tasteless. Of all people, Adler, the self-avowed socialist, is a big hit in the New World. But the "striving for perfection"[3] that he preaches simply fits in perfectly with the American way of life. If for Freud the ego is a battlefield of hidden wishes, resistances, and compromises, for Adler it plays a much more active role. "The psyche [. . .] is *an organic formative force*, which independently changes what has been appropriated."[4] Adler borrows this line from his philosophical role model Hans Vaihinger. The neurotic character differs from the healthy one in that it makes absolutes of its manner of thinking and feeling, its own life plan. The neurotic is characterized by "a stronger attachment to fictions, guiding principles, ideals, dogmas. These guiding principles float before the normal person also. But [. . .] he is not so involved in prejudice that when called upon to make a decision he cannot free himself from the abstract and reckon with reality. [. . .] The neurotic, however, [. . .] catches at the straw of his fiction."[5]

According to this view, the source of neurosis is neither suppressed libidinous energies nor an enforced conformity with societal norms. Rather neurosis is a means of escaping the demands placed on the individual by their family, job, or life in general. The neurosis fulfills a function: it frees the individual from the responsibility of fitting into society and contributing to it; and in so doing it narrows the neurotic's intellectual perspective. According to Adler, "one part of the neurotic way of life is to think in unshakeable dichotomies."[6]

He is influenced by the functionalistic thinking of his time and admires the neo-Kantian Vaihinger. In Vaihinger's 1911 book *The Philosophy of "As If,"* the human mind figures as a kind of fiction machine. The individual brings to life an attitude, formed through experiences, that cannot be justified on the basis of logic—the reason being that what counts is not truth but utility. Thus we treat intellectual constructions that are useful to us "as if" they were true—whether they be points of religious dogma, scientific principles, or abstract concepts like space and time. Vaihinger stresses that "the object of the world of ideas as a whole is not the portrayal of reality—this would be an utterly impossible task—but rather to provide us with an *instrument for finding our way about more easily in this world*."[7]

Neurotics, on the other hand, fixate on absurd fictions without really noticing that they are doing so. "Psychical illness is an unconscious flight from the tasks of life (work, love, and community)," says Adler. "What distinguishes the sick person from the healthy person is the greater magnitude of his *life lie* [*Lebenslüge*]."[8] The unwell person can only be helped by strengthening his social feeling. This for Adler means "a kind of feeling of solidarity, a social instinct."[9] Only by orienting oneself toward others can one overcome excessive narcissism, compulsiveness, or melancholy. In so far as this is the case, therapy is an education in cooperation.

Adler formulates this fundamental principle for the first time in 1914 in an article titled "Lebenslüge und Verantwortlichkeit in der Neurose und Psychose" ("Life-lie and Responsibility in Neurosis and Psychosis").[10] In the foreword to the third edition of *Über den nervösen Charakter*, published in 1922, he writes: "The views of our individual psychology require the unconditional dismantling of the striving for power and the development of the social feeling."[11] Solidarity and community are the crucial yardsticks, the "dividing lines between neurosis and normality."[12] For this argument, some consider Adler the social genius of his time, a "Confucius of the West."[13] To others, the concept of a social feeling seems as vague as "ethical haze."[14]

All this has little in common with Freud's intricate mechanism of drives. But on one point at least Adler resembles the professor on Berggasse: both demand unconditional loyalty from their followers. Dissidents are not tolerated for long, as one headstrong pupil will find out in 1927, when Adler rebukes him in the same way he himself was once rebuked by Freud. The name of the outcast, he too a Viennese doctor with ambition: Viktor Frankl. Unlike Adler, he regards neurosis as no mere expedient but rather the expression of a deeply unmoored ego cut off from its purpose in life. According to Frankl, this purpose, or meaning, is what keeps body and mind healthy.

REVISIONS

In the early 1920s, having lived through a horrible war in which two of his sons, Ernst and Martin, served as soldiers on the front lines, Freud carries off a spectacular turn. A quarter century has passed since he and Josef Breuer published their *Studies on Hysteria*. Freud's friendship with his older colleague, who is by now almost eighty years old, fell apart long ago, the casualty of an argument over money that Breuer once lent to Freud to open his practice. In the meantime, psychoanalysis has established itself both as a form of therapy and as a theoretical edifice, but its creator is unsatisfied with what he's achieved. He sets about making several revisions, one of which in particular will endure throughout the century and become known as *the* model of the human psyche. For it is now that Freud divides the personality into the three famous agencies: id, ego, and superego.[15] This triad emerges from his reflections on problems that resulted from his older distinction between conscious, unconscious, and preconscious mental activity. What were the considerations that led to Freud's epochal redesign?

It begins with a book that he publishes in 1920 called *Beyond the Pleasure Principle*. In it Freud argues, contrary to the dogma that he himself has bitterly defended for years, that alongside the libido there was a second drive present within the individual. This second instinct was directed towards the destruction and negation of life.

The book comes out in November 1920. In January of that year, Freud's admirer and patron Anton von Freund had died, followed days later by Freud's daughter Sophie, who was only twenty-seven years old. The latter death is particularly traumatic for him. Writing just a few years later, Freud's first biographer Fritz Wittels speculates that the sadness that followed these losses left its mark on the book. Freud dismisses this idea, noting that the manuscript was completed in 1919, before the deaths of von Freund and Sophie. This is true, but he also extensively revised the text in the summer of 1920.[16]

One aspect of the book that contributes to its gloomy tone is that it seems so irresolute, never arriving at a clear result. *Beyond the Pleasure Principle* is a probing attempt to venture out into new territory. Freud begins by examining the question of why the individual, despite striving for pleasure, repeats so many bad experiences in life. Those who have been traumatized replay what they've suffered again and again; children frequently relive fearful scenarios, like the loss of their parents; and many people continue to maintain relationships that cause them suffering rather than freeing themselves from negative patterns. Freud concludes from this that the instinctual impulse—*every* instinctual impulse—is directed in the first instance not at pleasure, but at recapturing an earlier condition. The condition that is ultimately sought is tension-less, inorganic nothingness—that is, death. The psyche, Freud says, harbors within it a yearning for self-negation, which if displaced onto other objects leads to aggression and hatred.

Among the evidence he brings forward, Freud includes examples drawn from biology. The supreme goal of all living things, from single-celled organisms to *Homo sapiens*, is to relieve tension, whether it is imposed on the organism from without or emerges from within. The end goal of life is to pass away, making it possible for new life to flourish. "The dominating tendency of mental life," Freud writes, "is the effort to reduce, to keep constant or to remove internal tension due to stimuli [. . .]—a tendency which finds expression in the pleasure principle; and our recognition of that fact is one of our strongest reasons for believing in the existence of death instincts."[17]

Freud's irresolution is on display in this passage. Reducing tension, keeping it constant, or eliminating it altogether are very different things. It remains unclear if the death and life drives whose existence Freud posits, and whose roots, he says, are the same, form a single entity or work counter to one another; or if the one operates in service of the other—Freud's book leaves all three possibilities open. And as if that weren't confusing enough, he ends the book by saying that future science will provide answers, "which will blow away the whole of our artificial structure of hypotheses."[18] Freud is thus already anticipating his own failure.

The ambiguous, not quite convincing arguments in *Beyond the Pleasure Principle* leave many of Freud's contemporaries baffled. Freud sets out to explain the greatest maladies in the life of the psyche—envy, grief, despair, sadism, and the longing for death—but he himself calls into question how far he can trust his assumptions. The last sentence doubles as a gesture of profound modesty: "What we cannot reach flying we must reach limping."

Many of those who come after Freud take this as an invitation to engage in grim speculation. According to pioneer of child psychoanalysis Melanie Klein, the infant wishes its mother dead out of envy for her omnipotence. And Jacques Lacan in France sees in the attempt to give verbal expression to inarticulate, animal instincts an inexhaustible source of self-hatred. *Beyond the Pleasure Principle* becomes famous not for its power to convince, but because with a stroke of the pen, Freud brushes aside the instinctual monism (everything is libido!) that he himself defended.

. . .

After destabilizing the old drive theory, Freud sets about reworking his notion of the ego. Three years after *Beyond the Pleasure Principle* he introduces the next radical revision, his theory of the three psychical agencies. *The Ego and the Id* (1923) draws on *Das Buch vom Es*[19] published that same year and written by the Baden-Baden sanatorium director Georg Groddeck. Groddeck understands the *Es* to be "some wondrous force which directs both what [man] himself does, and what happens to him. The affirmation 'I live' is only conditionally correct, it expresses only a small and superficial part of the fundamental principle, 'Man is lived by the It.'"[20]

The *Es* also makes an appearance in Eduard von Hartmann's *Philosophie des Unbewussten* from 1869. "That it is *not we* who think, but that *it* thinks *in us*, is clear to him who is wont to pay attention to the internal processes," writes the independent scholar from Berlin, who once derided his rival Nietzsche as a "trendy little philosopher." "This 'it' lies, however [. . .] in the Unconscious."[21] Once again Freud proves brilliant at discovering concepts that others have introduced before him but have not mined for their full utility.

If up to this point he has only described the dynamic interplay of instinctual forces, the hydraulics of the psyche's theater of illusion, as it were, now Freud constructs a topographical model consisting of three distinct spheres. First is the ego, which is made up of conscious and unconscious components. "[A]ll that is repressed is unconscious, but not all that is unconscious is repressed,"[22] Freud explains, and in doing so tacitly admits that not all of what is floating around in the darkness of the psyche is sexual in nature. While repression can be reversed—that is, while that which is repressed can be brought into waking consciousness—the mind's automatic mechanisms, intuitions, tacit conclusions, and preliminary perceptions necessarily remain unconscious.

First of all, then, the ego is not only conscious; it also contains unconscious emotions like guilt or envy, of whose existence the individual has no inkling, even though they influence his or her behavior. Secondly, unconscious ego-components can also extend "downwards" into the instinctual id, upon which the ego sits like a rider on a horse. The ego may believe it is acting rationally, but in truth it merely gallops off to wherever the id carries it.

Thirdly, moving "upwards," the ego finds its extension in the superego. This third agency, which Freud has referred to before now as the *Ego Ideal*, is formed from internalized duties and moral values, especially those impressed upon the individual by the father. Now, at last, Freud has put together an ensemble of psychical forces that can be summoned to explain all aspects of emotion and behavior. A person has trouble deciding? No wonder, their superego and id are vying for supremacy! Another person is outraged by others' homosexuality—a tendency that they secretly sense in themselves? A clear case of projection: they ascribe to other people the perceived immorality that their superego cannot tolerate; that way they can hate other people instead of themselves.

The ego, as the representative of reality, must constantly mediate and forge compromises between the superego and the id. It is "the actual seat of anxiety";[23] it is here that all the conflicting forces of the psyche converge. As such, it is constantly threatened from three sides: by the demands of the outside world; by the libido of the id; and by the rigidity of the superego. Freud's battlefield theory of the ego explains why it responds to the push and pull of desire and virtue, wish and reality, by summoning up the entire arsenal of tricks that characterizes our psyche. But help is on the way: "Psycho-analysis is an instrument to enable the ego to achieve a progressive conquest of the id."[24]

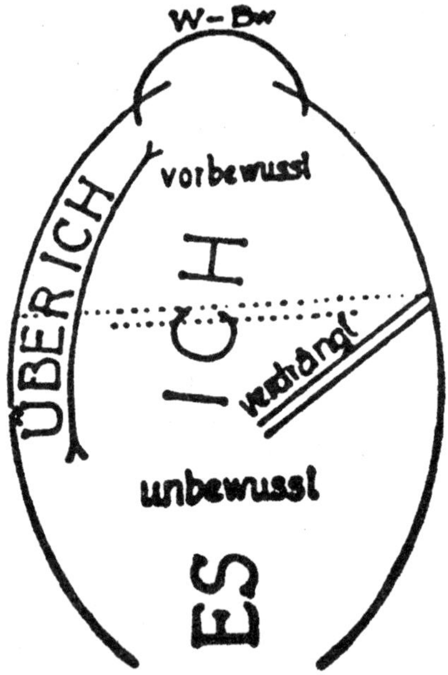

The topographical model: schematic rendering of the relationship between ego, id, and superego, as Freud imagined it in 1920.

A few days before the publication of *The Ego and the Id*, Freud undergoes surgery on his palate for the first time. Thus begins an ordeal that lasts more than sixteen years and ends only with his assisted suicide in London in September 1939. In February 1923 Freud notices a swelling on the roof of his mouth and consults his doctor, Felix Deutsch. After a thorough examination, Deutsch suspects a cancerous lesion, but reassures his patient, telling him it's probably just a harmless thickening of the oral mucosa (leukoplakia). Later Freud will be so furious over this lie that he drops Deutsch as his personal physician. A few weeks after discovering the tumor, Freud has it removed by the laryngologist Markus Hajek. Hajek removes a large portion of the palate under local anesthesia and has Freud taken to a room to recover. There he suffers a severe post-operative hemorrhage, and it is only thanks to the alertness of the patient in the bed next to his that the wound can be bandaged in time.

The brutal operation is not a success. In the fall a new tumor appears; Freud has to go back under the knife. This time he puts himself in the hands of the oral surgeon Hans Pichler, who removes parts of the soft palate and the upper jawbone. Afterwards Freud can neither swallow nor speak, has to be fed through a nasal tube and is in severe pain. As the wound gradually heals, Pichler implants a prosthesis that seals off the mouth from the nasal cavity. Over the years, this monstrosity, which resembles "a sort of magnified denture or obturator,"[25] has to be refitted and replaced several times. Even still, Freud often has trouble speaking and eating and is seldom free from pain. He bears his fate with stoic equanimity—and is soon smoking his first post-surgery cigar, because he can't work without it.

Only once does he lose heart, in June 1923, when his beloved four-and-a-half-year-old grandson Heinz, nicknamed "Heinerle," the son of Sophie, who passed away in 1920, dies of tuberculosis. "I am taking this loss so badly, I believe that I have never experienced anything harder," he writes.[26]

The 1922 Psychoanalytic Congress in Berlin will end up being the last in which Freud personally takes part. From now on he declines many invitations for health reasons, including an offer from Metro-Goldwyn-Mayer to come to Hollywood and make a movie about psychoanalysis. Freud withdraws into his study, receives a select few analysands and continues tirelessly adding to his body of work.

. . .

Freud's modern classic *Civilization and Its Discontents*, published in 1930, completes his metamorphosis from mind doctor to cultural theorist. The book begins by investigating the basis of religious feeling. Freud disputes the view that it comes from the desire to reach a higher sphere, to become one with a greater whole. Instead of this oft-cited "oceanic feeling," he sees something else, something typically Freudian, at work—an infantile wish fulfillment. To feel certain of being taken up into a protective, paternal power which repays the individual for their lifelong suffering—this is the true purpose of belief in God. By holding such a belief, the individual creates the consolation that he so bitterly needs in light of an existence full of want, impermanence, and danger. After all, the quest for pleasure meets with constant impediment. "[T]he intention that man should be 'happy,'" says Freud, "is not included in the plan for 'creation.'"[27]

The psyche has need of distraction and substitute forms of gratification. It avails itself of the doctrine of divine salvation in order to paint a dream image of reality that is far removed from reality itself but that is nevertheless reassuring: God sees everything and is all-powerful. Nothing happens without a reason. After one's death on earth, eternal life in paradise beckons. Religion for Freud is a kind of mass delusion, a collective neurosis, which serves the socially necessary aim of prompting the individual to renounce their drives. The price for this is high, however: nagging feelings of guilt stemming from one's own imperfection.

In addition to the religious, there are still other forms of sublimation—Freud specifically names the ideal of love, the aesthetic pursuits of art and literature, and the spirit of scientific inquiry. These all serve to channel the aggressive tendencies inherent in the pleasure principle into tolerable channels. In order to make this "sacrifice of their instincts," individuals have no choice but to turn their aggression inward, against themselves, to "introject" them and subordinate themselves to the power of the superego.

If we follow Freud's arguments to this point, we realize why, for him, the idea of giving free rein to the instincts is no solution to the problems of the psyche. Every human society is "built up upon a renunciation of instinct," he says. "This 'cultural frustration' dominates the large field of social relationships."[28] Contrary to what Wilhelm Reich argues in his last lecture before the Vienna Society in December 1929, Freud doesn't believe that one can ever fully root out neuroses. "The function of education is to inhibit, forbid, and suppress, and it has at all times carried out this function to admiration [. . .] It is a matter of finding out how much one may forbid, at which times, and by what methods."[29]

Nor is Freud convinced by the idea, advanced by the Communists, that doing away with private property will pacify society. The "narcissism of minor differences"[30] stands in the way: any dividing factor is sufficient to produce hate and hostility. It's no coincidence that the Christians of the Middle Ages so ruthlessly persecuted those who didn't share their idea of God, namely non-Christians; or that the Nazis, in their Aryan megalomania, declare the Jews their mortal enemies. The bourgeoisie serves the same purpose for the Communists. Freud's pessimism regarding humanity's ability to peacefully coexist is summed up in the famous words of the English philosopher Thomas Hobbes, which Freud cites: "*Homo homini lupus*. Who, in the face of all his experience of life and of history, will have the courage to dispute this assertion?"[31]

The note on which Freud ends his thesis is no less gloomy: "The fateful question for the human species seems to me to be whether and to what extent their cultural development will succeed in mastering the disturbance of their communal life by the human instinct of aggression and self-destruction. [. . .] Men have gained control over the forces of nature to such an extent that with their help they would have no difficulty in exterminating one another to the last man. They know this, and hence comes a large part of their current unrest."[32] Though written with the looming war in mind, these lines seem no less prophetic in our time of multiple threats.

Within ten years, Freud places his view of the human individual on a new foundation. At the same time he presents himself as the destroyer of old illusions by unmasking the general tendency toward self-delusion. Freud's three major works from this decade bear witness to his eloquence and keen powers of observation, but also to the imperfection of his speculative science. By claiming to dispense with illusion in elucidating the reality of the psyche, Freud creates a new illusion of his own.

SEE SCOTLAND AND DIE

Meanwhile Adler is ascending to the status of pop psychologist par excellence, becoming "the face of individual psychology, its top brand, its representative, its chief explainer."[33] A lecture tour to Oxford and Cambridge in the early 1920s is so successful that he decides to improve his English. Adler's warm tone of voice and his strong Viennese accent give him the air of a wise, slightly eccentric "German" philosopher peering down at the foundation of the psyche.

In November 1926, on board the RMS *Majestic*, he sets sail from Southampton on his first trip to the United States. It will help him achieve international fame, just as Freud and Jung's trip seventeen years earlier had for them. In New York Adler stays at the chic Gramercy Park Hotel, gives interviews, receives admirers. On January 11, 1927 he delivers a well-received lecture at the new main building of the New York Academy of Medicine; this is followed by appearances in Philadelphia, Boston, Chicago, Detroit, and still more cities. Unlike Freud, who when speaking at the anniversary celebration at Clark University addressed an academic audience, Adler also speaks in schools, to church groups and women's associations, and at homes for children.

In the years to come, the lecture tours that take him all over the US will become an important source of income for him. Alder often gives four or five talks a day, on top of the usual consultations, receptions, and conferences. In 1929 he travels from New York to Cleveland, then continues on to California to speak in Berkeley and Los Angeles. On February 16 he writes to his daughter Alexandra: "I think I've made about $2,500 this month, but have spent a lot. I've sent $700 to the Wiener Bankverein so that you all are covered."[34]

Eight years later, in 1937, he sends similarly good tidings from Manhattan: "My dear Ali, I can smell European air. I'm bringing you a pretty kimono and stockings. [. . .] There are now about 10,000 dollars in the bank. I'm doing very well. We are victorious everywhere we go." And indeed Adler is very much victorious. His ideas on will power and the individual's need to compensate for their weaknesses find fertile soil in a country in which everyone dreams of attaining success and prosperity by means of their own strength. It helps, too, that Adler's individual psychology has less of an intellectual air to it than psychoanalysis, and doesn't have the whiff of scandal about it. Where Freud tends to be adopted by the artistically-minded upper class, Adler's petit bourgeois social climber mentality speaks to the masses.

One pilgrim who comes to see Adler's New York lectures in the winter of 1927/28 is a man in his mid-twenties who has just dropped his pursuit of a theology degree in order to study pedagogy and psychology at Teachers College. Deeply impressed by the Viennese doctor, Carl Rogers wants to look for his own ways to give encouragement to people who are struggling, without patronizing them. This is precisely the challenge that Rogers will find himself faced with in his later work with "difficult" adolescents—and as we shall see, he will crib several ideas from the educational guidance offered by individual psychology.

. . .

In New York Adler gets to know the businessman Charles Henry Davis, who made a fortune in road construction and mining. He and his family live near Park Avenue, home to about half of the city's three thousand millionaires. Davis's oldest daughter suffers from depression. When her condition improves under Adler's care, Davis becomes his biggest champion. He even endows a professor's chair that Adler takes up on September 1, 1932. The position comes with an annual salary of $8,500 (about $165,000 today). Adler lectures every day but Sunday from 4 p.m. to 6 p.m.; on top of this he gives talks in the morning and evening on various topics like crime, love, self-actualization, community, and the meaning of life.

Adler's bestseller *Understanding Human Nature* is published in 1927. The first three editions sell a total of more than one million copies. By comparison, Freud's *Interpretation of Dreams* just sits on the shelves, selling a total of 11,000 copies for the entire decade of the 1920s. Adler, the gifted popularizer, is psychology's first commercially-successful self-made man. In just two years, 1929 and 1930, half a dozen books are published either by him or about him, from the *ABC of Adler's Psychology* to *The Science of Living*, *Guiding the Child*, and *What Life Should Mean to You*.

Over time Adler's interest shifts from psychopathology in the narrow sense to questions of personal growth and happiness, the roots of criminality, and how to raise strong and resilient children. He also establishes a business model that calls not only for addressing a general audience but also for passing his knowledge on, through workshops and training courses, to the growing cohort of social workers, marital and personal counselors, coaches, educators, and therapists.

All of this brings him considerable prosperity. Adler buys a villa, "Dreimarkstein 12," in Salmannsdorf just outside of Vienna. There is a grand piano in the salon; Adler's daughters, who are excellent pianists, often accompany their father as he belts out his beloved Schubert

Lieder. Along with music, Adler loves botany. He brings exotic seeds and seedlings back from his travels and quickly turns the sunny living room into a greenhouse. When a visitor compliments his cactus collection, Adler puts a finger to his lips and whispers: "Shhh! They think they're still in Texas!"[35] The reason he works so much, he jokes, is that he has to support a household of seventeen people—including in the tally not only his own family and siblings, but also their servants, gardeners, chauffeurs, and the German shepherd.

In 1930 Adler acquires his own private automobile. He gets his driver's license at age sixty. Seated behind the wheel of his new car, he travels to lectures in Germany, Poland, and Czechoslovakia. According to Alexandra, at the time her father was one of the first Viennese doctors who could afford his own vehicle. In 1930, the same year that Freud receives the Goethe Prize from the city of Frankfurt, Adler is named an honorary citizen of Vienna. It's a small consolation, at least, for the fragile ego of a psychologist who is only ever second best in the eyes of the cultural elite. Owing to unrest that brings Vienna to the cusp of a civil war, the ceremony doesn't take place until two years later, at the town hall. Mayor Karl Seitz commits a faux pas when he refers to the honoree as "Freud's most outstanding student." Adler is hugely offended. The sting of perceived inferiority implied by the mention of his former mentor sits too deep. It's no exaggeration to say that Adler's teachings are most apt when applied to one person: himself.

. . .

Unlike Freud, Adler isn't inclined to pessimism. Though he profits from capitalism like no other, he remains a socialist at heart and is filled with an unshakeable belief in progress. But fate has a hard blow in store for him.

The situation for Jews and avowed socialists in Austria is getting ever more precarious. After Adler is named a professor at Long Island College of Medicine in Brooklyn, he makes plans to move to New York for good. In October 1933 he applies for a visa. His wife Raissa and children Alexandra and Kurt don't follow until 1935. The strong-willed Raissa is long resistant to the idea of leaving. She is an independent, self-confident woman, a dedicated Communist who is personally acquainted with Leon Trotsky, who at the time resides in Vienna. Only after the Austrofascists take power in 1934 and she spends two days in police custody does she realize the danger she's in. Raissa follows her husband and emigrates to the United States.

Their eldest daughter, Valentina, remains in Europe, however. After completing her studies in political science she works in the women's secretariat of the German Communist Party in Berlin under Clara Zetkin and in 1925 marries the Hungarian journalist Julius Spitz, who after the wedding changes his name to Gyula Sas (*sas* is Hungarian for *Adler*, i.e., *eagle*). The bride's father sends a letter congratulating the newlyweds: "Please don't forget that marriage is a task that you both must work on, with joy. Remember that the monogamous form of life represents only the most beautiful flowering of sexual culture."[36]

The young couple moves to Moscow. At the height of the Stalinist purges, Valentine is arrested on suspicion of being a spy, and in 1937 suddenly disappears without a trace. All the family's inquiries come to nothing; what happens to her becomes clear only in the early 1950s, when it comes to light that Adler's daughter was sent to a penal camp in September 1937 for alleged conspiratorial activity. It's possible that her fate is sealed by her personal contact with Stalin's rival Trotsky during his time in Vienna. In all likelihood, Valentine Adler, like thousands of others, died of starvation in one of the Soviet Union's hopelessly overcrowded gulags.

The uncertainty over his eldest daughter's fate weighs heavily on Adler. On top of that, his enormous workload takes its toll. In early 1937, Adler is on a trip to the Netherlands when he feels a pressure in his chest. A doctor gives a diagnosis of cardiac arrhythmia and advises him to take a break. Adler makes plans to go on vacation—but only after that year's Summer School in Berkeley, which he wouldn't want to miss for the world. Before then there are still a few commitments to honor; the contracts were signed long ago, and he doesn't want to forego the income. Adler's "appointments book" bears witness to his immense workload: in January 1937 he gives a series of lectures in Texas, Oklahoma, Illinois, and Michigan. After a brief stop back in New York, by mid-February he is again crisscrossing the Midwest. These two months alone earn him fees totaling around $3,500. In

April come fifty-six lectures in France and a tour through Belgium, Luxembourg, and the Netherlands. Another planned lecture tour will take him through England and Scotland from mid-May through August. Everywhere he goes he gives lectures, makes visits, grants interviews. In late June he has twelve lectures in Edinburgh scheduled, then fourteen in Liverpool, and after that a dozen seminars in Exeter before he is set to leave from Southampton for California, where the Summer School awaits him beginning on August 15. But it's not to be.

On May 24, Adler arrives in Aberdeen, Scotland. In addition to giving readings, he makes daily visits to various hospitals. On the morning of the 28th, a Friday, he wakes up early as usual and after breakfast starts making notes for his next talk. At the front desk he hands over a telegram to be sent to Raissa, whom he plans to meet in London—they just need to decide on a hotel. The message ends with the words: "Tomorrow I'll know more. [I am having] great triumphs."

After that Adler goes out for a walk. Around half-past nine he is crossing Union Street. A passerby sees a man walking at a brisk pace who suddenly slips on the sidewalk. The observer, a theology student, had attended Adler's talk the day before; he recognizes him and hurries over. But Adler has already lost consciousness. The doctor who arrives on the scene can only confirm his death. As the cause he notes at 9:40 a.m.: "fatty degeneration of the heart"—a heart attack. Adler was sixty-seven years old.

In the coming weeks, a flurry of memorial notices appears in newspapers across the US and Europe. But one man at least doesn't shed any tears for the deceased. With unmasked disdain, Freud writes to Arnold Zweig: "For a Jew boy out of a Viennese suburb a death in Aberdeen is an unheard-of career in itself and a proof of how far he had got on. The world really rewarded him richly for his service in having contradicted psychoanalysis."[37]

LORD OF THE LISTS

Around this same time, in Germany, an author is making a name for himself by taking Adler's recipe for success in practical life advice and pushing it to its logical extreme. With staccato-style urgency, he hammers into his readers the idea that success and happiness are nothing but a question of the right method—the Grossmann method, to be exact, or GM for short. And the customers are lining up to be initiated into its secrets.

Gustav Grossmann's book *Sich selbst rationalisieren*—"Rationalizing Yourself"[38]—is published in 1927 by the small Stuttgarter Verlag für Wirtschaft und Verkehr ("Stuttgart Publishing House for Economics and Commerce") and starts selling like hotcakes. Where the first edition carried the modest subtitle "Nature and Preparation of Personal Success," the second edition in 1929 offers a full-throated promise: "Success in Life is Learnable." In the coming years the work will go through twenty-seven editions. Grossmann doesn't even try to sketch out a serious psychological theory. Instead, the book consists of a collection of concise, suggestive slogans like "All presence of mind, all quick-wittedness, all brilliance rests on the systematic preparation for success."[39]

Grossmann's prose strikes a nerve. According to sales records, over the years he licenses his method nearly 30,000 times. He also gives courses and seminars whose participants come away with one main lesson: planning is half of life—and the beginning of all success! Those who want to get ahead should make daily, weekly, monthly, and yearly plans, the more detailed the better; they should draw up step-by-step lists with all their essential goals for work and life, including all the intermediate stages they expect to pass through along the way; and they should keep track of what they've achieved in a happiness diary. In the diary it's important to set down what one can already do currently, what one wants to achieve next, and how one intends to execute one's plans with maximal "joy of success."

Ironically, Grossmann gives his followers a sense of meaning by declaring the search for it to be a waste of time. "Again that same old saw about the ultimate purpose of life! You know what I consider the ultimate purpose of life to be? [. . .] to be buried! Metabolizing, copulating, making money in business and padding your bank account: these are the true goals and means, the ones that have received objective recognition." These are not the words of a subtle thinker dedicated to dissecting the human psyche; they are the words of a man of action.

Raised on his parents' estate in Masuria, Grossmann studies psychology in Königsberg and receives his doctorate in 1920 with a thesis "On the Nature of the Satisfaction of Urges." Afterwards he works at the Institute for Industrial Psychotechnics in Berlin before becoming publicity manager for the Verlag Oldenbourg publishing house. The switch from the laboratory to the world of business is well suited to his temperament. Grossmann's pitch is based around a message that, in its thousands of variations, attracts customers to this day: you can achieve anything, all you have to do is want it! It's in your hands! Success is attainable! Use your potential, believe in yourself and be persistent, and everything you set out to do is guaranteed to work out!

Riding the wave of his success, Grossmann quickly publishes other books with outlandish-sounding titles like "The World of Doers," "Being Bigtime," "To Be Favored by Fortune," "Master Risks and Difficulties," and " . . . And Whatever He Touches Turns to Gold." And sure enough: Grossmann's method turns out to be a goldmine. "The Perpetual Personal Situation-analysis" (the title of another of his books) is a program studded with the kind of short, snappy formulas that Grossmann's books are bursting with: "Make money! How?"; "Increase your personal capacity for success! How?"; "Be able to influence people—how?" Concrete advice or suggestions for managing critical life situations tend to be the exception amidst a seemingly endless series of exaggerations. Grossmann's math has a pseudoscientific precision: "Most people use only a small portion of their talents. About 2 to 50 percent. Thus 50 to 98 percent of human talent isn't even developed."

Grossmann is a psychologist, but like John B. Watson, he's first and foremost an ad man. Both seem to take as their motto a simple precept: promise the moon and stars and people will love you for it! Like Watson, Grossmann is interested not only in the fate of the individual, but also in society as a whole: the whole nation, he feels, should profit from his advice and learn to tap into new sources of strength. Grossmann provides a "service to the suffering, downtrodden, and exhausted popular psyche"[40]—a pattern that will inspire many imitators.

Why does this carnivalesque bluster resonate so much with people? It hardly seems to deliver any evident value. Clearly it matters less *what* experts on the psyche say than *how* they say it, how much conviction and power of suggestion they display. Both Grossmann and Watson radiate a level of self-assuredness that those who hang on to their every word would themselves like to possess. If they had that much verve they could save the world, or at the very least their own psyche. The 1920s are a fertile ground not just for radical political slogans, but also for gurus of various stripes, convinced of the rightness of their mission.

THE THIRD FORCE

The teenage Fritz Perls hates school and loves the theater. His hero is Max Reinhardt, the Austrian theatrical genius who at the start of the century tears through Berlin's cultural scene like a tornado. In place of the sterile staging that had been the norm up to that point, with verse recitations between painted curtains and a backdrop of cardboard scenery, Reinhardt introduces a raft of dramatic innovations. For his production of *A Midsummer Night's Dream* at the Deutsches Theater in 1905 he puts a forest of actual tree trunks on the moss-covered stage, while in the background, backlit glass panels mimic the reflective surface of a lake. Reinhardt's sound and lighting effects, music, and costumes are no less legendary. This dramaturgical wizard—actor, director, and intendant all in one—is so successful that within a few years he has bought the whole theater and had it equipped with a rotating stage, lighting rig, and workshop.

Reinhardt's sensory theater of illusion is directed toward one thing above all else: unmasking. "Nowhere do human beings reveal themselves more authentically, in purer, more childlike form than in acting," he declares. "Bourgeois life is full of conventional lies. The actor's goal is the ultimate innermost truth, because his profession is not to mask but to unmask."[41] The seventeen-year-old Perls dreams of the same thing. He appears as an extra in theatrical productions and attends some of Reinhardt's acting classes, hoping to embark on a stage career himself. Theater for Perls becomes a place of revelation. It exposes the authentic nature of the characters—and he is thirsty for authenticity, for a glimpse behind the façade of discipline, duty, and constrictive morality.

Perls joins a company that performs on various open-air stages. He would rather spend time memorizing his lines than studying for school. Who cares what his parents think. His mother reaches for the carpet beaters in her effort to make him see reason, but as he later defiantly recalls: "She did not break my spirit; I broke the beaters."[42] His father is a womanizer masquerading as a faithful, caring husband. Once, when he takes his son along to a meeting of his Freemasons' lodge, young Fritz can barely contain his laughter; it seems so fake to him, all this secretive posturing. No, Fritz wants something else. The only question is, what?

. . .

Born in Berlin on July 8, 1893, the youngest child and only son of a Jewish wine merchant and his wife, Friedrich Salomon Perls, like many renowned psychologists, doesn't have an easy childhood. Materially speaking, the family is well off. They live in a four-room apartment in the Bayerisches Viertel in the posh southwest part of the city. But Perls's father is a monster, moody and domineering. He regularly calls his son a lazy, ungrateful "piece of shit." Perls's mother, in her helplessness, reaches for the belt and the cudgel whenever her son talks back. And this he does often.

When he reaches high school age, Perls first attends the authoritarian Mommsen-Gymnasium. After being held back a third time, he switches to the somewhat more liberal Askanisches Gymnasium. But there too, duty, loyalty to the emperor, and antisemitism are the rule. Jews like himself are considered second-class citizens, and the other children would rather not have all that much to do with them—learning this lesson is one of Perls's formative childhood experiences.

Friedrich, known as Fritz, regularly cuts class and roams around the neighborhood. When he's not appearing on stage himself, he is a passionate theatergoer. As fascinated as he is by the bohemian life, after graduating from high school he opts for a scientific course of study. Shortly before the outbreak of the First World War Perls enrolls at the Berlin University to study medicine. Diligence and determination are not exactly his strong suits, however. In 1916 Perls is drafted and experiences the horrors of the poison gas attacks at Ypres in Flanders. Back in Berlin, he finishes his studies; by the time he finally gets his medical degree, he's almost thirty.

In September 1926, Perls takes a position as an assistant physician under the neurologist Kurt Goldstein in Frankfurt. This will be the turning point in his life. Working for Goldstein, a cousin of the Hamburg philosopher Ernst Cassirer, Perls first encounters the concept of wholeness and of the innate capacity for self-actualization possessed by every individual. At the institute in Frankfurt he also meets the student Lore Posner, who is twelve years his junior. Sparks fly between the two of them during a course called "On Consciousness and the So-called Unconscious." Lore comes from a jeweler family in Pforzheim and writes her doctoral thesis on the perception of form (*Gestaltsehen*), with Goldstein's colleague Adhémar Gelb as advisor. She is well-read and is more systematic in her thinking than Fritz, whom she finds fascinating for that very reason: he's different from the others—"a mixture of a prophet and a bum," as she later puts it.[43]

The two of them have a shared passion: psychoanalysis. They admire Freud for having liberated sexuality from the taint of immorality and, by deciphering the unconscious, pointing the way to a more free and self-determined life. At the time many young progressives see things this way. Fritz and Lore set out to link Freud's ideas to gestalt theory. This theory rests on the insight that the individual perceives not only isolated stimuli or features in the environment, but rather whole entities: self-contained images or notions that, figure-like, stand out against the background. The visual organ, for example, connects a sequence of individual flickering points of light to form a single fluid motion; it automatically fills in fragmentary outlines to make geometric shapes. A melody, too, is far more than just a sequence of notes, which is why you can transpose it into a different key, changing each individual note without destroying the overarching structure. Gestalt theory says that the whole is greater than the sum of its parts.

Kurt Goldstein applies this idea to the treatment of ex-soldiers who have suffered brain damage, many of whom, nearly ten years after the end of the war, still need medical help. According to Goldstein, for them it's not merely a question of regaining a particular function like speech or the ability to walk. Rather they are striving to grow as an "organismic whole."

Goldstein draws on the work of Berlin gestalt psychologists like Wolfgang Köhler, Kurt Lewin, and Max Wertheimer, who argue that our cognitive apparatus constructs cohesive perceptions out of the fragmentary flow of impressions. Applying this principle to the personality reveals a tendency toward completion. Just as the sense of sight completes figures in the mind, the self too follows holistic principles. This self—the totality of a person's qualities, judgments, and tendencies embodied in a *gestalt* or figure—will become the byword for a new psychological way of thinking.

Fritz Perls became acquainted with psychoanalysis during his time studying medicine in Berlin. Before his year working under Goldstein in Frankfurt, when he was still just a budding neurologist, he began a training analysis with Karen Horney at the newly founded Berlin Institute. After his intermezzo at Goldstein's institute, other, rather disappointing courses of analysis follow, until on Horney's advice Perls finally knocks on Wilhelm Reich's door. Perls moves to Vienna in the fall of 1927 for the express purpose of undergoing analysis with him. Similar to Reich in temperament—they're both impatient and rebellious—he finds in him a congenial partner and eagerly adopts his technique of resistance analysis.

. . .

At first Perls's thinking remains within the bounds set by Freud, concurring for example with the view that anxiety emerges from repressed libido. Little by little however he begins to have doubts. Freud, according to Perls, "said that in a neurosis a part of our personality or our potential isn't accessible. But he had a funny way of saying it; he said, 'it *is* in the unconscious,' as if there were such a thing as *the* unconscious and not simply behavior or emotions that were unknown and simply inaccessible."[44] The pioneer of gestalt therapy refers to Freud derisively as the "usher," because he assigns every mental impulse a seat in the great theater of the ego, id, and superego. Perls, on the other hand, stresses the fluid, dynamic emergence of shifting gestalts that stand out against the Not-Known (*das Nicht-Gewusste*) (which Freud calls "preconscious" [*das Vorbewusste*]) like objects against a blurry background.

Perls's skepticism is also fueled by his dissatisfaction with Freud's conception of humanity—and Watson's as well. In psychoanalysis, as in behaviorism, the individual seems like a marionette, ruled either by impulses that he is unaware of and refuses to acknowledge, or by learned patterns that elude his control. The development of potential, self-actualization, growth—none of it factors in.

Perls, on the other hand, posits the existence of a constantly changing psychical agency that rests upon the experiences stored in the body's memory, in emotions, ways of thinking, and actions. It strives toward completion, and therapy is the attempt to make possible the development of such a living self. To reach this goal one must, per Perls, get in touch with one's environment, as well as with one's own needs. He and Lore base their approach on this claim, the individual's claim to holistic development. It will go on to be called "humanistic" and take its place as the third force in psychology alongside psychoanalysis and behaviorism.

Perls makes use of psychoanalytic concepts at first, but defines them differently: "Freud's catharsis notion is the emerging Gestalt. Not in the Unconscious, but right on the surface. The obvious is put on the throne."[45] His method is physical, immediate, and less cerebral than analysis. Perls practices applied phenomenology—the philosophical method founded by Edmund Husserl that devotes its attention to the subjective appearance of things in order to decipher their essence. An approach like Perls's doesn't even require a particularly refined technique. Gestalts emerge and cohere intuitively as soon as one gives room to one's physically rooted experiences. All aspects of the psyche will find their place, like pieces in a giant puzzle, if only one sheds the inhibitions that to this point have prevented this from happening.

Gestalt therapy thus clears away incrustation and inner resistance. Reich's influence becomes clear: only "disinhibited" individuals are at one with themselves and follow their purpose. And to help the individual on the road to self-actualization is at the same time to heal a neurotically inhibited society.

YOU ARE WHAT YOU THINK

If Mary Cover Jones is the mother of behavioral therapy, Joseph Wolpe can rightly be called the father. Born in 1915 in Johannesburg, he is descended from a family of Eastern European Jews. Around the turn of the century his grandfather emigrated from Ukraine to South Africa by way of Lithuania. The young Wolpe studies medicine at the University of the Witwatersrand and after receiving his MD in 1938 decides to specialize in psychiatry. At a clinic in Kimberley, a dusty day's journey southwest of Johannesburg, he encounters many soldiers who are traumatized from their experiences of war. Medical treatment for patients like them is almost non-existent at this time, and so Wolpe looks for ways to mitigate their panic attacks and flashbacks.

Frustrated by the failed outcomes produced by psychoanalytic treatment, Wolpe develops a different strategy. He has noticed that often his patients are most afraid *of their fear*—they're less frightened by the experiences themselves, the screams, explosions, or images of severed limbs, than they are of the prospect of losing control and being overcome by panic. Is it possible to get them to relinquish this fear, to "desensitize" them, step by step, by getting them used to situations that trigger their fear?

Before testing out his hypothesis on people, Wolpe first intends to gather data in an animal trial, as is standard practice in this type of research. But which species? Rodents strike him as unsuitable, since individual rodents' behavior is influenced too strongly by that of others of their species; cattle, goats, or apes meanwhile are costly and difficult to keep. Wolpe decides to go with cats.

In order to free the felines from neuroses, he first has to train them to acquire a few. To this end he builds a cage with a wire mesh floor through which he can send an electric current. Then he puts a cat inside and lets it explore the cage. After a while, the first electric shock is delivered, preceded by an audible signal. The animal startles, trying to escape the invisible foe, and retreats to a corner of the enclosure. After a few repetitions, the cat is cowering with fright, its fur standing on end. It won't eat, jumps at the slightest sound, and hisses as soon as it's brought anywhere near the cage, or even into the room where the experiment takes place.

High time for therapy! Wolpe puts the terrified animal back into the cage. Now some time passes and—nothing happens. As expected, the cat seeks shelter and gives every indication of being afraid. The signal that preceded the shock in the first round is sounded, but this time, the shock doesn't ensue. At first the observers see hardly any improvement; even after several repetitions the cat doesn't trust the ceasefire. Finally Wolpe puts food in the cat's cage and gives the signal again. As soon as the cat has eaten, its fear is visibly gone.

Wolpe's explanation: the reward stimulus, the food, competes with the panic reaction. By gaining the upper hand and suppressing the behavior that preceded it, the reward helps to gradually neutralize the fear. Wolpe first presents this principle of reciprocal inhibition in a 1954 article.[46] He sees in it the primary mechanism of all psychotherapy: the negative link between stimulus and reaction is overcome and replaced by a positive association.

In the years to come Wolpe devises a full course of cat therapy. But can the findings in his feline experiments be replicated in people? Humans differ from cats in two fundamental ways: first, it is often impossible to determine the concrete trigger for a person's fear, because sometimes people find creative ways to displace their reaction patterns onto other objects—they generalize their fear. And second, a human patient, unlike a cat, is aware of his fear, he thinks about it and forms expectations that can be divorced from particular circumstances. The result: he becomes afraid even if he is not threatened by any concrete danger.

To treat people who are deathly afraid of getting into a packed elevator or having a spider on their hand, Wolpe first induces a state of relaxation. For the next step, he confronts them with a weak fear-inducing stimulus—an empty elevator, say, or a fake plastic spider—and asks them to remain as relaxed as possible. Little by little the intensity of the stimulus is increased, verging on the very limit of the patient's tolerance. Voilà: the fear departs, the relaxation remains. Wolpe sees this as the fundamental principle behind all therapy—and reports a success rate of up to sixty-eight percent.

In the 1940s and 1950s, behaviorism dominates university psychology departments, especially in the English-speaking world. Pioneers like Watson and his younger colleague Burrhus Frederic Skinner ascribe all human and animal behavior to patterns of learning. Skinner places special emphasis on the role of operant conditioning. Working with pigeons, for instance, he manages to train his test subjects not only to give elementary responses to stimuli but also to carry out complex sequences of actions. Rather than having them just peck at a lever, he teaches the birds to perform astounding tricks, like turning pirouettes, in order to get food. In addition to the automatic association of stimuli with simple response patterns seen in Watson's paradigm of classic conditioning, multi-step sequences are also clearly learnable. People now start to tell themselves that it's not only mere reflexes that can be traced back to associative learning processes, like the flow of saliva in response to the ringing of a bell; rather it's the entire repertoire of human thought and action.

Skinner considers it a waste of time to delve into patients' thoughts and emotions when all they need is a suitable new learning paradigm. Every person is born an empty slate; all suffering is learned and has only to be unlearned.

To many, above all to therapists rooted in analysis, the behavioral therapy[47] that rests on such assumptions is a soulless form of dressage that doesn't do justice to deeper emotions. And in fact, according to strict behaviorist learning theory, there are only two ways to influence human behavior: positive or negative reinforcement, reward or punishment. In his novel *Walden Two*, Skinner lays out his vision of a society based on the principles of operant conditioning. Most of his readers take his book to be a realistic scenario—and a dystopia. Skinner himself, on the other hand, intends for the book to promote the idea of a scientifically-optimized commonwealth.

Freud's refined style and the prose of Skinner or Wolpe are literally worlds apart. The latter sounds like a dyed-in-the-wool technocrat when he defines the object of his research, neurosis, in the following terms: "Neurotic behavior is any persistent habit of unadaptive behavior acquired by learning in a physiologically normal organism. Anxiety is usually the central constituent of this behavior."[48] Behavioral therapists are concerned neither with difficult cultural criticism nor the liberation of the self; their dream is the effective modification of inappropriate behavior. Though Wolpe talks to his patients, it's mainly to ensure that he doesn't overlook anything important in their medical histories. He doesn't expect it to have any therapeutic effect.

. . .

Little Aaron is sick. Very sick. The doctors give him a fifty-fifty chance of making it. When the seven-year-old fell from the monkey bars at the playground his mother often takes him to, it seemed harmless enough at first. Aaron's parents—Ukrainians who found a new home in Providence, Rhode Island—love their son more than anything and keep a close watch over him. His mother has had two miscarriages; her first son, Aaron's older brother, died in infancy, and another daughter died of the flu shortly before Aaron was born. But Aaron, born in summer 1921, is a healthy, happy child, the youngest of five and the only one his parents have left.

After his fall, the boy gets up and knocks the dirt off his clothes. The shock is wearing off. His right elbow hurts, but it doesn't look too bad; it's probably fine. After a few days the aching gets worst; the doctor's advice is to wait and see. When the arm swells up and starts to become discolored, Aaron's parents take him to the hospital. The bone has become infected; the child is immediately given medicine for sepsis. He has to spend weeks in the hospital, and even when he gets back home he's instructed to stay in bed. On top of that, Aaron develops severe asthma. There are times when he's almost suffocating.

The boy misses so much school that when he finally goes back, he gets bumped down a grade. Eight years old and still a first-grader—the boy probably isn't the brightest! Aaron grows up knowing that he's the black sheep in the family. But he's not going to take it lying down. He studies hard, reads incessantly; after being sick for so long, he hardly has any friends left anyway. Year after year he gets a little farther ahead, till finally he ends up skipping a grade and graduating from Hope High School with top marks at age seventeen. Aaron gets himself admitted to Brown University and four years later moves on to Yale Medical School. His early experiences make a lasting impression on him: you can pull yourself out of even the worst mess, you just have to want it badly enough and adopt the right attitude.

Young Dr. Beck is dedicated. Girls, cars, alcohol—he's not interested in any of these things. The boy once thought to be of less-than-average intelligence, who came within a hair of being sent to remedial school, is now a promising young scientist. He completes a training analysis and tries his hand at therapy, working with patients who can't afford the fees of his more experienced colleagues. But something bothers him: the depth psychologists' understanding of depression—a condition that his mother also suffered from—is clearly at odds with the medical facts. Even the term, today the second-most-common psychiatric diagnosis after anxiety disorder, is not commonly used by analysts at this time; most prefer to speak of melancholy, taking their cue from a 1917 essay of Freud's. According to the psychoanalytic view, it's the price a person pays for *wanting* to be sick. Unconsciously, those who suffer from the condition have no interest in being healthy. They escape into melancholy, which, even if they can't manage to do anything else, at least relieves them of responsibility for their failure. The logical conclusion is that people with depression want to suffer, despair; they want to mope. Nothing cheers them up, everything seems dismal, the glass always half empty and the future uncertain.

According to Freud, depression is fueled by aggression turned against one's own ego. Aaron Temkin Beck thinks this is plausible, but feels that such a weighty claim needs a few tangible pieces of evidence to support it. He sets out to examine the accounts his depressive patients give of their dreams. If this analysis were to produce the finding that depressive individuals actually do have more "masochistic dreams" in which they direct aggressive impulses against themselves, then the theory would be confirmed. But a study of the dream accounts shows the exact opposite: depressives don't dream more often of self-directed violence than healthy individuals; rather their nights are more frequently filled with fantasies of protection, comfort, and rescue. Beck begins to have doubts about the psychoanalytic theory of depression.

In his early thirties, he decides to form his own sense of where the dark thoughts come from. How does it develop, this feeling that nothing in life has any value, that it would be better not to exist at all? Beck himself is no stranger to such thoughts. But he knows that they're false—he wants to pass them by, like Odysseus sailing past the island of the Sirens. Next Beck studies the patterns in his patients' way of thinking. He finds a negative default attitude that manifests in three different ways. Depressives have a fundamentally bleak assessment of themselves, the world, and the future. They believe that they are inferior to others, or that no one wants anything to do with them. What's more, they believe there's no point in trying to change this, because any attempt to do so would be pure wishful thinking.

According to Beck, depression is characterized by thoughts of this sort, no matter if it's the thoughts that trigger the depression or the depression that gives rise to the thoughts. Put another way: it isn't aggression directed against the self or a masochistic tendency that clouds the depressed person's thoughts; rather gloomy thoughts cause, exacerbate, or perpetuate the depressive emotional state. Maybe doctors should take more seriously what is going on in their patients' heads?

In 1954 Aaron Beck takes a research position at the University of Pennsylvania's medical school. It will be his academic home for more than thirty years. Here, the grounded, modest Beck will become the founding father of cognitive behavior therapy.

· · ·

Though eight years older than Beck, Albert Ellis begins his training as a psychologist at around the same time. Ellis already has a bachelor's in business, but balances and market analyses don't interest him in the least. He gives up his business career before it's even gotten started and at almost thirty, in the middle of the war, starts over again from scratch. He studies psychology in New York and gets his PhD in clinical psychology in 1947, a year after Beck. But his passion, if not to say obsession, is—sex. Ellis regards prudishness and hostility to pleasure as the largest source of mental suffering and advocates—in Wilhelm Reichian fashion, though without his Communist convictions—for free love and unlimited access to contraceptives. In 1952 he strikes out on his own and opens a practice in Manhattan. His trademark is "rational therapy," a term that he coins shortly after the war. For Ellis the key to happiness consists in gaining insight into false or irrational beliefs and translating that insight into practical action.

His career path resembles a kind of self-therapy. As a young man, Albert Ellis is ruled by all manner of inhibitions and self-doubt. His father, a banker, walks out on the family when his son is still in elementary school. His mother is pious but lacks warmth and affection. When, at the age of six, little Albert is hospitalized for weeks with a serious infection, his parents rarely visit him at all, leaving the boy in despair.

As a teenager Ellis is a habitual shoplifter and sexual predator. He is too shy to talk to women face to face, but has no scruples about pressing up against women's bodies in crowded restaurants or subway trains and rubbing his member against them—sometimes to the point of ejaculation. His behavior gets him slapped or yelled at, but some victims either don't notice or don't react. Ellis doesn't feel particularly guilty about this behavior, as he openly admits in his autobiography.[49]

According to him, many people stand in their own way by making irrational assumptions. The most common are: *I have to be good. Other people have to be good to me. Fate has to be good to me.* Anyone who places such unrealistic demands on themselves almost inevitably suffers. Ellis also regards the prevalence of black-and-white thinking as another product of irrationality. At the level of thought, he explains, neurotic fears and worries always consist of two parts: one understandable and plausible, the other pointless and counterproductive. To take as an example the statement "I have to be good," the rational part is: "I don't like it when I do something bad." But in most cases this is seamlessly accompanied by an irrational misjudgment: "If I fail, I'm worthless." Or: "Someone who does something bad can't be loved." Another example: "I want to be with person X." Here the irrational extension is: "If I can't be with X, everything is pointless."

Ellis develops what he calls the ABC model—for *activation*, *belief*, and *consequence*. According to the model, a mental crisis begins with a trigger, or activating experience, like a dismissive comment from one's boss, disinterest from one's partner or stress in one's daily life. These activate conclusions that are based on negative beliefs: "The boss doesn't like me." Or: "My relationship is beyond saving." Or: "I've failed." These thoughts in turn provoke their own emotional reactions, which seem inevitable to the person affected.

There are astounding parallels between Ellis's and Beck's approaches. Both argue that the most important step toward improvement is the realization that distressing feelings arise from distorted patterns of thinking and from misconceptions. The emotions triggered by this cognitive behavior are removed from reality, but nevertheless sew conflicts and a sense of being overwhelmed. In order to change this, patients must do more than merely understand that their thought patterns are one-sided, rigid, or exaggerated; they must, more than anything, practice alternatives.

Expressing yourself, gaining insights, feeling understood by another person—this is all well and good. But only those who make concrete changes to their behavior, bit by bit, will really benefit. In order to stress the connection between thinking and feeling, Ellis keeps tweaking the name of his theory: "rational therapy" becomes first "rational emotive therapy" before finally acquiring the name under which it is known today: "Rational emotive behavior therapy."

Unlike Ellis, Beck doesn't believe that it's always possible to say what's irrational and what's not. Many assumptions turn out to be irrational only after the fact, or under very particular circumstances. Maybe your boss really doesn't particularly like you; this only becomes a problem if you think people can't work well together unless they get along fabulously. According to Beck, the thoughts themselves shouldn't be regarded as irrational, only the effects that they have, the condition that they put a person in.

Cognitive behavior therapy, as developed by Aaron Beck and Albert Ellis—working, for the most part, independent of one another—aims at changing the patient's thinking and reasoning. Over time, however, it will turn out that in many cases it's enough for the patient to inwardly distance themselves from their thinking rather than eliminating it entirely. Acceptance-based approaches to therapy teach that unhelpful ideas and convictions don't necessarily have to be corrected; letting them pass on by and understanding that they are not inalterable truth is just as helpful—and easier to put into practice. Either way, the same principle holds: they're not truths, just thoughts.

Ellis considers it a crucial flaw of psychoanalysis that it declares the mere practice of making the patient conscious of hidden connections to be therapeutic. After all, understanding something in theory isn't at all the same as being able to implement it in practice. To Ellis, the idea that the patient's anxieties, compulsions, or other fixations will disappear once they have their eureka moment is a myth. After all, the thought patterns that are at the heart of the issue have usually developed over years or decades. Insight alone can't resolve them.

Here we can see how various approaches emphasize different aspects of the therapeutic process: of the three main factors that make psychological treatment successful for a patient—having new, positive experiences; gaining insights; and practicing alternative behavior—humanistic therapy aims primarily at achieving the first, psychoanalysis the second, and behavior therapy the third.

. . .

The field of psychotherapy in the first half of the twentieth century is like a circus with only two acts: the magician and the lion tamer. The one descends into the machinery of the psyche to work on unconscious traumas and conflicts; the other ignores inner processes completely and focuses solely on manipulating outward, observable behavior. Only over time does it become apparent that working on patterns of cognitive assessment is also a productive approach.

This insight is facilitated by the arrival of a new metaphor for the mind. The mechanical processing of information casts new light on the human psyche: instead of a pressure cooker filled with simmering drives or a puppet of the environment it begins to appear as a system that converts learning experiences into concepts, and these concepts into actions. The electrochemical exchange of signals between the brain cells saves complex programs in a way similar to computer chips. Beginning in the 1950s, therapists increasingly turn their gaze toward their clients' stalled thought paradigms. Instead of responding to failure by brooding—"Why can't you do anything right?!"—the goal is to think: "It's not so bad, it could happen to anybody!" At its core, the cognitive turn in psychology says no more and no less than this: you are what you think.

The consequences are far-reaching. Where the behaviorists assumed a direct relationship between stimulus and response and declared everything that went on in between to be a "black box," now a new agency appears on the scene—attribution. It determines how we react to stimuli. Bugs or a packed elevator only cause panic in someone who sees them as dangerous and thinks: *this can't end well.*

Cognitive behavior therapy targets such dubious judgments and tries to change them. In doing so it picks up on a two-thousand-year-old thought voiced by the stoic Epictetus: "It is never the things themselves that cause us unrest, only our own views of them."

TAKING SHAPE

In the early 1930s, Fritz and Lore Perls, like Annie and Wilhelm Reich, live on the Spree. They were drawn to the city by its cosmopolitan character and spirit of resistance. Nationwide the Communists get only about ten percent of the votes in the parliamentary elections of May 20, 1928, but in Berlin, one in four voters chooses the revolutionary cause. Another third of the capital's residents vote for the Social Democrats. Reich hopes to find more support for his sexual-political movement here than he did in Vienna; Perls, on the other hand, wants mainly to establish himself as a neurologist. He works at various clinics before

The calm before the storm: Lore and Fritz Perls at their wedding in Berlin, August 23, 1930.

opening his own practice. After he and Lore's wedding in August 1930, the newlyweds, with help from their parents, move into a seven-room apartment in the Bayrisches Viertel, the neighborhood that Fritz grew up in. The following year their daughter Renate will be born; it is a brief, carefree time before the world as they know it falls apart.

On the streets, Brownshirts and Red Front fighters clash in increasingly brutal battles. The world economic crisis ushered in by the Wall Street crash in the fall of 1929 exacerbates the tensions. Many people are faced with ruin; they've lost their jobs, their homes, and are forced to barter their last earthly possessions for food. And what then? Hunger and poverty are rampant, as is hatred. Its focus can be the Jews, the capitalists, the military, the landed nobility, the Communists, or—and here there is the broadest agreement—the Weimar Republic, the real culprit and cause of all this misery. As for what should replace it, that is completely up in the air. A restoration of the Emperor? A people's dictatorship on the Bolshevik model? Or a fascist state built on dreams of being a great power? Weimar is on the verge of collapse; the only question is who will deliver the coup de grâce.

Also in southwest Berlin, near an artists' colony popularly known as the "rote Tintenburg"—"the red ink fortress"—the Reichs find a small apartment for themselves and their two children, Eva and Lore, in the spring of 1931. In the morning the bedroom is arranged for receiving patients, as the apartment also serves as Reich's practice. At the nearby Breitenbachplatz U-bahn station, SA thugs often hang around, waiting to ambush the predominantly left-wing intellectuals who live in the neighborhood. When Perls comes to visit Reich, his training analyst, he feels like he's running the gauntlet.

When the aged German president Paul von Hindenburg appoints Adolf Hitler chancellor on January 30, 1933—and when, a month later, the Reichstag burns—the situation becomes life-threatening. Under the cover of an emergency order "for the protection of the people and the state," a wave of arrests begins; the Nazis consolidate power by suspending citizens' fundamental rights. Before the books of ostracized authors are burned on the square outside the Berlin opera house in May of that year, both the Reichs and Fritz and Lore Perls decide to flee. Many of those who hesitate, believing perhaps that Hitler won't remain in power for long, will later find themselves unable to escape.

While Reich flees first to Vienna and from there on to Copenhagen, where his wife and children join him, Fritz and Lore Perls decamp for Amsterdam in April 1933. A few months later Lore and Fritz board a ship bound for Cape Town. Ernest Jones, president of the International Psychoanalytical Association in London, has arranged for them to establish the first South African institute for psychoanalysis in Johannesburg. The country on the southern tip of Africa will be their home for the next twelve years.

. . .

Did Wolpe and Fritz Perls's paths cross in Johannesburg? They must at least have been aware of each other, especially since Wolpe underwent training in psychoanalysis as a young doctor.

But the pioneer of behavior therapy and the unorthodox ex-Freudian belong to two different camps that have long been united by a passionate mutual loathing. As was the case in Freud's heyday, a dim view of the competition makes the benefits of one's own approach appear in a better light. Thus on one side analysts find themselves subjected to the criticism that their lofty theorizing defies verification and verges nigh on quackery, while on the other side behavior therapists are held to be cold "psychotechnicians" who only tinker with symptoms rather than getting at the heart of the problem. This irreconcilable, cliquish thinking dominates the therapy scene for years, even though there are many who travel between the two worlds, especially in the US: psychologists who hold up the scientific principles of behavioral science in their academic positions while at the same time earning good money as psychoanalysts in private practice.

In the shadow of the feud between depth psychology and behaviorism, a third trend emerges that concerns itself with something that neither Freud nor Watson is particularly interested in: the individual's longing for self-realization. This humanistic brand of psychotherapy will be the first to be coupled with the promise, not merely of alleviating patients' suffering, but of helping them to find happiness in harmony with their own selves. Psychology at last becomes the royal road to a life of fulfillment.

. . .

Every school of therapy needs a manifesto, a kind of master plan that outlines that school's unique path to mental health. In the case of gestalt therapy, this manifesto appears in 1946 under the title *Ego, Hunger, and Aggression*.[50] Written by Fritz Perls, with substantial assistance from his wife, the book was completed five years earlier, in the winter of 1941. All the essential concepts of gestalt therapy can be found within, albeit in very disjointed, associative fashion. Perls touches on one topic here, another topic there, feeling his way along as if he didn't much trust his own ideas. "This book has many faults and shortcomings. Of this I am fully aware," he writes in the foreword. Perls wants to regard body and psyche, biology and psychology, as a comprehensive whole. And the key figure in all this is—the jaw.

To the use of teeth and food intake, or assimilation, Perls ascribes a considerable amount of influence on the homeostatic equilibrium of the organism. He also considers the act of eating to be psychologically formative, given that it is the individual's first, most immediate contact with their environment: it is here that the earliest damage occurs, for example when the infant is scolded for biting the mother's breast. The scolding causes the child to unlearn the ability to live out its natural aggression, and the foundation for neurosis is laid.

In the position occupied by Freud's unconscious libido and Adler's compensatory striving for power, Perls puts something that has been largely underestimated: hunger. Neurotics, he says, suffer from avoidance as a consequence of a dental inhibition. Perls's teacher Goldstein's concept of the "organism as a whole" shines through here: soma and psyche are inextricably linked, such that every physical process also has a psychological impact, and vice versa. This way of thinking might be unusual, Perls concedes, but it is indispensable.

In support of his theory he cites common expressions: we say we're *still chewing on* something, or that an idea is hasn't yet been *digested*. "Hunger for mental and emotional food behaves like physical hunger,"[51] he writes. A person who forgets how to *sink his teeth into things* usually shows abnormalities later in life: he might, for instance, greedily shove food into his mouth, displaying what Perls calls "oral frigidity," the inability to feel pleasure through the moderate use of the masticatory apparatus. In general, "our attitude towards food has a tremendous influence upon intelligence, upon the ability to understand things and get a grip on life and to put one's teeth into the tasks on hand."[52] In addition to the anal and genital inhibitions discovered by Freud, Perls sees above all oral inhibitions at work in the psyche.

For him, aggression is fundamentally good and desirable, as long as it is in the service of the ego and doesn't degenerate into raw destruction. "The use of the teeth is the foremost biological representation of aggression," he writes.[53] Viewing hunger and aggression as fundamental psychological needs and drawing parallels between physical and mental processes, Perls would also like to draw conclusions about the state of the psyche from physical phenomena like muscular tension or cramps. In this Perls's approach resembles that of his teacher, Wilhelm Reich. More than that, what from today's vantage seems an idiosyncratic argument is also a reflection of the times: when Perls is writing his book, Nazi Germany is taking over broad swaths of Europe, bringing war and misery in its wake. For millions of people, questions of hunger and aggression are existential.

There are two leitmotifs that recur throughout *Ego, Hunger, and Aggression*. The first is criticism of Freud. Freud, Perls writes, "treated his patients like children sitting on the chamber-pot, persuading, urging them to bring out whatever was in their minds without yielding to their embarrassment."[54] In truth, fear of excretion—anal resistance—isn't the problem; rather it's the inability to assimilate. What characterizes the neurotic is not that they are incapable of "letting it out," but that they avoid accepting the obvious, or, in Perls's terms, assimilating their intellectual nutrition.

Since his one, brief encounter with the master in Vienna in the summer of 1936, Perls has begun to distance himself more and more from orthodox Freudian doctrine. He does praise the founder of psychoanalysis for opening the field of therapy to cultivation, but he also castigates him for his mistakes and limitations. "By chewing psycho-analytical theories, however, and by pondering over every undigested morsel, I found myself becoming more and more capable of assimilating its valuable parts, and of discarding its errors and artificial constructions."[55]

The second leitmotif, typical for Perls, is the expansion of therapy's purview. He problematizes everyday traits, like the tendency to daydream, viewing them as the source of unhappiness and hidden conflicts. To be fully in the moment and recognize one's current needs—"figure formation," as it is called in the language of gestalt theory—is essential for finding inner equilibrium. "Self-realization is only possible if 'time-space awareness' penetrates every corner of our existence."[56] Just as it is obstructive to cling too tightly to the past, so is it harmful to revel too much in fantasies. This "avoidance of contact" stems from the world's demand that one be what one is not, and inhibits the development of the self.

Perls recommends practicing awareness. Only those who can free themselves from external demands can complete the shift to pursuing a more intensive existence. This becomes a key feature of humanistic therapy: curative treatment transforms into a universal guide for self-discovery.

In 1946, Fritz and Lore Perls, together with their now-adolescent children, emigrate again, this time to New York. The move is prompted by several considerations, from growing ethnic tensions in the apartheid state to Fritz and Lore's disillusionment with Jan Smuts, the philosopher who serves as South Africa's prime minister. Fritz and Lore were drawn to Smuts's holistic thinking at first, but over time it turns ever more into a theology of the "world soul," which holds little appeal for the two Germans. Finally, and not least among the reasons factoring into their decision, a new start in the United States promises to be economically attractive as well.

Together with Lore—who now calls herself Laura—and the libertarian and writer Paul Goodman, Fritz founds the Gestalt Institute of New York in 1952. The year before, a second foundational text had been published, *Gestalt Therapy*, the bulk of which was written by Goodman and Ralph Hefferline, a psychology professor at Columbia University. The explanations of concepts, at times difficult to understand, are leavened by lots of practical exercises and experiments. Goodman and Hefferline are responsible for most of the text; Fritz doesn't overexert himself, and Laura isn't even mentioned, even though she provided important ideas. Originally the book was supposed to be called "Concentration Therapy"; concentration, according to Perls, is the most effective remedy for neurotic avoidance of self. The title is changed, however, shortly before the book goes to print, probably in part to avoid the echo of Nazi vocabulary.

The program of gestalt therapy is now fully formulated: it reestablishes contact to the self, which is interrupted in cases of neurosis. Responsible for this interruption are five mechanisms whose names are borrowed from psychoanalysis: introjection, projection, confluence, retroflection, and egotism. Each represents a different channel taken by psychical tension that has no other means of escape. In the case of introjection—a term that Sándor Ferenczi coined in 1909—it is directed inwards; the individual lets the conflict "eat into" him and lives in a state of fearful-avoiding unease. In the case of projection, the opposite occurs: the individual shifts the conflict onto others and sees in them what he himself thinks or wishes but can't admit to. Confluence occurs when energy flows wildly in all directions, which causes the individual to act nervous and disoriented. In the case of retroflection, the energy is turned against one's self as aggression, and egotism is at play when the individual tends to overestimate themselves. All these phenomena have one thing in common: the connection to the self is disturbed.

AN ELYSIUM OF THE EGO

The Santa Lucia Mountains present to the visitor a landscape of dazzling beauty. The mountain range extends for more than a hundred miles along the Pacific coast, one peak rising after another. At their tallest the mountains soar to almost 6,000 feet above sea level, interspersed with grassland, cliffs, and ravines. To the west the land drops off sharply into the ocean. Here and there, narrow plateaus like small oases offer spectacular views of the rocky coast. On one such dream-like elevation, halfway between the sky and the sea, the land's original inhabitants, the Esselen tribe, once settled. The place was considered holy, for here, flowing together from three sources, was what was most precious to them: water. The surf mixed with the fresh water that flowed from farther inland, carving deep grooves into the rock, while on the plateau hot spring water bubbled through the cracks in the earth.

A man named Thomas Slate will find his way to this place in the late 19th century. The sulfurous springs help soothe his arthritis, and so Slate acquires the remote patch of earth in the middle of the great country of the south, the "gran país del Sur," as the Spanish called it. For years to come this section of the Big Sur coast will appear on maps as "Slate's Hot Springs."

In 1910 the Irish doctor Henry Murphy buys the land. He dreams of opening a spa here—but how, without roads or infrastructure? The region isn't opened up for development until 1937 with the completion of Highway 1. Planned as a giant job creation measure under Roosevelt's New Deal, the road along the Pacific coast links the Southern Californian cities of Los Angeles and San Diego with San Francisco in the north. Murphy opens a motel for highway tourists in the middle of the breathtaking landscape, but success fails to arrive. A quarter of a century later, in the same spot, roughly forty miles south of the fishing village of Carmel, a wooden sign will read: "ESALEN INSTITUTE – BY RESERVATION ONLY."

Here Murphy's grandson Michael, together with his friend from college, Richard Price, founds a retreat for dropouts and seekers. It is spring, 1962. The two men are in their early thirties, unmarried and unemployed. Like most other graduates of the elite Stanford University, all career paths are open to them. But the prospect of the usual suburban idyll, complete with house, car, and family, doesn't appeal to them. They see American society as mired in consumerism and outdated values, obsessed with competition and status, intent on the exploitation of nature and the repression of minorities—this isn't the life that Murphy and Price are dreaming of.

They studied philosophy and psychology, are interested in the wisdom teachings of the Far East and want to connect with their true selves. They draw their inspiration from Buddhism, from existential philosophy, and from the ideal of self-actualization. A new movement—the

Human Potential Movement—has captured the hearts and minds of many young US academics.

In this paradisical locale far from the noise and bustle of city life, Murphy and Price establish a center for personal growth. The program calls for bodywork: hot baths, massages, yoga, and meditation, plus workshops and lectures about spirituality and psychology. Murphy invites zen masters, quantum physicists, and consciousness researchers; explores the innermost layers of the psyche with the help of LSD and mescaline; organizes tantra sessions and encounter groups. Esalen—the place will soon gain a reputation that extends far beyond California as it becomes a center for a counterculture that seeks a new, freer way of living and thinking.

In the founding manifesto of the retreat, Murphy writes: "The Esalen Institute exists to promote the harmonious development of the whole person. It is a learning organization dedicated to continual exploration of the human potential, and resists religious, scientific, and other dogmas." The place draws dropouts, artists, and intellectuals from all over the world, like the English writers Aldous Huxley and Christopher Isherwood. In the first year, Esalen mainly plays host to bohemians and movie people from Hollywood. Still, there is a growing conviction among students at West Coast universities that happiness is a question not of wealth and career, but of one's own mental and spiritual attitude. More and more of them come streaming in to take part in the seminars and workshops that Esalen offers.

Fritz Perls sets foot in this little paradise for the first time around Christmas 1963. The gestalt therapist wanders the grounds in sandals and a worn-out jumpsuit and gives awareness seminars outdoors, high above the ocean. After a few weeks he announces his plans to move in permanently, taking his hosts completely by surprise. Murphy and Price are skeptical at first, but they quickly realize that the oddball German has the makings of a guru. In the years to come, Perls becomes a leading figure of the alternative youth movement and, at the same time, one of the driving forces at Esalen.

. . .

Right this way: street sign for the Esalen Institute, south of San Francisco on California's Pacific Coast.

As chance would have it, one summer evening in the early 1960s, another psychologist, this one a professor at Brandeis University, finds himself stranded in Big Sur. He and his wife Bertha are in the car headed south on the coastal road; in La Jolla, outside of San Diego, a prestigious fellowship awaits him. But once the sun sinks into the sea, every curve on the unlit road turns into an adventure. The pale moon, wreathed in fog, is the only source of light. Tired and hungry, the Maslows start looking for a place to spend the night. But the terrain to the left and right of the highway is nearly uninhabited. Suddenly the beam of the headlights lands on a sign: "Esalen Institute."

They turn down the steep drive that leads to the institute. Not knowing where they are, but believing they've found a hotel, Abraham Maslow and his wife start filling out the guest form. When the young man at the front desk sees the name, he reads it out loud in disbelief: "Ab-ra-ham . . . Mas-low? *The* Abe Maslow?!"

The man thus addressed is flattered, and all the more so when he finds out that at that same time the institute is offering a reading course centered around his new book, *Toward a Psychology of Being*. In it,

Maslow presents a theory of human needs that goes way beyond food, sex, and security. According to Maslow, other desires, like the wish for connection and to develop one's own talents, are rooted deep inside the individual. Do we not strive, above all else, for fulfillment? The way Maslow sees it, our various motives are governed by a hierarchical structure; as soon as one need is satisfied, we move on to the next highest.

Maslow arrives just in time to present his ideas in person to those enrolled in the course. The next day he gives his first lecture at Esalen; many more will follow. This community, in which so many like-minded people want to connect with each other and with the cosmos, will soon inspire Maslow to posit the existence of yet another motive, which he places at the top of his pyramid of needs: the need for self-transcendence. The path there leads through extraordinary altered states of being, or "peak experiences," as Maslow calls them. And where better to have such experiences than in a New Age commune at the far edge of the world?

. . .

Abraham Harold Maslow, born April 1, 1908 in New York, is fifteen years younger than Perls and, unlike his elder colleague, comes from a working-class family. He and his six siblings grow up in Brooklyn, where his parents settled after fleeing persecution in Kyiv. Maslow's relationship with his egocentric, less than empathetic mother is tense. Every day features some form of conflict. Abraham is delicate and often unhappy; he has few friends and finds an escape in books. Still, after he finishes high school his parents do make it possible for him to go to college. The idea is for him to become a lawyer, but after just a few semesters Maslow gives up his law studies in favor of psychology.

At nineteen he falls in love with his cousin Bertha Goodman. The two of them marry against the will of Maslow's parents and move hundreds of miles away to Madison, Wisconsin. There, at the University of Wisconsin, Abraham finds a position working for Harry Harlow. Harlow's famous experiments with animals make headlines: Harlow presents infant rhesus monkeys with a choice between a cloth-covered mother surrogate without food and a bare wire surrogate with a milk bottle. He observes that the baby primates remain with the cuddly ersatz mother almost the entire time and only climb over to the bottle for brief moments when they get too hungry. It seems that the need for warmth and security gives way to the need for food only when the latter becomes extreme.

After getting his doctorate in 1934, Maslow, along with Bertha and their two young daughters, moves back to New York to take up a job at Brooklyn College. At twenty-six he hears Alfred Adler's lectures at Columbia. The individual psychologist's theory that we are all trapped in a conflict between the will to power and the social feeling makes sense to him. His first scientific essay, "A Theory of Human Motivation," from 1943, formulates a model of hierarchically ordered physiological and psychological needs.[57] Maslow posits the existence of a series of motivations that build off one another, beginning with the desire for food and shelter and continuing on to abstract satisfactions like friendship and reputation. Fundamental needs must first be met before higher goals like self-actualization come into play. Because lower motives usually address a lack, Maslow calls them "d-motives" (for *deficit*); higher needs, on the other hand, are aimed at shaping an individual's own life (*being*), hence their name, "b-motives." There is an inkling here of the growth-based perspective that will propel Maslow to assume a leading role in the Human Potential Movement.

After sixteen years at Brooklyn College in New York, Maslow makes another move. In 1951 he becomes a professor at Brandeis University in Boston. His pyramid of needs is widely known by that point, but he continues to expand it, adding ever more motives: love, belonging, developing one's talents, experiencing purpose and happiness. Finally Maslow even posits the existence of a universal human need to believe in a greater whole or a divine authority.

Here the weakness of his model becomes apparent: it doesn't rest on survey data or other substantial observations; rather it is essentially speculative. Maslow himself concedes that there are sure to be many exceptions to the rules he lays out. One obvious one is that people experiencing hardship, whose essential needs remain unmet, are nevertheless often receptive to religious ideas. Indeed, for many, the hope of a better life in the next world is the only thing that makes the misery of their lives bearable. It remains unclear, then, just how there could be a hierarchically structured set of motivations.

In Esalen, Maslow finds what his academic home on the East Coast doesn't offer: drugs, meditation, body work. In his view, ecstatic experiences accelerate the process of self-actualization. Though he has little therapeutic ambition, the influence of Maslow's theories extends into this arena as well. Realizing your potential isn't a privilege of saints or wisemen, he declares; every individual has a natural drive impelling them toward fulfillment.

Maslow's winning manner, round face, and gentle voice make it easy to overlook the man's burning ambition. When he and Perls meet at Esalen, it quickly becomes clear that the two of them can't stand each other. For Perls, Maslow is a fraud and a "sugar-coated Nazi"; Maslow in turn sees Perls as nothing but a boorish egomaniac.

Things come to a head between them in early 1966. Perls has been living at Esalen for two years at this point. Maslow is a regular guest at the institute, but only ever for short periods; otherwise he continues to pursue his academic career. One day, Perls decides to sit in on one of Maslow's classes. Bored by Maslow's lecture, he interrupts to ask a

A man with ambition: Psychologist Abraham Maslow, the son of Ukrainian immigrants, did not have an easy start.

question: does Maslow seriously mean what he's saying? Why, Perls asks, does your stomach have to be full before you strive for transcendence? Don't many people endure hunger and suffering precisely *because* they have devoted themselves to their faith in God? "Don't be childish, Fritz," Maslow responds. Whereupon the Berliner gets down on his knees and crawls over to him on all fours, like an infant. While Perls, the gestalt teacher with the snow-white hair, whimpers and clutches at his pant legs, Maslow warns him that such escapades are harmful to Esalen's reputation. As for Perls himself, he's nothing but a fool.[58]

In 1967 Maslow becomes president of the American Psychological Association (APA),[59] opening the door for the scientific community's acceptance of humanistic psychology. But he isn't able to enjoy his fame for long. On June 8, 1970, while jogging in Menlo Park, near San Francisco, Maslow suffers a heart attack and dies.

DEATH IN PARADISE

From 1964 on, Perls gives regular gestalt seminars and awareness training sessions at Esalen, offering guidance on being present in the here and now. At this same time, so-called encounter groups are coming into fashion. Driven by the desire for open-minded, authentic communication, people convene for discussions that often last for several hours, approaching one another with openness and interest and talking about their personal experiences and emotions. Sometimes the sessions go on for days, hence their other name, "marathon groups."

It is the beginning of a psychocult that combines intense self-reflection with the attempt to be absolutely honest and real. One listens to one's inner self, looks to see what's there, and susses out one's needs and inhibitions. The slogan of the hour is: "Therapy is too good to be only for sick people." The perpetually supportive communal experience aims at actualization, at the free flow of psychical energy. To make this flow possible, you have to find yourself, going beyond the duties and distortions you were raised to accept. But being entirely yourself is often easier said than done. You never know exactly when you've reached the goal. Thus for many a sheer endless process of self-actualization begins.

You can always get just a little bit closer to your true self, feel even more intensely, and through talk, free love, and consciousness-expanding substances advance farther and farther on the path to self-liberation, without ever knowing where it ends.

This can be unsettling.[60] The therapist Irvin D. Yalom, himself a child of the 1960s New Age movement, describes the unique escalating logic of self-optimization: "If something is good, more is better. If self-disclosure is good in groups, then total, immediate, indiscriminate disclosure in the nude must be better. If involvement is good, then prolonged, continuous, marathon involvement must be better. If expression of feeling is good, then hitting, touching, feeling, kissing, and fornicating must be better."[61] The motto of more is better leads to all manner of unease.

"Esalen," Fritz Perls writes in his autobiography, "has become a symbol [. . .] for the humanistic-existential revolution, for finding and promoting new ways for sanity, growth, and the development of human potential."[62] The institute's celebrated mix of intellectuality and hedonism, nonconformity and wellness produces many classic techniques of the New Age scene: for example Rolfing, a deep-tissue massage developed by the biochemist Ida Rolf, or rebirthing, in which the participant relives the experience of their own birth, often with the help of drugs. The list also includes a special breathing exercise that aims at bringing about extraordinary states of consciousness through hyperventilation, as well as balancing, floating, and mindfulness. Nothing goes unattempted in the search for nirvana.

Perls's concentration-focused approach fits in seamlessly. What exactly does it involve? In his own words it sounds nebulous: "In Gestalt Therapy we start with *what is*, and see which abstraction, which context, which situation is there to be found and relate the figure, the foreground experience, to the background, to the content, to the perspective, to the situation, and they together form the gestalt."[63] For a person of average intelligence, trying to figure out what such a sentence means is a challenge. The whole thing easily devolves into a game of empty buzzwords, a simulation of therapy without beginning or end. "As soon as a gestalt is closed, a new, incomplete gestalt immediately emerges as a figure in the foreground. This process of closing and simultaneous opening of gestalts on the contact border is the crux of Perls's therapeutic approach," observes the psychologist Helmut Quitmann.[64]

At Esalen, Perls is one of the full-time teachers and lives in a wooden cabin with a grandiose view of the ocean. His seminars hinge on the element of surprise. You never know what to expect, what hijinks Fritz will have in store today. He's not exactly delicate—he says out loud what others don't dare think, interrupts participants, orders them around, reduces them to tears. Not everybody at Esalen likes this, but the German with the harsh accent commands respect. What if I fail? If behind my ego there's only emptiness? If I never make contact with my self?

The same Fritz who loved Reinhardt's theater of illusion as a young man puts on his own "circuses" at Esalen, as he ironically dubs the therapy sessions. Perls is a master of performance. "Lose your mind and come to your senses!" he suggests. From Jacob Moreno, the father of the psychodrama, Perls takes the technique of the "empty chair." Whoever faces the chair slips into another role and tries to describe the world from the point of view of the person imagined to be sitting there. What do you feel now? What do you see? What are you avoiding? Perls demands total attention and drills down deep, hoping to bring to the surface what lies within.

Part prophet, part bum: Fritz Perls at Esalen in the early 1960s.

The actor Jennifer Jones is a frequent guest at Esalen. In the summer of 1966 she throws a party at her house in Hollywood to introduce her show-business friends to Esalen founder Mike

Murphy. Rock Hudson, James Coburn, Shirley MacLaine, and Natalie Wood are there; the psychologist Carl Rogers comes too and leads an encounter group. Perls arrives late in the evening. He has traded the jumpsuit that is his trademark at Esalen for a tuxedo; otherwise he's as eccentric as ever. Around midnight a guest observes Perls giving Wood a private session by the pool. He orders her to stop playacting. Then he loses his cool and starts shouting at her: "You're nothing but a little spoiled brat who always wants to get her own way."[65]

The other guests stare at each other in shock. Who does this guy think he is? When Perls goes so far as to give Wood a symbolic spanking, she storms off in a fury. Around two a.m. the party breaks up. Perls has once again lived up to his reputation.

. . .

To be aware of yourself. In touch with your feelings. In the here and now. Holistic. Authentic. Alive. To develop your potential. Grow. Be connected. To this day, all these terms are part of the vocabulary of self-discovery. At the heart of the pursuit is the idea of setting aside the inauthentic, the conventional. Revealing your true self, bringing it out from behind the façade that your upbringing and society have forced on you. The individual is free when they stop putting on an act, stop simply doing what others want them to do. When they stop neglecting their inner needs in favor of all the external demands the world places on them.

The authenticity craze promises happiness and satisfaction for the individual and a better world to boot. If people paid more attention to themselves, they could relate to one another without hatred or competitiveness. Almost every philosophy of self-improvement contains one such element: a bleak negative image of the thing that must be overcome. As if the individual's happiness weren't enough, as if that happiness also, at the same time, had to be a vision for a new, improved society.

But what if this path doesn't actually get you anywhere? What if, despite living in a utopia, your own compulsions, anxieties, and sense of unease remain? In the late 1960s there is a series of suicides at Esalen and in the surrounding community. Nine young people take their own lives within a short time of one another. By the time Perls leaves the institute in late 1969, his confrontational style has precipitated mental crises in at least two women. They too take their own lives, but Perls denies any responsibility. He moves to Vancouver Island and founds a "gestalt kibbutz" modeled after Esalen. A few months later the seventy-six-year-old learns he has pancreatic cancer. Perls travels to Europe, visiting one city after the next, as if trying to make up for what he'd missed. But soon the pain becomes unbearable. On his way back to British Columbia he checks into a hospital in Chicago. When a nurse tries to tell him something, he snaps at her: "Don't tell me what to do!" A few days later Fritz Perls dies of a heart attack.

A memorial service fit for a hippie king is held for him in San Francisco. Hundreds of followers recite Perls's gestalt prayer: "I do my thing, and you do your thing. I am not in this world to live up to your expectations and you are not in this world to live up to mine. You are you and I am I. And if by chance we find each other, it's beautiful. If not, it can't be helped."[66]

Laura Perls lives for a good twenty years after her husband's death, during which time, in her quiet, persistent way, she does a lot for the dissemination of gestalt therapy. Today both Fritz and Laura are buried together in the Jewish Cemetery in Pforzheim. Their son Stephen, who becomes a psychotherapist himself, says on one occasion, looking back, that his father was always intent on lecturing him and his sister and hardly ever took them seriously. His praise for old Fritz is notably terse: "He did what he wanted to do and he did that extremely well. That is, basically, it."[67]

. . .

One morning in early November, Dick Price sets off on a hike through Hot Spring Canyon. The surrounding cliffs are blanketed in fog when he sets out. Price loves the quiet and the solitude, just him, the ocean, the mountains, and a path that seems to lead into nothingness. It rained during the night, the ground is sodden. Price could find his way even with a blindfold on, the path is so familiar to him. It leads along the hillside, then uphill for a short way before the rocky terrain slopes down into a ravine.

Price is still as captivated by the landscape as he was the first day that Michael, his friend from Stanford, brought him here. That was a quarter century ago. How naïve they were then! They wandered around for hours without any supplies; it was a miracle that they made it back to Slates Hot Springs. They checked out what was left of the motel that Michael's grandfather had built and decided that here, far from the hustle and bustle of San Francisco, they would "do their own thing." The Esalen Institute became a total success. In this magical place you can feel an intense cosmic energy. It's more intense here than anywhere else, and it inspires the thinking of all those who come here.

Ever since he was young Price has experienced hallucinations and delusions. More than once he has been institutionalized, given medication, electroshock therapy. The results were minimal, aside from the pain and shame. The hallucinogens that he experiments with at Esalen are his door to another world. Psychosis, as he sees it, isn't a disease; it's a way of being. One that seems threatening to the "normies." Now, at fifty-five, Price knows that the wild thinking is a part of him, and always will be. Thankfully the episodes aren't as frequent as they used to be—and by this point he sees them coming and can absent himself. He's not tormented by them anymore.

Esalen was easily the best idea he ever came up with. And he owes Michael a lot. Sometimes, though, it all gets to be too much for Price. All the questions, the visits from reporters, the rumors about orgies and mental crises, the accusations. Of course they have sex at Esalen, and quite a bit of it. Sure, sometimes tears are shed during their psychological workouts. But they look out for each other; nobody does anything they don't want to do. Even Fritz, when it came down to it, was just playing around with his guru image.

Price takes regular sabbaticals now. He travels to Asia, studies Far Eastern philosophy and seeks his own spiritual path. Thanks to all the guests who come flocking to Esalen, he doesn't have to worry about money. What good fortune, thinks Price, to meet so many inspiring people and to be able to make a living from it, too! A wave of gratitude surges through him.

Suddenly there's a rumbling. Price looks up at the sky. Is there a storm coming? Or did he just imagine the sound? A creeping suspicion comes over him. He looks for an outcropping that might offer shelter, spies a niche in a rockface a few steps away. At this moment the boulder hits him. It came loose from the cliff far above. Price doesn't know what hit him. He's killed on the spot.

5

OTHER PEOPLE

THE POWER OF COMPASSION

In June 1936, the city of Rochester, New York hosts a meeting of two men who will take psychotherapy in a completely new direction. This is the summer of the Berlin Olympics, during which the Nazis try to portray themselves as a peaceful dictatorship. For more than three years, Jews in Germany have been brutally marginalized and persecuted by Hitler's regime. Antisemitic ideology is prevalent, if not pervasive, in other countries as well. Meanwhile, in Spain, a murderous civil war rages. The world seems to be falling apart. In the midst of all these harbingers of looming disaster, these two psychologists develop a form of therapy that runs fully counter to the political zeitgeist. It rests on unconditional goodwill, understanding, and compassion.

One of the men is in his early fifties; he's short and rheumatic, with horn-rimmed glasses and a Viennese accent. The other is a lanky American from a strict religious home who is bursting with youthful energy. The older man was once Freud's favorite pupil and secretary of the Vienna Psychoanalytic Society until, in the mid-1920s, he began to distance himself from the master and his circle. For him, the primal, universal complex driving the individual isn't Oedipal incestual desire but rather the trauma of birth. Cast out of the protective uterus into a cold, hostile world, everyone strives to return to the womb, even if it's only in the act of coitus. Otto Rank has also long had doubts about Freudian analytic technique. Together with another dissident, the Hungarian Sándor Ferenczi, Rank developed "active therapy." In this approach the therapist takes an emotional interest in his client and sympathizes with his suffering, rather than remaining aloof and distant toward him, as classical analysis calls for.

The younger man, for his part, is at thirty-four still more or less an unknown quantity. He starts out studying agricultural science at the University of Wisconsin near his home town of Oak Park, Illinois. Raised by deeply religious parents, at the age of twenty he travels to Beijing for a conference of the World's Student Christian Federation. The piety and self-sacrifice of the Chinese Christians he meets leave such an impression on him that afterwards he transfers to the Union Theological Seminary in New York, planning to become a minister. Right across Broadway from the seminary is Teachers College, an institution for aspiring teachers and social workers. The two schools have a cooperative relationship, and soon Carl Rogers is taking his first seminars in education and psychology. Before long he has changed programs again, this time firmly resolved to become a psychologist.

In 1928, fresh out of college, Carl Rogers begins his first job in the city of Rochester on the banks of Lake Ontario. The Society for the Prevention of Cruelty to Children is looking for someone to put neglected, abused, and troubled youth on the right track. Eight years later, Rogers has risen to become the society's director and is following an approach that, while not orthodox psychoanalysis, is nevertheless derived from it. In conversations with the adolescents and their parents, he tries to make them see the unconscious motives and consequences of their actions—with middling success.

Rogers's colleagues at this time include a few social workers who attended the School of Social Work in Philadelphia, where Rank has been giving regular seminars since 1926. The women rave about Rank's vision of a "relational therapy" that requires love and devotion from the therapist. Instead of intellectual insight into the unconscious, the focus is on the relationship between two people. This, Rank says, is based above all on emotions—affection, trust, respect, and reliability on the one hand; envy, competition, fear, and authority on the other. Neurotic patients should feel secure in a protective atmosphere and accepted for who they are at that very moment; that way, Rank believes, they can build a stable attachment to their interlocutor. A person's current state matters more than what they may have experienced and repressed in the past. Sympathy instead of abstinence; opening one's self up and being present in the here and now instead of interpreting the past—for Freudians, these are downright blasphemous ideas.

To better get to know Rank and his approach, Rogers invites him to come to Rochester. Rank is there for just three days, but it's enough to get Rogers excited about relational therapy. From then on he's convinced that only through earnest sympathy and positive reassurance can the patient gradually come to their own realization of what they really want. After his meeting with Rank, this becomes Rogers's new guiding principle.

. . .

Who is Otto Rank? Born Otto Rosenfeld on April 22, 1884 in Vienna's Leopoldstadt neighborhood to the artisan jeweler Simon Rosenfeld and his wife Karoline, he is the youngest of three children. Otto's childhood is difficult, to put it mildly. His father, a drinker, is often violent and demands unquestioning obedience. Neither his wife nor his children are safe from his outbursts. Otto is intellectually gifted, but his talent is hardly nurtured. He is expected to become a tradesman like his father, and apprentices as a machinist. At nineteen Otto changes his name to Rank, after a character from Henrik Ibsen's *A Doll's House*. In the play, Nora, who dreams of being free and choosing her own path, is shut away from the world by her father and her husband, as if she lived in a doll house. The family doctor, Dr. Rank, is the only person she confides in.

On top of the problems he has with his family, Rank suffers from rheumatism and his, as he puts it, disadvantageous appearance. Young Otto grows up an anxious and melancholy bookworm. His loathing for his father, as well as his reading of the classics of philosophy—above all Nietzsche and Schopenhauer—lead to his interest in psychoanalysis.

As chance would have it, Rank gets to know Alfred Adler when Adler still has a practice on Czerningasse. Thus it comes to pass that one Wednesday evening the knowledge-hungry young man finds himself among the guests on Berggasse. After a lecture on the theme of incest in literature, the twenty-one-year-old becomes a member of the Wednesday Society. Rank wins Freud's affection as the minute-taker for the weekly meetings, and in turn, Freud becomes a second, better father to him. It takes twenty years for the eager pupil to work up the courage to go his own way.

Rank's departure from the true dogma begins long before his theory of birth trauma makes him persona non grata in Freud's circle. Like Ferenczi, he doubts the classical method. The abstinence rule dictates that the therapist maintain a distant relationship to his patients; indeed, he has to be invisible, to disappear into the shadows behind the couch. From this position, the therapist may guide the patient's free associating by asking follow-up questions; or he may present more or less convincing interpretations; but aside from that, instead of consolation, encouragement, or any kind of emotional response, the client is often met with nothing but silence. If he doesn't share the therapist's view, or if, worse still, he doubts the therapist's competence, that means only that he has yet to overcome his resistance.

By imposing the neutrality requirement after his failed treatment of Dora, as described in the "Fragment of an Analysis of a Case of Hysteria," Freud's aim was to head off the phenomenon of transference and countertransference. This dynamic occurs when the patient unconsciously puts the therapist in the place of the person he desires or fears. Freud regarded it as the biggest impediment to therapy: a patient who loves their therapist won't want to overcome their illness—and if they hate their therapist, this hatred scuppers the joint work of interpretation. Conversely, there is a danger that the therapist will abuse their power or have their judgment clouded. The abstinence requirement has a major downside, however: it turns patients into mere recipients of the analysts' insights, without allowing them to feel emotionally secure in the therapeutic environment. Rather than a sterile dissection of unconscious repression, Rank favors a trusting conversation between equals.

. . .

A month after Rank's flying visit to Rochester, two of his books appear in English translation. He first published them in German in 1929 and 1931, respectively, under frightfully verbose titles. *Die analytische Reaktion und ihre Konstruktiven Elementen* ("The Analytic Reaction and its Constructive Elements") was followed by *Die Analyse des Analytikers und seine Rolle in der Gesamtsituation* ("The Analysis of the Analyst and its Role in the Overall Situation"). Both are part of the multivolume overview *Die Technik der Psychoanalyse* ("The Technique of Psychoanalysis"). Rank's US publisher comes up with much catchier titles: published as *Will Therapy* and *Truth and Reality: A Life History of the Human Will*, Rank's books promptly meet with lively interest.

The author raises a central objection to psychoanalysis: "Where Freud met the will of the other he called it 'resistance.'"[1] Meaning: nothing the patient believes or wants has any validity because they have no clue what is truly going on within them. Rank, in contrast, is prepared to speak in the will's defense. Therapy must make patients capable of exercising their will in a courageous and proper manner. It's not a question of refining intentions and desires by revealing unconscious motives; these intentions and desires must first be developed. After all, the neurotic's main problem is self-denial. They can't bear the ambivalence inherent in life, and as a result can hardly bring themselves to make a decision.

Rank borrows a concept from the French existentialist philosophers Jean-Paul Sartre and Simone de Beauvoir which states that the condition of being cast into life produces fear. Every individual must shape their own life and in so doing accept the limitations of existence. This, Rank says, is a painful process: "The more strongly man feels his freedom and independence, the more intense on the other hand is the consciousness of guilt."[2] To decide is to become guilty; to pick one option is to rule out countless others. Only by exercising one's will can one actively assume the responsibility for self-invention that is imposed on every individual. It demands a "willing affirmation of the must,"[3] says Rank. Nietzsche's idea of *amor fati*—of loving the inevitable—can be glimpsed behind this thought.

But where does it lead? What does a therapy conducted in accordance with these premises look like? Rank gives only a vague answer.

"My technique consists mainly of the fact that I don't have one," he explains—and relies intuitively on "immediate understanding of experience," on the "emotional surrender to the present."[4] Rank listens, asks questions, receives the other person with patience and encouragement. No criticism, no lecturing—only sympathy and emotional mirroring are therapeutically effective, he believes. In *Die Technik der Psychoanalyse* Rank writes that "it is not intellectual knowledge but emotional experience in the analytic situation that forms the essential therapeutic factor in the cure."[5] In a 1929 lecture titled "The Psychological Approach to Personal Problems," Rank is even more explicit: "I don't think we can help these patients by making them more aware of their mechanisms. They need something else. They need an *emotional* experience."[6]

Anaïs Nin, the Parisian *bohémienne*, who begins therapy with Rank in 1933, describes his empathetic way of conversing as follows: "I talked to Rank as I talked to my journal . . . I feel his sympathy, a far-reaching one. I can tell him everything."[7] Freud believed Rank would never amount to much as a therapist because he was "too unsightly." But this very unsightliness becomes a virtue. Rank thinks of himself as an artist who turns his patients into artists of their own selves. Neurotics, as "artists manqués," must muster the courage to create themselves.

Concepts come into play here that will inspire generations of therapists to come: growth, self-discovery, relationships, the here and now. Rank figures as a central link between Freudian psychoanalysis and the humanistic school that takes off after World War II, above all in the US. With the lectures that he gives in the US between 1924 and 1938, the shy Otto becomes the spokesman for an emotionally-tuned therapy culture that will soon find its way back across the Atlantic to Europe. At the same time, Rank integrates numerous ideas from existentialist and cognitive therapy into his own approach.

Instead of rooting around in the unconscious, Rank attempts to change the *conscious* assumptions and convictions of the patient. "The individual is constantly interpreting himself," he writes, "his whole adjustment, maladjustment, *Weltanschauung* [world view] depends upon his interpretation of himself."[8] A whole range of approaches to therapy, each forming their own distinct school, have this one apostate to thank for important sources of inspiration.

. . .

As Europe hurtles toward a new war, Carl Rogers, inspired by Rank, develops a new therapeutic attitude of unconditional engagement and empathetic understanding. In his work with adolescents, Rogers makes an effort to listen in a fully open and interested manner, rather than criticizing. He has only one problem: to him personally, the youth he works with are often simply unlikeable, if not downright abhorrent. It's not uncommon for Rogers to deal with insolent, violent, or sadistic adolescents who point the finger at others and will seize on any excuse to avoid taking responsibility for their actions. Having grown up in a strict religious home, he has been accustomed to controlling his emotions from a very young age. Thus it's usually not hard for him to conceal his own discomfort. But is this game of hide-and-seek of any benefit to the therapy? Does he have to dissimulate to keep his interlocutors from losing their willingness to cooperate? Are engagement and empathy too much to ask for after all?

Out of such reflections, Rogers gradually develops a third pillar of what he calls his "client-centered therapy": the principle of congruence. If he can't respond with unreserved positivity, the therapist should be genuine and behave in a way that reflects his own feelings and is in harmony with his own self. To be sure, not merely pretending interest or putting on an act for the client's sake doesn't mean saying everything that pops into your head, without any filter. After all, a person's thoughts sometimes drift off to places that have no relation to the matter at hand: *did my wife remember to pick up the kids? I can't forget to buy milk on the way home.* Being congruent means putting your cards on the table and articulating your own doubts, reservations, and sources of irritation—but in small doses, and without jeopardizing the underlying attitude of engagement.

Only if therapist and patient are honest with each other can they work together. For Rogers, understanding grows out of empathizing with another person and considering their perspective. With his ideal of non-judgmental acceptance, Rogers comes fairly close to what today is considered indispensable for a successful course of therapy. At a time when psychotherapists often believed they had to educate their patients in a paternal manner, this is something completely new. Rogers takes the framework that Rank establishes with his relationship therapy and fills it with unconditional goodwill and authentic attentiveness.

A key experience from his own work with troubled youth makes it clear to him what little good it does to enlighten people as to their "true," repressed motives. The decision to change something about themselves has to come from within; the therapist is nothing more than a midwife. Rogers spends several weeks talking to a young woman about her behaviorally dysfunctional son and her strained relationship with him. The boy, according to the woman, is "something of a hellion."[9] Despite weeks of therapy, the situation hasn't changed; it's still as bad as it was before. Rogers suspects that the cause of the problems lies in the mother's subconscious rejection of her unwanted child, and tries to talk to her about this—in vain. Deeply frustrated, Rogers and the woman finally agree that the therapy probably isn't going to help the child; he wishes her luck, they shake hands and say goodbye.

As she's about to leave, the woman suddenly turns around and lingers in the doorway. "Do you ever take adults for counseling here?" the mother asks shyly. After he has said yes and she has sat back down, she confesses to him her strong feelings of guilt with regard to her son. Rogers neither condemns nor judges what she says, he merely repeats in his own words what she has told him. This way the woman finally recognizes herself what is to be done.

. . .

Just a short time after the meeting between Rank and Rogers, another encounter takes place in Vienna that isn't quite as edifying. In the summer of 1936, Fritz Perls travels from South Africa to the congress of the International Psychoanalytical Association in the Bohemian town of Marienbad (now Mariánské Lázně). There he speaks about the concept of oral resistances that he later spells out in *Ego, Hunger, and Aggression*. Perls draws parallels between the use of the masticatory apparatus and the patient's refusal to accept and "assimilate" objective facts. This inhibition is for him an indicator of a hidden early childhood trauma. But Perls's position meets with harsh criticism at the congress. According to orthodox theory, resistance is always anal, with the patient stuck at the phase of development situated between the oral and phallic phase.

Perls travels on to Vienna bearing the sting of this disappointment. He feels he's been unjustly treated and seeks clarification on the matter from the highest possible authority: Freud himself. At Berggasse he is first received by an older woman, probably one of Freud's sisters. No sooner has Perls stepped into the apartment than, as he remembers,

> a door opened about two and a half feet wide and there he was, before my eyes. It seemed strange that he would not leave the door frame, but at that time I knew nothing about his phobias.
>
> "I came from South Africa to give a paper and to see you."
>
> "Well, and when are you going back?" he said. I don't remember the rest of the (perhaps four-minute-long) conversation. I was shocked and disappointed.[10]

For the rest of his life, Perls will never grow tired of badmouthing Freud. "Interpret nothing!" is his mantra. Perls loathes lofty theorizing, what he calls "elephant shit." He has a deep aversion to everything conventional and despises the exchange of mere niceties, the verbal game of hide-and-seek. Under his guidance the client listens to their inner self, senses how they are moving, what positions they are taking. Even small gestures, a giggle here, a movement of the hand there, provide information about experiences that need processing. For some, the attempt to read their bodies' messages degenerates into a hunt for a chimera. For others Perls becomes an icon of the "counterculture" that pushes back against the societal pressure to conform. He wants to take "paper people" and turn them into living beings. Though he rejects authority, he himself acts very much like an authoritarian. In his sessions he tells his clients what to do, orders them to repeat words or gestures, or bombards them with questions. He doesn't mince words and sometimes goes too far. Many of his followers share his desire for authenticity, but they hardly feel empathized with or secure in his presence.

. . .

Meanwhile Otto Rank has to contend with the growing hostility of his former colleagues. As early as the summer of 1926, Freud is complaining that Rank's "whole behavior is evidently calculated to cut the tablecloth between us and him."[11] He also characterizes his once loyal disciple as an "imposter by nature" and a "huckster."[12]

Finally he cuts ties for good with the turncoat who dared to put the trauma of birth in the place of the Oedipus complex. Now, as far as Freud's entourage is concerned, it's open season on Rank. Even old friends like Ferenczi start to attack him; some call him mentally ill. Embittered, he, his wife Beata (nicknamed Tola), and their young daughter Helene leave Vienna for Paris, where as the former head boy among Freud's pupils he quickly finds his way into the art and literary scene. At that time, Freud and the unconscious are very much en vogue among the Surrealists.

In the spring of 1930—by this point Rank is already spending most of his time in America—attacks against him escalate even further. At the International Congress on Mental Hygiene in Washington, numerous members of the American Psychoanalytic Association (APA) led by Abraham Brill are present. Like most of his colleagues, Brill is vehemently opposed to "laymen"—such as educators, social workers, and lawyers, to say nothing of a trained machinist and literary scholar like Rank—being allowed to practice psychoanalysis alongside physicians. Now that Rank has fallen from grace, Brill sees his chance to cast him out. At an annual gathering of the APA that takes place in parallel to the congress on mental hygiene, he brings a motion to revoke Rank's honorary membership. The motion is approved. All of the Viennese exile's analysands must now find themselves a new training analyst and start their training over again. What's more, anyone who refers patients to Rank risks being cast out themselves. In short: Rank is stripped of his livelihood.

To make ends meet, he embarks on lecture tours, mainly in the US, where he feeds the Americans' hunger for anything that has to do with psychoanalysis. In the summer of 1935 Rank applies for citizenship, giving his parents Simon and Karoline Rosenfeld the name Rank on the application form. Despite all the obstacles that others have placed in his way, he decides to settle in New York—but not without his great

Parisian love: Anaïs Nin. In effusive letters he sets out to convince her to join him in opening up a practice. Fascinated by the idea of becoming an analyst herself, Nin finally gives in to his entreaties and bids adieu to her other lovers in Paris. Soon wild scenes are playing out in an apartment near Park Avenue. While Nin, who never underwent a training analysis, regularly seduces her patients and has sex with them on Rank's couch, Rank is in the next room plumbing his clients' emotional depths. The arrangement doesn't last long, as one can imagine. When Rank finally accepts that Nin will never be his alone, he ends his relationship with her, deeply depressed.

He had already put an end to his broken marriage with Tola in 1934 and left the family. Now Rank makes a new plan: he wants to move to California with his secretary, Estelle Buel, a young American with Swiss roots. He means to write one last book, to be called "Beyond Psychology," before he and Estelle begin a new life in Los Angeles. At Lake Tahoe in Nevada, where the couple stop over for a few weeks until Rank's divorce is finalized, he plugs away at the manuscript. "I merely want to give an impression of how I see human life," he writes. "The subjects of my former interest—the hero, the artist, the neurotic—all come back once more on the stage."[13] But he won't be able to complete the work.

On July 1, 1939, Estelle and Otto are finally able to get married. Two months later the German army attacks Poland, and three weeks after that Freud dies in London of an overdose of morphine. Rank is shaken—and in poor health himself. After a kidney stone operation he is given medication to prevent inflammation, but it has terrible side effects: in short order it drastically lowers his white blood cell count. Rank succumbs to an otherwise harmless infection. He dies on October 31, 1939 at only fifty-five years old. Shortly before his final breath he says just one word: "Strange."[14]

FACTS ARE FRIENDLY

Impressed by Rank, Carl Rogers is intent on further developing his own approach. When he takes a position at the University of Ohio in

1940, he uses the new space it affords him as an opportunity to hone his thoughts. His interpretation of the function of the therapeutic relationship differs from Rank's in one key respect. For Rank it was a means to an end: the patient feels secure within the bounds of a sympathetic encounter, which makes it possible for them to reveal things to themselves and their interlocutor that they wouldn't admit to otherwise. The relationship thus clears a path to insight, which in turn has a therapeutic effect. For Rogers, on the other hand, the relationship is itself the remedy. Through it, the client has a corrective experience. He senses—often for the first time—that someone else is taking an honest interest in him as a person, and is permitted to be just the way he is, with all his weaknesses and flaws.

"Client-centered therapy" first sees the light of day on December 11, 1940. On this date, Rogers first presents his concept to a group of psychologists, educators, and social workers. He then outlines the core elements of his approach in book form in the 1942 classic *Counseling and Psychotherapy*. From this point forward, instead of patients, he refers only to "clients." Therapy, as Rogers understands it, helps everyone continue to grow.

Rogerian therapists offer neither interpretations nor advice. They empathize; they try to understand and acknowledge their clients' feelings. They reformulate the client's thoughts as a way of strengthening the client's awareness of the thoughts' meanings. All of this has little to do with Freudian analysis. Psychotherapy becomes a form of encounter, an extension course for the psyche, which is meant not to relieve symptoms but rather "to assist the individual to grow."[15]

In using the term "client," Rogers stresses this sense of providing a service. Later he will go so far as to speak only of "person-centered counseling." His approach rests on three principles: congruence, acceptance, and empathy. The first refers to a manner of comporting one's self as a therapist that is authentic, honest, and relatable. The second term describes an unconditional esteem; the therapist doesn't criticize and doesn't raise concerns, but rather accepts clients exactly as they are. The third principle involves empathetic understanding. The clients set the topic and the tone, while the therapists, for their part, empathize with the client's perspective and through open, positive support contribute to the resolution of whichever issue is under discussion. Instead of treating the client in the medical sense, the therapist assists clients on their path to self-discovery.

Rogers's way of working can be seen in the case of Gloria, whom Rogers counsels live on camera as part of a 1965 film project. The single mother has a problem with her nine-year-old daughter Pam. She wants to be a good, honest mother and speak openly about everything. But at the same time, Gloria is looking for a partner and, well, she likes sex, as she tells Rogers openly. Gloria goes out and spends time with men, even those who aren't long-term partner material. She feels she has the right to have a little fun. But how is she supposed to tell Pam this?

Rogers lets Gloria talk. He asks questions, tries to understand exactly what she is trying to say, and summarizes what she has said. Their conversation is often punctuated by long silences; Rogers doesn't make any judgements and doesn't voice any opinions. While Gloria tries to find the right words, he just sits there and looks at her in a kindly manner. Gloria arrives looking for advice; she wants to know if it can hurt children to talk to them about sex. Could she even traumatize Pam by being

The good person from Oak Park: Carl Rogers as a young man.

open with her about her desire? But Rogers demurs: "It might seem to you as though I were being evasive, but if I understand you correctly, you are in a double bind. You want to be honest, and you feel you're not doing anything wrong when you sleep with men. You want to be loved and accepted by Pam the way you are. At the same time you're afraid that you don't deserve love and acceptance."

"Yes, that's right."

"And you'd like to hear from an authority figure: go ahead and do this or that, it's fine!"

"Exactly." Gloria sighs. "You know, Pam's daddy, from whom I'm separated, is always putting on a show for her. He's all goodness and light, and Pam adores him. I envy him for that. I'd like to have some of that glory myself. Pam doesn't have a clue what her father is really like; she only knows the image that he presents to her. But I want her to see me how I really am—and still love me."

"And you're not sure that's possible?"

"On the one hand, yes. But on the other hand, what's the point of hiding?"

"You think, if Pam's love and acceptance of you is based on a false picture of you, what the hell is the good of that?"

"Yes. But if I show her how I really am, she might hate me."

"You're afraid that she won't love you anymore if she finds out who you are and how you feel."

"You could say so."

Silence.

Rogers continues: "It's hard to take responsibility, isn't it? It's an awful risky thing to live."

"Yes. [pause.] Now I feel like, 'Now that's solved,' and I didn't even solve a thing, but I feel relieved."

"In my experience, it's no damn good telling people to do something that they haven't really chosen to do. That's why I am trying to help you find out what your own inner choices are."

"But I'm stuck in this double bind. I don't like what I want, that's why I'm afraid Pam won't like it either. What should I do?"

"At heart you wish for a situation in which you feel really comfortable about what you are doing."

"Yes. They always say listen to your feelings, do what feels right. But there's lots of moments in life where that's not at all clear. My feelings say one thing, but my conscience says something else."[16]

. . .

Rogers's open, attentive conversational style revolutionizes therapy. He himself is astounded by how much relief it brings people to feel that they are finally being taken seriously. Most of his clients are used to therapists who push back, point out errors or try to convince them to adopt another view of things. Not Rogers. He imagines what might be going through the client's head: "But now that I've shared with [the therapist] some of this bad side of me, he despises me. I'm sure of it, but it's strange I can find little evidence of it. Do you suppose what I've told him isn't so bad? Is it possible that I need not be ashamed of it as a part of me? I no longer feel that he despises me."[17] The experience of being with a therapist who, leaving his own judgments aside, merely engages and asks questions helps people who don't feel that they are worthy of love to develop a more positive self-image.

This type of conversational style is unusual because in our daily lives we usually do the opposite: we bombard one another with our views and with well-meaning pieces of advice. It's not long before the first jokes about Rogers's approach start making the rounds. Some therapists, as one joke has it, take the dogma of non-directive therapy so seriously that when asked for the time they merely reply: "So, if I understand you correctly, you would like to know what the clock says?"

In order to teach the client-centered approach to students, Rogers starts recording sessions on tape. At first he hides the microphone in the shade of his desk lamp, but once, when he puts the microphone out in the open on the table, he notices that it barely has an effect on the conversational atmosphere. From then on he obtains his clients' consent and records first isolated exchanges, then later entire sessions and full courses of therapy.

Rogers makes history with a two-hundred-page appendix included in his book *Counseling and Psychotherapy*: the case of Herbert Bryan is the first complete transcript of a course of psychotherapeutic treatment.

Never before had someone gone to the trouble to type out, word for word, everything that was said during eight full sessions of therapy, complete with extensive commentary and analysis.

In his seminars, Rogers stops the tapes at various points and lets the students think about how one could or should continue the conversation. Over time, he compiles several hundred transcripts. They serve yet another aim: Rogers is one of the first to assess the efficacy of his own method and to analyze outcomes. In his book *On Becoming a Person*, he writes: "We had to live with our failures as well as our successes, so that we were forced to learn. There was only one criterion [. . .], and that was, 'Does it work?' Is the method effective?"[18]

In this regard, Rogers also sets standards. He writes that "psychotherapy may become a science, applied with art, rather than an art which has made some pretense of being a science."[19] Robust efficacy tests are labor-intensive and expensive, however: a large group of test subjects must be compared with a control group so that it's possible to ascribe any changes that may result to the treatment itself and not merely to the passage of time or the expectation of improvement. What's more, one must define and track criteria for desired changes; from these criteria it's possible to draw more conclusions than from the usual anecdotal reports.

Clearly it does not concern Rogers that a rigorous examination of his methods could lead to disappointment. Quite the contrary, he stresses that facts are friendly—ultimately, they help practitioners to refine therapeutic conversational techniques. Rogers's research in the 1940s and 1950s consumes hundreds of thousands of dollars. Most of this funding comes from organizations like the Rockefeller Foundation or the Ford Foundation, or from the government-funded Public Health Service. Again and again, Rogers succeeds in convincing funders that the economy, the military, and society as a whole stand to benefit from a well-functioning psychotherapy. In Chicago, at his next academic post, he employs as many as thirty people at times, including several PhD candidates. Between 1943 and 1957, he and his collaborators produce more than two hundred scientific papers. Much of the work is still undeveloped, but as Rogers himself notes self-deprecatingly: "It isn't a good research in psychotherapy; it's just the best that there is."[20]

For all his scientific ambition, Rogers, the one-time seminarian, remains a spiritual person. At one point towards the end of his life he describes an ideal course of therapy: "When I am somehow in touch with the unknown in me, when perhaps I am in a slightly altered state of consciousness [in the relationship], then whatever I do seems to be full of healing. [. . .] Our relationship transcends itself and becomes a part of something larger. Profound growth and healing and energy are present."[21]

Rogers's conversational therapy is seen as belonging with the other humanistic approaches. It regards itself as an alternative to aloof psychoanalysis, but also to the behavioral therapy that comes out of behaviorism. Unlike these other schools, Rogers's method is dominated by an optimistic element. Be who you really are—it's possible! With this idea, Rogers's client-centered approach becomes a blueprint for the budding field of consultants and life coaches.

GODS LIKE YOU AND ME

A rabbi is in dialogue with the Almighty. "What exactly is the difference between heaven and hell?" he wants to know. "Come," says God, "I'll show you." He opens a door to a room in which many emaciated figures huddle around a large table. Each of the poor wretches has one hand chained to his chair; in the other he holds a spoon with an extra-long handle. The spoon can reach the delicious-smelling stew in the middle of the table, but can't be brought to the person's mouth. Helpless, they try again and again—in vain. The people starve while the room is filled with the most mouth-watering aroma. "This," says God, "is hell." Heaven is next door. A second door opens; in this room the rabbi sees another large table with a delicious stew in the middle, and sitting in a circle around it, chained figures with oversized spoons. But the people here are well-nourished and engaged in a lively conversation. The rabbi looks at God, puzzled. God answers: "Here they have learned to feed each other."

With this Hasidic parable the psychoanalyst Irvin D. Yalom illustrates how crucial the social element is for human well-being.[22] At a basic, elemental level, we are dependent on one another; without others we ourselves would be nothing. By extension, this means that psychological problems are almost always relationship disorders. They are rooted in internalized emotional and thought patterns that are often developed in childhood and shape the individual's relations with others. One child, neglected at a young age, learns to constantly set aside her own needs until at some point she isn't even aware of them anymore. Another, having to assume responsibility for his depressive father or alcoholic mother, "parents" the people in his life who are significant to him. Still others are plagued by self-doubts because from earliest childhood on they were never considered good enough. Either they undersell their abilities or they always try to act bigger than they are in order to get attention. It's hard to extract ourselves from the hold of such patterns. They become templates that we apply to every interpersonal relationship—after all, they've saved us once before. In this way, early influences often continue to hold sway in adulthood and are even passed on from generation to generation. Identifying this tendency in his important paper "Remembering, Repeating, and Working-through," from 1914, Freud terms it the compulsion to repeat.

If psychological maladies are rooted this deeply in interpersonal dynamics, is it not best to overcome them through interpersonal means? Talking to other people who have had similar experiences brings comfort and makes it clear that we're not alone with our sorrows, that many other people are going through the same thing. It can also be easier to recognize the influence of one's family or personal background if one discusses these factors with others or relives them through role play in a safe environment. Group therapy, which becomes especially popular in the US after the Second World War, is based on this premise.

It was first invented, however, in the 1920s, by yet another Viennese psychologist: Jacob Moreno. The eccentric young man begins frequenting the salons of the literary and art scene before the First World War. His extravagant appearance makes him a recognizable presence in the city's coffeehouses. Moreno has a scraggly Jesus-beard and long hair, goes hatless (which is highly unusual at the time) and wears an ankle-length green coat. Everything about him seems performative; there he is, striding messianically down the sidewalk as if he were acting upon a stage. And in fact, Moreno does regard himself as a messiah of spontaneity:

"I'm God, you're God, we're all God," he declares. For in the creative act, the individual, like God, creates himself and his own world.

Though enrolled as a medical student, his true calling is the theater, and specifically the improvisational theater. On April 1, 1921 he presents a memorable evening at the Wiener Komödienhaus. Moreno invites numerous friends and members of the cultural scene to a performance of a most extraordinary kind. Dressed in his Jesus getup, he steps out on stage and begins by reciting his own poetic inventions before calling on the audience to join in. Not everyone is amused by the mix of slapstick and exhibitionism; some, given the date, take it to be an April Fool's joke. The *Wiener Mittagszeitung* writes: "A doctor who considers himself a philosopher poet chose the first of April of all days to assemble a quite good-natured group of onlookers and impose on them his truly muddled trains of thought. Many noisily left the hall."[23]

This doesn't make a dent in Moreno's enthusiasm. He finds a small theater run by a female artists' organization and rents it out two evenings a week to put on his experimental shows. They aren't performances in the conventional sense; rather the audience members shout out prompts

Drama and Psyche: Jacob Moreno in Action

to the actors—including the future star of the stage Elisabeth Bergner and a certain Ladislaus Löwenstein, who from 1925 on will call himself Peter Lorre—who then improvise in response. Everyone is invited to participate in the proceedings. The point is to give free rein to your spontaneity while scenes from daily life or the headlines are being acted out on stage.

One evening two friends of Moreno's, the writer Georg Kulka and his wife, the actress Anna Höllering, act out their marital problems on stage. They bicker and quarrel, insult each other and make up, till finally, at the end, they are lying in one another's arms, laughing with relief. Here for the first time Moreno notices the cathartic effect of his brand of performance: it is capable of resolving even thorny conflicts and points of contention, and can get people who have been estranged for years to reconnect emotionally. This therapeutic effect doesn't necessarily last, of course. A few months after their onstage couple's therapy session, Höllering and her husband end up separating after all. The split is so destabilizing for Kulka that he takes his own life a few years later. When another depressive patient of Moreno's also resorts to suicide, the setbacks weigh on him. But he clings to his fundamental conviction: rehearsing one's actions, thoughts, and emotions, acting them out creatively helps to liberate the psyche. Thus the psychodrama is born, and from here on out Moreno will work diligently to refine it further.

. . .

The maverick Dr. Moreno's real name is Jacob Levy. As a young man he takes the name of his father, Moreno Nissim Levy, who deals in Turkish goods throughout Romania, Greece, and the Balkans. Levy, Sr. is away on business so much that his son barely ever sees him. As the first-born he slips into the role of substitute father; thus it seems only logical that he would take his name.

His father's side of the family is descended from Sephardic Jews who were driven out of Spain around the time Columbus sailed to America, eventually settling in the eastern Mediterranean and on the Black Sea. Later Jacob Moreno will spread the legend that he was born on board a ship somewhere on the foggy Black Sea on May 16, 1892, exactly four hundred years after the last Jews were expelled from the Iberian Peninsula. In truth—as written on his birth certificate, and as he himself stated when matriculating at the University of Vienna—Moreno was born on May 18, 1889 in Bucharest. Throughout his life he will trade in masquerades and mystifications; little of what he says about himself can be taken at face value.

His mother Paulina Iancu is just fifteen when she gives birth to Jacob. Her marriage to a traveling salesman nearly twenty years her senior was arranged by her brother. Paulina is an orphan who was raised in a convent; she is well-read, loves French, and usually calls her son Jacques. With her husband often away, she raises Jacob and his five younger siblings largely by herself. Moreno Levy's business is only moderately successful, and life in Bucharest with a half-dozen hungry mouths to feed is hard; their days are marked by poverty and antisemitism.

One of little Jacob's favorite activities, a way of escaping this oppressive reality, is to play God. In his autobiography he describes a Sunday afternoon when he was four or five years old: "My parents went out to visit friends. I stayed home and played with the neighbor kids. I thought about what game we should play and said: 'Let's play God and the angels!' But who will be God? 'I'm God and all of you are my angels,' I answered. The other kids agreed. We dragged chairs from all around the house, put them on the large oak table and started building one heaven after the other by tying chairs together and putting more chairs on top of them until we reached the ceiling. Then the other kids helped me climb to the topmost chair, where I sat quite comfortably. The children gathered around the table, flapping their arms like wings and sang. Suddenly one of them asked: 'Why aren't you flying?' I spread my arms out wide and gave it a try. A moment later I was myself back on the floor, my right arm broken. The psychodrama of the fallen God—this was, as far as I can remember, the first private psychodrama session that I ever led."[24]

When Jacob is six, the family moves to Vienna in the hopes of finding a better life. Eight years later, in 1903, the family moves again, this time to Berlin. Jacob is fourteen by this point and misses Vienna so much that after just three weeks he heads back on his own and stays with friends. He leaves school and starts working as a private tutor for various families, among them the Bergners. Their daughter Lisl, barely twelve years old at this point, shows great talent as an actress. Together with Lisl and some of her classmates, Moreno starts working with children he finds playing in Vienna's Augarten. He gets them to reenact scenes from their daily lives and spontaneously act out their worries and woes. Improv theater has long since become Moreno's mission when in 1909—without having finished school—he starts studying philosophy at the university. Two years later he has gone back and earned his *Matura* and enrolled in the medical school.

Before the war breaks out, probably in early 1914, Moreno hears Freud give a lecture. He gets into a conversation with the professor, who asks him what he's thinking of doing after he graduates. "I'll pick up where you leave off," is Moreno's self-assured reply. Rather than work in a private practice far removed from real life, he wants to help the needy in their everyday surroundings, just as he tried to do in 1913 with sex workers in Vienna's am Spittelberg red light district. There Moreno organized counseling and support groups for women on the fringes of society.

Thanks to his Turkish citizenship (which he inherited from his father), Moreno is let off from serving in the Habsburg army. He works in a displaced person camp in Mitterndorf and, beginning in 1920, as a company doctor in Bad Vöslau, less than forty kilometers south of Vienna. There he meets his first great love, Marianne Lörnitzo. The two of them move in together, and during this time he produces *The Words of the Father*, a poetic distillation of his worldview. It begins with the words: "I am God, / the father, / creator of the universe. // These are my words, / the words of the father."[25] He regularly commutes from Bad Vöslau to Vienna to indulge his artistic nature.

In many respects Moreno resembles Fritz Perls, who is just a few years younger. Both are eccentrics with a tendency towards arrogance and a taste for the provocative. Both play with the trope of the wise fool, and are fascinated by the power of spontaneity. "The truth of the soul can only be explored through action," Moreno believes. These could just as easily be Fritz Perls's words. Talking alone is not enough for the two pioneers: for them, the path to psychological health leads through the wisdom of the body.

. . .

In his therapeutic experiments, Moreno stages reenactments of early familial relationships. The emotions that surface are felt in the here and now and the participants can try out alternative ways of acting. First one participant is selected from the group; his or her story is to be the focus of the drama. Next secondary roles are assigned to the other participants—father, mother, siblings, or if need be other relatives or friends—and the actors take their places on stage. Now the improvised action begins.

The idea behind the psychodrama is that, by re-enacting interpersonal scenarios, one becomes conscious, through speech and movement, of the attendant emotions. It helps to have an "alter ego," someone whom the person at the center of the drama designates to portray her. While this designated person takes over her role, the central figure can step away from the scene and view it from the outside. Two other typical techniques of the psychodrama are doubling and role reversal. The latter calls for the central figure to take the place of another character, say the mother or the brother, and to attempt to view the scene from this person's perspective. Doubling means that another actor follows the protagonist like a shadow and suggests things the person can say or do in the situation. Also important for the therapeutic effect is the "sharing" session, the group discussion that follows the performance.

Moreno's successors further develop the concept of the psychodrama to include highly formalized approaches like family sculpting or constellation work. Family constellations staged in front of an audience, like the kind developed by the psychologist Bert Hellinger, reveal the dark side of the method: the particular nature of the group dynamic is such that the most mentally or emotionally vulnerable people risk being put on display or manipulated. There's often a fine line between re-enacting traumatic experiences and submitting to a charismatic facilitator intent on wielding power. In the best-case scenario, Jacob Moreno's techniques make relationships come alive and produce intense experiences. Terms like "doubling," "auxiliary ego," or "de-roling"—when a participant makes a symbolic gesture, like brushing themselves off or shaking their limbs, to cast aside the role they've been playing—find their way into group therapy textbooks.

In 1925 Moreno leaves Vienna for the United States. He has plans to patent a tape recorder invented by his brother-in-law, but the gadget is a flop, since more advanced technology is already available in the US. Moreno's medical degree isn't recognized in his new country; he has to sit for two separate examinations before he's allowed to work as a doctor. Moreno's philosophy of the "I-God" strikes many Americans as highly blasphemous, so he keeps it under wraps. Instead he comes up with lengthy questionnaires to measure social relationships and depict them graphically, a practice he calls sociometry. With an eye for publicity, he uses the data to predict things like the result of boxing matches: *World Champion Joe Louis proves to be unbeatable as a result of his superior spontaneity*. But the all too arbitrary sociometric technique fails to become an established scientific method.

Moreno's achievement is not that of a scientist, but of an artist and visionary. He founds a "religion of encounter," a form of creative role-playing, often with a spiritual overtone—in other words, a kind of "experimental theology."[26] Its creator considers himself God, and not just in a figurative sense—in his eyes, God is any individual who shapes his life and his relationships according to his own will.

TRAITOR, TRAITOR!

The auditorium is going wild. Not with enthusiasm, but with horror, indeed, with sheer rage. A chorus of boos fills the hall—something of a rarity at a scientific conference. Amidst the shouting, many attendees walk out. "Shut your mouth!" someone yells. There is even a shout of "Traitor, traitor!"

The man who is the focus of this collective disapproval puts on a show of innocence. All he's doing is presenting the facts, he says impassively, and the facts are clear. "I have seldom seen an audience behave in such an infantile manner," he says after the conference.[27] But of course he knew quite well that the facts he came to deliver would land like a bombshell. He repeats them calmly, almost with relish.

What is going on? On July 3, 1958, at a congress in London, the psychologist Hans Jürgen Eysenck delivers a talk on the fundamentals of behavioral therapy, something that he helped to develop. This is, he stresses, the "only *rational* theory of treatment available."[28] The *only* approach? As if that weren't insolent enough, Eysenck fires another salvo: psychoanalysis, says the researcher from Maudsley Hospital in South London, is quite simply ineffective. More than half a century of psychoanalytic research and therapy—all a waste? Here it's important to know that Maudsley is *the* center for behavioral and learning theory-oriented psychiatry in England. Eysenck belongs to the enemy camp, so to speak. But his criticism has to be taken seriously. After all, it rests not solely on resentment, but on very real study results.

Eysenck is speaking to members of the Royal Medico-Psychological Association of Psychiatrists, a group of clinicians most of whom practice psychoanalysis. An article of Eysenck's published prior to today's talk has already triggered heated debate.[29] In it, the author not only disputes psychoanalysis's status as science—something others had done before him—he also has the audacity to question the very core of analytic work, namely its success as a therapeutic measure. Eysenck contends that, based on the available data, psychoanalysis must be regarded as useless. The reason for this, he says, is that all studies that have carried out a before-and-after comparison of patients who had undergone treatment have been guilty of neglecting one crucial point: there will always be a certain number of cases of spontaneous healing, in the field of psychiatry, just the same as in somatic medicine. Time doesn't heal all wounds, but it does heal some, even without any form of medical intervention. Anyone who wants to show that a certain method of treatment is more effective than the wait-and-see approach has to take this into account.

Eysenck analyzed statistics on hospital stays in Great Britain and compared these with the health records of patients who went without treatment. Many of them were on the waiting list for a spot in a therapy program, at least for the span of time that Eysenck reviewed for his study. This group saw a considerable number of spontaneous remissions, the medical term for when an ailment disappears without proper therapy. According to Eysenck's highball estimate, in half of all cases—or even up to two-thirds, depending on the disorder—the passage of time alone has a curative effect. According to this finding, mentally ill patients need only wait, then they'll feel better on their own.

What gets the psychoanalysts in attendance so up in arms against Eysenck isn't so much the substance of Eysenck's words as the implicit challenge conveyed in them. The far greater danger to their profession is the assertion that every medical intervention must prove that it can do more for the patient than the passage of time or the mere expectation of positive results. It must, in other words, offer more than the placebo effect. The success of a method isn't proven by saying that *x* number of people improved after receiving it. Rather the success rate must exceed the rate of those who show improvement without medical intervention or after receiving a placebo treatment.

Eysenck's analysis found that, while treatments that relied on various other methods, chief among them behavioral therapy, had an average improvement rate of sixty-five percent, psychoanalysis managed only forty-four percent.[30] Given a nearly fifty percent rate of spontaneous remissions, that means that a person who undergoes analysis has a *worse* chance of recovering than if he does nothing at all!

Eysenck concedes that the data his findings are based on are sparse. But this, he says, is primarily a result of psychoanalysts' unwillingness to subject their work to a substantial review. Herein lies the true provocation: Eysenck demands of psychoanalysis that it be able to prove its utility, just like every other method. Going back to Freud's day, analysts have tended to cite their personal impressions of the course of an analysis and to relate anecdotal case histories. Some even regard a worsening of the patient's condition as a "positive reaction," reasoning that the road to recovery often leads through an initial crisis. And besides, what do symptoms reveal? Questionnaires and weighted responses can't possibly capture the unconscious. Humanistic psychologists often have a similar attitude: their approach is too complex and subtle for its success to be measured in objective terms.

Eysenck becomes famous for calling out such claims. To him they're merely excuses: some therapists only hide behind grandiose theories as a way of refusing an actual test of effectiveness. As harsh and overblown as Eysenck's criticism occasionally is, its jarring impact is salutary. True, a few analysts just stick their heads in the sand—but many more realize that a method that wishes to be regarded as legitimate and covered by insurance companies must be proven to help. Instead of a sense of mission, what is needed is a transparent, rational approach.

The road from eminence to evidence has a few travelers by this point: psychoanalytically oriented institutions like the Tavistock Clinic in London or the Menninger Sanatorium in Topeka, Kansas are gradually beginning to keep track of and evaluate treatment outcomes. In 1967, less than ten years after Eysenck's general reckoning, the psychiatrist Annemarie Dührssen, on the basis of several major studies, convinces statutory health insurers in Germany to cover psychoanalytic treatments of up to two hundred fifty hours. By doing so the healthcare system saves money in the long term, she argues, because continuous support of psychologically vulnerable patients is cheaper than other forms of treatment, like that for addiction, which would often become necessary otherwise—not to mention the costs associated with missing time at work. It's worth noting of course that minimizing cost is the crucial consideration here, rather than the imperative to heal.

In that sense, something good did come out of the feud between analysts and humanistic psychologists on the one side, behavioral therapists on the other. The latter camp, represented by Eysenck and Wolpe, bet on treatments whose effects could be measured objectively.[31] Their colleagues from the other therapeutic schools could no longer avoid this requirement.

Eysenck's eagerness to provoke is revealed by yet another episode that occurs years later at a different conference. After a lecture by the Berlin-born British psychologist, an older gentleman, seemingly an analyst himself, steps up to the microphone. Speaking English with a strong European accent, the man asks: "Professor Eysenck, I don't understand, how can you doubt the obvious success of Freudian therapy . . . ?" The man has barely finished talking when Eysenck stands up and, in his own strong accent, retorts: "That's right, you don't understand!" And having delivered this withering response, he sits back down without another word.[32]

. . .

As the son of two successful actors, Hans Jürgen Eysenck is born with a flair for the dramatic. His father, Eduard Eysenck, is a cabaret performer from the Rhineland; his mother Ruth Werner has a career on stage and in silent films under the pseudonym Helga Molander. Hans is born on March 4, 1916, in Berlin. His parents just don't have the time to raise a child, and two years after Hans's birth the artist couple splits up. Their son is raised by his maternal grandmother. The five-year-old Hans proves his acting talent in a minor role in one of Molander's films. After separating from Hans's father his mother falls in love with a film producer named Max Glaß and moves in with him. The two can't get married, since Glaß's wife refuses to grant him a divorce. Glaß is a Jew and finds himself in trouble after the Nazis seize power. Molander's mother has Jewish roots as well. The couple see no future for themselves in Germany and flee first to Paris, then on to Brazil. Hans's father Eduard, on the other hand, gets in the fascists' good graces and profits from the fact that many of his non-Aryan colleagues are barred from performing.

According to the Nazis' racial ideology, Hans is a "quarter Jew." After finishing high school in 1934, he wants to study physics at the University of Berlin, but is expected to join the party or the SS in return. He refuses. From an early age, Hans has often had to fend for himself. Now the eighteen-year-old says goodbye to his grandmother and moves to England, a country he's visited several times before on trips to improve his English. He sees his grandmother one last time, on a visit to Berlin in 1937. She is deported in 1943 and dies in Theresienstadt.

In London, Eysenck wants to devote himself to his beloved physics, but ends up studying psychology by mistake. Because University College doesn't recognize his German school credentials, Eysenck has to pass several matriculation exams to gain admission. To enroll as a physics student, he would need to take two exams in the natural sciences; Eysenck only takes one, with the rest in history, languages, and literature. As a result, the only scientific course of study open to him is psychology, which is grouped with the rest of the humanities. "Try it, you'll like it," says the admissions officer who signs him up.[33] And as it turns out, he's right.

As a psychologist, Eysenck strives to emulate the model of precise research set by the rest of the sciences. In his case that includes objective measurement of psychical variables, controlled experiments, and statistical data analysis. It is in this latter field above all that he makes a name for himself, developing an approach called factor analysis. Eysenck investigates which fundamental traits make up the personality and what causes it to change. Like his boss, Cyril Burt, who studies intelligence, Eysenck sees the genes as the dominant factor and downplays the influence of environment and upbringing. Burt is a charismatic but controversial teacher. Years after his death it comes to light that he very likely invented data for comparative studies of twins that purported to show both that IQ was hereditary and that white people have higher cognitive capacity than black people.

Eysenck becomes an eager student of Burt's—and is just as creative in his use of sources. Ironically enough, the man who accuses psychoanalysts of methodological failures later himself comes under suspicion of having manipulated research results. If he likes a theory, Eysenck has a strange knack for hitting upon the data to back it up. Late in life he co-authors several scientific papers with a controversial Heidelberg psychosomatic epidemiologist that purport to show that tobacco consumption doesn't increase a person's cancer risk, while the personality very much does have an influence on the development of tumors. These papers have since been withdrawn owing to a grave lack of transparency.

When he himself is almost an old man, Eysenck publishes an article in the far-right *National-Zeitung* about the "charlatan Freud," in which he attributes the psychoanalyst's alleged shiftiness to his being Jewish. He also develops far-fetched theories about how the orbit of the planets shapes character or why white people can think more clearly than other ethnicities. There are, in other words, more than a few blots on his record; Eysenck's thinking, especially in his later years, veers off into racist territory. Though far from being a shining example of scientific probity, he must nevertheless be credited with an important achievement: his sharp criticism of psychoanalysis's methodology contributed to a shift. Thanks in part to his efforts, psychoanalysis could no longer exempt itself from modern effectiveness research.

THE UNKNOWN BEING

In Freud's universe, the human individual is a solitary being. His psychical apparatus functions like a complex machine: psychical energy flows through all manner of circuitous routes and channels, always with the goal of discharging internal tension, which the organism experiences as a gain in pleasure. Other people certainly play a role in this dynamic, for example as representatives of the internalized moral conscience, the superego, or as screens on which to project libidinously-charged desires that the individual ascribes to others because they cannot admit them to themselves. Aside from that, however, the Freudian model of the psyche envisions a largely autonomous entity.

On the other hand, the psychoanalytic theory of neurosis rests on the assumption that a person's psychological makeup is a product of their individual history, in particular their early childhood experiences. If Freud's two central premises are accurate, first, that the repressed memory of childhood traumas makes you sick, and second, that everything pertaining to the psyche—whether it be dreams, slips of the tongue, or symptoms of mental illness—points to a deeper truth that is waiting to be discovered, then one can't help but suspect that even the imaginative world of the infant must have a decipherable subtext. Shouldn't the work begin with the youngest children, so as to prevent the formation of neuroses before it starts? Freud himself was too fatalistic in his thinking to draw this conclusion; for him neurosis was the inevitable price we pay for acquiring civilization. Thus it was left to a few of his students to turn psychoanalysis into a means for rescuing the child's psyche, and with it, ultimately, that of society as a whole.

Freud's youngest daughter, Anna, born in 1895, is the only one of his children to show sustained interest in the theoretical edifice he had spent so many years building. After earning her *Matura* she first starts working as an elementary school teacher in Vienna. Even without a medical degree, Freud considers her eligible to complete a training analysis. And why not do it with him? Anna's training begins in 1918. For almost four years, she and her father wrestle with questions of repression and transference, Oedipal libido, the castration complex, and penis envy.

Early on, Freud's daughter turns to the study of the child's psyche, which unlike that of adults is still terra incognita. The object of study poses special difficulties. Children, especially younger children, can't express what is going on inside them; in vain does one seek from them insight and interest in the analytical process. As a result, the emphasis usually lies on the pedagogical, preventative character of the treatment. In 1923 Anna Freud opens her own practice right next door to her father's. That same year, after Freud first undergoes surgery for oral cancer, Anna soon grows into the role of surrogate, giving lectures and appearing at other occasions on her father's behalf.

Around the same time, Anna meets the love of her life: Dorothy Burlingham. In the summer of 1924 the American and her four children spend their vacation in the idyllic town of Semmering in a house next door to Villa Schüler, where the Freuds are staying. Burlingham's father is Louis Tiffany, heir to the famous New York jewelry store. At twenty-three years old, Dorothy marries a surgeon who soon afterward develops what now would be called bipolar disorder. Life with a man who vacillates constantly between rage and depression becomes so challenging for her that she finally leaves him and takes her children as far away as possible—to Europe.

Burlingham's ten-year-old son Bob sees Anna for treatment of his psychosomatically induced asthma. When the therapy works, Dorothy is convinced of the validity of Freudian theory. She feels drawn to Anna, and the two of them begin spending a great deal of time together; they vacation together and immediately become a couple, albeit covertly. In 1928, Burlingham moves into the building on Berggasse, one floor above the Freuds. From then on until her death in 1979, she and Anna Freud live under the same roof. The two of them purchase a small weekend home outside of Vienna and found a school in the Hietzing district, where they teach and treat children from their social circle in accordance with psychoanalytic principles. In 1927, Anna's essay collection *Introduction to the Technic of Child Analysis* is published. She becomes secretary of the International Psychoanalytical Association and founds a group that advocates for the dissemination of psychoanalysis in pedagogy, child-rearing, and social work. The group's members work intensely on the question of how the psychological makeup of the child,

Father and daughter forever: Anna Freud, born 1895, with her Herr Papa.

that unknown being, can be rendered accessible—and how it can be shielded from unhealthy psychological development.

"The therapeutic analyses of adult neurotics left no doubt about the detrimental influence of many parental and environmental attitudes and actions," Anna Freud writes, "such as dishonesty in sexual matters, unrealistically high moral standards, overstrictness or overindulgence, frustrations, punishments, or seductive behavior."[34] But how do you treat phobias, compulsions, sleep problems, bedwetting, aggression, or masturbation (which at the time is considered potentially dangerous) if the patient won't talk about these things? Free association is usually not an option, says Freud's daughter; young children especially don't possess the necessary capacity for reflection. "The history of child analysis is at bottom nothing other than an endless chain of attempts to replace the absence of free association with other technical means."[35] But what means could those be?

. . .

The first person to devote herself to child psychoanalysis is a noblewoman, Hermine Hug Edle von Hugelstein, who is inspired by the case history of "Little Hans." She is born in Vienna in 1871. Her father is a lieutenant colonel in the army and raises his daughter with a firm hand, inculcating a sense of duty and moral probity. After finishing school, the bright young Hermine first works as a teacher until, at age twenty-six, frustrated with the educational profession, she begins studying philosophy and physics at the University of Vienna. While working on her doctoral thesis on the phenomenon of radioactivity, she meets the doctor Isidor Sadger and undergoes analysis with him. Through Sadger she also comes in contact with Freud's circle. In 1913, Hug-Hellmuth, as she now calls herself, becomes just the third woman to join the Vienna Psychoanalytic Society, after Margarete Hilferding and Sabina Spielrein.

Hug-Hellmuth's personal involvement with the psychological life of the child begins with a death in the family. When her half-sister Antonie dies unexpectedly in 1915, Hermine assumes responsibility for the care of her illegitimate eight-year-old son Rudolf, nicknamed Rolf. She doesn't show much affection for the boy, however. Visitors report that Hug-Hellmuth probably speaks more with the cat than she does with the child, and that she subjects Rolf to "crazy child-rearing methods."[36] She constantly dictates to him what he must wear, eat, or say, and often forbids him from meeting friends or indulging in sweets. Hug-Hellmuth is a buttoned-up woman with little warmth to offer—and as the daughter of a noble family that lost its fortune in the Vienna stock market crash of 1873, also extremely thrifty.

In part in response to his aunt's emotional frigidity, Rolf, when he reaches puberty, starts to steal from her and becomes insolent, even aggressive. The worse he behaves, the more Hug-Hellmuth criticizes him. She fails to recognize that the boy's behavior is merely his way of masking his own nagging self-doubt. When he's fifteen, Rolf steals a large sum of money that Hug-Hellmuth had kept sewn inside her petticoat. As punishment, Hug-Hellmuth takes the boy out of trade school and puts him in a home for difficult youth. Rolf is beside himself with resentment. He harasses his aunt with ever more brazen demands for money until finally she forbids him from setting foot inside her apartment.

The tragedy takes place on the night of September 9, 1924. Rolf, determined to take what he feels is his, breaks into his aunt's upper-ground-floor apartment at Lustkandlgasse 10. Hug-Hellmuth is frightened by the noise and cries for help, and at this point her nephew grabs her and clamps down on her throat until she stops moving. The next morning he is picked up by the police not far from Vienna. At trial the seventeen-year-old testifies that, as far as his aunt was concerned, he was only ever a guinea pig. The court finds him guilty of murder and robbery, and sentences him to twelve years in prison. He must also spend a full day in darkness every September 8, the anniversary of the crime.

After the trial a debate rages in the press, centering on the question of how dangerous psychoanalysis is for children. Does it ruin a child's character to tell him at an early age about unconscious conflicts and infantile-sexual lust? In Rolf's case, to be sure, what fueled the boy's rage was presumably less the content of Hug-Hellmuth's lectures than it was her callous and didactic treatment of him—even if this in no way excuses his horrible deed.

Hug-Hellmuth had already set off a public scandal in 1919 when she published a book called *A Young Girl's Diary*. With this purportedly authentic document of the first stirrings of the libido in a twelve-year-old girl, the newly-founded Psychoanalytischer Verlag makes quite a splash. It's not long, however, before doubts start to emerge as to whether a girl that age could elaborate on sexual desires and practices in such fashion. Hug-Hellmuth, billed as the editor of the diary, is suspected of having invented the whole thing. The book does in fact contain numerous discrepancies. Not only do the thoughts and mode of expression of the young narrator Rita seem all too grown up; she is also graded at school on a grade scale that isn't introduced until years later, and uses a telephone that hadn't been invented yet at the time the events of the diary are meant to be taking place. There are several other happenings described in the book that only occurred after the purported date of the manuscript, and the parallels between Rita's life and Hug-Hellmuth's own are quite striking.

This diary, one reviewer writes, is at best an "inextricably tangled mix of fiction and truth."[37] There is much to indicate that the editor forged this first-hand account of a child's experiences in order to garner more recognition for Freud's theory. Freud himself quickly drops the book from the publishing house's list and envelops the matter in a cloak of silence.

. . .

It's not easy to be this woman's daughter. No, it's more than a person can stand! For as long as she can remember, her mother was either absent entirely or off somewhere brooding. Feelings of neglect and emptiness have been with her always. Too often, she and her two younger brothers were left in the care of their overwhelmed grandmother. And what choice did the older woman have but to look after her grandchildren, what with her son-in-law being away on business most of the time and her daughter hardly being up to the task.

It might be unfair for a daughter to resent her own mother for suffering from depression. But even after her mother had recovered somewhat, following her first run of psychoanalysis in Budapest, the children

A terribly nice family? Melanie Klein and her children Melitta and Hans.

were of interest to her mainly as objects of study. She peppered them with questions, took note of all their emotions, compared her theories about the mental life of children with what they said while at play or in their interactions with her. Melanie Klein's ambition was to refine the technique of child analysis, and Melitta, Hans, and Erich were the test cases. And once she had seen enough to satisfy her curiosity, she moved away, first to Berlin, then later to distant London.

Melanie Reizes, the youngest of four children, is born on March 30, 1882 on Tiefer Graben in Vienna's city center. The Reizes family comes from the Hungarian part of the Burgenland. Melanie's father, Moriz Reizes, is a doctor and comes from Lviv, her mother, Libussa Deutsch, from the small town of Warbotz in present-day Slovakia. When Melanie is five, her older sister Sidonie dies of tuberculosis. Her beloved brother Emmanuel dies of heart failure at twenty-five, not long after the death of her father. From childhood on, Melanie must bear the loss of people she loves.

At twenty-one she marries the chemical engineer Arthur Klein, a friend of her brother's who first proposed to her when he was just seventeen. The couple moves away from Vienna, going first to Rosenberg to live with Arthur's parents. It is here that their children Melitta (1904) and Hans (1907) are born. Next the family relocates to Budapest, after Klein's company transfers him there. From the time of Hans's birth, Melanie begins suffering from severe depression. She feels unloved, broods constantly, is often on the verge of tears. Her mother Libussa now runs the household and looks after the children while Melanie is away on one of her many cures or desperate escapes from everyday life. When she becomes pregnant for the third time in late 1913, she's on the verge of a total breakdown. In May 1914 Erich is born, and a few months later the war begins. Melanie's dream of becoming a doctor fades far into the distance.

The deaths in the family, her joyless marriage, the duty of bearing children, and on top of that her patronizing mother Libussa, on whose help she is nevertheless dependent—all of this takes its toll on Melanie. She feels like a failure. Her distant, dismissive manner might well be what provokes from her own children the fury that Klein declares to be an inevitable part of a child's development. Like other pioneers, she too ignores a fact that her colleague Helene Deutsch expresses thus: "Children want to be loved, not observed."[38]

One day Melanie can't take it anymore and walks into the office of a neurologist who had been recommended to her. In the consultation room she is received by a tall man with slightly graying hair, round glasses, and a gentle gaze. Sándor Ferenczi is a student of the famous Dr. Freud of Vienna. Melanie tells him of her woes and begins a course of analysis that will change her life completely. In the coming years Ferenczi is called up repeatedly to serve as a soldier on the front, but he continues Klein's analysis throughout almost the entire length of the war. Ferenczi praises her sensitivity and observational talents and encourages her to study her children from a psychological standpoint. Klein immerses herself in Freud's work and is fascinated by his 1901 paper "On Dreams," which Carl Gustav Jung had also read with excitement. Klein decides to become a psychoanalyst herself.

She joins the Hungarian Psychoanalytic Society with a lecture in which she describes her analysis of her five-year-old son Erich. Karl Abraham, whom she meets at the Psychoanalytic Congress in Budapest in 1918, invites her to Berlin to report on her experiences with child analysis. When the "White Terror" unleashed by the right-wing regime in Budapest begins in 1919, she accepts the offer, while her husband Arthur flees to Sweden and her children stay with their grandparents. The children, and Erich in particular, suffer greatly from the separation.

Klein is only one of many exiles who flee the pogroms in Hungary. To her colleagues in Berlin she presents her object relations theory, the rough tenets of which she has already worked out by that point. The theory states that every child develops a symbiotic relationship to their first caregiver, usually the mother. The baby-mother dyad forms the nucleus of psychological development, and the relationship patterns internalized early on, above all with the mother, shape the child's character—with the important proviso that the child's "inner" image of their parents need not have much relation to who they are in reality. Though Klein has never studied medicine and only worked for a short time as a kindergarten teacher, Karl Abraham accepts her as a candidate for a training analysis.

When Anna Freud publishes her *Introduction to the Technic of Child Analysis* in 1927, the differences between the two women's views come to light for the first time. But by that point Klein is already living in London, where her theories are better received than in Vienna and Berlin, cities dominated by Freudians. When Sigmund and Anna Freud themselves go into exile in England more than ten years later, there is a sharp clash of opposing views. Several controversial debates center on arguments for and against Klein's theories. Klein's daughter Melitta, now a psychoanalyst herself and full of resentment toward her mother, vehemently criticizes her. The prevalence of anger and violence in small children, Melitta argues, is not a law of nature; in fact, these traits can usually be traced back to parental neglect, above all neglect by the mother. This attack is a thinly-veiled accusation leveled at Melanie herself.

One question lies at the center of the dispute between the Anna Freudians and Kleinians: at what age can children start to be analyzed? The Freuds, Sigmund and Anna, believe that infants and very young children are incapable of giving voice to their inner conflicts and desires, and even if they were they would have little to report, because the superego, which acts as the agent of repression, only develops when the Oedipus complex is overcome, sometime between the ages of five and six. Until that point the little ones are ruled only by the amoral pleasure principle; they seek out pleasant things and avoid unpleasant things, without worrying about morality or the demands of their environment.

In Klein's view, on the other hand, even in diapers we are driven by hate and destructive revenge impulses that result from the conflict between instinct and conscience. This is an inevitable consequence of the frustration that the infant experiences when their demands persistently go unmet. Babies want to nurse and yet must wait; they want to have their mother all to themselves and must share her with others; they want to walk, talk, exert power, but they can't. This, according to Klein, triggers a blind thirst for revenge on those whom they actually love: their parents. They envy their omnipotence, want to punish, indeed, destroy them. This in turn produces a wave of guilt that washes over the child. "Thus the child's destructive impulses are directed against the very people he loves most; and this gives rise to the struggle between love and hatred which is the deepest source of unhappiness in children, or for that matter in adults. This conflict can be mitigated by the parents' love and understanding, but can never be eradicated."[39]

In Klein's view, the worst can be avoided through early sex education. An account by Karen Horney's daughter Renate gives us a clue as to how this psychological prophylactic measure might play out in practice. In the mid-1920s, the Horneys and the Kleins live not far from one another in southwest Berlin. Horney wants all three of her daughters to be analyzed by Klein so that they don't become neurotic in adulthood. Brigitte, the eldest, refuses, but for her younger sisters Marianne and Renate, going to see Klein at her house is part of their daily lives for years. Renate, looking back, describes the experience: "As I lay on the hard, ominous couch, Melanie asked me to talk about my thoughts and dreams. Being a lively, healthy eight-year-old, I told of climbing trees and playing Indians. The therapist's long reply startled my innocent ears. All my thoughts, she said, had to do with penis envy and anus play. Although proud of having been told to make the long trip by bus and subway to her office alone, I soon found a way to get there ever so slowly. Arriving late, I would dive not onto but underneath the terrible couch, with my fingers pressed firmly in my ears."[40]

. . .

For Freud's eightieth birthday in May 1936, Anna Freud gives her father a special gift. She hands him her book *The Ego and the Mechanisms of Defense*, in which she revisits the arsenal of psychical forms of resistances that her father postulated. With it she proves herself, in his eyes, to be a worthy successor. Adler, Jung, Stekel, Reich, Rank, and Ferenczi—all betrayed him, all strayed from the true doctrine. Not Anna.

But even she can't prevent the further fragmentation of the psychoanalytic movement in the years during and after the Second World War. In London, three separate groups form under the mantle of the British Psychoanalytical Society: Freudians, Kleinians, and a so-called Independent or Middle Group for those in between. How did it come to this?

The superego, in Freud's view, only emerges through the overcoming of the Oedipal complex around age six—but Klein moves its emergence up to a far earlier stage in the child's development. According to this theory, a "paranoid-schizoid position," in which the two-to-four-month-old infant is still completely one with their mother and knows of no distinction between themselves and others or inside and outside, gives way to a second phase, which Klein terms the "depressive position." Here the little ones first distinguish between good and evil and feel guilt in response to their fantasies of violence and killing. Klein draws this conclusion from a technique that she employs with infants that are only a few weeks old: the symbolic interpretation of childplay. The method, like so many others in psychoanalysis, has just one little flaw: it can't be refuted. Even if the positions Klein postulates had no basis in reality, they could still be used to explain any behavior a child might display. Klein constructs post hoc causal connections; coming to her conclusions after the fact, her theory allows her to attribute any given action or utterance to some determining factor. In the bright light of her theory, everything appears meaningful. What Klein and many of her colleagues lack is epistemic modesty. The Socratic maxim "I know that I know nothing" gives way to in-depth psychological speculation masquerading as rigorous scientific assessment.

What exactly motivates the child, that unknown being? Are instances of anxiety, crying, waking up at night, or temper tantrums always attributable to parental behavior? Or are these phenomena inevitably driven by an instinctual conflict that can only be resolved by "making it conscious"—bringing the conflict into conscious awareness? And if that is in fact the case, how do you carry this out with a small child who can't articulate their thoughts? According to the Anna Freudians, psychoanalysis requires a minimum of linguistic and emotional development, which rules out analyzing children younger than elementary school age.

Klein, however, believes that instincts (drives), conscience, guilt, and aggression are all present at birth, or at the age of a few weeks at the latest. These aspects of the psyche merely find different forms of expression in the infant than they do in the adult. The first movements of the head and limbs, and above all child play, can be interpreted as forms of communication, even in the youngest children. If in fact it's possible to draw conclusions about unconscious mental life based on what can be observed in pre-lingual developmental stages, then the textbooks for pediatricians will have to be rewritten.

But not everyone is convinced by Klein's theories. In London in the early 1940s there are bitter disputes between Kleinians and their critics. The latter camp argue that Klein's understanding of infantile object relations opens the door to arbitrary interpretations. Klein for her part accuses the Anna Freudians of ignoring the instinctually-driven character of early stages of development. Klein's daughter Melitta sides with Freud and at the fiercest moment of the debate calls her mother the "Goebbels" of child analysis. In the end the Psychoanalytical Society is cleft in two: from now on candidates for a training analysis must choose the dogma that will guide their instruction. The question is no longer who has the better arguments, but rather who can assemble the larger group of followers.

. . .

In the mid-1930s the exodus of German Jews and the return of American expats who had learned the analytic craft in Europe leads to the arrival on US shores of many well-trained experts on the psyche. They all need to make a living, and in doing so they transform America into a Mecca of therapy and self-help. The image of the expert shrink with the X-ray gaze, combined with the prospect of overcoming the strictures and conformism of consumerist society, attracts many to therapy, above all young people. Psychoanalytic institutes and clinics start popping up all over the place. Meanwhile the tradition of internecine strife continues, with new rifts leading to ever more new approaches, all of which are in competition with one another. The greater the supply, the greater the pressure to present one's own path to psychological salvation as the only one worth its salt. Thus the therapy profession expands at a breakneck pace.

There is also a corresponding rise in criticism of Freud's patriarchal approach. The master held that identification with the father creates the superego, while women find their purpose in suffering. Karen Horney is one of the dissidents who put forward a female perspective to counter the theory of penis envy and the castration complex. Horney, for her part, posits that men feel "womb envy." Tracing the course of Horney's career gives a sense of the dynamic that prevails in this period: in ten years, between 1932 and 1942, she switches "clubs" a half dozen times. First her colleague from the Berlin Institute Franz Alexander brings her on as Co-Director of the Chicago Psychoanalytic Institute. Horney's daughters come to the US with her; only Brigitte, already a successful actress at that time, stays in Berlin. After falling out with Alexander, Horney moves in 1934 to New York and there joins the New York Psychoanalytic Institute. Here another exile sets the agenda: Sándor Radó, who takes a critical view of Horney's feminine psychology. Her disputes with Radó limit Horney's freedom to work as a training analyst.

In 1941, Horney leaves the New York chapter of the American Psychoanalytic Association and, along with other like-minded analysts, founds the Association for the Advancement of Psychoanalysis (AAP), with its own affiliated institute. Just two years later, in 1943, Erich Fromm, Frieda Fromm-Reichmann, and Harry Stack Sullivan split off to form the William Alanson White Institute—Fromm especially had clashed with Horney, insisting on his right to teach despite not having a medical degree. In 1944 yet another group grows fed up with the grande dame and leaves to join the New York Medical College. Only a few colleagues remain with Horney. Finally, in the early 1950s, colleagues raise the idea of a Karen Horney Clinic. But Horney doesn't live to see the founding of the institute bearing her name. She dies on December 4, 1952 of gall bladder cancer.

6

MEANING

THE SPIRIT MOVES

The human individual is a mystery to themselves—but the exact nature of that mystery has always been a matter of dispute. Goethe and Romantic writers like Schelling and Novalis once praised the unconscious as a mysterious power that brings forth premonitions and creative energy. For Freud it becomes a closet full of skeletons, or, to be more precise, a dark sphere to which memories and desires are banished so they won't cause any trouble. But because the repression never succeeds entirely, phobias, compulsions, and other neuroses are the result.

Carl Gustav Jung, for his part, favored a less lurid view of the unconscious, and describes its role in the life of the psyche as follows: "We are a psychic process which we do not control, or only partly direct. Consequently, we cannot have any final judgment about ourselves or our lives. If we had, we would know everything—but at most that is only a pretense. At bottom we never know how it has all come about."[1] This *not knowing* "how it has all come about" is the basic element in our everyday experience of the unconscious: we simply don't know where our thoughts, associations, feelings, and desires come from; they're just there, all of a sudden—and this gap in knowledge, our own insurmountable mysteriousness, we fill with all manner of theories.

One man who refuses to tolerate this not-knowing is a doctor of philosophy who moves from Vienna to Berlin—with a brief stop in

Weimar—before the turn of the century to take up a post as editor of the *Magazin für Litteratur*. On the side, in various clubs and schools for adult education, he gives courses in history and rhetoric and lectures on Goethe's understanding of nature and Nietzsche's nihilism. His choice of subject matter and his rhetorical gifts make this independent scholar quite popular, judging for instance from the list of students enrolled at a workers' school founded by Karl Liebknecht where he regularly taught. But the money Rudolf Steiner makes from his two jobs isn't nearly enough to make ends meet. The capital of the German Empire is an expensive place to live. To save money, Steiner rents a room from a mother of three who keeps house for him in the bargain so that he can concentrate fully on his intellectual work. From 1899 on, he and this woman, Anna Eunike, share a bond of warmth and devotion, maybe even love.

Soon after the dawning of the new century, he is presented with the opportunity to embark on a new and promising career. The opportunity arrives in the form of Count and Countess von Brockdorff. In the fall of 1900 they invite Steiner to give a lecture in their library on Friedrichstraße, one of the premier addresses in Berlin. Royal Prussian Cavalry Captain Cay Lorenz Count von Brockdorff leads the Berlin lodge of the Theosophical Society. He and his wife Sophie number among the most zealous supporters of the esoteric movement, beloved above all by ladies of the upper class. Its devotees strive for "divine wisdom"—*theo sophos*. The society was founded in 1875 in New York by a strong-willed Russian woman with German roots. Helena Blavatsky makes a name for herself as a medium and author of devotional literature, and organizes numerous séances, working alongside the spiritualist Henry Steel Olcott. The topics discussed at such events range from clairvoyance, telepathy, and reincarnation to making contact with the beyond.

In late September 1900, Steiner delivers a lecture on Nietzsche to a handpicked audience assembled in the Brockdorffs' library. He makes a big impression. A week later he makes another appearance before the occultists, this time to offer his reading of Goethe's *Kunstmärchen* "The Green Snake and the Beautiful Lily." Here, for the first time, as Steiner recalls in 1923, he speaks "very esoterically. It was an important experience for me." And on it goes from there: in October he is booked for a lecture series on medieval mysticism; this is followed, in 1901, by eighteen talks on "Christianity as Mystical Fact."

What exactly makes this an "important experience" for Steiner? Presumably it is learning what a profound impression he can make on people with an interest in the spiritual world. Or finding out that he knows how to give them the very thing they're thirsting after. The skilled speaker grows intoxicated with the power of his own words; the audience is like wax made supple by the fiery intensity of his thoughts.

At this time, though, he himself is more or less a stranger to theosophy; before now he's had scarcely anything to do with occultists. Steiner is a free spirit and a literary man who soaks up Berlin's cultural life and blazes his way through the salons and stages of the city, at least to the extent his wallet allows. Rather than hunting for higher states of being, he preaches a pure knowledge of the self, which is at the same time knowledge of the world. Very much in the spirit of his great idol, Johann Wolfgang von Goethe, he devotes himself to the "language of things that are spoken in the inner chambers of man."[2]

Steiner's friend Ludwig Jacobowski starts a group of philosophers and artists in Berlin called "Die Kommenden"—"The Coming Ones"—of which Steiner is a member. When Jacobowski dies of meningitis at just thirty-two years old in December 1900, Steiner takes over leadership of the debate club. At a meeting at the Nollendorf casino he gives a lecture on the "history of humanity's development from the most ancient oriental times to the present, or anthroposophy." Here for the first time he uses the term that will come to be inextricably linked to his name.

Riding the wave of success brought about by his appearances in the Brockdorffs' library, Steiner gives up the underpaid editor job in September 1900. His plan now is to make a career as a spiritual-intellectual teacher and traveling speaker. His list of admirers will soon include a young actor who only just joined the Brockdorff circle of occultists. The young Baltic German Marie von Sivers hears Steiner speak about mysticism for the first time in the spring of 1901. Is it love at first sight? Whatever the case, from then on the younger woman barely leaves Steiner's side—to the chagrin of Steiner's landlady Anna Eunike, who waits back home on Kaiserallee in Berlin's Westend neighborhood, doing his laundry and warming up his dinner for him when he comes back late at night from his high-minded business in town.

Steiner recognizes the opportunity that has presented itself to him, and he is determined to seize it. Plagued by in-fighting, the theosophists alone can't possibly satisfy the spiritual hunger of bourgeois Wilhelmine society. Leadership of the movement is in the hands of a small group of fanatics, each offering their own world-explaining myth and accusing all the others of charlatanism. Meanwhile Berlin at the turn of the century stands alongside London, Mumbai, Liverpool, and Rochester, New York as one of the centers of the esoteric movement.

The movement has three aims: first, to promote "universal brotherhood" among men; second, to fuse religion, philosophy, and science into a unified global doctrine; and third, to investigate the secret natural forces that lie behind the world of phenomena. This last aim is particularly prized by those who regard the rationalist spirit of the times with skepticism. Scientific breakthroughs like Charles Darwin's theory of evolution or Albert Einstein's theory of relativity leave many people feeling unnerved. Something within them resists accepting the notion that humans evolved from the animal kingdom or that space and time are not immutable, despite appearances to the contrary. They seek shelter in communion with supernatural forces, and the charismatic Steiner strikes them as just the right person to guide them through this spiritual realm. Within a quarter century, until his death in March 1925, he rises to become the leader of a spiritual movement whose adherents are profoundly devoted to him, a movement that will come to compete with psychology in the early twentieth century's marketplace of meaning.

. . .

Steiner isn't from Vienna, but he comes from the vicinity. He is born in late February 1861, five years after Freud, in Kraljevec, a whistlestop two hundred kilometers south of the capital on the Croatian-Hungarian border. His father Johann is the town stationmaster. The family doesn't stay put for long, moving every few years as Johann Steiner is posted to different towns in the Vienna Basin, from Mödling to Pottschach and on to Neudörfl on the Leitha river, just across the border from Hungary.

At that time the railroad is the epitome of progress and mastery over nature. Johann Steiner's job is on the Budapest-Trieste line, whose spectacular tunnels and viaducts are the object of much admiration. The transport of people and products, communication via telegraph wires that run alongside the tracks—these innovations shape young Rudolf's image of the world: everything is on the move and out to make a profit. Steiner experiences the flow of goods and information from up close, but he himself is fixed in place, like a rock in a rushing river.

As a sixteen-year-old student in Wiener Neustadt, Steiner buys a copy of Kant's *Critique of Pure Reason*. His history teacher's lessons are so monotonous that the teenager tears apart the cheap Reclam paperback edition and slips the individual pages into his textbook so that he can read during class without getting caught. Some pages he must have studied twenty times, he says, but Kant's doubt of knowledge independent of experience leaves him confused. According to his biographer Helmut Zander, Steiner's career can be understood as a lifelong attempt "to undo what Kant had set in motion: expulsion from the paradise of an unmediated access to the world."[3]

In 1879 the family moves again, this time to Brunn, close enough to the capital that Rudolf can commute to the university there. He lives with his parents until the fall of 1887, when he is twenty-six years old. An ambitious and solitary student, he writes to a lovesick friend: "This is true love, when one is satisfied with the image and doesn't need the flesh, indeed one suppresses it. Then there's no grief, no sorrow."[4] Here is a man with both feet planted firmly in Victorian soil, his urges very much under control.

But Steiner happens to pursue his studies in the capital of transgression. He opts to study natural sciences at the Technische Hochschule Wien, planning to do as his father had hoped and take up a career as a railroad engineer. Soon, however, influenced by the Germanist Julius Schröer, he switches to literature and philosophy. Then, in the fall of 1882, the lexicographer Joseph Kürschner assigns him the task of overseeing the volume of Goethe's scientific writings for a planned edition of the poet's collected works. Imagine it: a twenty-one-year-old undergraduate with no completed degree and no philological experience is supposed to produce a critical edition of the work of the German national poet! Kürschner for his part is happy to have found anyone at all for this Herculean task. The young man throws himself into the task—and is soon in over his head. He is not at all faithful to Goethe's work, instead refashioning it into a bulwark against Kantian skepticism.

Goethe is Steiner's go-to authority in the search for what he calls the "absolute truth." For him there are no limits to what can be known; in order to arrive at true knowledge, one only has to look *truthfully*. "By taking possession of the idea, thought fuses with the primordial basis of world existence; that which seems exterior enters into the spirit of man: he becomes one with objective reality at its highest level of potency. Awareness of ideas in reality is the true communion of man."[5]

In Steiner's "science," there is no uncertainty, no incremental advance or careful consideration. This is one key difference between Steiner's method and true scientific inquiry, which asks questions, forms hypotheses, tests these hypotheses and sometimes rejects them, and in so doing steadily inches its way forward. Compared to Steiner's knowledge-as-pathos, even Freud's theory of the unconscious seems like textbook science.

Things turn out as they must: Steiner overextends himself, caught between his editorial tasks, philosophical ambitions, and the necessity of making a living. Because his work on the Goethe volume doesn't bring in enough money, in 1884 he starts working as a private tutor. In the summer of 1888 Steiner falls in love with the twenty-year-old Radegunde Fehr, but the relationship remains platonic. "We loved each other and both seemed to know it quite clearly; but neither of us could overcome our shyness to tell each other of our love."[6]

Finally Steiner leaves Vienna and, after a brief stop in Weimar, where he tries unsuccessfully to establish himself as a Goethe scholar, moves to Berlin. It is 1897. To make ends meet, Steiner does a lot of things that go against his convictions. He hates Jews, but gives lectures at the "Society for the Fight against Antisemitism." His views are German nationalist and yet he speaks alongside Rosa Luxemburg at the opening of a school for workers in Berlin-Spandau. The less recognition he receives, the harder he works to create an untouchable aura around himself. His mission: to save the world of ideas from the poison of skepticism.

. . .

The key break for Steiner's career comes in early 1902: when the elderly Count von Brockdorff relinquishes his position as leader of the Berlin theosophical lodge, Steiner inherits it. On January 17 he joins the Theosophical Society and by October he's already become general secretary of the German chapter. He holds this office for a decade, until he leaves to found his own Anthroposophical Society.

The catalyst for the split is a bizarre tale featuring a new messiah: in 1910, the leader of the Theosophical Society, Annie Besant of Britain, moves the society's headquarters to Adyar, a suburb of the Indian city of Madras. Seeking to justify the choice of so remote a location for the center of the movement and to build a mystique around the place, Besant and her right-hand man, Olcott, come up with a bold plan: they declare a fine-limbed fifteen-year-old boy named Jiddu Krishnamurti to be the reincarnation of Jesus Christ. Besant goes so far as to have the boy's father grant her custody and founds the "Order of the Star in the East." At first the gambit seems to have succeeded: numerous media outlets in Europe and the US run stories on the dark-skinned Jesus from the East and Besant and her faction receive global attention. But ultimately Besant's maneuver only accelerates the trend toward schism.

Steiner's response is hesitant at first, then outraged. The idea that an "Indian boy" would be named the new Christ is "something that isn't to be taken seriously," he says.[7] The head of the German lodge will have no truck with such exoticism, and in December 1912 he cuts ties: at a theosophical congress in Cologne he proclaims the founding of his own "anthroposophic" society.

Steiner's somnambulant aura attracts many followers. "A hypnotic power lay in his dark eyes," writes the writer Stefan Zweig, half fascinated, half leery, "and I listened to him better and more critically when not looking at him, for his ascetic, thin face, carved by spiritual suffering, was well disposed to be convincing—and not only to women."[8] It is chiefly ladies from the upper ranks of the bourgeoisie who fall for Steiner's "mix of pedantry and demonic power," as the writer Max Halbe puts it.[9] The school of intellectual-spiritual perfection is meant to raise man to a higher plane of being, beyond his material-bound existence. Herein lies the therapeutic element of anthroposophy: Steiner doesn't diagnose, nor does he possess a treatment method in the narrow sense; nevertheless his teachings aim for spiritual-intellectual transformation through the development of the higher being that dwells within man. Steiner is neither a doctor nor a scientist; he doesn't want to heal and certainly doesn't want to follow the example of analytical, critical science by bringing specific bits of knowledge to light. Clairvoyance is his method. Nevertheless, for many followers, the higher truths that he reveals have a therapeutic effect.

Thus there are conspicuous similarities between psychoanalysis and anthroposophy, two popular early-twentieth-century movements. Both promise to help people overcome unknown but essential forces hidden within the human mind. And both grant the "master" ultimate authority, deferring to his interpretation on matters of dispute. Steiner speaks of the "path of reverence"[10] that the assiduous student must tread, and demands respect for his authority, even if he lacks the taste for controversy clearly evident in Freud. But even the founder of psychoanalysis quickly loses interest in a discussion as soon as he senses a challenge to the ultimate authority he possessed at the early Wednesday gatherings. Despite the mutual loathing that divides the two camps, esotericists on the one side, analysts on the

Aiming high: Rudolf Steiner, founder of anthroposophy.

other, their love-hate relationship, says Steiner's biographer Zander, is based "more on affinity than on difference."[11]

Steiner likewise has plenty in common with Adler. Being Hungarians by birth, the two are actually foreigners in the Habsburg empire, and both are raised in simple circumstances. They are rhetorically gifted and driven by a manic work ethic. A lecture workload consisting of thousands of appearances, sometimes several on a single day in different locations, not only speaks to the two figures' shared sense of purpose—it also ruins their health over the long term. Adler dies of heart failure at sixty-seven; Steiner, who is ten years older, dies at just sixty-four, probably of cancer. The cause will never be conclusively determined; Steiner preached the view that mistletoe extract prevents the degeneration of tissue, and so it was out of the question that cancer be given as the cause of death on the coroner's report. Steiner's last partner, the doctor Ita Wegmann, makes sure this doesn't happen.

While Freud and Adler are at pains to show how they deduced their theories and to substantiate them with satisfactory evidence, the anthroposophist Steiner retreats into the world of whispers. Nevertheless, one common thread remains: a fondness for Goethe, Steiner's idealistic role model. Jung believed—spuriously—that he was related to the privy councilor of Weimar, and Freud, who had little sympathy for the spiritualists, decided to study medicine after hearing a lecture on the fragment "Die Natur." The poetic text mistakenly attributed to Goethe contains a passage that reads: "Nature! [. . .] We live in her midst and know her not. She is incessantly speaking to us, but betrays not her secret."[12]

LINES OF DEMARCATION

A desk made of dark oak. Behind its polished surface sits a man with a beard and thinning hair. Without looking up from his papers he raises one hand, gesturing for the guest to come in and sit down. Then there is silence. The visitor wants to begin a training analysis. He fidgets nervously in his seat. Suddenly the bearded man leans forward, looks him straight in the eye, and says in a high-pitched voice: "So, Herr Frankl, what is your neurosis?"[13]

The young man thus addressed is still in high school, but already he has read a lot about psychoanalysis. An essay by the nineteen-year-old even appeared, on Freud's recommendation, in the *Zeitschrift für Psychoanalyse*.[14] In it Viktor Frankl traces the gesture of nodding one's head to the rhythmic movements made during intercourse; shaking one's head, on the other hand, stems from the act of turning one's face away in moments of disgust. It was Freud who sent him here, to his colleague Paul Federn. Let Federn see if the schoolboy, despite his youth, is analysand material.

The candidate stammers something out about having observed anal character traits in himself, and about his anxiety; but Frankl needn't say anything further. Federn has passed his verdict, and the conversation ends as abruptly as it began: the young man should come back when he's received his medical degree—before then there was nothing to be done.

Back out on the street, Frankl can barely suppress his anger. Who does this squeaky-voiced clown think he is? No hello, not even a trace of interest, just the assumption that he, the candidate, naturally must have a neurosis. Frankl is too proud to stand for such treatment. If this shrink thinks he can arbitrarily attest to the presence of an unprocessed psychological problem in anyone he sees, he's got another thing coming to him.

Not long after this disappointment, Frankl suddenly finds himself standing before the master himself, in the middle of Berggasse in the ninth district. Frankl is on his way home from the community college where he, though a student himself, often lectures, when by chance he runs into Freud. By this time the older man's reputation as a genius of epochal stature is firmly established. Frankl, overcome by shyness, gives a polite nod to the architect of the ego, id, and superego—but can't manage to say a word. It will be the only in-person meeting between the two men. It is not only the difference in age, half a century, that separates them; a massive gulf lies between their two ways of seeing the world.

. . .

Viktor Frankl is born on March 26, 1905 in Vienna's Leopoldstadt neighborhood. The Frankls live at Czerningasse 6. Alfred Adler lives and works right across the street, at number 7, until 1911, when he moves to an address on the Dominikanerbastei in the first district. It's possible that little Viktor encounters him, the busy Herr Doktor, while playing out in the street. Years later, Adler's individual psychology will be a great influence on the gifted youth.

Frankl's father Gabriel moved to Leopoldstadt, the neighborhood of Jewish merchants and clerks, from his home in South Moravia; his mother Elsa is from Prague. The elder Frankl is a civil servant working for the Ministry of Social Affairs, while his wife looks after the household and raises the couple's three children. Viktor is a good student, bright and hard-working. His older brother Walter and younger sister Stella often call him "Bocki"—"little billy goat"—because he's always disobeying their parents. When Viktor's natural history teacher remarks at one point that life is essentially nothing more than an ongoing process of combustion, Viktor is outraged: "But what's the point of that?" Even as a boy, he is preoccupied with the question of what this life of ours, so weighted down with hardship and pain, is good for.

He reads a lot, including works by the philosopher Arthur Schopenhauer. Too clever for his own good, Viktor doesn't share Schopenhauer's view that the individual spends his entire life oscillating between two basic states: misery and boredom. He prefers a dictum coined by another great thinker, Friedrich Nietzsche: "He who has a Why in life will endure any How."[15] To have a goal, a mission or a task that lends one's own life meaning—even as an adolescent, Frankl sees this as the crucial challenge awaiting every individual. Each person must only find the question that is personally addressed to them, and then answer it, as best they can. Otherwise they risk a feeling of existential emptiness.

Frankl isn't yet seventeen when he gives his first lecture on the meaning of life at the Wiener Volkshochschule, Vienna's community college. He doesn't yet suspect that his *own* mission in life will be to found logotherapy, a coinage based on the Greek word *logos*, for meaning, reason. According to Frankl's approach, the true illness afflicting the psyche is a lack of devotion to a cause. Where psychoanalysis has the will to pleasure and individual psychology has the will to power, Frankl has the will to meaning.

Frankl's father Gabriel once had to break off his study of medicine in order to help support his family. He entered the civil service as a stenographer and worked his way up over the years to a position as a ministerial official. He wants his son Viktor to be better off and to finally make good on his own desire to become a doctor.

. . .

Three years before Frankl, in the summer of 1902, another Vienna native who will place his own stamp on modern thought first glimpses the light of day. At eighteen, in the midst of political upheaval, he ponders the question of how the individual arrives at true knowledge. In 1920, on his first attempt to get his *Matura* and graduate high school, the young Karl Raimund Popper fails Latin and logic, even though at just sixteen he had begun attending lectures in mathematics, physics, history, and philosophy at the university. Two years later he finally passes, to the joy of his parents. Rosa Graf, one of Freud's sisters, is friends with the Poppers; through this connection, Karl's father, the jurist Simon Popper, occasionally attends meetings of the Vienna Psychoanalytic Society.

For a few months in early 1919, Simon Popper's son is a dedicated Marxist. He wants to live as a simple worker, but the drudgery of working in construction is too much for him. Nevertheless, still wanting to learn something practical, he begins an apprenticeship as a carpenter—and studies music at the conservatory on the side. Disgusted by the snobbery of his bourgeois friends, Karl makes a plan to become a teacher. If the need arises he can make chairs and desks for his students himself. With the psychologist Karl Bühler as his thesis advisor, he studies the laws of thought and in the mid-1920s starts to write essays on rigorous learning and deductive reasoning. Meanwhile, Popper starts helping out at a "red Vienna" child guidance center run by Alfred Adler. Karl becomes friends with Adler's children Valentine and Kurt, who often go on hikes in the mountains with their dear "Karli."

One evening Karl is consulting with the boss on the case of a difficult youth. Adler immediately diagnoses the boy with an inferiority complex. Taken aback, Popper asks how he could be so sure, he hasn't even seen the boy. Adler responds that his "thousandfold experience" leaves no doubt. "And with this new case, I suppose, your experience has become thousand-and-one-fold," Popper dryly responds.[16] Adler takes the criticism in stride, but Popper's impudent manner rubs others the wrong way. The philosopher Moritz Schlick, for example, prudently declines to invite him to the meetings of his Vienna Circle, fearing that the combative Popper will stir up trouble.

But the discussions at this club of logicians and linguistic philosophers don't particularly interest him anyway. Popper is captivated by the exciting discoveries in physics: Einstein's theory of relativity, the dualism of wave and particle, the budding field of quantum mechanics. As improbable as these theories might seem, it's astounding how well they can be empirically substantiated. The young skeptic, however, has his doubts about whether this is enough.

Measurements and positive evidence are all well and good, but they can never sufficiently prove a hypothesis on fundamental grounds. The true position of the stars measured during the solar eclipse of 1919 does confirm the deflection of light by large bodies of mass that Einstein predicted. Nevertheless, it doesn't constitute actual proof that he was right.

Prophet of modesty: Karl Popper founds critical rationalism.

The reason has to do with something the Scottish philosopher David Hume pointed out in the eighteenth century, namely that inductive logic, which establishes a general rule based on an observation, can't be substantiated: even if on countless occasions the sun has risen at the exact time it was calculated to rise, that doesn't mean, in purely logical terms, that it will also do so tomorrow. Could it be that there is no absolute truth, no firm foundation on which knowledge rests?

One reason Popper is looking for such a foundation might be that the difficult years after the First World War are marked by so much insecurity. "Most of us had no prospects and no plans," he remembers of his student days in Vienna. "We lived in a very poor country in which civil war was endemic, flaring up in earnest from time to time. We were often depressed, discouraged, disgusted. But we were learning, our minds were active and growing. We were reading ravenously, omnivorously; debating, changing our opinions, studying, sifting critically, thinking."[17]

Popper makes this his mission in life: to separate the chaff from the wheat of knowledge; humbug from reason; pseudoscience from true science. Where is the border, the line of demarcation between the two? The place to go looking for it must be in the method by which hypotheses and laws of causality are formed. Does science produce nothing more than provisional theories that await testing? Xenophanes, Popper's favorite pre-Socratic philosopher, knew the answer: "And of course the clear and certain truth no man has seen [...] But opinion is allotted to all."[18]

Among Popper's Marxist friends there are many who believe in the inevitability of revolution. History will follow the course predicted by Karl Marx, and as such the uprising of the proletariat is unavoidable. Popper considers this a fatal illusion. The more firmly one believes that revolution is imminent, the less probable it becomes. After all, if something is inevitable, there's no need to fight for it. For Popper, the course of history is fundamentally unforeseeable. To claim the contrary is only to display intellectual hubris.

Popper promotes a philosophy of modesty. Science, to him, is a method for critically examining one's own theories and searching for new, better answers. Contrary to what people for centuries now have led themselves to believe, it doesn't produce eternal truth; it only gives provisional hypotheses. Popper's philosophy of critical rationalism holds that scientific theories must be formulated in such a way that they can *fail* in the face of experience. In line with this core criterion of refutability, or falsifiability, it is a typical characteristic of pseudoscientific theories that they leave no room for doubt and refuse to submit to empirical verification. On a fundamental level, one cannot establish anything in purely *positive* terms, as Freud attempted to do with his case histories and deductions. Only by exposing yourself to the risk of refutation can you incrementally approach the truth—though at no point will you attain it.

Popper draws a distinction between two complementary kinds of thinking: one dogmatic, the other critical. The one forms connections, the other refutes them or limits their scope. In order for the interplay of the two to lead to ever better theories, it is necessary for the terms used to be well-defined and to contain testable criteria. A number of psychology's model assumptions, which at best can be understood metaphorically, run afoul of this requirement.

According to Popper, psychoanalysis is resistant to empiricism because it uses ambiguous terms and eludes examination. Worse still, it turns objections into putative proof of its own validity. By not acknowledging their sexual desires, a patient only confirms that they are repressing them. Psychoanalysis is one of those theories that "is able to feel bolstered by every objection against it," as Dieter E. Zimmer puts it. "The more wrong someone thinks it is, the more correct it believes itself to be."[19] Every denial is a secret confirmation—resistance is futile.

Popper illustrates this faulty logic using the following example. Let us imagine two men: one pushes a child into a lake in order to drown him; the other jumps in the water to save him. In the first case a psychoanalyst could explain that the man's murderous impulses stem from the Oedipal conflict: because the man cannot kill his own father, he would have the child die in his place. The individual psychologist, on the other hand, says that the man is trying to compensate for his feelings of humiliation by showing that he has power over life and death. Either of these can just as well be turned around and applied to the rescuer: per Freud he is sublimating his instinctual conflict through the performance of a moral act; per Adler he is driven by the desire to be a hero. Whichever way one looks at it, the theory is always right.

A frequent criticism made of the principle of falsifiability is that it's difficult to maintain in practice. No one throws out a theory simply because certain things seem to contradict it. It's just as easy, often even easier, to cast doubt on the validity or significance of the data or to try to save one's theory with ad hoc additions. And in fact there are many reasons to cling to a cherished viewpoint—such as personal vanity, wishful thinking, or the fear of having backed the wrong horse for too long. When it comes to psychotherapy, there's another important point to consider: in order for the therapy to be beneficial, what is needed isn't so much scientific but rather *subjective* certainty. What the therapist says doesn't have to be correct, so long as what they say is useful to the patient. What the patient believes is a crucial factor contributing to the therapeutic effect. It's for this reason that psychologically-effective explanations often seem so overweening: where certainty heals, there's little room for doubt and questioning.

SEX MAGIC, CONCRETE, AND MISTLETOE

In Dornach bei Basel, the anthroposophists' new home base, Steiner's leadership mandate is put to a difficult test in late 1914. His marriage to his partner of many years, Marie von Sivers, comes as a bitter disappointment to many of his followers. A woman named Alice Sprengel who is part of the Dornach sect is particularly resentful of the new "Frau Steiner." In an open letter, she accuses the head of the anthroposophists of breach of faith. Sprengel also complains of Steiner's having broken a promise to guide her soul, which she believes to be karmically linked to his, on its spiritual path.

Another member of the anthroposophical commune, a man named Heinrich Goesch, criticizes Steiner's authoritarian leadership style. Goesch is a free spirit and a professor at the Dresden Academy of Applied Arts. He plays an active role in life in the commune and has many ideas to share, often provocative ones, including some that Steiner will not tolerate under any circumstances, because they run counter to his idea of spiritual-intellectual purity.

A few years prior, Goesch underwent psychoanalysis with none other than Otto Gross, and since that time has been plumbing the depths of his own unconscious. Inspired by Gross's utopianism, he promotes the liberating power of physical love and practices what he preaches, conducting many love affairs. Together with Hannah Tillich, the wife of the theologian Paul Tillich, he engages in orgiastic exercises as a way of searching for buried memories of an earlier life.

Goesch the maverick espouses a sexual magic that Steiner has already fallen for once. In search of freemasonic rituals that he could include in his manual of enlightenment, he once entered into a contract with one Theodor Reuß, leader of an irregular masonic lodge. Reuß had made a business of selling occult titles and offices and had a reputation even among fellow esotericists as a notorious con artist. This doesn't stop Steiner from paying Reuß a lot of money to explain to him the many intricacies of the Rite of Memphis-Misraïm. Steiner was all too eager to gain insight into the ancient knowledge of Egyptian mysticism, but Reuß abused his power and conducted sexual rites with female followers for purported "soul-cleansing" purposes. With stunning naïveté, Steiner, in a guide called "Wie wird man Anthroposoph?"—"How Does One Become an Anthroposophist?"—borrows from Reuß the concept of the Kundalini fire, which must be stoked in order to attain knowledge of the higher realms. What Steiner doesn't know is that he is citing a concept taken from the Buddhist tradition of Tantra, where the "Kundalini fire" represents sexual potency. In later revisions of his writings Steiner expunges all mentions of the Kundalini; he doesn't want his teachings to be associated with exercises like the retention of semen during coitus.

Now in Dornach he comes down with full force on those who are making the case for the unbridled libido. He won't allow anyone to question his authority and bring the anthroposophist cause into disrepute with their wanton actions. Steiner expels Goesch, his wife, and Alice Sprengel from the sect—though without getting his hands dirty. Lest it look like an act of personal revenge, he leaves it to a committee, convened by him, to carry out the expulsion. Eroticism and lies are the greatest threats to the community, Steiner's wife declares. The doctrine of rebirth, she says, seduces some into cultivating a kind of "incarnation-exclusivity."[20]

During the first years of the war Steiner extensively revises many of his earlier writings. Just as he once transformed from an exponent of a Christian-mystic worldview into an atheistic follower of Nietzsche and dyed-in-the-wool materialist, now he completes a turn to karma, metempsychosis, and florid fantasies of the world beyond. "Only the malicious can regard this as a reversal of my thinking," he writes, in clear denial of the facts. Whether it was inner conviction or calculating business sense that brought about the doctrinal shift is hard to say; the motivations are difficult to disentangle. What occurs is likely another demonstration of the human individual's talent for sincerely believing in what brings them renown and gratification.

. . .

New Year's Eve, 1922: the home of the new man is burning. At first there are only thin wisps of smoke rising from a hill near Dornach, but then thick billowing clouds begin issuing from the cupola of the Johannesbau, which for two years has served as the spiritual home of the tight-knit community. Their leader, Rudolf Steiner, is at a dance performance and doesn't return to his home until around nine-thirty, when he sees the smoke rising over the "University of the Humanities." Several members soon gather outside the building—and make a grave mistake: with an axe they cut a hole into the building's wooden exterior, hoping to extinguish the fire they suspect is smoldering within. But as soon as the axe has cut through the façade, the fire, with a howl, sucks more air in through the opening and eats its way through the rafters with greater speed. When the fire brigade arrives shortly before eleven, flames are shooting out of the windows and gables. The building is beyond saving. By midnight, when the bells of the surrounding churches ring in the new year, the anthroposophists no longer have a place to worship.

Whether it was a short-circuit or arson that started the blaze is never determined, though that doesn't stop Steiner from accusing radical opponents of his teachings of having lit the spark. Either way, he quickly overcomes his initial shock, transforming it, as he so often does, into fresh energy. Just weeks later Steiner, with the help of deep-pocketed donors, is planning a new building made of a more sturdy, modern building material: concrete. The Goetheanum that Steiner helps design becomes the new headquarters of his community.

. . .

Steiner is the shining light of anthroposophy. Any resistance he meets only fans the flame of his enthusiasm. The autodidact strives toward an objective idealism in which the self and the world fuse into one. In Steiner's view, truth reveals itself not to the senses, but only to the "inner spirit." And he regards his teachings not as a religious doctrine but rather as a method for acquiring absolute knowledge.

The goal for Steiner is to become one with the higher realm. Where established science is silent, he provides answers. What happens after death? Is our fate pre-determined? Where is humanity headed? His eagerness to offer explanations runs fully counter to the credo of the physiologist Emil du Bois-Reymond, who, in his lecture "Über die Grenzen des Naturerkennens"—"On the Limits of Knowledge of Nature"—put it this way: "With regard to the mystery of what matter and energy are and how they might be capable of thinking, man must resolve once and for all to issue this verdict: 'Ignorabimus.'" Or put plainly: we'll never know! This kind of humility isn't Steiner's thing. He regards Immanuel Kant's *Critique of Pure Reason*, in which the Königsberg philosopher and Enlightenment figure placed narrow limits on the possibility of attaining knowledge, as the product of a lower mind. According to Steiner, for this foolishness, Kant was sure to have been reincarnated as a "negro."[21]

Steiner's dispute with Max Dessoir, a professor of psychology at the University of Berlin, gives a sense of his ability to inoculate himself from criticism. The controversy takes place in 1917. Dessoir has coined the term "parapsychology" for the view that there are mental phenomena with an existence outside the psyche. The idea that the human individual is made up of a physical etheric body and a spiritual astral body, is bound by karmic fate and will be reborn in a different incarnation, Dessoir considers a delusion. He regards Steiner's esoteric doctrine as a "mix of false interpretations of certain psychical processes and falsely understood leftovers of a vanished worldview."

Steiner is incensed at Dessoir's dismissal of himself and his teachings. Contrary to his custom, he decides to respond: the academic psychologist, he says, has put words in his mouth, crediting him with theories that he doesn't at all subscribe to only to point out their absurdities. When, for example, Dessoir finds fault with Steiner's unfounded idea that when a limb falls asleep, the etheric and astral bodies have temporarily separated, the anthroposophist counters by saying that Dessoir has simply misunderstood him, having taken a quote out of context.

On one point, however, Steiner defends himself, rather than merely deflecting. Knowledge, the anthroposophist declares, is inner contemplation of the spirit. But if that's the case, how can delusion and superstition be distinguished from actual truth? Not even Steiner denies that there are false conceptions. But differentiating between illusion and truth is very easy: one must simply trust the judgment of the initiated! What is true is what the initiate recognizes as such—here is the textbook definition of esotericism.

In his dispute with Dessoir, Steiner vehemently distances himself from science, with its analytic, dissecting character. Soon afterward he also comes up with an alternative theory of sickness and healing that he presents in 1920 in one of his innumerable lectures. In "The Humanitics-based Foundations of Physical and Mental Health," he writes: "The path that the natural sciences has followed over the past three to four centuries, to the benefit of so many fields, can never become a salutary one for the treatment of the sick individual." Steiner's therapeutic approach is based on "intuitive medicine." He describes it in a way that is reminiscent of the language of psychoanalysis: "In the therapeutic operation, one works out of life and into consciousness, and consciousness becomes a collaborator in the therapeutic process." Unlike psychoanalysis, where the aim is for the analyst's interpretations to have an effect within the patient's psyche, Steiner of course considers consciousness a bridge to other spheres. The claim to divine wisdom makes his teachings attractive to many, even if it remains an open question how one recognizes his wisdom, what it consists of, and what one must do to obtain it.

What Steiner imagines his own role in this performance to be can be surmised from the eight-meter-high wooden sculpture "The Representative of Humanity." One arm raised up to heaven, the other

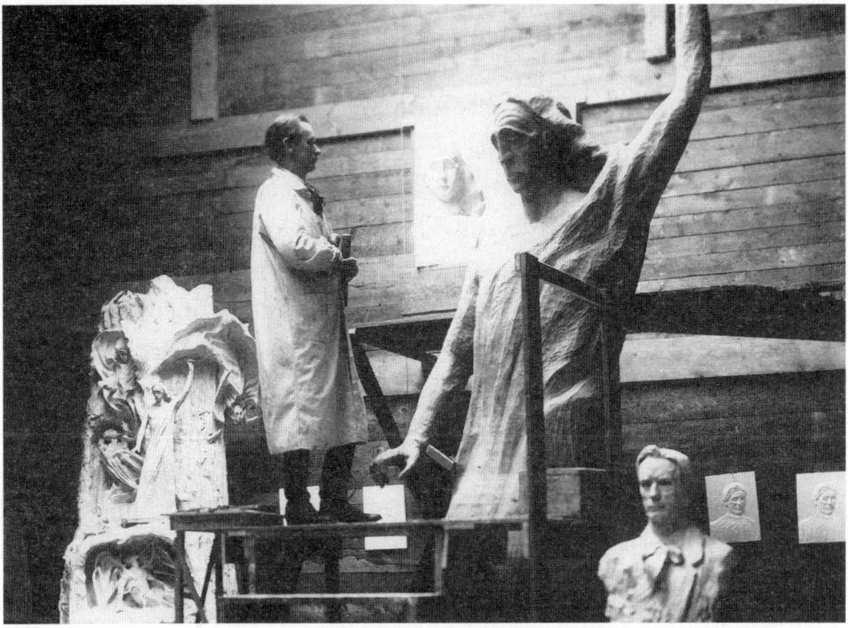

An image of a man: Steiner at work on the eight-meter-high wooden sculpture "The Representative of Humanity."

pointing imperiously downward, the figure depicts a modern messiah who will save humanity from its suffering. Built for a house of worship, the sculpture bears a strong resemblance to Steiner. "There is much to indicate that the 'Christ' Steiner left for posterity was shaped in his own image," writes Steiner's biographer Helmut Zander. The monumental sculpture was still unfinished at the time of the fire, and as a result escaped the flames.

Steiner is neither a psychologist nor a therapist and isn't interested in healing in the medical sense. Nevertheless, numerous followers look to his teachings for support. Feeling connected to a purposeful higher power gives them confidence and direction. The market for salvation has always included spiritual movements that offer something to counter the modern individual's sense of uprootedness: the feeling of self-efficacy. For time immemorial people have looked to talismans, rituals, or mantras to help them take control of their fate; everything will work out fine, if one can only find the magic formula. Steiner, the staunch esotericist, liberally doles out this balm to his disciples.

HE WHO HAS A WHY

One evening in the spring of 1927, Alfred Adler and his followers gather in a lecture hall at the University of Vienna's Histological Institute. A few psychoanalysts are present as well, as spectators. They will be witnesses to a dramatic spectacle. The individual psychologists Rudolf Allers and Oswald Schwarz each give lectures in which they openly disagree with the boss. They cast doubt on the dogma that the striving for power and recognition are fundamental constants in mental life. After this general reckoning, Allers and Schwarz announce their resignation from the Society for Free Psychoanalytic Research. An awkward silence fills the hall. Adler sits in the front row, next to other suspected rebels. Now he stands up, looks around for a moment, and says: "Well, you heroes?"[22]

Viktor Frankl speaks up. He begins by agreeing with the speakers, but then draws a completely different conclusion: individual psychology, he says, has within itself the ability to overcome its psychologism, its fixation on a single all-explaining mechanism. He for his part sees no reason to leave the society. Over the next few weeks, Adler tries repeatedly to get him to resign before finally excommunicating him. The reason: "unorthodox behavior (asking about meaning)."

Frankl's crime is to have formed a different conception of the individual's primary motive—namely to strive for coherence and a feeling of security and comfort within a greater whole. This idea exists in Adler's model as well, but he associates it with communal ties, the social feeling. Because of these parallels, Frankl's approach is at first considered a variant of individual psychology. Similarities aside, though, in expelling Frankl, Adler is less concerned with matters of substance than he is afraid of losing his authority. Through his actions he signals that he alone will decide on the direction of the movement.

At a congress in September 1926, Frankl uses the term "logotherapy" for the first time. He is convinced that people must imbue their suffering with meaning in order to overcome it. While Adler regards neurosis as a means to an end, a way of escaping the demands of society, Frankl sees it as an authentic expression of inner emptiness. One doesn't have to instruct patients in ways to develop will power, as Adler believes, but rather should show them how they can take responsibility for their lives.

Frankl pushes back against the determinism that both Freud and Adler espouse: the individual is free to choose whatever source of meaning they want—whether it be creative effort or devotion to abstract values or religious belief. The question to ask is not what makes a person happy, but rather how to deal with the inevitable defeats and setbacks they will encounter. The individual has to answer the questions that life puts to them. Borrowing from the nascent field of existential philosophy, Frankl calls his approach, premised on the individual's search for their own system of values, "existential analysis."

Frankl is a transcendentalist. He is fascinated by the "*Übersinn*," or "greater meaning," the individual's need to devote themselves and their life to a greater cause. He also does not regard the release of tension, which according to the theory of drives results from the discharge of libido, as a goal worth striving for. Tension and conflict are not pathological; rather they are a motor for change. According to Frankl, the individual is cursed with responsibility; therapy must be directed toward making them aware of this burden.

Adler doesn't just drive Frankl out of his society; one can assume that, from that point forward, he doesn't even speak to him when they run into each other on the street. After Frankl has cut ties with individual psychology, he continues to study medicine until 1930. On the side he counsels Viennese schoolchildren whose struggles in class lead to suicidal thoughts, and gives lectures to hone his talents as a speaker. His self-confident air draws the admiration of a number of young ladies. He invites one of them to a lecture by someone he describes as a "gifted speaker"—and on arriving in the auditorium steps up to the podium himself, enjoying the astonished look on her face as he speaks about the meaning of life. Even in his younger days, Frankl's character is marked by a generous portion of narcissism.

. . .

In 1933, the newly-minted neurologist and psychiatrist is put in charge of Pavilion 3 at Vienna's Am Steinhof mental hospital, also known as the "suicide pavilion." There he encounters hundreds of suicidal patients, many of whom are Jews who bear the brunt of society's hate and resentment. Frankl is all too familiar with the weight of depression: he himself often feels empty, is prone to brooding, and drifts from one day to the next.

In this time Frankl begins to experiment with a technique that yields good results in certain patients, and also in himself. Only years later will he first describe it in a scientific paper as "paradoxical intention."[23] It calls for the patient to try to do the exact opposite of what their fears prompt them to do. If for example they are afraid of getting stuck in an elevator or breaking out in a sweat in front of other people, they should actively imagine this very scenario and say to themselves: lose your mind with terror as soon as you step inside the elevator! Start sweating like mad when people look at you! Frankl believes that by imagining the worst possible outcome of their anxieties, the patient learns that there's really nothing to fear. They become aware of the absurdity of their own phobias and can distance themselves from them. The more one amplifies the anxiety in one's head, while at the same time the feared catastrophe fails to result, the more the feeling of dread disappears. This method of confronting what triggers the fear and enduring it in supportive company will find its way into cognitive behavior therapy.

But how can a patient undertake to do something that terrifies them to so great an extent? They might be able to pretend, but can they *really* imagine the catastrophe? At one point in the classroom, Frankl's student Alfried Längle struggles with this idea and probes further: "How can someone who is afraid of fainting wish that he will faint?" As Längle remembers it, Frankl responds with impatience. "*What do you mean, it's obvious how it works: you have to act it out.* He wouldn't tolerate anything that undermined what he was teaching."[24] Mastering one's fear by "acting as if"—this, according to Frankl, must be the goal.

He himself is afraid of heights as a child—and so, when he is in college, he starts forcing himself to go hiking in the mountains on a regular basis. On via ferratas and ridgelines he overcomes his fear little by little, until finally he becomes an enthusiastic alpinist. What is true for physical ailments also holds true for the psyche: too much rest and avoidance only reinforce the problem. If someone constantly avoids unpleasant situations because they consider them impossible to handle, then in doing so they prove to themselves that the avoidance is necessary, that doing otherwise would be too great a risk. In treating such a condition, therapists quickly find themselves in a bind: on the one hand, the therapist mustn't encourage the patient's evasive behavior; on the other, if they insist too strongly—if they confront the patient with their fear—then they lose the patient's willingness to cooperate. Some people would rather keep living with their fear than go through hell, and will break the therapy off before it has properly begun.

In his autobiography, Frankl describes how the technique of paradoxical intention helped delay his deportation. One day he is summoned by the Gestapo. The Nazi who is interrogating him asks if he's a psychiatrist. When he says yes, his interrogator tells him he has a friend who suffers from agoraphobia—what should he do about it? Frankl recommends his method of paradoxical intention. "Whenever he has an attack of his phobia, he should say to himself: 'I am afraid I could collapse on the street. Fine then, that is exactly what I want. I will collapse and a crowd will gather around me. Worse than that, I will have a heart attack and a stroke to boot.'"[25] Clearly the recommendation bears fruit; in any case, Frankl is spared further interrogations.

If a person succeeds in willing something that they have long avoided, they experience a break with their own expectations: nothing happened to me! There's another way! Here Frankl recognizes something that is a fundamental factor in many therapies: experiencing an alternative, a different way of doing things, helps the patient learn to mistrust what the voice in their head is telling them, rather than confusing it with reality. This is often a big step toward recovery.

Another trick from Frankl's repertoire is dereflection. The point of the technique is to interrupt the infinite loop of brooding thoughts and to understand that just thinking about problems doesn't actually solve them. Dereflection aims at getting the patient to stop tormenting themselves with questions that are unanswerable. But how does it work? Frankl recommends becoming active. The individual experiences a sense of purpose by doing something meaningful, pursuing a passion, showing devotion to a cause.

Frankl has ample clinical material to draw on. He works at the Steinhof Mental Hospital for four years, until 1937. The Austrofascists under Chancellor Kurt Schuschnigg also stoke antisemitism, and the acts of humiliation and attacks against Jews rise sharply even before Austria's "Anschluss" in March 1938. Frankl's clinic is just about flooded with patients who have attempted suicide. Over the years he will treat thousands of them.

The situation gets even worse with the occupation of Austria by German troops. Frankl is forced to close the practice he has just opened and loses his professional status. As "Jew Practitioner Viktor Israel Frankl," as a Nazi order puts it, he moves to the Israelitisches Kulturbund's Rothschild Clinic. Working there provides him with a livelihood while at the same time shielding his parents from deportation. But Frankl is aware of the danger. He applies for a visa to the United States and waits impatiently for it to be approved.

Seeker in a white smock: Viktor E. Frankl as a young doctor.

Finally the news of his salvation arrives: he can emigrate. Frankl's visa is at the consulate, ready to be picked up. But what will become of his parents? And what about Tilly, a nurse he has fallen in love with and wants to marry? Late one evening Frankl walks into St. Stephen's Cathedral to think. He covers the Star of David on his coat with his scarf. But the answer won't come to him. At home his father greets him with a piece of marble that he found in the rubble of the synagogue that had recently been burned down. The fragment comes from the inscription of the Ten Commandments. Frankl's father believes it contains part of the fourth commandment: "Honor thy father and thy mother: that thy days may be long upon the land which the Lord thy God giveth thee." He decides then and there to stay with his family; the visa expires.

For a time Frankl is able to continue practicing medicine. The Rothschild hospital is the last clinic that is still permitted to treat Jews. On December 17, 1941, Frankl marries Tilly Grosser at the Leopoldstadt registry office. Soon afterwards she becomes pregnant. Because Jewish women who are expecting a child face immediate deportation to a concentration camp, she must get an abortion. The young couple is devastated. In summer 1942 the Rothschild hospital is finally closed. With its closure, Frankl and his family lose their protection against deportation. On September 25 they leave Vienna in a cruelly overcrowded train, bound for Theresienstadt.

. . .

Conditions in the "model ghetto" northwest of Prague (in present-day Terezín) are abysmal: the food strictly rationed, medical supplies practically non-existent. On top of that, the residents of the ghetto are subjected to abuse by guards and the SS. After a work detail in the "Small Fortress," a camp on the outskirts of Theresienstadt, Frankl is dropped off back home. He can barely walk; his body is covered with cuts and bruises. At the sight of him, Tilly bursts into tears: "For heavens sake, what have they done to you?"[26]

Frankl's father dies shortly after being deported. The elder Frankl has pulmonary edema; a vial of morphine which his son carries with him for emergencies eases his father's suffering. "Do you still have pain?"

he asks the eighty-one-year-old in farewell. "No."—"Do you have any wish?"—"No." He doesn't see his father again.

"*Wie Gott will, ich halt still*"—God's will be done, I'll keep silent. The deeply devout Gabriel Frankl had spoken this mantra to himself and the other deportees to keep their courage up on the journey to Theresienstadt. This stoic attitude also illustrates one of the flip sides of Frankl's therapeutic ethos, which sees the solution only in enduring, in the search for some sort of meaning behind the suffering. To be sure, under oppressive rule or in a concentration camp there's hardly an alternative; to rebel is to risk death. But someone who is living under normal conditions in which alternatives are very much available and yet is only ever intent on finding meaning "in spite of everything" often gives up the desire to change something about the circumstances that oppress him. He who has a why endures any how—this maxim also contains an element of lost agency.

In October 1944, Frankl's family is torn apart completely. His mother and his brother Walter are sent to Auschwitz. Shortly thereafter, Viktor and Tilly are also put on a transport to the extermination camp. In closed cattle cars they travel across the countryside for two days and nights. Before the "disinfection," Frankl is forced to hand over his hastily finished manuscript "Ärztliche Seelsorge," along with his few other remaining possessions. He is given the clothes of a dead man. In the inside pocket he finds a page ripped out of a Jewish prayer book, which gives him hope.

Frankl stays in Auschwitz for three days. At the selection led by camp doctor Josef Mengele he is first placed in the line of those who are headed to the "shower." When he spots a familiar face in the other group of prisoners judged capable of work, he seizes a moment when Mengele's back is turned to go over and join him. This saves him from certain death.

Theresienstadt, Auschwitz, Kaufering III, Türkheim. Frankl survives four camps in three years. On April 27, 1945, shortly before the German surrender, the US army liberates Türkheim. The suffering comes to an end; the burden on the psyche remains.

. . .

After the war ends, Frankl first works at a field hospital for concentration camp survivors. Many of the liberated prisoners are so debilitated that they die within weeks. Frankl hopes to find Tilly, his mother, and his brother in Vienna, and quits his post soon after regaining his strength. Then he sets out on the five-hundred-kilometer journey back home. In Vienna he wanders around aimlessly. He visits familiar spots, keeps a lookout for familiar faces. His mother, he learns, was killed shortly after her arrival in Auschwitz. Tilly, who when they parted at the train station promised him that she would do everything she could to stay alive, was sent to Bergen-Belsen. There, in the Lüneburg Heath, she was liberated by British soldiers on April 15, 1945, and taken to a hospital. She died shortly thereafter from the effects of her imprisonment. Walter, too, did not survive his time in a forced labor camp near Auschwitz. "Thus I am now left all alone," Frankl writes on September 14, 1945. "I am unspeakably tired, unspeakably sad, unspeakably lonely."[27] Only his sister Stella survives. She had immigrated to Mexico before the war and will die in Australia at an advanced age, a few years before her brother.

Frankl finds an apartment on Mariannengasse, next to the university. He gets a job at the Polyclinic, which he knows from his student days. He also acquires a typewriter.[28] At Türkheim Frankl had made notes using pencil stubs on scraps of old camp forms. Now that he's got a solid roof over his head, he rewrites his lost manuscript within a few weeks. *Ärztliche Seelsorge* is published in 1946 at almost the same time as his memoir *Ein Psycholog erlebt das KZ.*[29]

Frankl remains astoundingly unresentful of the Viennese, who looked on as their neighbors and colleagues were deported, some actively denouncing others or participating in the persecution directly. He has no time for the notion of collective guilt. "This or that person has remained a human being and does what he can," he writes in the play "Synchronisation im Birkenwald," which appears as a kind of afterword to his memoir of his time in the camps. "What do you call just?" Frankl asks in the play. "To answer hate with hate—injustice with injustice? For us to do the same thing that the others have done? That's not justice. That only perpetuates the injustice."[30]

Frankl also visits an old mentor, Otto Pötzl, who was a long-time member of the Nazi party. Later he co-authors an article with Pötzl about near-death experiences in mountain climbing. Despite all his bitter experiences, the personal matters more to Frankl than abstract historical guilt.

Frankl's conciliatory attitude, combined with his pronounced self-praise, draws criticism. The historian Timothy Pytell claims that Frankl unconsciously sympathized with the Nazis, if not outright collaborated with them. In his book *Viktor Frankl: Das Ende eines Mythos?*,[31] Pytell delivers a harsh verdict on the founder of logotherapy. The main charge: Frankl was actually fascinated by fascism. As proof, Pytell points for example to the fact that Frankl was a member of the Vaterländischer Front, the ruling party under Austrofascism from 1934 to 1938. But all doctors working for the state in Austria were automatically enrolled in the party, whether they wanted to be or not. Frankl also had a "weakness for borderline experiences," according to Pytell. It took being deported for him to be able to work out his logotherapy. This is a grotesque accusation to make of someone who only barely survived the Nazi terror. Even if Frankl did first develop his "defiant power of the spirit" in the concentration camp; that most certainly doesn't mean that the suffering was to his liking.

In Frankl's conception of psychotherapy, self-transcendence plays a special role. Our life is always pointing at something that extends beyond it. "Nothing does so much to impel an individual beyond himself, nothing is capable of activating him, nothing allows him to overcome ailments and difficulties so much as the consciousness of personal responsibility, the experience of a particular mission."[32] One night, as he wanders through the Kaufering III camp, hungry and with "frozen and festering feet," he has this experience first-hand. "My situation seemed bleak, even hopeless. Then I imagined that I stood at the lectern in a large, beautiful, warm and bright hall. I was about to give a lecture to an interested audience on, 'Psychotherapeutic Experiences in a Concentration Camp'. In the imaginary lecture I reported the things that I [was then] living through."[33]

His gifts as a speaker become an escape for Frankl. The thought of one day speaking before a large audience and sharing his experiences nourishes his desire to survive. And so it comes to pass: after the war, Frankl gives innumerable lectures all over the world and is admired for his courage and resilience. His appearances make him one of the most influential voices pleading for decency and humanity. Alfried Längle, his former student in Vienna, describes in blunt terms his old boss's egocentricism: "He liked nothing more than to hear himself talk."[34] Frankl's autobiography, *Recollections*, also reveals the strong need for recognition. At one point Frankl relates: "I was once given the Rorschach inkblot test by a psychologist at an Innsbruck psychiatric clinic. He claimed that he had never seen such a range between rationality and deep emotions."[35] At another point he writes: "I have always been amused when I heard that others had an idea that I had had a long time before. [. . .] I suspect that I would not have cared if others had received the Nobel Prize for ideas that had occurred to me also."[36]

The US-American psychoanalyst Irvin D. Yalom, a practitioner of "existential therapy," centered on the fleetingness of life, meets Frankl during his time as a visiting professor in Vienna. Yalom invites Frankl to visit him in California. In Stanford Frankl presents a few clinical cases to medical residents who have been trained in the client-centered tradition of Carl Rogers. The doctors are horrified by the visitor from Vienna. "His logotherapy demonstration," says Yalom, "consisted, for the most part, of his determining, in a ten- to fifteen-minute inquiry, what the patient's life meaning should be, and prescribing it to the patient in authoritarian fashion."[37] Even if Frankl wasn't, as it seems, an especially empathetic therapist, his ideas still live on today.

SICKNESS AS A WEAPON

It is summer in Wiesenbach, an idyllic rural town just outside of Heidelberg. After the heat of the day a cool night breeze drifts in, the stars twinkle in the sky, crickets chirp, a stream burbles softly in the distance. It's not just any summer. A whiff of revolution hangs in the air, now that so many young people have started dreaming of overthrowing the current system. Down with capitalism! It turns people into slaves and makes them sick. Out with the old authorities! Stale leftovers of a thousand years of mustiness and decay. Throw off the constraints of the parental home, the bourgeois family, the imbecilic ideal of the good citizen! Break out into the open air, into life, into clear consciousness!

It's still night when they set out on their way to meet Wolfgang, who lives out here in this postcard idyll. Somewhere close by, well-hidden in the woods, is everything they need for the revolutionary struggle: money, weapons, detonators and explosives, fake IDs. The first houses of Wiesenbach come into view, the car turns a corner, and suddenly they see cops at the entrance to town, waving their traffic paddles. Police checkpoint. What now? After the first surge of panic they slow down and keep driving. Two cops on patrol—they can handle 'em, it'll be a cinch. Sergeant Brand studies the people inside the car in the light of his flashlight. Long hair, unkempt, what are they doing in the Odenwald at this hour? A suspicion starts to dawn on Brand, then it happens. He is just speaking the words "license, registration" when a shot is fired, followed by another. Without warning the man in the passenger seat had drawn a pistol and pulled the trigger. *It's his own fault, the pig!* The silence is broken sharply by the squealing of tires, the roar of the engine.

Sergeant Brand doesn't know what hit him; all he notices is a burning sensation in his arm. He falls to the ground, but he's lucky. Only one of the bullets reached him, and it struck him in the shoulder—painful, but not life-threatening. His partner unholsters his pistol and fires at the car as it speeds away, but he misses his target. By the time he starts pursuit, the perpetrators are already out of sight. He calls for backup; minutes pass before the ambulance comes. By dawn a helicopter is hovering over the town.

Police comb the surrounding area. Their search quickly leads them to a house where Dr. Wolfgang Huber from the Heidelberg Polyclinic lives. Huber is a known rabble-rouser. In March he founded the Socialist Patient Collective (Sozialistisches Patientenkollektiv – SPK) after the university administration had barred him from treating patients in accordance with the tenets of Marxism-Leninism. He wants to make them aware of the roots of their suffering, the pathological conditions of capitalism, which he regards as a continuation of fascism by other means. He wants to convince his patients to join the revolutionary struggle; they should use their "sickness as a weapon," as one SPK flyer puts it.

A few days after the shootout in Wiesenbach, Huber is arrested. The suspicion that the perpetrators were members of Huber's patient collective is hardening. In the basement of an apartment that Huber's girlfriend is renting under a false name, investigators find guns, ammunition, and tons of flyers.

The thirty-five-year-old Huber was, up until a short time ago, a respectable member of the Heidelberg medical profession—but that was before he began working to "call the shit system to account." The exploitation of the individual, the pressure to consume and compete, alienation from labor, forced monogamy, obedience and oppression inside the family . . . Huber believes that in order to truly be free, one must first bring down the system. After much hemming and hawing, the university administration had placed an apartment in a prime location in the city center at his disposal, where Huber, who had left the polyclinic over the dispute, could continue his revolutionary form of group and individual therapy.

Marx and Hegel for the psyche: for the doctor Wolfgang Huber, head of the Socialist Patient Collective, it wasn't the individual who was sick, but society as a whole.

The SPK brings together dropouts and the unemployed, alcoholics and students, oddballs and seekers. Even retirees and housewives are part of the group—how many members there are exactly, no one knows. Some come for hour-long therapy sessions; others, above all young runaways and homeless people, camp out on mattresses on the floor. Huber is eloquent. Many in the collective would like to be like him, self-confident and sure of his judgments. Those who come to the SPK for help are, for the most part, lost souls; some are victims of domestic violence or neglect. Huber has affairs with several women he treats. And why not? After all, sex is the best way to free yourself from outdated dogmas. Sick or not, it makes no difference; it's not the individual who is sick, but rather the society in which he lives.

At times there are a dozen or more members living in the roomy apartment. A therapy session, usually conducted within the group, costs five Marks; all funds are pooled. To cope with the demand, Huber names some of the patients co-therapists. Treatment mainly involves studying Hegel, Marx, and Engels. One patient reports: "Understanding Marxist theory and dialectic serves as the foundation for the treatment's success." Another says: "The freed-up energy is converted into Marxism. By means of the Dialectic Interpretation of Symptoms, the inhibition vanishes."[38]

University rector Rolf Rendtorff, an evenhanded theologian and member of the Social Democratic Party, asks a group of psychiatrists for a professional assessment of Huber's revolutionary approach. For them the matter is clear: Huber isn't crazy, but what he's doing is nevertheless irresponsible and dangerous. He holds his patients hostage to his own project of political agitation, including some who suffer from schizophrenic psychosis and suicidal ideation. Huber puts on a guru act, smoking like a chimney and often staring silently at his patients during therapy sessions—either that, or demanding that they answer his questions about the end of capitalism based on their reading. Huber isn't licensed to prescribe medication; for the most part he limits himself to lecturing. According to Huber, working on the individual is pointless. Only by overcoming the fascist form of society—if necessary with violence—can the individual become healthy.

By declaring societal conditions to be the sole cause of psychological suffering, Huber turns his patients' hatred and anger outward, toward cops, fat cats, and reactionaries. In April 1971 a woman takes her own life in the woods overlooking Heidelberg. She doesn't want to be buried with Marx and Engels, she writes in a suicide note; she feels guilty and forlorn. After the woman's death Huber circulates a pamphlet that declares Rendtorff, Culture Minister Wilhelm Hahn, and the "Doctor Pigs" to be murderers. The woman's death was their fault—he himself couldn't have been responsible, notwithstanding his unempathetic, overaggressive way of treating her.

Then, on June 24, 1971, the shots are fired in Wiesenbach that herald the beginning of the end of the SPK. The whole country is in an uproar. Students are demonstrating against the Vietnam war, against old Nazis in influential positions—and in support of sexual self-determination and the right to an abortion. For them, the Federal Republic of Germany harbors fascists at every level of government. The system has to go! The day is not far off when the working class will rise up and socialism will triumph.

Where is the line between utopian fantasy and madness? After the patient collective has dissolved and the apartment has been cleared out by the police, a handful of members go underground. Some are involved in the attack on the German embassy in Stockholm in April 1975. Huber himself provided Gudrun Ensslin and Ulrike Meinhof of the Red Army Faction with money and a hideout. He is sentenced to four and a half years in prison for membership in a criminal organization.

He who stands up for people's liberation must be prepared to make sacrifices. There's only one thing he must not do: question himself. Is the struggle just? Will it stir up the masses? Bring down the system? Is there even a point? Does any of it mean anything? Meaning, thinks Huber in his bare prison cell, is merely a construct of the bourgeoisie. All psychologists have done so far is to interpret the individual in different ways; what it really comes down to is changing society. Whether society is ready for it or not.

AFTERWORD

SO WHAT DOES IT ALL ADD UP TO?

Welcome to the here and now! Now that we've reached the end of our journey through the early days of psychotherapy, you might be asking yourself what's left of all these theories and techniques? Is Freud's theory of the repressed libido still in fashion? Has Adler's concept of the inferiority complex held up? And what about their many successors and competitors, from Reich's character analysis and Perls's gestalt therapy to Moreno's psychodrama, Rogers's conversational therapy, and Frankl's logotherapy, and on from there to Wolpe and Cover Jones's behavioral therapy and Beck and Ellis's cognitive approaches—what should we think of all these efforts from our present-day perspective? There's no overarching answer to this question. The groundbreaking ideas from the early days of psychotherapy have rapidly evolved and above all diversified: thus over the years ever more variations, off-branchings, and counter-developments have come along to form a tangled web of hundreds of therapeutical methods, so many that it's scarcely possible to keep track. And their number is constantly growing.

The reasons for this dizzying abundance are in part technical, and have to do with advances in clinical psychology and psychiatry. But they are also rooted in the fact that psychotherapy obeys the economic logic of supply and demand.

One of the technical reasons is this: we look at psychological problems today in a much more nuanced fashion than we did a hundred years ago. There is no longer a *single* neurosis; rather there is a large spectrum of disorders and syndromes with numerous subtypes. According to the most recent diagnostic handbooks, depression alone embraces more than two dozen variations, such as seasonal depression, prolonged grief disorder, and bipolar disorder. Because many treatment programs tackle certain problems in a "disorder-specific" fashion, it's only logical that there would be a fairly broad diversity of methods.

Psychotherapy began when physicians gave up the dogmatic view that every illness, even mental illness, must have a physical cause. Phobias, compulsions, restlessness, unexplained pains or melancholy couldn't be ascribed to brain anomalies or organ defects and yet were clearly more than "malingering." The idea that symptoms might be caused by fantasies, memories, emotions, and patterns of thought of which patients weren't even necessarily aware was a revolutionary insight that threw new light on the question of what makes the human individual "tick": the psyche became the stage for a suite of hidden processes which a guild of young experts promised to decipher. Peering behind the scenery of the psychical theater, they provided help, theoretically at least, by facilitating self-knowledge. What's more, their work made the boundary between sick and normal fluid. Rather than assume that there is a fundamental difference between pathological and healthy mental activity, the pioneers of psychotherapy posited a continuum: everyone harbors more or less amoral wishes, is occasionally depressed, nervous, compulsive, or anxious; whether these add up to illness is determined only by the degree of the symptoms' intensity and the amount of suffering associated with them.

The second reason for the miraculous proliferation of therapeutic methods lies in a simple capitalist imperative: someone who wants to establish themselves in the market of psychotherapy needs an attractive brand, a niche, a unique selling point. Distinguishing yourself from others by coming up with your own label and your own nomenclature is a way of putting forth an attractive product that speaks to the zeitgeist. Psychotherapy has always been characterized by a particular tension: on the one hand it provides important help and relief, often more effective than medication. On the other hand it is a profession that trades in the hope that everyone can cast off their misery and find happiness. This is the promise of the therapeutic narrative, and Western culture has sucked it up like a sponge.

Today psychotherapy is booming like never before. Attentively focusing on one's self and its condition, averting dangers and strengthening one's resilience—these concepts pervade all aspects of life. This heightened sensibility certainly has its good side, helping to detect problems earlier and leading to less stigmatization. Another consequence, however, is that some emotions that are merely unpleasant quickly begin to appear pathological. For cases such as these, Viktor Frankl recommended "dereflection"—doing instead of thinking, acting instead of brooding. The hype around therapy tends to produce the opposite reaction, however: a state of hyperreflectiveness in which one's thoughts constantly revolve around themselves. This comes out in a widespread language of vulnerability whose vocabulary is teeming with blocked energies, repressed trauma, and inner children.

The relationship between therapist and patient has also profoundly changed since Freud's day. The image of the knowing therapist, who by dint of his insights helps his patients achieve better self-control, is now passé. Thanks in part to clients' growing self-awareness, it's no longer an option for therapists to make pronouncements from on high, diagnosing their clients' problems and telling them what they have to do to solve them. Someone who goes into therapy today often has at least a rough idea of what's wrong and what needs to be done.

At the same time, therapists for their part realized that explanations alone aren't enough to overcome disorders. Thus rather than coolly dissecting inner conflicts, practitioners developed approaches that foregrounded the attendant emotions. The focus was now on facilitating positive experiences in the context of a therapeutic relationship between equal partners, and on rehearsing new habits. Therapy providers today are far less dogmatic or ideologically rigid than the early pioneers, and—not coincidentally—they are much more likely to be women. They no longer try to cure mental distress by presenting an incontestable truth, as Freud, Adler, or Jung did; rather they pragmatically support their clients in better coping with their day-to-day lives.

Anything that helps achieve this goal is welcome. The search for the source of the trouble, however, only plays a minor role. In most cases there's no saying what exactly caused a disorder, because a lot of factors are at play—genetics, background and life experience, social hardship, losses and setbacks, and other stress factors. Mental problems have multiple causes; they cannot be traced back to individual factors like a buried trauma. More important than asking "Where did this come from?" is asking "Where do I go from here?"—and finding the means to obtain relief. One solution might well be learning to live with the issue. More recent approaches in acceptance and self-distancing have contributed a great deal to the de-ideologization of therapy.

It is striking that the major schools, with the exception of behavioral and cognitive therapy, developed for a long time outside of the academic and scientific field of psychology. Often therapists would even carry out a kind of self-marginalization by portraying themselves as the exponents of a truth that was rejected by the mainstream. This is another narrative that began with Freud, who claimed that the ignorant masses resisted his insights. Dogmatic postulations about the power of the libido, the need to compensate for feelings of inferiority, or the effects of blocked energy flows helped form the original image of the psychotherapist as someone who brings the secrets of the psyche to light. Only little by little did this cliché disappear from serious psychotherapy; its influence persists however in the approaches of many consultants and life coaches.

One thing is for certain, and it's that psychotherapy has traveled a long way from eminence to evidence, from the psychodynamism of charismatic luminaries to a pragmatic medical practice. Many of its early thinkers, from the publicity-hungry John B. Watson to the guru of gestalt therapy Fritz Perls, coined suggestive concepts that evaded clear definition. As a result, it took a long time for critical evaluation of the effects of treatment to finds its way into therapeutic thinking. It was above all the practitioners of cognitive behavior therapy who set the standard in this regard. No other method can put forth such substantial proof of its efficacy; not for nothing are behavioral therapeutical interventions considered the gold standard today.

As in the past, research in the field of psychotherapy continues to face the problem that those who test a method are usually also applying it professionally and profiting from it. No one wants to bite the hand that feeds them—to the contrary, practitioners, whether consciously or unconsciously, defend their methods beyond what is justifiable and try to make them seem as efficacious as possible.[1]

As comprehensive reviews, so-called meta-analyses, show, psychotherapy on average is effective in the long term for about half of patients.[2] It doesn't magically make symptoms disappear, it won't make a new man or woman of someone who tends toward phobias or anxiety, but it can help attenuate the most severe effects. Meta-analyses also show that for around one in ten cases, undesirable side effects occur: during or after therapy patients feel worse than before, or they become dependent on the therapy.[3]

And there's yet another number that many like to ignore: a good half of the effectiveness factor in psychotherapy can be chalked up to empathetic attention, to the good feeling that results from being in competent hands and having the opportunity to speak openly and without shame—in short: to the placebo effect.[4] This is not a scandal, but an opportunity. It's no doubt true of a broken leg or an infection that the more one trusts the treatment, the better the injury heals. But what in somatic medicine is only a supportive factor is nothing short of a prerequisite in psychotherapy: the "expectation colored by faith"[5] on the part of patients that even Freud called for.

Where faith heals—or contributes to the healing—in such a way, there is every reason to place your trust in the method and put any critical questions aside. This is likely one reason why some providers project a bewildering self-certainty, and why not a few of their clients hang on to their every word. But often, as the degree of conviction grows, so too does the pressure for both parties to immunize themselves against doubt. Highlighting this dilemma was a guiding motivation in selecting the figures portrayed in this book. They came up with extraordinary ideas and powerful therapeutic approaches and were at the same time prisoners of their theories and their egos.

Recent research, however, provides evidence of something astonishing: the usefulness of a therapy has little to do with the underlying theory.[6] Clearly the question of *which* explanation you find valid is less important than the mere fact of having landed on an explanation that you find convincing. It provides support and unburdens the psyche, whether it's true or not. In this sense Frankl's motto does apply: "He who has a why in life will endure almost any how."

We live today in a culture of self-improvement, in which one goal is omnipresent: becoming who you really are; identifying your true self and living accordingly.[7] But we should be wary of oversimplified explanations ("It's your parents' fault") or full-throated promises ("Success guaranteed!"). They can entrench suffering and exacerbate it. Someone who believes that they were traumatized as a child but repressed the memory of the trauma seldom does themselves a favor. As much relief as it can bring to have someone or something to assign blame to, it would be better to let the question of blame go. Scientists who study memory have long since exposed the Freudian pattern—make buried memories conscious in order to get rid of them for good—as a myth: in our memories, facts and fictions fuse together into a knot that is impossible to untangle.

The early psychotherapists provide wonderful examples of the power of stories. The founders of the psychodynamic, humanistic, and learning-theoretical schools helped shape a narrative without which our therapy-dominated society would be utterly unthinkable. It is them we have to thank for the idea that one must attentively observe and interpret one's psyche in order to forge resilience; that everyone should investigate themselves instead of merely functioning; and that these insights will benefit not only the individual, but also society as a whole. By facing the unconscious, "letting ourselves in," and being open and authentic, the world as a whole becomes just a little more free, more peaceful, more self-determined. Therapists of various stripes continue to belabor this cliché. It was pushed to its most absurd extreme in the utopian visions of the '68 generation, which provide this account with its closing chapter.

With inspired ambition, Freud, Adler, Jung, and others each turned their own particular brand of psychodynamism into a profession. They didn't discover the unconscious, but furnished it with secrets to be brought out into the light of day. In so doing they established a way of thinking that lives on today. But if we measure our well-being according to their standards alone, if we base our idea of health on our ability to overcome unconscious resistances, attain complete awareness, or achieve orgastic potency, we might well suffer twice over: from the burden of our own existence and our incapacity to overcome it.

In the century of psychology, the image of the psyche underwent a fundamental transformation. A worldview became a science, a controversial service a pillar of the healthcare system. Psychotherapy as we know it today provides us with a good means of helping people face life's challenges. We can correctly assess its promise only if we know how it all began.

ACKNOWLEDGMENTS

A book, like the psyche, is always a collective work. And as in the realm of the psyche, in writing too we are often blind to the many ties and connections that make our work turn out the way it does. I thank my literary agent Michael Gaeb and his team, above all Andrea Vogel and Bettina Wißmann, for their enthusiasm and their valuable suggestions. Without the constructive criticism from my editor Charlyne Bieniek this book would likewise have hardly been possible; my sincere thanks to her and to the team at dtv for their enthusiastic support. For help orienting myself in this subject I thank first and foremost: Michael Schröter, Katrin Angst, Erich Seifritz, Eva-Lotta Brakemeier, Bernhard Strauss, and Winfried Rief. I thank Daniel Lingenhöhl, the editor-in-chief of *Spektrum der Wissenschaft*; my colleagues at *Gehirn&Geist*; and Corinna Hartmann for the opportunity to take a sabbatical to complete the manuscript. Last but not least I thank my wife and my daughter Mira for their emotional support. All of you gave me something incredibly helpful, and not just for writing a book: knowledge, patience, and confidence.

BIBLIOGRAPHY

Abraham, Hilda C. and Ernst L. Freud, eds. *Sigmund Freud, Karl Abraham – Briefe 1907–1926*. Frankfurt: S. Fischer, 1965.

———. *A Psycho-Analytic Dialogue: The Letters of Sigmund Freud and Karl Abraham 1907–1926*. New York: Basic Books, 1965.

Adler, Alfred. *The Neurotic Constitution*. Trans. Bernard Glueck and John E. Lind. New York: Dodd, Mead, 1926.

———. *Social Interest*. Trans. John Linton and Richard Vaughan. London: Faber and Faber, 1938.

———. *Studienausgabe*. 7 Vols. Ed. Karl Heinz Witte. Göttingen: Vandenhoeck and Ruprecht, 2007.

———. *Understanding Human Nature*. Trans. Walter Béran Wolfe. Cleveland: World Publishing Co., 1942.

Aschaffenburg, Gustav. "Die neueren Theorien der Hysterie." *Deutsche Medizinische Wochenschrift* 33, no. 44 (1907): 1809–1813.

Bair, Deirdre. *Jung: A Biography*. New York: Little, Brown, 2003.

Beck, Hall P., Sharman Levinson and Gary Irons. "Finding Little Albert: A Journey to John B. Watson's Infant Laboratory." *American Psychologist* 64, no. 7 (2009): 605–614.

Bloch, Ernst. *Das Prinzip Hoffnung*. In: *Gesamtausgabe*. Vol. 5. Frankfurt: Suhrkamp, 1985.

Boadella, David. *Wilhelm Reich: The Evolution of His Work*. London: Arkana, 1985.

Bocian, Bernd. *Fritz Perls in Berlin 1893–1933: Expressionismus, Psychoanalyse, Judentum* / Wuppertal: Peter Hammer, 2007.

———. *Fritz Perls in Berlin: 1893–1933: Expressionism, Psychoanalysis, Judaism*. Trans. Philip Schmitz. Bergisch Gladbach: Verlag Andreas Kohlhage, 2010.

Bos, Jaap, Leendert Groenendijk, Johan Sturm, and Paul Roazen. *The Self-Marginalization of Wilhelm Stekel: Freudian Circles Inside and Out*. New York: Springer, 2007.

Bruder-Bezzel, Almuth. *Alfred Adler: Die Entstehungsgeschichte einer Theorie im historischen Milieu Wiens*. Göttingen: Vandenhoeck and Ruprecht, 1983.

Buchanan, Roderick D. *Playing with Fire: The Controversial Career of Hans J. Eysenck*. New York: Oxford University Press, 2010.

Buckley, Kerry W. *Mechanical Man: John B. Watson and the Beginnings of Behaviorism*. New York: Guildford Press, 1989.

Canetti, Elias. *Die Fackel im Ohr: Lebensgeschichte 1921–1931*. Munich: Hanser, 1980.

———. *The Torch in My Ear.* Trans. Joachim Neugroschel. New York: Farrar, Straus & Giroux, 1982.

Carotenuto, Aldo, ed. *A Secret Symmetry: Sabina Spielrein between Jung and Freud. The Untold Story of The Woman Who Changed the Early History of Psychoanalysis*. New York: Pantheon, 1982.

———, ed. *Tagebuch einer heimlichen Symmetrie: Sabina Spielrein zwischen Jung und Freud*. Freiburg im Breisgau: Verlag Traute Hensch, 1986.

Clarkson, Petruska and Jennifer Mackewn. *Frederick S. Perls und die Gestalttherapie*. Cologne: Edition Humanistische Psychologie, 1995.

Cooper-White, Pamela and Felicity Brock Kelcourse. *Sabina Spielrein and the Beginnings of Psychoanalysis: Image, Thought, and Language*. London: Routledge, 2019.

Cover Jones, Mary. "The Elimination of Children's Fears." *Journal of Experimental Psychology* 7 (1924): 382–392.

———. "A Laboratory Study of Fear: The Case of Peter." *Journal of Genetic Psychology* 152, no. 4 (1924): 462–469.

———. "A Laboratory Study of Fear: The Case of Peter." *Pedagogical Seminary* 31 (1924): 308–315.

———. "Albert, Peter, and John B. Watson." *American Psychologist* 29 (1974): 581–583.

Crews, Frederick. *Skeptical Engagements*. New York: Oxford University Press, 1986.

Cuijpers, Pim, et al. "Was Eysenck right after all? A reassessment of the effects of psychotherapy for adult depression." *Epidemiology and Psychiatric Sciences* 28, no. 1 (2018): 1–10.

Davis, Timothy L. and Clara E. Hill. "Spiritual and Non-Spiritual Approaches to Dream Work: Effects on Clients' Well-being." *Journal of Counseling and Development* 83, no. 4 (2005): 492–503.

Deutsch, Helene. *Confrontations with Myself.* New York: Norton, 1973.

Dragioti, Elena, et al. "Does Psychotherapy Work? An Umbrella Review of Meta-analyses of Randomized Controlled Trials." *Acta Psychiatrica Scandinavia* 136, no. 6 (2017): 236–246.

Dührssen, Annemarie. "Katamnestische Ergebnisse bei 1004 Patienten nach analytischer Psychotherapie." *Zeitschrift für Psychosomatische Medizin* 8 (1962): 94–113.

Dührssen, Annemarie and Eduard Jorswieck. "Eine empirisch-statistische Untersuchung zur Leistungsfähigkeit psychoanalytischer Behandlung." *Der Nervenarzt* 36. 1965. 166–169.

Eissler, Kurt R. *Freud und Wagner-Jauregg vor der Kommission zur Erhebung militärischer Pflichtverletzungen*. Vienna: Löcker, 1979.

Ellenberger, Henri F. *The Discovery of the Unconscious*. New York: Fontana Press, 1970.

Ellis, Albert. *All Out! An Autobiography*. Amherst: Prometheus Books, 2010.

Eysenck, Hans Jürgen. "The Effects of Psychotherapy: An Evaluation." *Journal of Counseling Psychology* 16 (1952): 319–324.

Fallend, Karl and Bernd Nitzschke, eds. *Der "Fall" Wilhelm reich. Beiträge zum Verhältnis von Psychoanalyse und Politik*. Gießen: Psychosozial-Verlag, 2002.

Federn, Ernst and Gerhard Wittenberger, eds. *Aus dem Kreis um Sigmund Freud. Zu den Protokollen der Wiener Psychoanalytischen Vereinigung*. Frankfurt: Fischer, 1992.

Ferenczi, Sándor and Otto Rank. *Entwicklungsziele der Psychoanalyse: Zur Wechselbeziehung von Theorie und Praxis*. Leipzig, Vienna, Zurich: Internationaler Psychoanalytischer Verlag, 1924.

Flournoy, Théodore. "Quelques faits d'imagination créatrice subconsciente. Par Miss Frank Miller de New York." *Archives de Psychologie* 5 (1905): 36–51.

Frank, Leonhard. *Heart on the Left*. Trans. Cyrus Brooks. London: Arthur Barker, 1954.

———. "Zur medikamentösen Unterstützung der Psychotherapie bei Neurosen." *Schweizer Archiv für Neurologie und Psychiatrie* 17 (1939): 26–31.

———. "Philosophie und Psychotherapie. Zur Grundlegung einer Existenzanalyse." *Schweizerische Medizinische Wochenschrift* 69 (1939): 707–709.

———. *Dem Leben Antwort geben: Autobiographie*. Weinheim: Beltz, 2017.

———. *Es kommt der Tag, da bist du frei: Unveröffentlichte Briefe, Texte und Reden*. Munich: Kösel, 2015.

———. *Frühe Schriften 1923–1942*. Vienna: Maudrich, 2017, 188.

———. *Recollections: An Autobiography*. Trans. Joseph and Judith Fabry. New York: Plenum, 1997.

Freud, Anna. *Normality and Pathology in Childhood*. New York: International Universities Press, 1965.

———. *Wege und Irrwege in der Kinderentwicklung*. Stuttgart: Klett-Cotta, 1965/1968.

Freud, Sigmund. *Briefe 1873–1939*. Ed. Ernst L. Freud. Frankfurt: Fischer, 1960.

———. *The Complete Letters of Sigmund Freud to Wilhelm Fliess 1887–1904*. Ed. Jeffrey Moussaieff Masson. Cambridge: Belknap Press, 1985.

———. *Gesamtausgabe*. Ed. Christfried Tögel. 23 Vols. Gießen: Psychosozial-Verlag, 2015–2023.

———. *The Interpretation of Dreams*. Trans. Joyce Crick. Oxford: Oxford University Press, 1999.

———. *Letters of Sigmund Freud*. Ed. Ernst L. Freud. Trans. Tania and James Stern. New York: Dover, 1992.

———. *The Standard Edition of the Complete Psychological Works of Sigmund Freud*. 24 Vols. Trans. James Strachey. London: Hogarth, 1953–1974.

———and C.G. Jung, *Briefwechsel*. Eds. William McGuire and Wolfgang Sauerländer. Frankfurt: Fischer, 1974.

———and C.G. Jung, *The Freud/Jung Letters: The Correspondence between Sigmund Freud and C.G. Jung*. Ed. William McGuire. Trans. Ralph Mannheim and R.F.C. Hull. Princeton: Princeton University Press, 1974.

———and Lou Andreas-Salomé. *Letters*. Ed. Ernst Pfeiffer. Trans. William and Elaine Robson-Scott. New York: Harcourt Brace Jovanovich, 1972.

Furtmüller, Carl. *Denken und Handeln. Schriften zur Psychologie 1905–1950. Von den Anfängen der Psychoanalyse zur Anwendung der Individualpsychologie*. Ed. Lux Furtmüller. Munich: E. Reinhardt, 1983.

Galton, Sir Francis. *Inquiries into Human Faculties and Its Development*. London: J.M. Dent, 1911.

Gay, Peter. *Freud: A Life for Our Time*. London: J.M. Dent, 1988.

Graf-Nold, Angela. *Der Fall Hermine Hug-Hellmuth: Eine Geschichte der frühen Kinder-Psychoanalyse*. Munich: Verlag Internationale Psychoanalyse, 1988.

Green, Martin. *Else und Frieda—die Richthofen-Schwestern*. Munich: Kindler, 1976.

Groddeck, Georg. *Das Buch vom Es: Psychoanalytische Briefe an eine Freundin*. Leipzig: Internationaler Psychoanalytischer Verlag, 1923.

———. *The Book of the It*. Trans. V.M.E. Collins. New York: Vintage, 1949.

Gross, Otto. "Zur Überwindung der kulturellen Krise." *Die Aktion* 3 (1913): 384–387.

Gross, Werner. *Wie man lebt, so stirbt man. Vom Leben und Sterben großer Psychotherapeuten*. Berlin: Springer, 2021.

Großmann, Gustav. *Sich selbst Rationalisieren: Lebenserfolg ist erlernbar*. Grünwald: Ratio-Verlag, 1927/1993.

Halbe, Max. *Jahrhundertwende: Erinnerungen an einer Epoche*. Munich: Langen Müller, 1935.

Handlbauer, Bernhard. *Die Freud-Adler-Kontroverse*. Frankfurt: S. Fischer, 1990.

Harris, Ben. "Whatever Happened to Little Albert?" *American Psychologist* 34, no. 2 (1979): 151–160.

Highhouse, Scott. "A History of the T-Group and Its Early Applications in Management Development." *Group Dynamics Theory, Research, and Practice* 6, no. 4 (2002): 277–290.

Hoffman, Edward. *The Right to Be Human: A Biography of Abraham Maslow*. Los Angeles: Jeremy P. Tarcher, 1988.

Horney, Renate. *Lazarus, What's Next? A Memoir by the Daughter of Noted Psychoanalyst Karen Horney*. Laguna Beach: Laurel Press, 1999.

Hübl, Philipp. *Der Untergrund des Denkens: Eine Philosophie des Unbewussten*. Reinbek: Rowohlt, 2017.

Hurwitz, Emanuel. *Otto Gross—Paradies-Sucher zwischen Freud und Jung.* Zürich: Suhrkamp, 1979.

Illouz, Eva. *Die Errettung der modernen Seele: Therapien, Gefühle und die Kultur der Selbsthilfe.* Frankfurt: Suhrkamp, 2009.

Jones, Ernest. *The Life and Work of Sigmund Freud.* 3 Vols. New York: Basic Books, 1953.

Jung, Carl Gustav. *The Collected Works of C.G. Jung.* 20 Vols. Eds. Herbert Read, Michael Fordham, and Gerhard Adler. New York: Pantheon Books, 1953.

———. *Erinnerungen, Träume, Gedanken.* Olten: Walter, 1961/1990.

———. *Gesammelte Werke.* 20 Vols. Zurich: Rascher, 1958.

———. *Memories, Dreams, Reflections.* Ed. Aniela Jaffé. Trans. Richard and Clara Winston. New York: Vintage, 1989.

———. *Studies in Word-Association.* Trans. M.D. Eder. London: William Heinemann, 1918.

Kauders, Anthony D. *Der Freud-Komplex: Eine Geschichte der Psychoanalyse in Deutschland.* Berlin: Berlin Verlag, 2014.

Kerr, John. *A Most Dangerous Method: The Story of Jung, Freud, and Sabina Spielrein.* New York: Knopf, 1993.

Kiell, Norman. *Freud without Hindsight: Reviews of His Work 1893–1939.* Madison: International UP, 1988.

King, Vera, Benigna Gerisch, and Hartmut Rosa, eds. *Lost in Perfection. Zur Optimierung der Gesellschaft und Psyche.* Frankfurt: Suhrkamp, 2021.

Kirschenbaum, Howard. *The Life and Work of Carl Rogers.* Ross-on-Wye: PCCS Books, 2007.

———. *On Becoming Carl Rogers.* New York: Delta Books, 1979.

Klein, Stefan. *Träume: Eine Reise in unsere innere Wirklichkeit.* Frankfurt: S. Fischer, 2014.

Kluy, Alexander. *Alfred Adler: Die Vermessung der modernen Psyche.* Munich: DVA, 2019.

Kramer, Robert. *The Birth of Relationship Therapy.* Gießen: Psychosozial-Verlag, 2002.

Kripal, Jeffrey J. *Esalen: America and the Religion of No Religion.* Chicago: University of Chicago Press, 2007.

Längle, Alfried. *Viktor Frankl: Ein Porträt.* Munich: Piper, 1998.

Laska, Bernd A. "Otto Gross zwischen Max Stirner und Wilhelm Reich." *3. Internationaler Otto-Gross-Kongress, LMU München.* Eds. Raimund Dehmlow and Gottfried Heuer. Marburg: Literaturwissenschaft.de, 2003: 125–162.

———. *Wilhelm Reich.* Reinbek: Rowohlt, 1981.

Lazarus, Arnold A. "New Methods in Psychotherapy: A Case Study." *South African Medical Journal* 32 (1958): 660–664.

Leidinger, Hannes, Christian Rapp, and Birgit Mosser-Schuöcker. *Freud, Adler, Frankl. Die Wiener Welt der Seelenforschung.* Vienna: Residenz Verlag, 2022.

Lieberman, E. James. *Acts of Will: The Life and Work of Otto Rank*. New York: The Free Press, 1985.

———and Robert Kramer, eds. *The Letters of Sigmund Freud and Otto Rank: Inside Psychoanalysis*. Baltimore: Johns Hopkins University Press, 2012.

Lieberman, Morton, Irvin D. Yalom, and Matthew B. Miles. *Encounter Groups—First Facts*. New York: Basic Books, 1973.

Linden, Michael and Bernhard Strauß, eds. *Risiken und Nebenwirkungen von Psychotherapie*. 2nd edition. Berlin: Medizinisch Wissenschaftliche Verlagsgesellschaft, 2018.

Lindenberg, Christoph. *Rudolf Steiner*. Reinbek: Rowohlt, 1992.

Loeb, Jacques. *The Mechanistic Conception of Life*. Chicago: University of Chicago Press, 1912.

Lohmann, Hans-Martin. *Sigmund Freud*. Reinbek: Rowohlt, 1998.

Lück, Helmut E. *Die psychologische Hintertreppe: Die bedeutenden Psychologinnen und Psychologen in Leben und Werk*. Freiburg im Breisgau: Herder, 2016.

Makari, George J. *Revolution der Seele: Die Geburt der Psychoanalyse*. Gießen: Psychosozial-Verlag, 2011.

Mann, Thomas. *Freud und die Psychoanalyse: Reden, Briefe, Notizen, Betrachtungen*. Ed. Bernd von Urban. Frankfurt: S. Fischer, 1991.

Maslow, Abraham H. "A Theory of Human Motivation." *Psychological Review* 50, no. 4 (1943): 370–396.

Misik, Robert. *Das große Beginnergefühl: Moderne, Zeitgeist, Revolution*. Berlin: Suhrkamp, 2022.

Moreno, Jacob. *The Words of the Father*. Beacon: Beacon House, 1941.

Mosser-Schuöcker, Birgit. "Viktor Frankl—Auf der Suche nach dem Sinn." *Freud, Adler, Frankl: Die Wiener Welt der Seelenforschung*. Eds. Hannes Leidinger, Christian Rapp, and Birgit Mosser-Schuöcker. Vienna: Residenz Verlag, 2022.

Musil, Robert. *Der Mann ohne Eigenschaften: Aus dem Nachlaß*. 2 Vols. Reinbek: Rowohlt, 1943/1987.

Nietzsche, Friedrich. *Götterdämmerung oder Wie man mit dem Hammer philosophiert*. Leipzig: C.G. Naumann, 1889.

———. *The Twilight of the Idols: Or, How to Philosophise with the Hammer*. Trans. Anthony M. Lodovici. Edinburgh: T.N. Foulis, 1911.

Nitzschke, Bernd. "Vorwärts zur Freiheit! – 'Zurück zur Natur'? Wilhelm Reich (1897–1957) zum 50. Todestag." *Zeitschrift für Sexualforschung* 20 (2007): 199–209.

Nunberg, Herrmann and Ernst Federn, eds. *Protokolle der Wiener Psychoanalytischen Vereinigung*. 4 Vols. Gießen: Psychosozial-Verlag, 2008.

Perls, Frederick S. *Das Ich, der Hunger und die Aggression*. Stuttgart, Klett-Cotta, 1969.

———. *Ego, Hunger and Aggression*. London: Allen and Unwin, 1947.

———. *Gestalt Therapy Verbatim*. Lafayette: Real People Press, 1969.

———. *Grundlagen der Gestalt-Therapie. Einführung und Sitzungsprotokolle.* Stuttgart: Klett-Cotta, 1976.

———. *In and Out the Garbage Pail.* Lafayette: Real People Press, 1969.

———. *Gestalt, Wachstum, Integration. Aufsätze, Vorträge, Therapiesitzungen.* Ed. Hilarion Petzold. Paderborn: Jungfermann, 1980.

Perls, Stephen. "Frederick Perls: A Son's Reflections." *The Gestalt Journal*: https://gestalt.org/Stephen.htm. Accessed 5.13.25.

Popper, Karl R. *Conjectures and Refutations.* London: Routledge, 1963.

———. *Unended Quest: An Intellectual Autobiography.* London: Routledge, 1992.

Powell, Russell A., et al. "Correcting the Record on Watson, Rayner, and Little Albert: Albert Barger as 'Psychology's Lost Boy.'" *American Psychologist* 69, no. 6 (2014): 600–611.

Pross, Christian. *Wir wollten ins Verderben rennen—Die Geschichte des Sozialistischen Patientenkollektivs Heidelberg.* Cologne: Psychiatrie-Verlag, 2016.

Pytell, Timothy. *Viktor Frankl: Das Ende eines Mythos?* Innsbruck: Studien-Verlag, 2005.

Quitmann, Helmut. *Humanistische Psychologie: Psychologie, Philosophie, Organisationsentwicklung.* Göttingen: Hogrefe, 1996.

Rank, Otto. *Das Trauma der Geburt und seine Bedeutung für die Psychoanalyse.* Leipzig: Internationaler Psychoanalytischer Verlag, 1924.

———. *Will Therapy: An Analysis of the Therapeutic Process in Terms of Relationship.* Trans. Jessie Taft. New York: Knopf, 1936.

Rattner, Josef. *Alfred Adler.* Reinbek: Rowohlt, 1972.

Reich, Wilhelm. "Libidokonflikte und Wahngebilde in Ibsens 'Peer Gynt' [Antrittsvortrag in der Wiener Psychoanalytischen Vereinigung am 13. Oktober 1920]." *Frühe Schriften 1.* Vol. 1. Cologne: Kiepenheuer & Witsch, 1977.

———. "Trieb-und Libidobegriff von Forel bis Jung." *Zeitschrift für Sexualwissenschaft* 9 (1922): 17–19, 44–50, 75–85.

———. "Der Ausschluss Wilhelm Reichs aus der Internationalen Psychoanalytischen Vereinigung." *Zeitschrift für politische Psychologie und Sexualökonomie* 2 (1935): 54–61. (Published anonymously.)

———. *Charakteranalyse. Technik und Grundlagen für Studierende und praktizierende Analytiker.* Self-published, 1933.

———. *Die Sexualität im Kulturkampf.* Copenhagen: Sexpol, 1936.

———. *Massenpsychologie des Faschismus. Zur Sexualökonomie der politischen Reaktion und zur proletarischen Sexualpolitik.* Copenhagen: Verlag für Sexualpolitik, 1933.

———. *The Discovery of the Orgone: The Function of the Orgasm.* Trans. Theodor P. Wolfe. New York: Noonday, 1942.

———. *Die Funktion des Orgasmus.* Cologne: Kiepenheuer & Witsch, 1942/1969.

———. *Die Funktion des Orgasmus: Zur Psychopathologie und zur Soziologie des Geschlechtslebens.* Leipzig: Internationaler Psychoanalytischer Verlag, 1927.

———. *Die Sexuelle Revolution. Zur charakterlichen Selbststeuerung des Menschen.* Frankfurt: Europäische Verlagsanstalt, 1966.

Rief, Winfried. "Was kann die Psychotherapie vom Placeboeffekt lernen?" *Psychotherapeut* 67 (2022): 191–194.

Rogers, Carl. *On Becoming a Person: A Therapist's View of Psychotherapy.* Boston: HarperOne, 1995.

Roudinesco, Elisabeth and Michel Plon. *Wörterbuch der Psychoanalyse.* Vienna: Springer, 2004.

Rubin, Lore Reich. *Erinnerungen an eine chaotische Welt.* Gießen: Psychosozial-Verlag, 2019.

Schönpflug, Wolfgang. *Kurze Geschichte der Psychologie und Psychotherapie (1783–2020). Paradigmen und Institutionen: Vereint oder getrennt?* Berlin: Peter Lang, 2022.

Schorske, Carl E. *Wien: Geist und Gesellschaft im Fin de Siècle.* Frankfurt am Main: S. Fischer, 1982.

Schröder, Christina. *Der Fachstreit um das Seelenheil: Psychotherapiegeschichte zwischen 1880 und 1932.* Frankfurt: Lang, 1995.

Schröter, Michael. *Auf eigenem Weg: Geschichte der Psychoanalyse in Deutschland bis 1945.* Göttingen: Vandenhoeck and Ruprecht, 2023.

———, ed. *"Ich bin zuversichtlich, wir erobern bald die Psychiatrie": Sigmund Freud, Eugen Bleuler—Briefwechsel 1904–1937.* Basel: Schwabe, 2012.

Sharaf, Myron. *Fury on Earth: A Biography of Wilhelm Reich.* New York: St. Martin's Press, 1983.

Smith, Mary L. and Gene V. Glass. "Meta-analysis of Psychotherapy Outcome Studies." *American Psychologist* 32, no. 9 (1977): 752–760.

Sperber, Manes. *Alfred Adler: Der Mensch und seine Lehre.* Berlin: Springer, 1926.

Spielrein, Sabina. "Die Destruktion als Ursache des Werdens." *Jahrbuch für psychoanalytische und psychopathologische Forschung* 4 (1912): 465–503.

Steiner, Rudolf. *Rudolf Steiner Gesamtausgabe.* 354 Vols. Dornach: Steiner Verlag, 1961.

———. *Soul Economy and Waldorf Education.* Trans. Roland Everett. Spring Valley: Anthroposophic Press, 1986.

Stekel, Wilhelm. "Über Coitus im Kindesalter. Eine hygienische Studie." *Wiener Medizinische Blätter* 16 (1895): 247–249.

Straub, Jürgen. "Selbstoptimierung als Rationalisierung der Lebensführung: Gustav Großmanns Exzess als Paradigma: Buchhalterische Existenz für zweckrationale Zwangscharaktere." *Lost in Perfection: Zur Optimierung von Gesellschaft und Psyche.* Eds. Vera King, et al. Frankfurt: Suhrkamp, 2021.

Vaihinger, Hans. *Die Philosophie des Als Ob: System der theoretischen, praktischen und religiösen Fiktionen der Menschheit auf Grund eines idealistischen Positivismus.* Leipzig: Felix Meiner, 1911/2021.

———. *The Philosophy of 'As If'.* Trans. C.K. Ogden. New York: Harcourt, Brace, 1924.

von Hartmann, Eduard. *Philosophy of the Unconscious.* Vol. 1. Trans. William Chatterton Coupland. London: Trübner and Co., 1884.

Voswinckel, Ulrike. *Freie Liebe und Anarchie: Schwabing – Monte Verità. Entwürfe gegen das etablierte Leben.* Munich: Alitera, 2009.

Wampold, Bruce E. and Zac E. Imel. *The Great Psychotherapy Debate: The Evidence for What Makes Psychotherapy Work.* London: Routledge, 2018.

Watson, John B. *Behaviorism.* Chicago: University of Chicago Press, 1930.

———and Rosalie Rayner Watson. "Conditioned Emotional Reactions." *Journal of Experimental Psychology* 3, no. 1 (1920): 1–14.

———. "Studies in Infant Psychology." *The Scientific Monthly* 13, no. 6 (1921): 493–515.

———. *Psychological Care of Infant and Child.* New York: Norton and Company, 1928.

Wittels, Fritz. *Sigmund Freud: Der Mann, die Lehre, die Schule.* Leipzig: Tal, 1924. (English: ———. *Sigmund Freud: His Personality, His Teaching, and His School.* Trans. Eden and Cedar Paul. London: Allen & Unwin, 1924.)

Wolpe, Joseph. "Objective Psychotherapy of the Neuroses." *South African Medical Journal* 26, no. 42 (1952): 825–829.

———. *Psychotherapy by Reciprocal Inhibition.* Stanford: Stanford University Press, 1958.

Xenophanes of Colophon. *Fragments.* Trans. J.H. Lesher. Toronto: University of Toronto Press, 1992.

Yalom, Irvin D. *Becoming Myself: A Psychiatrist's Memoir.* New York: Basic Books, 2017.

———. *Theory and Practice of Group Psychotherapy*, 4th Ed. New York: Basic Books, 1995.

Zander, Helmut. *Rudolf Steiner: Die Biographie.* Munich: Piper, 2011.

Zeller, Uwe. *Psychotherapie in der Weimarer Zeit—die Gründung der "Allgemeinen Ärztlichen Gesellschaft für Psychotherapie" (AÄGP).* Tübingen: MVK, 2001.

Zenaty, Gerhard. *Sigmund Freud lesen.* Bielefeld: transcript Verlag, 2022.

Zimmer, Dieter E. *Tiefenschwindel: Die endlose und die beendbare Psychoanalyse.* Reinbek: Rowohlt, 1986.

Zweig, Stefan. *Die Welt von Gestern: Erinnerungen eines Europäers.* Frankfurt: S. Fischer, 1942/1985.

———. *The World of Yesterday.* New York: Viking, 1943.

NOTES

All citations from Freud's works use the Standard Edition translated by James Strachey, with the exception of those taken from The Interpretation of Dreams, *for which I've relied on Joyce Crick's translation.—Trans.*

1: THE UNCONSCIOUS

1 Alexander Kluy, *Alfred Adler: Die Vermessung der modernen Psyche* (Munich: DVA, 2019), 24. Cf. Carl E. Schorske, *Wien: Geist und Gesellschaft im Fin de Siècle* (Frankfurt am Main: S. Fischer, 1982).

2 The mark will be hit in 1910; Vienna has around the same number of residents today.

3 In 1904, Alfred Adler, along with his two daughters, secretly converted to Protestantism.

4 Robert Misik, *Das große Beginnergefühl: Moderne, Zeitgeist, Revolution* (Berlin: Suhrkamp, 2022), 112.

5 Hans-Martin Lohmann, *Sigmund Freud* (Reinbek: Rowohlt, 1998), 125ff.

6 In fact, a remarkable twenty-two reviews of *The Interpretation of Dreams* appear in newspapers and trade journals between 1899 and 1902. Most physicians expressed criticism, but among literary figures, artists, and feulletonistes the work was well received. That the book was met with "deathly silence" is a myth conjured up by Freud. (Cf. Norman Kiell, *Freud without Hindsight: Reviews of His Work 1893–1939* (Madison: International UP, 1988).)

7 Sigmund Freud, *Studies on Hysteria*, SE 2:7.

8 Freud first begins using the term in 1896.

9 Freud, *Selbstdarstellung*, *Sigmund Freud Gesamtausgabe*, ed. Christfried Tögel, Vol. 18 (Gießen: Psychosozial-Verlag, 2021), 106. (English: Freud, "An Autobiographical Study," SE 20:8.)

10 Freud, *Studies on Hysteria*, SE 2:305.

11 Josef Breuer and Freud, *Studien über Hysterie*. Freud's word is "Mohrenwäsche," literally "moor-washing."—Trans.

12 Freud, *Interpretation of Dreams*, 151.

13 Freud to Martha Bernays, 22 August 1883. Cited in Peter Gay, *Freud: Eine Biografie für unsere Zeit* (Frankfurt: S. Fischer, 1989), 53. (English: Freud, *Letters of Sigmund Freud*, ed. Ernst L. Freud, trans. Tania and James Stern (New York: Dover, 1992), 43.)

14 Freud, *Selbstdarstellung*, 106. (English: Freud, "An Autobiographical Study," SE 20:9.)

15 Freud to Fließ, 11 March 1902. Freud, *Briefe 1873–1939*, ed. Ernst L. Freud (Frankfurt: Fischer, 1960), 243. (English: Freud, *The Letters of Sigmund Freud*, 246.)

16 Carl Gustav Jung to Sabina Spielrein, 21 or 22 September 1911. Aldo Carotenuto, ed. *Tagebuch einer heimlichen Symmetrie: Sabina Spielrein zwischen Jung und Freud* (Freiburg im Breisgau: Verlag Traute Hensch, 1986), 202. (English: Aldo Carotenuto, ed., *A Secret Symmetry: Sabina Spielrein between Jung and Freud. The Untold Story of The Woman Who Changed the Early History of Psychoanalysis* (New York: Pantheon, 1982), 182.)

17 Freud to Jung, 12 October 1911. Freud and Jung, *Briefwechsel*, eds. William McGuire and Wolfgang Sauerländer (Frankfurt: Fischer, 1974), 493. (English: Freud and Jung, *The Freud/Jung Letters: The Correspondence between Sigmund Freud and C.G. Jung*, ed. William McGuire, trans. Ralph Mannheim and R.F.C. Hull (Princeton: Princeton University Press, 1974), 447.)

18 Freud, "Psychische Behandlung (Seelenbehandlung)," 1890. (English: Freud, "Psychical (Or Mental) Treatment," SE 7.)

19 Kerry W. Buckley, *Mechanical Man* (New York: Guildford Press, 1989), 1. Buckley, 1.

20 Ibid., 15.

21 Ibid., 11.

22 Jacques Loeb, *The Mechanistic Conception of Life* (Chicago: University of Chicago Press, 1912), 232.

23 John B. Watson, "The New Science of Animal Behavior," *Harper's* 120, 1910, 346–353.

24 Watson, "Psychology as the Behaviorist Views It," *Psychological Review* 20, 2, 158–177.

25 Ibid., 158.

26 Ibid., 160.

27 William James, *Psychology: Briefer Course* (New York: Fawcett, 1963), 407.

28 Breuer and Freud, *Studien über Hysterie*, *Sigmund Freud Gesamtausgabe*, ed. Christfried Tögel, Vol. 5 (Gießen: Psychosozial Verlag, 1895/2015), 141. (English: Freud, SE 2:7.)

29 Ibid., 54. (English: Freud SE 2:34.)

30 Peter Gay, *Freud: Eine Biographie für unsere Zeit*, 54. (English: Freud, SE 2:34–35.)

31 Breuer and Freud, 169. (English: Freud, SE 2:41.)

32 Henri F. Ellenberger, *Die Entdeckung des Unbewussten*, Vol. 2 (Bern: Huber, 1973), 667. (English: Henri F. Ellenberger, *The Discovery of the Unconscious* (New York: Fontana Press, 1970), 484.)

33 An allusion to Goethe's *Faust, Part Two*.—Trans.

34 Freud to Stefan Zweig, 2 June 1932. *Briefe*, 406. (English: *Letters of Sigmund Freud*, 413.)

35 Breuer to Auguste Forel, 21 November 1907.

36 Sir Francis Galton, *Inquiries into Human Faculties and Its Development* (London: J.M. Dent, 1911), 135.

37 Ibid., 145.

38 Jung, "Die Hysterielehre Freuds: Eine Erwiderung auf die Aschaffenburgsche Kritik," *Gesammelte Werke*, Vol. 4 (Zurich: Rascher, 1958), 6. Cited in George J. Makari, *Revolution der Seele: Die Geburt der Psychoanalyse* (Gießen: Psychosozial-Verlag, 2011), 246. (English: Jung, "Freud's Theory of Hysteria: A Reply to Aschaffenburg," *The Collected Works of C.G. Jung Vol. 4: Freud and Psychoanalysis*, trans. R.F.C. Hull (New York: Pantheon, 1961), 7.)

39 Gustav Aschaffenburg, "Die Beziehungen des sexuellen Lebens zur Entstehung von Nerven- und Geisteskrankheiten," *Münchener Medizinische Wochenschrift* 53, 1793–1798.

40 Jung, "Psychoanalyse und Assoziationsexperiment," *Journal für Psychologie und Neurologie* 7, 1–24. (English: Jung, *Studies in Word-Association*, trans. M.D. Eder (London: William Heinemann, 1918).)

41 Jung, *Collected Works Vol. 2*, 298–303.

42 Aschaffenburg, "Die neueren Theorien der Hysterie," *Deutsche Medizinische Wochenschrift* 33 (44), 1811.

43 Ibid., 1812.

44 Jung, *Diagnostische Assoziationsstudien: Beiträge zur experimentellen Psychopathologie* (Leipzig: Barth, 1906), 286. (Jung, *Collected Works Vol. 2: Experimental Researches*, trans. Leopold Stein and Diana Riviere, ed. (Princeton: Princeton University Press, 1973), 316.)

45 Jung, *Erinnerungen, Träume, Gedanken* (Olten: Walter, 1961/1990), 137. (English: Jung, *Memories, Dreams, Reflections*, ed. Aniela Jaffé, trans. Richard and Clara Winston (New York: Vintage, 1989), 116.)

46 Deirdre Bair, *Jung: A Biography* (New York: Little, Brown, 2003), 97.

47 Ibid., 63.

48 Ibid., 117. [See also Jung, *Memories, Dreams, Reflections*, 155.]

49 Jung, *Erinnerungen, Träume, Gedanken*, 171. (English: Jung, *Memories, Dreams, Reflections*, 150.)

50 Ibid.
51 Jung, *Memories, Dreams, Reflections*, 120.
52 "Die schönsten Fälle der Psychoanalyse sind die Felle des alten Eitingon." The line is frequently attributed to Freud, but was probably coined by his student Theodor Reik.
53 Freud, "Bruchstück einer Hysterie-Analyse," *Monatschrift für Psychiatrie und Neurologie* 18 (4), 283–310 and 18 (5), 408–467. (English: Freud, "Fragment of an Analysis of a Case of Hysteria," SE 7:3–124.)
54 Freud, "Bruchstück einer Hysterie-Analyse," *Gesamtausgabe*, Vol. 10, ed. Christfried Tögel (Gießen: Psychosozial-Verlag, 2018), 134ff. (English: Freud, SE 7:47–48.)
55 Dieter E. Zimmer, *Tiefenschwindel: Die endlose und die beendbare Psychoanalyse* (Reinbek: Rowohlt, 1986), 129ff.
56 Freud, "Bruchstück," *Gesamtausgabe*, 163. (English: Freud, SE 7:80.)
57 Zimmer, 341.
58 Ibid., 27
59 Frederick Crews, "The Freudian Way of Knowledge," *The New Criterion 6*, 1984, 7–25. Cited in Zimmer, 131. (Crews, "The Freudian Way of Knowledge," *Skeptical Engagements* (New York: Oxford University Press, 1986), 60.)
60 Freud, "The Question of Lay Analysis," SE 20:256.
61 Freud, "Bruchstück," *Gesamtausgabe*, 198. (Freud, SE 7:122.)
62 This article is one of the few that Freud first published in English: Freud, "A Note on the Unconscious in Psycho-Analysis," *Proceedings of the Society for Psychical Research* 24, 312–318. (SE 12:264–265.)
63 Freud, *Die Traumdeutung, Gesamtausgabe*, ed. Christfried Töge., Vol. 7 (Gießen: Psychosozial-Verlag, 2017), 21. (English: Freud, *The Interpretation of Dreams*, trans. Joyce Crick (Oxford: Oxford University Press, 1999), 7.)
64 Freud to Werner Achelis, 30 January 1927. In: Freud, *Briefe*, 372. (*Letters of Sigmund Freud*, 375.)
65 Ibid.
66 Ernest Jones, *Das Leben und Werk von Sigmund Freud* (Stuttgart/Bern: Huber, Bern, 1960), Vol. 1, 379. (English : Ernest Jones, *The Life and Work of Sigmund Freud*, vol. 1 (New York: Basic Books, 1953), 324.)
67 Freud, *Die Traumdeutung*, 121. (English: Freud, *The Interpretation of Dreams*, 97.)
68 Ibid., 277, 312. (English: Freud, *The Interpretation of Dreams*, 235.)
69 Freud to Wilhelm Fließ, 8 March 1895. (English: Freud, *The Complete Letters of Sigmund Freud to Wilhelm Fliess 1887–1904*, ed. Jeffrey Moussaieff Masson (Cambridge: Belknap Press, 1985), 117.)
70 Freud to Fließ, 12 June 1900. In: Freud, *Briefe*, 237. (English: Freud, *The Complete Letters of Sigmund Freud to Wilhelm Fliess 1887–1904*, 417.)

71 Freud, *Die Traumdeutung*, 55. (English: Freud, *The Interpretation of Dreams*, 38.)

72 Stefan Klein, *Träume: Eine Reise in unsere innere Wirklichkeit* (Frankfurt: S. Fischer, 2014), 166.

73 Freud didn't publish this paper in his lifetime; he only sent it to his friend Fließ to get his opinion. It was published posthumously in 1950 in a volume titled *Aus den Anfängen der Psychoanalyse*. (English: Freud, SE 1:283–398.)

74 Philipp Hübl, *Der Untergrund des Denkens: Eine Philosophie des Unbewussten* (Reinbek: Rowohlt, 2017), 168.

75 Breuer and Freud, *Studien über Hysterie*, 278. (English: Freud, SE 2:160.)

76 Hermann Nunberg and Ernst Federn, *Protokolle der Wiener Pschoanalytischen Vereinigung*, four volumes (Gießen: Psychosozial-Verlag, 2008).

77 Cited in Helmut E. Lück, *Die psychologische Hintertreppe: Die bedeutenden Psychologinnen und Psychologen in Leben und Werk* (Freiburg im Breisgau: Herder, 2016), 97.

78 There's no record of how the two first came to know each other. According to later hagiographers, Freud became aware of Adler after the younger man published an ardent defense of *The Interpretation of Dreams* in the *Freie Neue Presse*, countering previous negative reviews. In the paper's archive, however, there is neither a damning review nor the reply purportedly penned by Adler.

79 Adler, *Der Arzt als Erzieher*, in: Adler, *Studienausgabe*, ed. Karl Heinz Witte (Göttingen: Vandenhoeck and Ruprecht, 2007), Vol. 1, 33.

80 Freud, "Analyse eines Phobie eines fünfjährigen Knaben," *Gesamtausgabe*, Vol. 11, 318. (Freud, "Analysis of a Phobia in a Five-Year-Old Boy," SE 10:140.) Only after the First World War will Freud revise his view on this point and, in *Beyond the Pleasure Principle* (1920), postulate the existence of an independent death drive.

81 The idea that consultations with artists from the nearby Prater helped Adler to formulate his concept of overcompensation might be one of the many distortions offered after the fact.

82 Nunberg and Federn, Vol. 1, 36.

83 Bernhard Handlbauer, *Die Freud-Adler-Kontroverse* (Frankfurt: S. Fischer, 1990), 50.

84 Nunberg and Federn, Vol. 1, 135.

85 Ernst Bloch, *Das Prinzip Hoffnung*, in: *Gesamtausgabe* (Frankfurt: Suhrkamp, 1985), Vol. 5, 65.

86 Robert Musil, *Der Mann ohne Eigenschaften: Aus dem Nachlaß* (Reinbek: Rowohlt, 1943/1987), Vol. 2, 1176.

87 Bair, 161.

88 Jones, *The Life and Work of Sigmund Freud*, Vol. 2, 57.

89 Jung, *Erinnerungen*, 179. (English: Jung, *Memories*, 158.)

90 Adler, *The Neurotic Constitution*, trans. Bernard Glueck and John E. Lind (New York: Dodd, Mead, 1926), 112.

91 Adler, *The Neurotic Constitution*, 66–67.

92 Adler, *Über den nervösen Charakter*, in: *Studienausgabe*, Vol. 2, 32.

93 Cf. Almuth Bruder-Bezzel, *Alfred Adler: Die Entstehungsgeschichte einer Theorie im historischen Milieu Wiens* (Göttingen: Vandenhoeck and Ruprecht, 1983), 90ff.

94 Adler, *Der Sinn des Lebens*, in: *Studienausgabe*, Vol. 6, 147. (English: Adler, *Social Interest*, trans. John Linton and Richard Vaughan (London: Faber and Faber, 1938), 252.)

95 The quote comes from a paper, "A Note on the Unconscious in Psycho-Analysis," that Freud wrote in English in late January 1912 for the "Proceedings of the Society for Psychical Research" (Vol. 24, 1913, 312–318). (Freud, SE 12:260).

96 Freud, "A Note on the Unconscious in Psycho-Analysis", 113. (English: SE 12:262)

97 Ibid.

98 Ibid., 115. (English: SE 12:264.)

99 Freud, writing here in English, uses the term "foreconscious." Later, "preconscious" will become the standard translation of the German *vorbewusst.*—Trans.

100 Ibid.

101 Elisabeth Roudinesco and Michel Plon, *Wörterbuch der Psychoanalyse* (Vienna: Springer, 2004), 815.

102 The last neurological work from Freud's pen, "Die infantile Cerebrallähmung," was published in 1897.

103 Not only the name, but also the chief symptoms of the condition—restlessness, mental impairment, delusion and hallucinations, as well as, in many cases, a reduced emotionality—are included in medical diagnostic manuals to this day in similar form. The cause, however, is now viewed differently: by this point, schizophrenia is primarily regarded as an impairment of the brain that is genetic in origin. Difficult familial relationships, drugs, and trauma are thought to contribute to the development of the condition, but they are not viewed as causational factors.

104 Mithras was originally a Persian god and was likely adopted by the Romans in the first century AD. The Mithras cult, which Emperor Marcus Aurelius is thought to have had ties to, was considered in the early 19th century to be an early competitor of Christianity. According to more recent religious scholarship, however, it seems to have been more of a loose, esoteric male organization. Nevertheless, both the celebration of Christmas and the word "Sunday" can likely be traced back to the sun god Mithras.

105 Johann Jakob Honegger, the father and namesake of Jung's colleague, was also a psychiatrist and employed at the Burghölzli. After the onset of what is presumed

to be schizophrenia, the doctor was himself kept at the clinic for years as a patient.

106 Thus the title of the original edition, which appeared in book form in 1912. A later revision received from Jung an abbreviated title: *Symbole der Wandlung.*

107 Jung, *Wandlung und Symbole der Libido* (Munich: DTV, 1912/1991), 8. (English: Jung, *Collected Works Vol.* 5, trans. R.F.C. Hull (New York: Pantheon, 1956), xxiii.)

108 Théodore Flournoy, "Quelques faits d'imagination créatrice subconsciente: Par Miss Frank Miller de New York," *Archives de Psychologie* 5, 1905, 36–51.

109 Jung to Freud, 2 March 1910. Cited in: Freud and Jung, *Briefwechsel,* 339. (English: *The Freud/Jung Letters,* 298–299.) The description refers to the contents of a lecture given in January 1910 at a conference of physicians in Herisau in which Jung discussed the different manners of thinking.

110 Jung, *Wandlungen und Symbole der Libido,* 9. (English: Jung, *Collected Works Vol.* 5, xxiv.)

111 In his study of da Vinci Freud falls victim to a translation error that brings his whole argument crashing down: Freud analyzes a vision da Vinci had when he was young in which a vulture puts his tail feathers in da Vinci's mouth. Vultures, according to Freud, were regarded in Ancient Egypt as a symbol for the mother. But in reality, da Vinci's account refers to a kite (*Milan*), a bird of the genus Milvas. Freud took the German mistranslation from a historical novel in which the kite was turned into a vulture.

112 Jung to Freud, 8 May 1911. Freud and Jung, 465. (English: *The Freud/Jung Letters,* 421.)

113 Jung, *Wandlungen,* 370. (Cf. John Kerr, *A Most Dangerous Method: The Story of Jung, Freud, and Sabina Spielrein* (New York: Knopf, 1993), 388–415.)

114 Fred to Jung, 3 January 1913. Freud and Jung, 598. (English: *The Freud/Jung Letters,* 539.) Cf. Kerr, 437.

115 Jung to Freud, 6 January 1913. Freud and Jung, 600. (English: *The Freud/Jung Letters,* 540.) Cf. Kerr, 437.

116 Freud to Ferenczi, 8 May 1913. Cited in Gay, *Freud,* 237.

117 Kerr, 344.

118 Freud to Ferenczi, 8 May 1913. Cited in Gay, *Freud,* 237.

119 Fritz Wittels, *Sigmund Freud: Der Mann, die Lehre, die Schule* (Leipzig: Tal, 1924), 133ff. Cf. Kluy, 71. (English: Fritz Wittels, *Sigmund Freud: His Personality, His Teaching, and His School,* trans. Eden and Cedar Paul (London: Allen & Unwin, 1924), 130.)

120 Eugen Bleuler to Freud, 4 December 1911. Michael Schröter, ed., *"Ich bin zuversichtlich, wir erobern bald die Psychiatrie": Sigmund Freud, Eugen Bleuler—Briefwechsel 1904–1937* (Basel: Schwabe, 2012), 151.

121 Kerr, 511.

2: SEX

1 As one might imagine, Spielrein doesn't reveal the precise nature of her intimate relationship with Jung. Her surviving letters and diaries refer to it only indirectly. Nevertheless, she does write on June 11, 1909 to Freud: "Four and a half years ago Dr. Jung was my doctor, then he became my friend and finally my 'poet,' i.e., my beloved. Eventually he came to me and things went as they usually do with 'poetry.' He preached polygamy; his wife was supposed to have no objection, etc. etc." (Carotenuto, 93.) Later she says that Jung "could stand it no longer and wanted 'poetry.' For many reasons I could not and did not want to resist" (Ibid., 96). Her experiences with her family suggest a masochistic tendency, though this is speculative (cf. Kerr, 223–227).

2 Jung to Freud, 25 September 1907. McGuire and Sauerländer, eds., 99. (English: *The Freud/Jung Letters*, 90.)

3 Cited in George J. Makari, *Revolution der Seele: Die Geburt der Psychoanalyse* (Gießen: Psychosozial-Verlag, 2011), 278.

4 There was only one other full member who was a woman, Margarete Hilferding. A follower of Adler, she left the Society in 1911.

5 Christine Schmidt, "Sabina Spielrein: Frauen-Biographieforschung Fembio e.V. online," 17.11.2023, https://www.fembio.org/biographie.php/frau/biographie/sabina-spielrein/.

6 Ibid.

7 Freud, *Jenseits des Lustprinzips*, in: *Gesamtausgabe*, Vol. 16, 440. (English: Freud, *Beyond the Pleasure Principle* SE 18:55.) See also Kerr, 499.

8 Spielrein, "Die Destruktion als Ursache des Werdens," *Jahrbuch für psychoanalytische und psychopathologische Forschung* 4, 1912, 503.

9 Cf. Kerr, 498–502.

10 Carotenuto, 107. (English: Carotenuto, 107.)

11 Jung to Freud, 10 July 1909. McGuire and Sauerländer, 265. (English: *The Freud/Jung Letters*, 240.)

12 Freud to Jung, 18 June 1909. McGuire and Sauerländer, 259. (English: *The Freud/Jung Letters*, 235.)

13 Freud, "Wege der psychoanalytischen Therapie," in: *Gesamtausgabe*, Vol. 16, 224. (English: Freud, "Lines of Advance in Psycho-analytic Therapy," SE 17:162.)

14 Cf. Jaap Bos, Leendert Groenendijk, Johan Sturm, and Paul Roazen, *The Self-Marginalization of Wilhelm Stekel: Freudian Circles Inside and Out* (New York: Springer, 2007).

15 Wittels, 116. (English: Wittels, 132.)

16 This is the common translation of the German term *Aktualneurosen*. The German word conveys the idea that such neuroses stem from current—*aktuell*—causes. Though the sense implied by the English "actual neuroses"—that these neuroses

are "actual" (i.e., real), whereas others are not—is present in the German term, it is not the principal meaning.—Trans.

17 Wilhelm Stekel, "Über Coitus im Kindesalter: Eine hygienische Studie," *Wiener Medizinische Blätter* 16, 1895, 247–249.

18 Otto Gross, "Zur Überwindung der kulturellen Krise," *Die Aktion* 3, 1913, 384.

19 Cited in Anthony D. Kauders, *Der Freud-Komplex: Eine Geschichte der Psychoanalyse in Deutschland* (Berlin: Berlin Verlag, 2014), 57.

20 Cited in Dieter E. Zimmer, *Tiefenschwindel: Die endlose und die beendbare Psychoanalyse* (Reinbek: Rowohlt, 1986), 15. (English: Freud, SE 16:432–433.)

21 Cited in Ulrike Voswinckel, *Freie Liebe und Anarchie: Schwabing – Monte Verità. Entwürfe gegen das etablierte Leben* (Munich: Alitera, 2009), 53. (English: Leonhard Frank, *Heart on the Left*, trans. Cyrus Brooks (London: Arthur Barker, 1954), 12–13, 31.)

22 Today psychiatrists refer to this mental and emotional disorder as schizophrenia—a term that Jung's boss Bleuler introduced in 1908. Its cause is primarily genetic; the condition is accompanied by paranoia and hallucinations.

23 Michael Schröter, *Auf eigenem Weg: Geschichte der Psychoanalyse in Deutschland bis 1945* (Göttingen: Vandenhoeck and Ruprecht, 2023), 253.

24 Freud, "Lines of Advance," SE 17:168.

25 Karl Abraham to Freud, May 16, 1909. Hilda C. Abraham and Ernst L. Freud, eds., *Sigmund Freud, Karl Abraham – Briefe 1907–1926* (Frankfurt: S. Fischer, 1965), 86. (English: Hilda C. Abraham and Ernst L. Freud, eds., *A Psycho-Analytic Dialogue: The Letters of Sigmund Freud and Karl Abraham 1907–1926* (New York: Basic Books, 1965), 79.)

26 Bernd A. Laska, *Wilhelm Reich* (Reinbek: Rowohlt, 1981), 11.

27 There are different accounts of the precise sequence of the tragic events in the Reich home. I am relying here on the biography by Reich's student Myron Sharaf, among other sources. (Cf. *Fury on Earth: A Biography of Wilhelm Reich* (New York: St. Martin's Press, 1983).)

28 Wilhelm Reich, *Die Funktion des Orgasmus* (Cologne: Kiepenheuer & Witsch, 1942/1969), 31. (This book, Reich's "scientific autobiography," written in exile in the US in 1942, is not identical with the 1927 work of the same name in which he lays out his basic principles. The book was published in English as *The Discovery of the Orgone: The Function of the Orgasm*, trans. Theodor P. Wolfe (New York: Noonday, 1942), 4.)

29 Cited in Sharaf, 57.

30 It's possible that psychoanalysis found its footing so quickly in the US because for prudish Americans Freud's "sex stories" were especially sensational and titillating.

31 Sharaf, 72–73.

32 Sharaf, 73.

33 Reich, *Reich Speaks of Freud*, ed. Mary Higgins and Chester M. Raphael (New York: Farrar, Straus & Giroux, 1967), 40. (Cf. Laska, 29.)

34 Reich, *Die Funktion des Orgasmus: Zur Psychopathologie und zur Soziologie des Geschlechtslebens* (Leipzig, Vienna, Zurich: Internationaler Psychoanalytischer Verlag, 1927), 32.

35 Freud to Lou Andreas-Salomé, 9 May 1928. In: Freud and Lou Andreas-Salomé, *Letters*, ed. Ernst Pfeiffer, trans. William and Elaine Robson-Scott (New York: Harcourt Brace Jovanovich, 1972).

36 Sharaf, 25.

37 Lore Reich Rubin, *Erinnerungen an eine chaotische Welt* (Gießen: Psychosozial-Verlag, 2019), 25ff.

38 *Reich Speaks of Freud*, 56.

39 Freud, *Das Unbehagen in der Kultur*, in: *Gesamtausgabe*, Vol. 19, 74. (English: Freud, *Civilization and its Discontents*, SE 21:76.)

40 Freud to Federn, 10 October 1930. Sharaf, 155.

41 Sharaf, 188.

42 In 1957 Reich is sentenced to two years in prison in the United States for contempt of court and dies of a heart attack on November 3 of that same year.

3: FEAR

1 *Wiwimacher*. Lit. "wee wee maker."—Trans.

2 Freud, "Analyse der Phobie eines fünfjährigen Knaben," *Gesamtausgabe*, Vol. 11, 239. (English: Freud, "Analysis of a Phobia in a Five-year-old Boy," SE 10:41–42.)

The other quotes in this passage are from the standard edition, though I have changed Strachey's "puts his hand to/put your hand to" to "puts his hand there/put your hand there"—Trans.

3 Ibid., 291. (English: Ibid., 102.)

4 Freud, "Neue Folge der Vorlesungen zur Einführung in die Psychoanalyse. XXXI. Vorlesung: Die Zerlegung der psychischen Persönlichkeit," *Gesamtausgabe*, Vol. 19, 347. (English: Freud, *New Lectures on Psychoanalysis*, SE 22:80.)

5 Christina Schröder, *Der Fachstreit um das Seelenheil: Psychotherapiegeschichte zwischen 1880 und 1932* (Frankfurt: Lang, 1995), 176.

6 Kurt R. Eissler, *Freud und Wagner-Jauregg vor der Kommission zur Erhebung militärischer Pflichtverletzungen* (Vienna: Löcker, 1979), 31–34.

7 Buckley, 124.

8 Breuer and Freud, 410. (English: Freud, SE 2:305.)

9 Watson, "Psychology as the Behaviorist Views It," *Psychological Review* 20, 1913, 158–177.

10 This conclusion comes from a re-examination of the historical record that Russel Powell, Nancy Digdon, and others conducted in 2014. An earlier theory held that "little Albert" was Douglas Merritte, a boy of nearly the same age who at the time of the experiment is believed to have suffered from a neurological disorder. He died six years later of meningitis. (Cf. Russel Powell, Nancy Digdon, Ben Harris, and Christopher Smithson, "Correcting the Record on Watson, Rayner, and Little Albert: Albert Barger as 'Psychology's Lost Boy,'" *American Psychologist* 69 (6), 2014, 600–611.)

11 Buckley, 124.

12 Watson, *Behaviorism* (Chicago: University of Chicago Press, 1930), 104.

13 Elias Canetti, *Die Fackel im Ohr: Lebensgeschichte 1921–1931* (Munich: Hanser, 1980), 130. (English: Elias Canetti, *The Torch in My Ear*, trans. Joachim Neugroschel (New York: Farrar, Straus & Giroux, 1982), 119–120.)

14 Recently doubt has been cast on some of Mayo's results. Though it is true that the attention workers received merely by virtue of being studied did have a measurable effect on them, this influence was weaker than Mayo's team initially claimed.

15 Otto Rank, *Das Trauma der Geburt und seine Bedeutung für die Psychoanalyse* (Leipzig, Vienna, Zurich: Internationaler Psychoanalytischer Verlag, 1924).

16 Sándor Ferenczi and Otto Rank, *Entwicklungsziele der Psychoanalyse: Zur Wechselbeziehung von Theorie und Praxis* (Leipzig, Vienna, Zurich: Internationaler Psychoanalytischer Verlag, 1924).

17 Michael Schröter, *Auf eigenem Weg*, 506.

18 Mary Cover Jones, "The Elimination of Children's Fears," *Journal of Experimental Psychology* 7, 1924, 389.

19 Ibid. A more in-depth description of Peter's treatment appeared shortly thereafter: Mary Cover Jones, "A Laboratory Study of Fear: The Case of Peter," *Pedagogical Seminary* 31, 1924, 308–315.

20 Watson, "The Behaviorist's Utopia," typescript, John B. Watson Papers, Manuscript Division, Library of Congress, Washington, D.C., 2. Cited in Buckley, 162.

21 John B. Watson and Rosalie Rayner Watson, *Psychological Care of Infant and Child* (New York: Norton, 1928), 81ff. Cited in Buckley, 162.

22 Watson, "The Behaviorist's Utopia," 5. Cited in Buckley, 163.

23 Watson, "Why I Don't Commit Suicide," undated manuscript, Library of Congress, Washington, D.C. Cited in Buckley, 179.

24 Buckley, 182.

25 B.K. Reiss, "A Biography of Mary Cover Jones," Unpublished doctoral dissertation, the Wright Institute, Los Angeles, 1990. Cited at feministvoices.com/profiles/mary-cover-jones, accessed July 8, 2025.

26 Cited in Anthony D. Kauders, *Der Freud-Komplex: Eine Geschichte der Psychoanalyse in Deutschland* (Berlin: Berlin Verlag, 2014), 101.

27 Thomas Mann, *Freud und die Psychoanalyse: Reden, Briefe, Notizen, Betrachtungen*, ed. Bernd von Urban (Frankfurt: S. Fischer, 1991), 21ff. Cited in Kauders, 79.

28 After being forced into exile in London in June 1938, Freud describes his relationship to Vienna in these words: "One has lived in a prison for so long, and yet one did love it dearly."

29 Cited in Schröter, 589.

4: THE EGO

1 Adler, *Menschenkenntnis*, in: *Alfred Adler Studienausgabe*, ed. Karl Heinz Witte, Vol. 5 (ed. Jürg Rüedi) (Vandenhoeck & Ruprecht), 63. (English: Adler, *Understanding Human Nature*, trans. Walter Béran Wolfe (Cleveland: World Publishing Co., 1942), 57–58.)

2 Kluy, *Alfred Adler: Die Vermessung der menschlichen Psyche*, 281.

3 Adler, *Religion und Individualpsychologie*, in: *Alfred Adler Studienausgabe*, ed. Karl Heinz Witte, Vol. 6, 198.

4 Hans Vaihinger, *Die Philosophie des Als Ob: System der theoretischen, praktischen und religiösen Fiktionen der Menschheit auf Grund eines idealistischen Positivismus* (Leipzig: Felix Meiner, 1911/2021), 2. (English: Hans Vaihinger, *The Philosophy of "As If,"* trans. C.K. Ogden (New York: Harcourt, Brace, 1924), 2.)

5 Adler, *Über den nervösen Charakter*, in: *Alfred Adler Studienausgabe*, Vol. 2, 66. (English: Adler, *The Neurotic Constitution*, 29–30.)

6 Kluy, 91.

7 Vaihinger, 14. (English: Vaihinger, 15.)

8 Josef Rattner, *Alfred Adler* (Reinbek: Rowohlt, 1972), 55.

9 Carl Furtmüller, *Denken und Handeln. Schriften zur Psychologie 1905–1950. Von den Anfängen der Psychoanalyse zur Anwendung der Individualpsychologie* Lux Furtmüller, ed. (Munich: E. Reinhardt, 1983), 53–73. Cited in Kluy, 179.

10 Adler, "Lebenslüge und Verantwortlichkeit in der Neurose und Psychose: Ein Beitrag zur Melancholiefrage," *Zeitschrift für Individualpsychologie 1*, 1914, 44–53.

11 Adler, *Über den nervösen Charakter*, Vol. 2, 32.

12 Kluy, 180.

13 This expression is coined by Adler fan Philip Mairet, because *yen*, a key concept in Confucianism, is frequently translated as "affection for others" and recalls Adler's concept of the social feeling.

14 Manès Sperber calls it this in his Adler biography. (Cf. Manès Sperber, *Alfred Adler: Der Mensch und seine Lehre* (Berlin: Springer, 1926).)

15 *Es*, *Ich*, and *Über-Ich*. A literal translation might be It, I, and Over-I. Joan Riviere, translator of the first English edition of *The Ego and the Id*, chose to

substitute the Latin pronouns, and James Strachey preserved Riviere's choice in his Standard Edition. While the German *ich*, on its own and lowercase, is the first-person nominative pronoun, "Das Ich," capitalized and with a direct article, means "the self." Thus an alternative rendering of Freud's triad could be: It, Self, and Over-self.—Trans.

16 Freud dismisses Wittels's suspicion by asserting that "What seems true isn't always the truth" (Wittels, 252). But Freud neglected to mention that in summer 1920 he added to the first draft of *Beyond the Pleasure Principle* the chapter in which the death drive first appears. Thus presumably the melancholy that took hold in response to the blows that fate had dealt him did very much leave its mark on the work.

17 Freud, *Jenseits des Lustprinzips, Gesamtausgabe*, Vol. 16, 440. (English: Freud, *Beyond the Pleasure Principle*, SE 18:56.)

18 Ibid., 444. (English: Freud, SE 18:60).

19 Published in English as *The Book of the It.*

20 Georg Groddeck, *Das Buch vom Es: Psychoanalytische Briefe an eine Freundin* (Leipzig: Internationaler Psychoanalytischer Verlag, 1923), 287. (English: Groddeck, *The Book of the It*, trans. V.M.E. Collins (New York: Vintage, 1949), 11.)

21 Cited in: Gerhard Zenaty, *Sigmund Freud lesen* (Bielefeld: transcript Verlag, 2022), 290. (English: Eduard von Hartmann, *Philosophy of the Unconscious*, Vol. 1, trans. William Chatterton Coupland (London: Trübner and Co., 1884), 41. In the first half of the quote, von Hartmann is citing Adolf Bastian's *Beiträge zur vergleichenden Psychologie.*)

22 Freud, *Das Ich und das Es, Gesamtausgabe*, Vol. 17, 277. (English: Freud, *The Ego and the Id*, SE 19:18.)

23 (English: Ibid., 57.)

24 Ibid., 309. (English: Ibid., 56.)

25 Jones, *The Life and Work of Sigmund Freud*, Vol. 3 (New York: Basic Books, 1957), 95.

26 Freud to Kata and Lajos Levy, June 11, 1923. Cited in Gay, 421.

27 Freud, *Das Unbehagen in der Kultur, Gesamtausgabe*, Vol. 19, 74. The title originally intended for the book was *Das Unglück in der Kultur* (*Unhappiness in Civilization*); before the book went to print, Freud softened it to "Discontent." (English: Freud, *Civilization and Its Discontents*, SE 21:76.)

28 Ibid., 93. (English: SE 21:97.)

29 Freud, SE 20:191–192. Cited in David Boadella, *Wilhelm Reich: The Evolution of His Work* (London: Arkana, 1985), 77.

30 Freud, *Das Unbehagen in der Kultur*, 107. (English: Freud, SE 21:114.)

31 Ibid., 104. (English: Freud, SE 21:111.) *Homo homini lupus*: "Man is a wolf to man."

32 Ibid., 134. (English: Freud, SE 21:145.)

33 Kluy, 202.

34 In terms of purchasing power, $2,500 is the rough equivalent to between $40,000-$50,000 today. (Cf. Kluy, 221.)

35 Ibid., 243.

36 Ibid., 240.

37 Jones, *Life and Work of Sigmund Freud*, Vol. 3, 208. Cf. Kluy, 311.

38 Published in English as *The Formula for Success: The Grossmann Method of Self-Rationalization*.

39 Gustav Großmann, *Sich selbst Rationalisieren: Lebenserfolg ist erlernbar* (Grünwald: Ratio-Verlag, 1927/1993), 125.

40 Jürgen Straub, "Selbstoptimierung als Rationalisierung der Lebensführung: Gustav Großmanns Exzess als Paradigma: Buchhalterische Existenz für zweckrationale Zwangscharaktere," *Lost in Perfection: Zur Optimierung von Gesellschaft und Psyche*, Vera King, et al., eds. (Frankfurt: Suhrkamp, 2021), 310.

41 Max Reinhardt, *"Es ist nicht die Welt des Scheins . . . " Max Reinhardt über das Theater* (Berlin: Deutsches Theater Berlin, 1993), 82. Cited in Bernd Bocian, *Fritz Perls in Berlin 1893–1933: Expressionismus, Psychoanalyse, Judentum* (Wuppertal: Peter Hammer, 2007), 79. (English: Bocian, *Fritz Perls in Berlin: 1893–1933: Expressionism, Psychoanalysis, Judaism*, trans. Philip Schmitz (Bergisch Gladbach: Verlag Andreas Kohlhage, 2010), 70.)

42 Cited in Bocian, 53. (English: Bocian, 280.)

43 Kripal, 161. Citing Perls, *In and Out*, 43, 95.

44 Friedrich S. Perls, *Gestalt, Wachstum, Integration. Aufsätze, Vorträge, Therapiesitzungen*, ed. Hilarion Petzold (Paderborn: Jungfermann, 1980), 92.

45 This quote is taken from a brief chronology of Perls's life, written for the 1969 edition of *Ego, Hunger, and Aggression* but ultimately omitted. The chronology is available online at https://gestalt.org/fritz.htm.

46 Joseph Wolpe, "Reciprocal Inhibition as the Main Basis of Psychotherapeutic Effects," *Archives of Neurologic Psychiatry* 72, 1954, 205–226.

47 Wolpe's student Arnold Lazarus first uses the term in 1958 in his paper "New Methods in Psychotherapy: A Case Study," *South African Medical Journal* 32, 1958, 660–664.

48 Wolpe, *Psychotherapy by Reciprocal Inhibition* (Stanford: Stanford University Press, 1958), 32.

49 Albert Ellis, *All Out! An Autobiography* (Amherst: Prometheus Books, 2010), 302–303. There he writes, among other things: "Did I commit any 'really' immoral sex acts? To be honest, I certainly did. A few? No, many. In fact, hundreds. [. . .] frotteurism was a ubiquitous part of my life from my fifteenth year to my nineteenth year [. . .] an easy, quick, and painless way to get hundreds of subway orgasms."

50 The German translation, *Das Ich, der Hunger und die Aggression*, didn't appear until the late 1960s, after Perls had gained renown in the US through the Human Potential Movement.
51 Perls, *Ego*, 132. (English: Perls, 110.)
52 Ibid., 136. (English: Ibid., 115.)
53 Ibid. (English: Ibid., 114.)
54 Ibid. [English: Ibid., 112–113.)
55 Ibid., 146. (English: Ibid., 123.)
56 Ibid., 247. (English: Ibid., 206.)
57 Abraham H. Maslow, "A Theory of Human Motivation," *Pyschological Review* 50 (4), 1943, 370–396.
58 Cf. Edward Hoffman, *The Right to Be Human: A Biography of Abraham Maslow* (Los Angeles: Jeremy P. Tarcher, 1988), 289–291.
59 This organization, founded in 1892, for a long time represented the interests of academic psychology, which in the late 19th century started to branch off into various scientific disciplines. The various schools of psychotherapy were for a long time organized independently of academic psychology.
60 A classic study conducted by Morton Lieberman and colleagues in 1973 found that, out of 170 college students who had taken part in encounter groups, one in five (18 percent) felt less psychologically grounded afterwards. Because those participants who didn't make it to the end of the twelve-week seminars weren't included in the analysis, the number of those who experienced undesirable side effects was presumably even higher. This is a common problem: if studies don't classify the breaking off of therapy as a failure, they tend to exaggerate the therapy's efficacy. (Cf. Morton Lieberman, Irvin D. Yalom, and Matthew B. Miles, *Encounter Groups—First Facts* (New York: Basic Books, 1973).)
61 Irvin D. Yalom, *Theory and Practice of Group Psychotherapy*, 4th Ed. (New York: Basic Books, 1995), 501.
62 Perls, *In and Out the Garbage Pail* (Lafayette: Real People Press, 1969), 262.
63 Perls, *Gestalt Therapy Verbatim*, 60. Cited in: Helmut Quitmann, *Humanistische Psychologie: Psychologie, Philosophie, Organisationsentwicklung* (Göttingen: Hogrefe, 1996), 127.
64 Quitmann, 137.
65 Jeffrey J. Kripal, *Esalen: America and the Religion of No Religion* (Chicago: University of Chicago Press, 2007), 209.
66 Perls, *Gestalt Therapy Verbatim*.
67 Stephen Perls, "Frederick Perls: A Son's Reflections," *The Gestalt Journal*, https://gestalt.org/Stephen.htm, accessed 5.13.25. (German: "Meine Eltern, die Gestalttherapeuten: Gedanken eines Sohnes," *Gestaltkritik*, 1998, 1–99.)

5: OTHER PEOPLE

1 Rank, *Will Therapy: An Analysis of the Therapeutic Process in Terms of Relationship*, trans. Jessie Taft (New York: Knopf, 1936), 13. Cited in Robert Kramer, *The Birth of Relationship Therapy* (Gießen: Psychosozial-Verlag, 2002), 77.

2 E. James Lieberman and Robert Kramer, eds. *The Letters of Sigmund Freud and Otto Rank: Inside Psychoanalysis* (Baltimore: Johns Hopkins University Press, 2012), 271. (German: E. James Lieberman and Robert Kramer, eds. *Sigmund Freud und Otto Rank: Ihre Beziehung im Spiegel des Briefwechsels 1906–1925* (Gießen: Psychosozial-Verlag, 2014), 304.)

3 Lieberman, 356.

4 Lieberman, *Acts of Will: The Life and Work of Otto Rank* (New York: The Free Press, 1985), 359. (German: *Otto Rank: Leben und Werk*, 2nd Ed. (Gießen: Psychosozial-Verlag, 2014), 454.)

5 Lieberman and Kramer, 257.

6 Ibid., 276–277.

7 Ibid., 261.

8 Ibid., 277. Brackets original to source.

9 Rogers, *On Becoming a Person*, 11.

10 Kripal, 160.

11 Lieberman and Kramer, 260.

12 Freud to Eitingon, 2 July 1926. (Cf. Lieberman and Kramer, 264 and 281.)

13 Lieberman, 387.

14 Lieberman, 389. Rank is reported to have said "Komisch," which like the English word "funny" can mean both "comical" and "strange"—Trans.

15 Howard Kirschenbaum, *On Becoming Carl Rogers* (New York: Delta Books, 1979), 113. (Cf. Kramer, *The Birth of Relationship Theory* (Gießen: Psychosozial-Verlag, 2002), 92.) Cited here in Howard Kirschenbaum, *The Life and Work of Carl Rogers* (Ross-on-Wye: PCCS Books, 2007), 109. *The Life and Work of Carl Rogers* is an updated edition of *On Becoming Carl Rogers.*

16 *Three Approaches to Psychotherapy*, dir. Everett L. Shostrom, 1965. Transcript: Transcripts of Carl Rogers' Therapy Sessions, edited by Barbara T. Brodley and Germain Lietaer, Vol. 12. Not a verbatim rendering of the session.

17 Carl Rogers, *On Becoming a Person: A Therapist's View of Psychotherapy* (Boston: HarperOne, 1995), 67.

18 Rogers, *On Becoming a Person*, 26.

19 Kirschenbaum, *The Life and Work of Carl Rogers* (Ross-on-Wye: PCCS Books, 2007), 197.

20 Ibid., 208.

21 Ibid., 478.

22 A paraphrase of a passage in Irvin D. Yalom, *Becoming Myself: A Psychiatrist's Memoir* (New York: Basic Books, 2017), 184–185.

23 Dorothea Marcus, *Besser handeln als reden*, SWR2 Feature "Therapien für die Seele," 3 CDs, Beltz, Weinheim, 2007.

24 Cited in Marcus, 2007.

25 Jacob Moreno, *The Words of the Father* (Beacon: Beacon House, 1941), 5.

26 Psychodrama expert Christoph Hutter coined this term.

27 Roderick D. Buchanan, *Playing with Fire: The Controversial Career of Hans J. Eysenck* (New York: Oxford University Press, 2010), 209.

28 Ibid., 208.

29 Hans Jürgen Eysenck, "The Effects of Psychotherapy: An Evaluation," *Journal of Consulting Psychology* 16, 1952, 319–324.

30 This low number comes from the fact that Eysenck classified as therapeutic failures both instances in which symptoms got worse and instances where there was an interruption of therapy—even when the interruption was precipitated by the patient moving away or the patient's death. So radical a position is hardly justifiable.

31 Joseph Wolpe, "Objective Psychotherapy of the Neuroses," *South African Medical Journal* 20 (42), 1952, 825–829.

32 Cf. Buchanan, 218.

33 Buchanan, 38.

34 Anna Freud, *Wege und Irrwege in der Kinderentwicklung* (Stuttgart: Klett-Cotta, 1965/1968), 14. (English: Anna Freud, *Normality and Pathology in Childhood* (New York: International Universities Press, 1965), 4.)

35 Ibid., 37. (While the previous quote is taken from the English edition of *Normality and Pathology in Childhood*, this quote is my translation of a passage from the German edition.—Trans.)

36 Angela Graf-Nold, *Der Fall Hermine Hug-Hellmuth: Eine Geschichte der frühen Kinder-Psychoanalyse* (Munich: Verlag Internationale Psychoanalyse, 1988), 286.

37 Ibid., 260.

38 Helene Deutsch, *Confrontations with Myself* (New York: Norton, 1973), 137.

39 Melanie Klein, "Copy of Script Broadcast in French on European Service," October 21, 1944: www.melanie-klein-trust.org.uk.

40 Renate Horney, *Lazarus, What's Next? A Memoir by the Daughter of Noted Psychoanalyst Karen Horney* (Laguna Beach: Laurel Press, 1999), 18.

6: MEANING

1 Jung, *Erinnerungen*, [9th Ed.], 18. (English: Jung, *Memories*, 4.)

2 Cited in Christoph Lindenberg, *Rudolf Steiner* (Reinbek: Rowohlt, 1992), 71.

3 Helmut Zander, *Rudolf Steiner: Die Biographie* (Munich: Piper, 2011), 22.

4 Ibid. 35.

5 Rudolf Steiner, "Grundlinien einer Erkenntnistheorie der Goetheschen Weltanschauung," 1886. Cited in Zander, 49.

6 Zander, 36.

7 Lecture given on December 23, 1921 in Dornach (cf. Steiner, "Die gesunde Entwickelung des Menschenwesens: Eine Einführung in die anthroposophische Pädagogik und Didaktik," *Gesamtausgabe*, Vol. 303 (Basel: Rudolf Steiner Verlag, 1922/1978). The lecture is available in English in: Steiner, *Soul Economy and Waldorf Education,* trans. Roland Everett (Spring Valley: Antrohposophic Press, 1986), 1–14.)

8 Stefan Zweig, *Die Welt von Gestern: Erinnerungen eines Europäers* (Frankfurt: S. Fischer, 1942/1985), 141. (English: Zweig, *The World of Yesterday* (New York: Viking, 1943), 115.)

9 Max Halbe, *Jahrhundertwende: Erinnerungen an einer Epoche* (Munich: Langen Müller, 1935), 135.

10 Zander, 248.

11 Ibid., 244.

12 Taken from the first lines of the fragment "Die Natur," which appeared anonymously in 1783 in the "Tiefurter Journal" and was ascribed to Goethe, though it probably was written by the Swiss pastor and writer Georg Christoph Tobler (1757–1812). English translation by T.H. Huxley, *Nature*, Nov. 4, 1869, Vol. 1, Issue 1, 9.

13 Cited in Alfried Längle, *Viktor Frankl: Ein Porträt* (Munich: Piper, 1998), 56.

14 Viktor E. Frankl, "Zur mimischen Bejahung und Verneinung," *Internationaler Zeitschrift für Psychoanalyse* 10, 437–438.

15 Nietzsche's original quote is: "Hat man sein w a r u m? des Lebens, so verträgt man sich fast mit jedem w i e? – Der Mensch strebt n i c h t nach Glück; nur der Engländer thut das." Friedrich Nietzsche, *Götterdämmerung oder Wie man mit dem Hammer philosophiert* (Leipzig: C.G. Naumann, 1889), §12. In Anthony M. Ludovici's English translation: "If a man knows the wherefore of his existence, then the manner of it can take care of itself. Man does not aspire to happiness; only the Englishman does that." Friedrich Nietzsche, *The Twilight of the Idols: Or, How to Philosophise with the Hammer*, trans. Anthony M. Lodovici (Edinburgh: T.N. Foulis, 1911), 2.

16 Karl R. Popper, *Conjectures and Refutations* (London: Routledge, 1963), 35.

17 Popper, *Unended Quest: An Intellectual Autobiography* (London: Routledge, 1992), 39. (German: Popper, *Ausgangspunkte: Meine intellektuelle Entwicklung* (Munich: Piper, 1974), 6th Ed., 49.)

18 Xenophanes of Colophon, *Fragments*, trans. J.H. Lesher (Toronto: University of Toronto Press, 1992).

19 Zimmer, *Tiefenschwindel*, 11.

20 Cf. Zander, 338.

21 Zander, 22.

22 "Und nun, ihr Helden?" Frankl, *Recollections*, 63.

23 Frankl, "Zur medikamentösen Unterstützung der Psychotherapie bei Neurosen," *Schweizer Archiv für Neurologie und Psychiatrie* 17, 1939, 26–31.

24 Cited in: Birgit Mosser-Schuöcker, "Viktor Frankl—Auf der Suche nach dem Sinn," in: Hannes Leidinger, Christian Rapp, and Birgit Mosser-Schuöcker, *Freud, Adler, Frankl: Die Wiener Welt der Seelenforschung* (Vienna: Residenz Verlag, 2022), 229.

25 Frankl, *Dem Leben Antwort geben: Autobiographie* (Weinheim: Beltz, 2017), 103. (English: Frankl, *Recollections: An Autobiography*, trans. Joseph and Judith Fabry (New York: Plenum, 1997), 84.)

26 Frankl, *Recollections*, 93. Following quotes in this passage also from *Recollections.*

27 Frankl to Wilhelm and Stepha Börner, 14 September 1945. Cited in Frankl, *Es kommt der Tag, da bist du frei: Unveröffentlichte Briefe, Texte und Reden* (Munich: Kösel, 2015), 48.

28 Mosser-Schuöcker, 216.

29 *Ärztliche Seelsorge* is published in English in 1955 as *The Doctor and the Soul: an Introduction to Logotherapy*. The first edition of *Ein Psycholog erlebt das KZ*, Frankl's memoir of his time in the concentration camps, appeared without an author's name on the title page. Later the book bore Frankl's name and the title *. . . trotzdem Ja zum Leben sagen*. (The English edition was first published as *From Death Camp to Existentialism: A Psychiatrist's Path to a New Therapy*. Later editions bore the title: *Man's Search for Meaning.*)

30 Mosser-Schuöcker, 218.

31 Timothy Pytell, *Viktor Frankl: Das Ende eines Mythos?* (Innsbruck: Studien-Verlag, 2005). The book is the German translation of a 1997 dissertation written in English, "The Man Who Would Be King: Viktor Frankl's Struggle for Meaning." Pytell published a revised version of the biography in English in 2015: *Viktor Frankl's Search for Meaning: An Emblematic 20th-Century Life.*

32 Frankl, "Philosophie und Psychotherapie: Zur Grundlegung einer Existenzanalyse," *Schwizerische Medizinische Wochenschrift* 69, 1939, 707–709. Cited in: Frankl, *Frühe Schriften 1923–1942* (Vienna: Maudrich, 2017), 188.

33 Frankl, *Dem Leben Antwort geben*, 121. (English: Frankl, *Recollections*, 98.)

34 Längle, *Viktor Frankl: Ein Porträt*, 122ff.

35 Frankl, *Dem Leben Antwort Geben*, 9. (English: Frankl, *Recollections*, 22.)

36 Ibid., 18. (English: Ibid., 33.)

37 Yalom, *Becoming Myself*, 161.

38 Both quotations taken from Christian Pross, *Wir wollten ins Verderben rennen—Die Geschichte des Sozialistischen Patientenkollektivs Heidelberg* (Cologne: Psychiatrie-Verlag, 2016), 235.

AFTERWORD

1 There are several different reasons for this. A few important ones: studies that show the effects of treatment to be too weak or negative often disappear into researchers' desk drawers instead of being published. Samples are often distorted because, for example, those who discontinue therapy (so-called dropouts) are not included in the evaluation, even though this group includes many who did not profit from the treatment. And the control groups used (if they are in fact used) usually consist of patients who are urgently waiting for a spot in therapy, for which reason their psychological condition is often subject to additional strain. As a result, the distance between the average condition of those receiving treatment and those in the control group ends up being greater.

2 See, for example, Constantin Yves Plessen, et al., "Exploring the Efficacy of Psychotherapies for Depression: a Multiverse Meta-Analysis," *British Medical Journal (Mental Health)* 26 (1), 2023, e300626 or Lena Dragioti, et al., "Does Psychotherapy Work? An Umbrella Review of meta-Analyses of Randomized Controlled Trials," *Acta Psychiatrica Scandinavia* 136 (3), 2017, 236–246.

3 Michael Linden and Bernhard Strauß, eds., *Risiken und Nebenwirkungen von Psychotherapie*, 2nd Ed. (Berlin: Medizinisch Wissenschaftliche Verlagsgesellschaft: 2018).

4 Winfried Rief, "Was kann die Psychotherapie vom Placeboeffekt lernen?" *Psychotherapeut* 67, 2022, 191–194.

5 Freud, "On Psychotherapy," SE 7:257.

6 E.g. Pim Cuijpers, et al., "Was Eysenck right after all? A reassessment of the effects of psychotherapy for adult depression," *Epidemiology and Psychiatric Sciences* 28 (1), 2018, 1–10. A good overview can be found in Bruce E. Wampold and Zac E. Imel, *The Great Psychotherapy Debate: The Evidence for What Makes Psychotherapy Work* (London: Routledge, 2018), 2015.

7 More on this in Eva Illouz, *Die Errettung der modernen Seele: Therapien, Gefühle und die Kultur der Selbsthilfe* (Frankfurt: Suhrkamp, 2009).

IMAGE CREDITS

p. 7 © akg-images / Marion Kalter

p. 15 © Wellcome Library, London. Wellcome Images: images@wellcome.ac.uk, http://wellcomeimages.org (https://upload.wikimedia.org/wikipedia/commons/1/18/Freud_family_group._Photograph%2C_c.1876._Wellcome_V0027598.jpg) "Freud family group photograph, c. 1876", public domain

p. 15 © Unknown Austrian Photographer (https://commons.wikimedia.org/wiki/File:Sigmund_Freud_as_a_child_with_his_father.jpg), "Sigmund Freud as a child with his father", public domain

p. 25 © Unknown Photographer (pre-1923 photo) (https://commons.wikimedia.org/wiki/File:John_Broadus_Watson.JPG), "John Broadus Watson", public domain

p. 30 © Unknown Photographer (https://commons.wikimedia.org/wiki/File:Pappenheim_1882.jpg), "Pappenheim 1882", public domain

p. 34 © Baugeschichtliches Archiv der Stadt Zürich / Ganz Rudolf

p. 41 © New York Public Library / Science Source

p. 52 © Unknown Photographer (https://commons.wikimedia.org/wiki/File:Die_Traumdeutung_(Congress_scan).jpg), "Die Traumdeutung (Congress scan)", public domain

p. 69 © Unknown Photographer (https://commons.wikimedia.org/wiki/File:Hall_Freud_Jung_in_front_of_Clark_1909.jpg), "Hall Freud Jung in front of Clark 1909", public domain

p. 81 © Unknown Photographer (https://commons.wikimedia.org/wiki/File:Eugen_bleuler.jpg), "Eugen Bleuler", public domain

p. 87 © Becker & Maass (https://commons.wikimedia.org/wiki/File:Freud_and_other_psychoanalysts_1922.jpg), "Freud and other psychoanalysts 1922", public domain

p. 92 © Prints & Photographs Division Library of Congress (https://commons.wikimedia.org/wiki/File:Jung_1910-crop.jpg), "Jung 1910-crop", public domain

p. 97 © Unknown Photographer (https://commons.wikimedia.org/wiki/File:Sabina_Spielrein.jpg), "Sabina Spielrein", public domain

p. 105 © Unknown Photographer (https://commons.wikimedia.org/wiki/File:Otto-gross.jpg), "Otto Gross", public domain
p. 107 © Fondazione Monte Verità, Fondo Harald Szeemann
p. 112 © Deutsche Kinemathek / Hans Casparius
p. 125 © Ludwig Gutmann (https://commons.wikimedia.org/wiki/File:Wilhelm_Reich.jpg), "Wilhelm Reich", public domain
p. 146 © Vibha C Kashyap (https://upload.wikimedia.org/wikipedia/commons/c/ce/Albert_experiment.jpg), "Albert experiment", licensed under CC BY-SA 4.0
p. 168 © Austrian Archives / brandstaetter images / picturedesk.com
p. 176 © Sigmund Freud; photographical reproduction by Rolf Nemitz (https://commons.wikimedia.org/wiki/File:Freud,_Second_topography,_1933.jpg), "Freud, Second topography, 1933", public domain
p. 201 © Christof Weber
p. 210 © Richard Mittleman/Gon2Foto / Alamy
p. 213 © Bettmann / Getty Images
p. 216 © Pam Walatka / Getty Images
p. 233 © Everett Collection
p. 239 The rights holders could not be located
p. 252 © World History Archive / Alamy
p. 255 © Wellcome Library, London. Wellcome Images: images@wellcome.ac.uk, http://wellcomeimages.org, (https://upload.wikimedia.org/wikipedia/commons/9/96/Melanie_Klein%2C_her_daughter_Melitta_Schmideberg-Klein%2C_and_Wellcome_L0028506.jpg), "Melanie Klein with her daughter Melitta and one of her sons. Photograph by Hegedus", public domain
p. 270 © Otto Rietmann (https://commons.wikimedia.org/wiki/File:Steiner_um_1905.jpg), "Steiner um 1905", public domain
p. 275 © Mohr Siebeck GmbH & Co. KG
p. 283 © Rudolf Steiner Archiv / Otto Rietmann
p. 288 © Viktor Frankl Archiv / brandstaetter images / picturedesk.com
p. 295 © Rhein-Neckar-Zeitung

INDEX

Locators in italics indicate an image (*168*). Locators followed by n and a number indicate an endnote in that page (315n8). Titles of articles, books, and lectures are found under their authors. Titles are given in their English translation where available.